Burma at the Turn of the Twenty-First Century

Burma at the Turn of the Twenty-First Century

Edited by

Monique Skidmore

University of Hawai'i Press

HONOLULU

Library of Congress Cataloging-in-Publication Data
   Burma at the turn of the twenty-first century / edited by
Monique Skidmore.
      p. cm.
   Includes bibliographical references and index.
   ISBN 13: 978-0-8248-2857-8 (hardcover : alk. paper)
   ISBN 10: 0-8248-2857-7 (hardcover : alk. paper)
   ISBN 13: 978-0-8248-2897-4 (pbk. : alk. paper)
   ISBN 10: 0-8248-2897-6 (pbk. : alk. paper)
   1. Ethnology—Burma. 2. Burma—Social conditions. 3. Burma—
Politics and government—1962–1988. 4. Burma—Politics and
government—1988– . 5. Burma—Social life and customs.
I. Skidmore, Monique.
   GN635.B8B87 2005
   306'.09591—dc22

7698 D   2005003440

Designed by University of Hawai'i Press production staff

Printed by The Maple-Vail Book Manufacturing Group

Contents

Part 3: Public Performance

Part 4: The Domestic Domain

Acknowledgments

Not many editors can say that an edited volume was a pleasure to put together, but this has been true for *Burma at the Turn of the Twenty-First Century*. The Burmese scholarly community is small and welcoming, and Burmese conferences seem more like family reunions and *pwes* (festivals), than numbing days of paper presentations. The 2002 Burma Studies Conference in Gothenburg, Sweden, afforded me the opportunity to plan this volume with its Canadian, French, American, Australian, English, and Japanese participants. I wish to sincerely thank all of the participants for entrusting their work to my care, and also to thank Pamela Kelley at University of Hawaiʻi Press for enthusiastically and professionally guiding the volume to publication.

A very special thank you from all of the authors to John Okell, who not only gave many of us our first Burmese lessons, but who graciously rewrote all of the Burmese romanization using the Okell method (1971). I am also very grateful to Robert Weber who has graciously consented to the use of his photographs in the volume.

Parts of several essays in this volume have been previously published. Parts of chapter 11 were published in *Worlds of Music;* parts of chapter 4 were published in *Bulletin de l'École française d'Extrême-Orient;* and parts of chapter 7 were published as Chapter 15 in "Mental Culture in Burmese Crisis Politics: Aung San Suu Kyi and the National League for Democracy." Each chapter in this book has, however, been wholly or substantially reworked.

The research for this grant was enabled by the Rockefeller Foundation and an Australian Research Council Discovery Grant. I am grateful to the Joan B. Kroc Institute for International Peace Studies at the University of Notre Dame for the research and writing time in which to expeditiously complete the volume; to the University of Melbourne, Faculty of Arts, for granting me leave; and to Colin and Isabelle Rieger, for giving up a year of their lives to accompany me to Burma and to Notre Dame so that this volume could come to fruition.

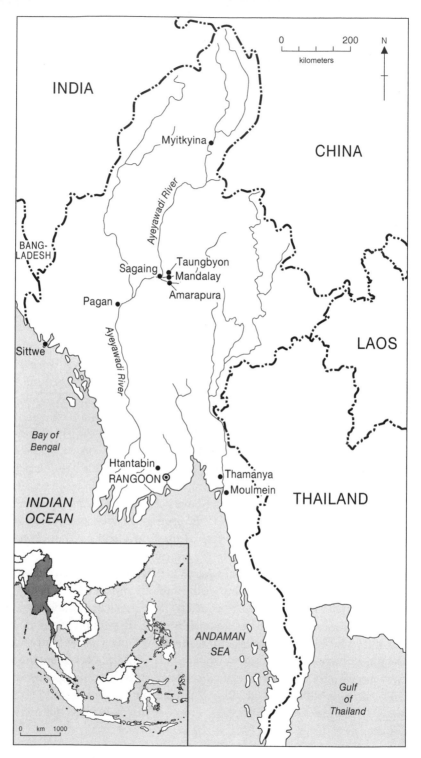

Map 1. Burma (Myanmar)

Introduction

Burma at the Turn of the Twenty-First Century

Monique Skidmore

*B*urma at the Turn of the Twenty-First Century is the first collection of essays about everyday life in Burma in forty years. The anthropologists and scholars of religion who have contributed to this volume show how everyday negotiations about culture, power, and group and individual identity play out in contemporary Burma. The essays together demonstrate how the state is not one monolithic rational entity and how the Burmese people participate or manufacture some of the conditions of their own subjection. In this way the volume provides a context for, and corrective to, the totalizing discourses of the military state and the necessarily grim portrayals of repression documented by human rights observers. The authors portray the dynamism, activity, and fragile flux in Burmese popular space and imagination through a survey of micro institutions and macro-level connections that have come to exist at least since the military coup of 1962.

The forty-year lacuna since the last edited volume of everyday (village) life in Burma—Manning Nash's 1965, *The Golden Road to Modernity: Village Life in Contemporary Burma*—encompasses not only the period of Burmese Independence (from 1948 to the present), but also the period of military rule (from 1962 to the present). The anthropologists who contributed to Nash's volume conducted fieldwork prior to Gen. Ne Win's coup of 1962 and since that time access for researchers to this country has been severely limited.

Not only is it almost inconceivable for there to be such a long time between published collections of such work,[1] but it is also extraordinary that this current volume about everyday urban and peri-urban life does not contain the work of any Burmese citizens. All those approached to contribute either quietly ignored the request or pleaded the continued safety of family and friends within Burma or their ability to return to the country. A very limited number of works documenting the lives and literature of the Burmese people have appeared in the past two decades, and there is a small cohort of Burmese expatriates, largely political refugees, who write about conditions within Burma, but without the benefit of contemporary immersion in a rapidly changing nation.[2]

Before Gen. Ne Win's military coup in 1962, researchers collaborated on religious, rural, agricultural, political, and culture and personality studies, especially within mainland Southeast Asia. The past few years have seen an easing of some restrictions on scholarship, and a new generation of students is conducting fieldwork over extended periods of time in Burma. Burmese studies thus tends to be represented by researchers at either end of the age spectrum, although a number of midcareer researchers have managed to conduct research about religion, ritual, art, and archaeology.[3]

The most established field of Burmese studies concerns religion and ritual, and Burma has been included in a number of edited volumes that survey these themes across Southeast Asia. Within Burmese studies proper, the fields of political science and economics are frequently represented in contemporary manuscripts and edited volumes. *Burma at the Turn of the Twenty-First Century* brings together most of the anthropologists and scholars of religion who are actively working in contemporary urban and peri-urban central Burma. All of the contributors have conducted extensive field research in Burma, a fact that would be assumed in a book about the other nations of Southeast Asia, but is unusual in a volume about Burma. Together, then, these essays provide the first detailed analysis of the ways in which the Burmese people actively manage and create lives for themselves despite the shadow that military dictatorship throws across Burma's religious, political, and social life.

History and Landscape: The Union of Myanmar

Lying immediately to the south of the Himalayas, Burma has always been a trade and information route between Indian and Chinese civilizations. Surviving architectural forms, medical practices, and Indian weights and measures constitute but a fraction of the evidence of the infusion of Indian, Chinese, Tibetan, and Thai practices and knowledge into the Burman empire. The chapters of this volume are set in the cities and towns of the central riverland plains and surrounding hills, home to the ethnic Burman population, and in the south, home to the Karen and Mon populations. The book thus does not survey the entire social landscape, but only those urban and peri-urban areas of central Burma. A great deal more scholarly research will, we hope, be permitted in the coming years in the mountains, forests, jungles, and coral atolls where Burma's more than a hundred minority groups live. This volume, however, focuses on the Burman empire: a Buddhified landscape of green paddy fields and thatched bamboo huts sheltering among tracts of palm trees, dusty plains dominated by the ruins of thousands of pagodas, deserted cities and palaces of now-deposed Burmese kings, and the muddy brown Ayeyarwadi River, flowing through centuries of conquest and submission. From the ascendancy of the Buddhist kings (1057–1824), to the period of British colonization (1824–1937), through the growth of nationalism to the brief burst of Independence and democracy (1948–1962), and onwards to more than four decades of military dictatorship, this central landscape has been continually recruited to the tasks of resistance, rebellion, memorialization, and nation-building.

The years 1962–1988 constituted the "Burmese Road to Socialism," during which time Gen. Ne Win's Burma Socialist Programme Party (BSPP) managed to bankrupt a country that was, like Asia's "tiger" economies, set to take advantage of the prosperous latter part of the twentieth century. During this time Burma was dubbed the "hermit nation" as the new military government nationalized the economy and withdrew from the international political and economic spheres. Standards of living, the export economy, and health indicators relative to other nations plummeted during these years and have recovered only slightly under successive military regimes, with Burma being granted Least Developed Country status in 1987. Steinberg (1982:92) notes that per capita income did not reach prewar levels until 1976. For example, GDP per capita in 1900 was $647; it fell to $396 in 1950 and stands now at US$1,700 (Central Intelligence Agency 2003). On the Human Development Index, Burma is ranked 131 of 175 nations (2002 ranking, UNDP 2003). Life expectancy at birth has increased only slightly, from 53 years in 1978 (Steinberg 1982: 130) to 55.8 years in 2003 (CIA 2003). Burma's other health statistics are just as dire, with an estimated 40 percent of the country not covered by basic medical services, and in these areas infant mortality rates are almost 400 percent higher than in areas where basic health services exist (UNICEF 1995).

The demonetization of the Burmese currency, the kyat, in 1987 was for many urban people the factor that drove them to participate in the pro-democracy uprising that began in 1988 when farmers liberated rice trucks in the delta areas. The resignation of Gen. Ne Win, who had ruled the country since 1962, was a further factor in this nationwide uprising against military rule. The pro-democracy protests and their brutal suppression resulted in a group of generals forming a ruling council, the State Law and Order Restoration Council, or SLORC. From its inception, the SLORC intensified the project of modernization that has transformed Rangoon and Mandalay into "modern" and "developed" cities. This project was continued under the rule of the State Peace and Development Council, the SPDC, which was constituted in 1997. The SPDC represents a reshuffle in the military council but continues the rule of the president, Gen. Than Shwe, and his quest to modernize the country while keeping the military as the pivotal social, economic, and political institution.

In conjunction with this selective modernization, an ideological program to "unify" the many peoples of Burma as a "Union of Myanmar" has occurred. The name of the country was changed in 1989, as were most other colonial place and street names. Rangoon, for example, became Yangon, and the Burmese language became Myanmarese. Other aspects of the military government's program have included the adoption of new architectural and spatial relationships with the land and the environment and the production of official histories (Houtman 1999). Most significantly, this agenda has involved four decades of civil war where pacification of all those groups who will not submit to unification of the nation occurs through the might of the armed forces, the Tatmadaw (Fink 2001; Skidmore 2003a; Smith 1991).

As part of the narrowing definition of model persons and appropriate citizens, new universities[4] have been created in which to train Buddhist missionaries, for the state seeks, often coercively, to convert Christians, Muslims, and animists to Buddhism. New rules deny citizenship to Burmese who are not ethnic Burmans and relegate them to the status of "residents." Model villages have been created in an enormous internal relocation process (Skidmore 2004), a recurring theme in twentieth-century Burmese history (Scott 2002).

Internal relocation has taken place for many reasons in different parts of the country. In the cities it has allowed a project of urban modernization to occur in which large sections of the cities are demolished and then rebuilt in a "huts to highrise" scheme. This undertaking has occurred concomitant with an opening of the country to select foreign companies and capital and an easing of restrictions upon tourism. The last decade and a half (1990–2005) has thus seen enormous changes to everyday urban life and the results of these changes can also be traced in the growth of religious retreats such as monasteries, nunneries, and meditation centers. Theravāda Buddhism, the religion of 89 percent of the population, has become an ambiguous element in daily life. The Burmese people can feel deeply ambivalent about the obvious Buddhist beliefs of the ruling council, and the concrete merit-making opportunities newly afforded to Buddhists by the military regime. While new venues for merit-making are being created by the military junta, Buddhist retreats are also providing refuge for political opponents in the face of authoritarianism (Houtman 1999). The ambivalence with which urban residents view the state-supported renewal of Buddhist infrastructure is evident in Keiko Tosa's chapter in this volume, "The Chicken and the Scorpion," where she documents Burmese suppositions about the possible conflicting motivations for the intensification of the military council's patronage of Buddhism as they are conveyed through rumor.

One very visible aspect of the urban remodeling endeavor is the Golden Façade project (Skidmore 2004), the repairing of ancient pagodas and monasteries and the building of enormous new pagodas and monasteries in the city suburbs. "Upgrading" of existing pagodas, such as the Shwedagon pagoda has involved new metal work and precious gems, the liberal use of yellow paint as a substitute for gold leaf, and the inclusion of modern conveniences such as elevators (Jordt 2003). The Golden Façade scheme is part of an amplification in the funding of Buddhism and Buddhist infrastructure by which the ruling generals seek to take over the mantle of Buddhist moral authority that was invested, before British colonialism, in the Burmese monarchy.

The Burmese people do not sit idly by while these sweeping forces change their sociopolitical and religious landscapes. This book surveys not just the social topography, but also the moral topography of the contemporary nation state. Many of the chapters here concern the process of creating a moral consensus within particular social, religious, economic, and political domains. This diffuse moral consensus is sometimes at odds with the forms of moral legitimation claimed by the ruling generals. More often, however, the moral consensus is ambivalent, qualified, and complicit. This ambiguous moral understanding is carried through travelers, pilgrims, rumors, and the deliberate voluntary participation in cultural and religious forms deemed worthy of respect by the populace.

Military Rule

Any examination of everyday Burmese life over the past four decades is necessarily encompassed by the framework of military rule and the economic consequences and social suffering it has generated. The remarkably stable troika (the president, the head of Military Intelligence, and the military) of the SLORC and, since November 1997, of the State Peace and Development Council (SPDC) resulted in one of the most enduring military states of the twentieth century. As we go to press, Khin Nyunt, the prime minister and head of Military Intelligence, has been sacked, and it is not yet known what kinds of changes this event presages. The past decade has seen a decrease in violence in areas where the civil war has been commuted to a system of pacification as rebel armies have signed peace agreements with the increasingly strong military state. Torture, disappearances, rape, and extrajudicial killings documented by human rights observers in the now-pacified regions have also decreased. Suffering has also been slowly reduced in the peri-urban areas where around 1.5 million Rangoon (Yangon) and Mandalay residents were forcibly relocated. Demonstrable decreases in previous rates of mortality in the peri-urban areas can be charted over the past decade. Infrastructure such as roads has slowly been created (largely through forced labor) to link former paddy fields and villages to urban centers, and land speculation has resulted in the voluntary resettlement of many urban residents to these "New Fields" (Allott 1993; Skidmore 2004). In other parts of the country, however, heroin and amphetamine production, the trafficking of women and children to Thailand, China, and India, and the forcible recruitment of children and youth as soldiers in armed combat situations continues unabated.

Within the urban and peri-urban areas of Burma that are the subject of this volume, the military regime seldom needs to send its tanks, riot police, and military intelligence officers into battle. With the exception of demonstrations in late 1996 and early 1997, and a smaller uprising in 1998, the student movement has been largely silenced. Similarly, the continued arrest (largely as house arrest) of Aung San Suu Kyi, the pro-democracy figurehead in Burma and party secretary of the National League for Democracy (NLD), and the jailing of other political opponents of the military junta have meant that almost all political opposition in central Burma has been suppressed.

Mechanisms used to repress the population include fear, propaganda, censorship, surveillance, strategic and symbolic acts of violence, and the inculcation of a permanent state of alert and vulnerability in the populace (Skidmore 1998; 2003a; 2004). The issuance of personal identity cards (that from 1990 have included ethnicity and religion), the creation of the *Fundamental Rules of Organization of the Sangha* (monastic order), and the 1993 *Development of Border Areas and National Races Law,* are all methods of regulating and controlling the flow of people as citizens, "residents," and "official" monastic sects (Liddell 1999:58–67). These are some of the key ways in which the military juridical apparatus has acted to stop freedom of speech, association, and assembly, and to repress all forms of political opposition and mobilization. This, then, is the political climate in which anthropologists and scholars of religion have had to work since 1962.

A significant reason for producing this book, however, is to demonstrate that despite the entrenchment of military rule, there is no all-powerful military state here, no black-and-white understandings, and certainly no monolithic Orwellian entity overseeing all the Burmese people. Instead, as each chapter makes apparent, forms of association, elements of free speech, and collectivities of moral opposition are clearly apparent. The chapters show how the Burmese people have sought to maintain certain key values and beliefs, while deliberately employing strategies of complicity, collusion, or ambivalence regarding the changes to the urban and peri-urban landscapes. With the improved transportation infrastructure, for example, came the relaxing of rules regarding movement, and the Burmese people have used the new infrastructure to create business opportunities and to engage with peri-urban and rural religious communities in order to make merit, money, and auspiciousness.

Everyday Life in the Popular Domain

The subjects of this book exist within the domain designated as *popular,* which came into existence long before the pro-democracy uprising was repressed in 1988. The current regime's rules of engagement with political and social life, and the burden or fear, censorship, and surveillance that the Burmese people shoulder daily, should not blind us to the furtive creativity and industry invested in making a future for Burmese children.

Where does this work for the future occur? In political science, "civil society" is a European concept that has recently begun regaining its currency in contemporary theorizing. Political scientists have often been concerned with the elusiveness of civil society in Burma (Kramer and Vervest 1999). It can be defined narrowly as nongovernmental organizations (ibid.),[5] or more widely to include any voluntary association, formal or informal, that exists between the level of the family and the level of the state. In this broader sense, civil society is civic life, the ways in which individuals come together in groups larger than the family for any purpose whatsoever, apart from political affiliations. Even this is a vague notion, however, as trade unions and business associations, for example, often have strong political ties. Htun Aung Kyaw, founder of the activist expatriate Civil Society for Burma organization defines it as

> that realm of organized social life that is voluntary, self generating, (largely) self supporting, autonomous from the state and bound by a legal and or a set of shared rules. In this context, citizens act collectively in a public sphere to express their interests, passions, and ideas, exchange information, achieve mutual goals, make demands on the state and hold state offices. . . . Civil society in the western sense has no equivalent in the Burmese lexicon (Htun Aung Kyaw n.d.).

Besides being an allochthonous concept, civil society is a term that brings with it certain assumptions. This view is described by Martin Smith as the belief that the military regime's "on-paper" support for "a 'market-oriented,' 'open-door,' 'multi-party' system of 'democratic' government . . . are elements that are generally considered essential building blocks in the development of civil society" (Smith 1999:17). Although this implies linear progression from civil society to democracy and pluralism, such has not occurred, for example, in Burma's northern neighbor, China, where the postsocialist state has engineered the linking of economic openness with more subtle, but equally coercive, forms for the distribution of power through society (Wang 2001). As a consequence, rather than use the term civil society, I have searched for a term that is accurate and applicable to the sphere of interpersonal interaction these authors examine but that does not imply or assume a domain that is an embryonic form of liberty, democracy, or pluralism. I use the term "popular domain" to designate the sense of popular imagination and the forging and reforging of a social moral consensus. This is a domain that is, as Farquhar (2001:107) has written for China, "neither remote nor small nor grounded in a community of people who share a local history and mundane conditions of life." Nor is it a space impermeable to the state or set apart from it.

The genealogy of the "popular" throughout the modern period is inextricably linked to the state and to the modernization of China, and East Asia more broadly. Burma has a series of "localities," some of which are defined by the state, others in negotiation or conflict with the state (and other states such as China), and yet others more thoroughly entangled in the state's introduction of transnational, illegal, and laundered capital into the country, most particularly on the nation's geographic periphery. There is no isolated subculture to be sniffed out and revealed by anthropologists and no unofficial site where nongovernmental organizations flourish. Rather, there is oftentimes a consenting nexus and a circulation of individuals within and outside of bureaucracies, villages, transnational border zones, peri-urban factories and sweatshops, military "tax free" zones, and monastic territories (to name but a few localities), who are tied together through forms of association. In a conversation with me in 2002, Guillaume Rozenberg likened these forms of association to a previously unknown degree of elasticity within reciprocal, hierarchical, patron-client, and kin-based relationships.

Our focus on the popular means that the interpenetration of political life with the social world is not dichotomized. In particular, it affords us an opportunity of scrutinizing the complicitious and imbricated ways that almost all Burmese people have come to participate in sociopolitical life. The encompassing domain of the popular is infused with power and with commodification: the penetration of capitalism and dictatorship into even the most intimate provinces of personal relations is an increasing reality in daily life. It is possible for a Burmese citizen to be a government employee and a member of that particular department's football team, a member of a religious order during the rainy season, an aficionado of Burmese heavy metal music, and an occasional smuggler of contraband from Thailand or China. Such a person has multiple positionings within the popular domain and a variety of strategies, rationalities, and logics that justify and guide his or her participation at certain moments, to a greater or lesser degree, in each of these subspheres.

The Acceleration of Modernization

The title of Nash's 1965 collection, *The Golden Road to Modernity*, is consistent with his interest in modernization, industrialization, and the changing dynamics of rural life as villagers come to be more tightly linked to urban areas.[6] The intervening decades of isolation and economic mismanagement have meant that these issues continue to be pertinent in Burma at the turn of the twenty-first century. It is a central premise of this book that specific modes of contemporary modernity in Burma are channeled through long-standing relations between villages and towns encircling larger polities, and are in part constituted through the connection of polities via intermediary nodes of economic and religious activity.

For tourists to Burma, modernity must appear as the increased circulation of quantity, not quality. In the lurid and cheap plasticware that floods over the Chinese border and spreads along the laminated tables of street vendors in Rangoon and Mandalay, for example, we see the increased circulation of low-quality material goods. But there is a more complex rendering of modernity occurring with the selective liberalization of the economy in the 1990s, the creation of expanded infrastructure for tourism and travel, the development of industrial and manufacturing zones, and the changes that have occurred in living units and family arrangements due to the processes of relocation, urban remodeling, and limited industrialization.

Each of the chapters in this volume necessarily discuss aspects of Burmese modernization, "the measurable material processes of industrialization, technological innovation, expanding capitalist markets, and rapid urbanization" (Kendall 2002: 2). Unlike Western nations, the past fifty years have seen only very limited industrialization in Burma and now the economy is moving directly from, for example, paper filing systems to digital cash registers and electronic visas, and from windup telephones scattered across the country, to cellular phones and satellite and Internet provision through a military hub. In addition, Burmese people now not only watch, but also produce and appear on television which reports state-controlled ceremonies and nation-building activities. Television was introduced by Gen. Ne Win as a conduit for disseminating state ideology, and it is now in at least 320,000 homes (CIA 2003).

The effects of these recently accelerating changes for urban and peri-urban Burmese are significant. Freed from the restraint against traveling within the country, urban residents now flock to moral and economic centers of activity, and rural men are increasingly becoming ensnared in day laboring, cash cropping, and seasonal work in faraway provinces. Young women migrate to peri-urban factories and sweatshops. In the regular "ferry" boats that ply the Hlaing and Pun Hlaing rivers, in the high-speed buses hurtling along the potholed asphalt roads that connect the cities to one another via newly constructed bridges over the Ayeyarwadi, and in the pickup jeeps that traverse muddy jungle hills linking Mandalay to dusty Thai and Chinese border towns, chickens, ducks, soldiers, men, women, children, and vegetables endlessly move between villages, towns, and cities.

Each author in this collection places a particular node or subdomain of activity under the microscope. One purpose for bringing these experienced Burma scholars and fieldworkers together is to allow readers to examine one segment of Burmese life closely and simultaneously to expand the magnification so they can glimpse the ways that these different centers of activity connect the Burmese people and moral and religious discourses into the particular conformation of contemporary Burmese social life.

The responses of the Burmese people and the active ways in which they manage and create lives for themselves are often described by these authors in terms of discourses of moral legitimation. For more than a decade now, anthropologists and scholars of religion have been engaged in discovering those places and processes within the popular domain from which a sense of moral reality and public consensus emerges. In each essay the answer emerges not from traditional anthropological subjects or civil society organizations, but from nodes of possibility, from the places where the Burmese people find it possible to nourish forms of popular imagination that circulate, like the material accoutrements of modernity, along newly established transportation routes and information conduits.

Organization of the Book

Where, then, are the particular areas in which Burmese people engage with each other, as individual and collectivities, within the popular domain? It is difficult to conduct research in the current political climate so many fieldworkers choose established centers of religious and ritual activity as their focus. This strategy means following Burmese people to the spaces where moral discourses are constructed and economic and religious activities are transacted. The meditation center and monastery, the state bureaucracy, the home, the tea circle, the literary circle, the *pwe* (or *bwe*) (festival), the public performance, and the pagoda: these are some of the localities into which the anthropologists and scholars of religion have inserted themselves.

Within these arenas a number of key themes and distinctions are apparent. The book is accordingly divided into four parts: spirituality, pilgrimage, and economics; political and moral legitimation; public performance; and the domestic domain. No one essay fits entirely within its own section. There is enormous overlap, in part because the military gaze penetrates the entire popular domain, but also because no individual has only one role to fill, or one mode of engagement.

Part 1, Spirituality, Pilgrimage, and Economics, consists of four essays. Like the Burmese people themselves, many of the chapters trace journeys that crisscross the country, circumambulate the nation, and follow regional linkages and connections. We travel with Guillaume Rozenberg from Rangoon to cities and towns in search of clues to the winning numbers of the Burmese and Thai lotteries. In his "The Cheaters: Journey to the Land of the Lottery," dozens of cars and pickup trucks line the winding dirt roads to forest monasteries, and hundreds of Burmese can be found seated in teashops along the route, to listen to the sermons of the "lottery monks." Hopeful individuals drive between major cities and the forest monasteries and the lottery vendors and bankers move between the major cities, their activities reaching a frenzied climax from the third to the tenth of every month when gambling on the illegal lottery is afoot. Rozenberg notes the enduring values of pilgrimage and reciprocity between monks and laity that is apparent even in the commodified domain of contemporary lottery practices, and the fine line that monks, laity, lottery bankers, and paid policemen walk between legal and religious proscriptions on economic behavior.

The porous nature of analytical constructs, such as institutional versus noninstitutional space, and the location of all Burmese institutions firmly within the public domain are clearly portrayed by Ingrid Jordt in "Women's Practices of Renunciation in the Age of Sāsana Revival." Jordt reviews several ways in which women have, over the last century, practiced renunciation. This has included the adoption of institutional, noninstitutional, vocational, and nonvocational roles. The phenomenal growth of the "new laity" of the mass meditation movement not only challenges the traditional idea that religious renunciation occurs in institutions, as opposed, for example, to its taking place in a popular domain that is both religious and secular, but also it challenges the place of women in wider gender hierarchies and Buddhist cosmologies. Many urban Buddhist women are engaged in the struggle for greater institutionalization, and hence spiritual status, through their renunciation practices and their association with meditation centers. They have effectively created shadow institutions in order to approximate the male Sangha, thereby transcending gendered social roles by challenging the spiritual supremacy of the Sangha and the broader gender structure of Burmese Buddhist society.

Only ten kilometers north of Burma's second city, Mandalay, is the village of Taungbyon, the epicenter of the cult of the *nat* (spirits), the possession cult that is part of the Burmese religious system in the shadow of Buddhism. In "The Taungbyon Festival: Locality and Nation-Confronting in the Cult of the '37 Lords,'" Bénédicte Brac de la Perrière describes the wide-ranging ritual cycle throughout the "nat belt" of central Burma that involves three festival periods each year. Taken together, this vast ritual complex unifies central Burma, tying the rural areas to the precolonial administrative royal center of Mandalay. Here too a series of identity negotiations occur in the face of modernizing city centers and the centralization and consolidation of military rule extending from Rangoon and Mandalay outward towards the nation's geographic peripheries.

The infrastructure of this festival waxes and wanes according to the fortunes of the Burmese centralized economy. Brac de la Perrière has been studying the festival for more than fifteen years. She charts the growth of the festival beyond its original boundaries and the economic implications of secondary dance sites, hereditary guardianship of Nat palaces, and the rapid growth of the population of urban spirit mediums organized in performing troupes. Community conflict has followed the growth of the festival among the local population as there is no central organizing body. Rather, in fulfilling their customary duties within their designated domains, and in seeking to maintain control and profit from the cycle of spirit festivals, local communities engage in power struggles between spirit mediums, palace guardians, and villagers where eventually a new status quo is reached as local economies adapt to changing circumstances.

In the final chapter in this section, "Respected Grandfather, Bless This Nissan: Benevolent and Politically Neutral Bo Bo Gyi," we travel with Mandy Sadan to principal pagoda sites in Rangoon, Mandalay, and their environs, tracing the pilgrimages that urban dwellers take to seek protection, amelioration, and good fortune in their dealings with such aspects of uneven urban development and modernization as traffic accidents, limited tertiary education, and poverty. Sadan layers three processes in her depictions of Bo Bo Gyi, a revered spirit common in many parts of the country. The first is the development from autochthonous animist spirit to nat and then to legendary Buddhist wizard in the figure of Bo Bo Gyi, a process of Buddhification and centralization that took place over centuries of Buddhist rule in central Burma. Overlaid is the pilgrimage of individual Burmese to sites where Bo Bo Gyi is honored, as they search for culturally valued traits such as wisdom, benevolence, and longevity. Finally, the military regime is also in the process of visiting Bo Bo Gyi statues, but only for the purpose of removing them from "tourist" sites so that they can be replaced with bronzed images taken from their cult of victorious warrior kings and generals. Sadan analyzes the political appropriateness of veneration of these different kinds of statues, noting the compromises the Burmese make in order to participate in public veneration of Bo Bo Gyi.

Part 2, Political and Moral Legitimation, presents three essays concerning political beliefs and practices by the military regime and moral communities that form in opposition to the linking of Buddhist patronage with political legitimacy. Both Schober and Houtman document this debate through the international media and in particular through Aung San Suu Kyi's "Letters from Burma." In "Buddhist Visions of Moral Authority and Modernity in Burma," Schober describes the different forms of modernity that are encapsulated in the National League for Democracy's use of Buddhism to secure moral and hence political legitimacy in the absence of secular forms of authority, such as a constitution and a judiciary system. Both institutions draw upon modern Buddhist forms of practice to transform national communities into religious communities through their speeches, rituals, and appeals to rationalist Buddhist visions of moral authority.

And like the new-style writers (see Leehey, this volume), both the NLD's and SPDC's forms of "Buddhist modernism intersect in distinct, hybrid ways with Euro-American, post-enlightenment political thought." Burmese modernization has thus allowed a variety of groups to conduct a dialogue with global society for both national and international agendas, highlighting the fact that the hybrid forms of Buddhist modernities and modernisms do not exist in a hermit nation but instead rapidly propagate through a diversity of media, radiating outwards from individual centers of practice to connect Burmese people to each other and then to elements of Asian and global society.

Gustaaf Houtman documents the pilgrimage made by Burmese Buddhists to various Buddha images believed to have a sudden and magical thickening of the right side of the shoulder, indicative of Aung San Suu Kyi's spiritual (Buddhist) qualifications to take political office. These pilgrims are searching for evidence of Buddhist moral legitimacy in the figure of Aung San Suu Kyi, and Schober, Sadan, and Tosa similarly note the outrage of Buddhists at the alleged interference by the ruling council with important Buddhist images and pagodas throughout the country, especially the Mandalay Mahamuni Buddha image. In "Sacralizing or Demonizing Democracy? Aung San Suu Kyi's 'Personality Cult,'" Houtman notes the circulation of rumors about these Buddha images in addition to rumors of Aung San Suu Kyi's supernatural nature as being part of a personality cult centered on the democracy figurehead. The cult is not local, nor regional, being also apparent in the international media.

State media vociferously denounce the personality cult and this leads to intense teashop discussions on the forms of religious legitimacy claimed by both the NLD and the ruling council.

The most common sites for the production of narratives about the impacts and meanings of modernity, modernization, and national and global influences upon Burmese society are the "tea circles," those ubiquitous rings of (often childhood) friends who gather in teashops to discuss everything from philosophy and literature to political forecasts and international events as seen through the micro lens of the local. In "The Chicken and the Scorpion: Rumor, Counternarratives and the Political Uses of Buddhism," Tosa discusses the continual re-creation of a sense of moral consensus and ongoing assessments of the truth that spread through the political rumors that circulate in Burma's teashops.

Tosa demonstrates how Burmese people analyze the political uses of Buddhism with reference to an old system of folk knowledge known as *lawkī pyinnya,* or this-worldly discourse. Delicate resistance is promulgated in the forging of a consensus as to the meaning of actions of members of the military council. Tea circles exist also in village communities (Tamura 1997: 122), in markets, and in workplaces. In the last fifteen years, women have become more frequent tea circle participants and a series of unspoken rules guide the discussion of tea circles in towns and cities. These rules relate to what can be said in public, and the way in which discussions must be phrased. Rules denying freedom of assembly and the discussion of political matters, in conjunction with the prevalent fear of political informers, means that the deconstruction of political rumors and the creation of moral consensus occurs cautiously and only among intimates. Like Houtman's informants, there is no one subculture that conveys these thoughts and reaches consensus. Instead, political rumors move along the modernized transportation and communication networks, connecting key contemporary figures such as Hsayadaw Thamanya, Aung San Suu Kyi, and former Prime Minister Khin Nyunt, in new ways.

In Part 3, Public Performance, trust, intimacy, and authenticity are the key themes. Burma's literary, artistic, and musical communities struggle to express, in politically allowable forms, the difficulties of self-expression and a sense of personal identity within the framework of a militarized public domain. In "Writing in a Crazy Way: Literary Life in Contemporary Urban Burma," Jennifer Leehey describes the refusal of a particular school of writers to publish work that conforms to the regime's ideological dictates about what is conveyed by terms such as trust, intimacy, and authenticity. In the "new style" literary circle, itself a subset of the broader Burmese literary world, or *sa-pay lawka,* Leehey charts the changing value of intellectuals (literary workers) under the Burma Socialist Programme Party and subsequent regimes to their current small circles of colleagues. The new-style writers have been progressively isolated as fewer magazines are able to publish their works without censorship and because these writers were linked with pro-democracy activities during the December 1996 student demonstrations.

These writers reject the view of reality promulgated by the regime and refuse to give coherency and unidirectionality to their writings. Drawing inspiration from the postmodern literary movements of the West and from tenets of poststructuralist theory, these writers challenge the older generation of writers who believe that realism can exist in the current climate and who feel a duty to portray it. Congregating in certain teashops, they promulgate magical realism and fantastic imagery using techniques that defy logic, rhyme, or meter, and prose that does not make sense. They refuse to write coherently about nonsensical topics that will pass the Press Scrutiny Board. They refuse to be complicit in the war on truth. Rather than presenting alternate truths, they prefer instead to remain outside the truth paradigm where freedom of expression, and not truth, is at issue.

The key public performance venue in Burma is the *pwe*, or festival. After the rice paddy has been harvested, villagers gather under tamarind and banyan trees or in the shade of pagodas to participate in an annual cyclical series of pagoda, spirit, harvest, comedy, and marionette *pwes*. Two pwes are described in this volume: Keeler describes a *zat*-pwe and Brac de la Perrière describes a *nat*-pwe. In Keeler's "'But Princes Jump!': Performing Masculinity in Mandalay," the zat-pwe provides a public space for performances of contemporary masculinity and is set in the center of the former royal capital of Mandalay. The national image of Mandalay as the epicenter of Burmese "culture" and tradition is increasingly one of a nostalgic, mythical, simpler, and purer Burma, contrasted in time and space, with the lights and pace of Rangoon. Keeler's chapter reveals the negotiating of a modern male identity that occurs alongside the dominant "we'll always have Mandalay" cultural stereotype. Typical of the "everyday" nature of the subject matter in the volume, the focus within the zat-pwe is on the urban cultural processes and forces at work in reinvesting the Burmese masculine world with meaning in the face of rapid social change in the popular domain.

Consistent with the primacy of Mandalay's courtly style, the version of masculinity embodied by the aristocratic prince has until recently been the central feature of the zat-pwe. Keeler charts the emergence of the rock star, the angry rapper, and the "romantic lovelorn crooner," as conscious attempts to reinvent masculinity in Burma in the model of an imagined Western modern autonomous manhood. The costumes, songs, and subject matter of Keeler's zat-pwe increasingly move away from the officially sanctioned images of performing arts as described in Douglas's chapter. Like Leehey's new-style writers, the artists look outwards from Burma for models by which to express themselves in the public eye.

Gavin Douglas's "Who's Performing What? State Patronage and the Transformation of Burmese Music" is set in the newly created state arts institutions and performance halls and describes the workings of the University of Culture and the annual state performing arts competition. Within the state media there is a voluminous discourse regarding the authentic and unique attributes of the Union of Myanmar, and "Culture" and "Tradition" are some of the main areas in which the remaking of the past is occurring. Many of the contributors in this volume chart aspects of this process of reconnecting the past and repackaging it as an authentic, unbroken history carrying into an imagined militarized future.

Even the state employees engaged in creating the official definitions of Burmese culture are scathing in their criticism of the effects of coopting music and performance for ideological purposes. The winners of the performing arts competitions cannot earn a living as musicians because the public refuses to grant them status and credibility. Conversely, on the final day of the annual performing arts competition, a genuine and voluntary audience arrives at the new state performance venues. They come to listen to the one form of musical performance that does not derive from the royal court tradition patronized by the military regime. In their enjoyment of the drumming of the paddy-planting tradition, the audience makes clear their opposition to the usurpation of music, performance, and entertainment as a forum for the regime's culture-making program.

The final section of the volume, Part 4, The Domestic Domain, contains only one essay, reflecting the difficulty anthropologists have when they work among the general public without the facilitation of an institutional space or recognized activity such as a festival. The domestic domain of Burmese Buddhists is the subject of much Burmese literature. It is often romanticized or idealized, especially the power of the female with regard to running the household and the deference of adult males towards this female domestic expertise and authority. Relatively little has been written about children, but Asian childhoods and forms of socialization have not been immune to transnational marketing and state agendas. We can see this in China's One Child policy, Singapore's Family Values campaign, and the growth of the youth leisure industry. In this final section individual Burmese were asked to articulate their fundamental beliefs about value, worth, and a meaningful life. In "The Future of Burma: Children Are Like Jewels," those Burmese interviewed gave unequivocal answers regarding these issues, and their answers revolved around the inestimable value and worth of children. In contemporary Burma the home remains the domain of children and the locus of family life, even though representations of what constitutes the ideal modern family and ideal parental conduct is increasingly depicted in urban locales as conforming to a pan-Asian consumerist ideal. Women are told by the military council to expend more effort "safeguarding" Burmese traditions and morals and the "nation's youth" are endlessly being exhorted to uphold the good traditions of the nation. Burmese children are educated in "union spirit" and required to become members of parastatal organizations such as the Union Solidarity and Defense Organization (USDA) and to attend innumerable opening ceremonies and other state-sponsored spectacles.

In the privacy of their homes, however, the current generation of Burmese children continue to learn an alternate system of value that is divorced from the modernized urban dream promulgated in the state media and by trans-Asian marketing companies. This is a soft and quiet form of resistance, a deliberate focus upon self-directed values, directly at odds with the incorporation of model families into a modern authoritarian state structure scaled down even to the level of shared rice pots.

In the various activity centers that constitute the province of popular space and popular imagination, and in the information channels between them, the individual authors of this volume portray complex fragments of daily life. In Jing Wang's (2001:11) words, "only in juxtaposition with these essays can the absent signifier of the people . . . be re-embodied." We are all acutely aware of the malnutrition that stalks much of Burma, of the rampant inflation that sends basic commodities out of the reach of many families, and of a public health system that is impotent against the spread of infectious diseases such as AIDS and hepatitis and unaffordable for people with serious illnesses such as cancer. Many of us have written about these topics in other places. We do not intend to downplay the suffering occasioned by more than four decades of military rule, economic calamity, and civil war, but rather to focus on active hotspots in the moral terrain and thus understand a little better how accommodation, complicity, collusion, resistance, intimacy, trust, and moral legitimation operate in Burmese everyday life at the turn of the twenty-first century.

Notes

1. A short volume of social and political assessments was compiled by Josef Silverstein (1989) from papers presented at the fortieth annual meeting of the Asian Studies Association.

2. These students, academics, and activists have used the Internet, sometimes

from within the jungles and mountains that border the country, to wage a public relations war against the junta and to document human rights violations committed by the regime. This activist diaspora has been successful in applying relentless economic and political pressure upon the regime through their demonstrations, human rights lobbying of politicians and the U.N., organization of consumer boycotts, and their effective call for sanctions against organizations doing business with the regime and against tourism to Burma. In addition, they have created an alternative government in exile and developed nongovernmental organizations and societies to discuss issues such as civil society and the environment in a future democratic Burma.

3. A young generation of scholars are moving beyond ethnic Burman culture and locating their studies among the "national races," as they are designated by the military regime, and in the coming years they will bring forth a corpus of work that will reflect upon the engagement of minority cultural groups with the nation state. In addition, a generation of Burmese peace activists are being trained in public health, peace and conflict studies, international politics, and reconciliation and international development modeling. These Burmese students will be at the forefront of policy formation for a postregime or postaccord society.

4. In contrast, the continued political mobilization of students from 1988 to the present has led to the closure of almost all urban tertiary institutions throughout most of the 1990s.

5. Steinberg (1999, 2–5) qualifies the search for civil society in Burma by noting that it generally did not exist at the village level before Independence.

6. Nash was the first anthropologist to use a factory as a field site.

–2–

The Cheaters

Journey to the Land of the Lottery

Guillaume Rozenberg
TRANSLATED BY ANNABELLE DOLIDON

[The anthropologist] is also working within the limits imposed by the culture of the people he is studying. If they are pastoral nomads he must study pastoral nomadism. If they are obsessed by witchcraft, he must study witchcraft. He has no choice but to follow the cultural grain.
    —E. E. Evans-Pritchard

During the two days of my journey deep into the Burmese archipelago of the lottery, I wasn't able to stop thinking about the short but striking story by Shway Yoe (1963:528–30), alias James Scott, concerning the introduction of the lottery to the suffering Burmese kingdom of Mandalay. After two Anglo-Burmese wars and the British occupation of several provinces, the weak young king Thibaw (r. 1878–1885) was left with a drained treasury and a kingdom reduced to just the northern part of Burma. The days for what was left of independent Burma were numbered: not only were mercantile and political forces in London and Calcutta lobbying for its invasion and annexation, but the kingdom was in a deep financial crisis and the monarchy was bankrupt. Thibaw tried different methods to replenish the royal reserves. Beginning in 1879 he issued lottery licenses in exchange for cash. The capital rapidly filled with lottery offices for the ruler had granted their management and their benefits to ministers and other high royal officials. The officers had to manage their individual lotteries on their own, and so they began to compete seriously with each other in order to attract gamblers, using methods that were more or less legal: shows in offices, drinks, cigars and betel for gamblers, and even threats if the gamblers bought their tickets somewhere else. The lottery rage devastated the capital.

> Neither buyers nor sellers were to be seen in the bazaar. Cultivators sold off their farming stock and implements, and launched all their money in the state lotteries. Fathers sold their daughters, and husbands their wives, to have a final try for fortune, until the lottery managers issued a notice that they would give no more tickets in exchange for women. (Shway Yoe 1963:530)

After some time, however, because of lack of money or disillusionment, the fever subsided. King Thibaw tried other means of procuring money, but he couldn't prevent the fall of Mandalay in 1885 and the end of the Burmese monarchy. It was as if the entire society, feeling that it was on the brink of catastrophe, rushed to its end and gave itself, through the game, a great dramatic, exultant finale.

Can history repeat itself? An observer of Burmese contemporary society, and Burmese people themselves, cannot help but be struck by the invasion into their daily lives of lottery practices. Since the midnineties, a spectacular intensification of lottery practices has occurred in Burma. Everywhere in the country—in the streets, in homes, in monasteries, in shops, in popular papers and magazines, and on the phone—people think and speak the lottery. A good part of Burma's 50 million people live according to the rhythm of the draws.

Some will say that this is the symptom of a social pathology linked to the economic crisis the country has been going through since 1997, after a too-brief moment of euphoria. Burmese people themselves favor such an interpretation and frequently explain their all-consuming passion by the lack of anything to do because of the sluggish economy and general underemployment. Moreover, the illegal lottery bankers find a comfortable income in the game at a time when opportunities for economic investment are limited and risky. There is no need to be a Burmese scholarly expert to guess the political reasons behind the phenomenon. Here again many Burmese seem aware of the game's implications and clearly understand, in this matter as in others, the way they participate in their own subjection. Through their betting on the outcome of the Thai and Burmese lotteries, they cast a particular but striking light on the *la-boetian* paradox that has been questioned a thousand times but never entirely solved: that of voluntary servitude. In effect, contemporary Burmese society never ceases, in one way or another, to confront the observer with this paradox.

Although current psychological, economic, and political conditions can be used to explain the intensification of lottery practices, we can also see that similar circumstances in other societies would have created different phenomena. It therefore seems necessary to speculate on the deeper reasons why the lottery has gripped Burmese society so quickly and with such an absolute hold, and to look more closely at the way lottery practices fit within and operate upon the very cultural foundations of this society. One peculiar aspect of the phenomenon requires immediate attention: lottery practices penetrate even into the one domain—Theravāda Buddhism—that constitutes "the dominant site of symbolic production"[1] for Burmese society. From this domain come the major cultural categories that imply the various modalities of social organization and activities.

How precisely do lottery practices articulate with Burmese religious categories, and how should we interpret such a configuration? This question is relevant not only to Burmese society: the articulation of lottery practices with Buddhist categories also appears to be a structural tendency throughout mainland Buddhist Southeast Asia.[2] The extent and the weight of the phenomenon in the Theravādin region thus make examination of the Burmese case even more pressing.

Looking for Numbers: The Forest of Predictions

We leave Rangoon around nine, this Monday in October 2001. The weather is pleasant and the rainy season is ending. There are four of us in the car. Ma Aye, who has been an inveterate player for two years, is the expedition's guide; she is also a broker of administrative documents and stands as an intermediary between citizens and civil servants who are not very zealous because of the poor state of public service and its miserable wages. Ko Kyaw Kyaw, an acquaintance, is a mechanic. He was attracted by our destination and decided to leave the small garage that he owns for a day. Then there is the driver and myself. Tomorrow, around 3:30 p.m. Burmese time, just as on every first and sixteenth day of the month, the results of the Thai lottery draw *(che)*[3] will be announced. The last three numbers constitute the object of illegal Burmese bets. The countdown has started. Burma starts waiting.

We are very early. The sermon that Daing Pyay Hpongyi ("The Monk Who Makes the Bankers Run Away"; in French "le moine qui fait fuir les banquiers") gives each month on the day before the draw doesn't take place before afternoon, and the city of Htandabin, near which he resides, is only a few dozen kilometers from Rangoon. This monk, who has recently become famous, was given his nickname by his followers because on several occasions he has indirectly predicted the winning number of the lottery and therefore aroused great fear among the *daing*—the bankers who control the networks of the illegal lottery and who have lost money because of his predictions.

Once outside of Rangoon, we decide to make a detour to the site of Shwe Zedi, the "golden pagoda," in a small village near the township of Mingaladon. Letkhattaung Hsayadaw—*hsayadaw* means both abbot and venerable monk— recently took charge of the complete renovation of this huge pagoda. It was begun by a local monk who died in 2000 at the age of ninety-six. The original pagoda is attributed to legendary Mon king Okkalapa, who built the most venerated Burmese pagoda, the Shwedagon of Rangoon. Before the renovation only the foundations were left intact. Relics attributed to a saint are on display under a large bamboo pavilion, and they will be enshrined in the pagoda when the renovation is complete. There are also numerous statues and the diamond ornament *(hti)* that will be placed on top of the pagoda. Three laymen are receiving gifts from visitors. Letkhattaung Hsayadaw himself is not here. He passed by a few days ago for a quick inspection of the renovation. He never stays long and moves regularly around the country to further his religion propagation activities or else he resides in his main monastery near Mudon, in the Moulmein area of Mon State.

The forty-seven-year-old hsayadaw gained his reputation because of his predictions as to the winning last three numbers of the Thai lottery. He has acquired a significant clientele of generous donors who finance his religious building projects with part of their winnings, principally at the Mudon and the Shwe Zedi sites. According to rumors, his prediction practices also gained him a temporary imprisonment last year (one month, so the rumors say). Monks who are members of official monastic institutions[4] ordered him to stop making public predictions, but he didn't comply, and his disobedience forced political authorities to arrest and incarcerate him. The hsayadaw was not forcibly disrobed during his prison sentence and resumed his religious activities when released.

Our visit to Shwe Zaydi wasn't in vain. Lay people in charge of the pavilion had that morning received a call from Mudon. An assistant of the hsayadaw related to them a sentence that the hsayadaw had stated on the occasion of the forthcoming lottery draw: "Pagoda of the sun and of the moon, Son of Friday." Ma Aye carefully writes down the expression in her notebook. Just to see, Ko Kyaw Kyaw immediately tries the most simple and common deciphering method that any Burmese can master. Each of the twenty-eight letters of the Burmese alphabet corresponds in this system to a day of the week that corresponds itself to a number according to the ordinary sequence of the week, starting with Sunday: the *hpa* of 'pagoda' corresponds to Thursday, and thus to the number 5.[5] By applying this method to the seven letters in Letkhattaung

Hsayadaw's expression, Ko Kyaw Kyaw arrives at the two following groups of numbers:

nay la hpaya (pagoda of the sun and of the moon):   **7 4 5 4**
thagya-tha (son of Friday):   **6 2 6**

A complete work of interpretation still needs to be done. These figures allow numerous combinations in the choice of a definitive number, not to mention that there are concurrent deciphering methods. The written form of some letters or signs are linked, for example, to one of the Arabic numerals that Burmese people know and use all the time. This way, the word Theravāda *(Htera-wada)* can be deciphered in at least two ways and can give two possible series of numbers:

7 4 4 7   (using a correspondence between letters and days of the week), or
6 8 7 0 3   (using a comparison between signs and letters and occidental numbers; in Burmese "T," for example, looks like a horizontal "8," and "r" looks like "7").

To multiple deciphering methods are added games of affinity between numbers. Some numbers seem to exist in pairs according to series that circulate in various tables.

With our first indication in hand, we leave Shwe Zedi and arrive in Htandabin around 12:30 p.m., where we stop for a short while to eat. We start visiting monasteries to find new clues. These monasteries are called "forest monasteries" *(tawya kyaung)* and their monks are famous for their predictions. They live near the city, but outside of it, away from inhabited zones, and they are accessible through dirt roads that peel off from the main road. The sermon of the Monk Who Makes the Bankers Run Away won't begin until around three or four in the afternoon so we have enough time to sound out other monks.

Shortly after leaving town, we turn left. At the crossroad, an army of sidecars are waiting for gamblers without their own transportation to take them on the narrow road that snakes between paddy fields towards a monastery about two kilometers away. The monastery is a permanent structure, with two main buildings and a pagoda. The hsayadaw is resting; his sermon is not scheduled until three that afternoon. His second in charge, who is about forty, welcomes visitors who regularly come to collect clues. The small crowd of ten to fifteen people in the room is constantly changing according to the rhythm of departures and arrivals. Others wait patiently outside for the hsayadaw to wake up and give his sermon. Ma Aye writes in her notebook three sentences and Arabic numbers (see Figure 2.1) that the hsayadaw received in a dream and wrote on a piece of cardboard for followers unable to listen to his sermon. The translation of the third part—everything can be destroyed *(akon pyet-thwa-naing-de)*—was difficult for Burmese themselves because several translations are possible and none was making any sense. In these circumstances it is common for the monk to address his audience in enigmatic terms not immediately apparent to his devotees.

We set out again for Htandabin. We turn back onto the main road but instead of going back to town, we head further into the countryside, this time to a dirt road on the opposite side. At the beginning of the trail there is a donation post managed by a layman to finance some sort of new religious building. Ma Aye puts a bill in the donation pot that the man is holding out to us and to greet him, she says only, "numbers" *(ganan)*. Without hesitation the man gives her a scrap of paper. Four three-digit numbers are written on it. He probably got it from a monk around here. Ma Aye copies them into her notebook.

The trail goes through a bamboo forest where there are several independent monasteries. Some are famous for predictions by their hsayadaw, and that is where the crowd of disciples goes today. Others, like a nearby large center for monastic studies, remain empty because the hsayadaw refuses to make lottery predictions. "Monks come to the forest to be left alone and meditate quietly," Ma Aye says to me, "but lay people follow them here and create problems *(dokkha)* by asking them for lottery numbers."

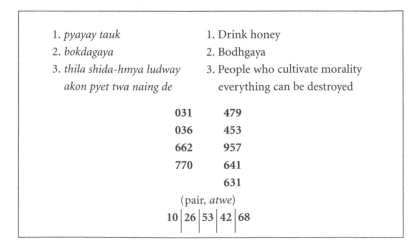

1. *pyayay tauk*	1. Drink honey
2. *bokdagaya*	2. Bodhgaya
3. *thila shida-hmya ludway*	3. People who cultivate morality
akon pyet twa naing de	everything can be destroyed

031	479
036	453
662	957
770	641
	631

(pair, *atwe*)

| 10 | 26 | 53 | 42 | 68 |

Figure 2.1. Forest Monk's Predictions

It is about 2 p.m. when we arrive at the monastery of the Monk Who Makes the Bankers Run Away. In a cleared space, without walls, there is a large pagoda and a sermon building with two floors *(dhamma-yon)* that had been recently built. There is also the monk's house, a very modest hut protected by a fence. Next to the hut the monk's two cars are parked, one of which is a huge, brand new 4 x 4. Recently three teashops opened next to the monastery to welcome gamblers, who always arrive early because the sermon never occurs at the same time each month. Coming from Rangoon and the surrounding area, they sit at tables in small groups and wait while sipping their tea and talking about the lottery.

Ma Aye meets an acquaintance, a forty-five-year-old woman who doesn't work but whose husband must soon leave to be a factory worker in Malaysia. The woman offers to lead us to another monastery about half a mile away. This hsayadaw must have already begun his sermon. On the approach to the monastery, mobile vendors have set up fruit and vegetable stalls. Suddenly we hear loud laughter. Our guide explains that the monk is famous for his sense of humor. Now forty years of age, he became a monk late in life and moved to this site three years ago. The monastery's yard is full of people who can't fit in the completely packed sermon room; however, an exterior speaker allows them to hear the sermon. The monk has been organizing sermons before the lottery draws for the past two years and he is now quite famous. Most of the audience, two to three hundred people, is composed of women. They grab bits and pieces of the sermon to write in their notebooks, especially formulas containing numbers, for enumerations abound in Buddhist terminology, such as the Four Noble Truths, the Nine Supreme Virtues of the Buddha, and the Five Precepts. The monk himself is sometimes suggestive, sometimes direct, accentuating the pronunciation of one sentence or telling his audience to remember this or that. He smokes a cigarette when he preaches, a very unusual action, maybe even shocking. For orthodox Buddhists, smoking cigarettes is considered highly inappropriate for monks. If, in reality, a certain number of them do smoke, they never do so during their formal religious activities, as these require solemnity. Is the cigarette by any chance a 555, the label of a foreign and prestigious cigarette manufacturer?

I ask the lay assistant for permission to take photographs. Refused. Any other day, but not today.

The sermon lasts forty-five minutes and at its conclusion the monk writes the following on a white board:

18316/-	18316/-
edalay	This
hto ba	Bet

The five-digit number is written directly in Arabic numerals. It corresponds to the amount of a donation made to the monk. One letter of the word "this," the "d" *(da)*, is underlined with a double line. Next to the board that the monk then hangs on the wall, an earthen pot with a plant is also suspended and apparently refers to a number. The crowd quickly disperses in the hubbub of first conjectures.

We return to the monastery of the Monk Who Makes the Bankers Run Away. The three teashops are now full, and the sermon room starts to fill up. Without success, I try to have a private interview with the monk. Ma Aye, who has known him for twenty years, gives me some information about his past. About forty years old, he is a former engineer, married, and the father of two children, she says. He progressively detached himself from his professional and family life at the end of the 1980s to live the life of a professional semireligious astrologer in a pagoda in Rangoon's suburbs, where he had some success. Around 1995 he decided to definitively renounce the world and authorized his wife to remarry. He left her with a significant amount of money and told her the winning number for the Thai lottery in order to ensure her material comfort. The man continued to vacillate between hermit and novice status before deciding, less than a year ago, to become a monk.

Thanks to the money he earned as an astrologer, in 1996 he bought land in this place next to Htandabin to live as a forest monk. However, he has been popular for only two or three years because of verified predictions of lottery numbers. Significant donations that he then received allowed him to start an ambitious building project in Ayeyarwadi Division: a 108-cubit-high pagoda (about fifty meters), where relics (strands of Buddha's hair) will be enshrined. These strands of hair are from a pagoda destroyed during the Second World War. Another one of these strands is located in a pagoda recently built on the site of today's sermon.

The monk finally appears at around 4:45 p.m. He comes out of his hut, walking in front of four or five donors. One of them beats a gong regularly. Three or four hundred people are waiting. The enormous hall is packed and many people must sit outside. The monk takes his place in an armchair on the stage, slightly off the ground. Ma Aye invites me to come to the front ranks. On my right sit a dozen people holding small cassette recorders with which they will tape the whole sermon. They are mostly women, lavishly dressed and wearing much jewelry. Ma Aye whispers in my ear that the predictions of the Monk Who Makes the Bankers Run Away have allowed these devotees to win significant amounts of money. They sometimes bet 100,000 kyat (twenty times the official monthly salary of a high civil servant) on one number.

The monk takes advantage of my being here to briefly remind his audience of the story of the piece of hair enshrined in the pagoda, and then launches into a classical lecture regarding insight meditation practices *(wipathana)*, the surest and most direct route to Nirvana. Ko Kyaw Kyaw and the driver both felt that the speech was clear and incisive.

The audience members write down all or part of the sermon, as well as many details, such as the fact that the monk holds a string of Buddhist beads around his wrist and the color of his robe. At the end of the sermon, as he stood up to go back to his hut, the Monk Who Makes the Bankers Run Away asks Ma Aye for her notebook and, as an unexpected favor, writes on one page:

wipathana shu gyi ba	Practice insight meditation
(yathay)	Hermit
layhsaung–761	Gift–761
751	751

The first two letters of the word "insight meditation" (the *'wipa'* of *wipathana*) are underlined with one line. In addition, the word "gift" is written with a probably intentional spelling mistake that shows an *ay* (*lay* instead of *let*) that could refer to the number "6."

Outside, there's almost a riot. As we try to return to our car, the shouting crowd closes around Ma Aye, forcing her to show them the clues that the monk wrote in her notebook.

When we return to Rangoon, at around 6:30 p.m., the pages of Ma Aye's book are photocopied for each of us. The whole evening will be devoted to making copies and distributing them among other gambling acquaintances. A final hint is added to our rich harvest: there is a rumor that says that the *break*, according to the English word Burmese people use, will be 15. In other words, the sum of the last three digits of the winning number that will be drawn tomorrow shouldn't be more than 15.

The whole evening is consumed by consultations with experts in numerology, astrology, and other esoteric logic systems. People also refer to the charts of winning numbers, draw results that go all the way back to 1969. A significant part of the night is used to feverishly crosscheck all calculations, sometimes by candlelight because of the frequent power shortages. But some will just gamble with the numbers of their birth date or will count on numbers that have appeared to them in their dreams.

Bankers and 'Commission Eaters': Living on the Illegal Lottery

The day after, Tuesday, day of the draw, in a Rangoon apartment, at around 11 in the morning. There are six people in the living room with the telephone beside them; they are sitting on sofas around a coffee table with the notebooks on it. First, there is the apartment owner, U San Lwin, about sixty years of age: he is the *daing*, the game banker, the one who takes on the financial risk in an illegal lottery business. Such a position requires him to have sufficient capital to be able to pay immediately when a gambler wins. In return for the financial risk he's taking, the banker is also the main beneficiary of the game, receiving about 75 percent of the sum of all the bets. The banker's financial capital and his personal solvency together determine the maximum amount of the bets he can accept on any one number. U San Lwin is an experienced banker, and he enjoys a solid financial situation. He can accept up to 2,300 kyat for a bet on any one number. This amount represents the possibility of a 1,265,000 kyat loss (550 times the bet in case of a correct bet on the three digits in the correct order).

U San Lwin only recently moved to Rangoon, having spent most of his life in Moulmein. Moulmein is the main city of southeastern Mon State. It is also the capital of the illegal lottery. A pioneer city in its gambling practices, it sets the tone at the national level. Thanks to their banking and selling experience and their general know-how, Moulmein people contributed greatly to the spread of gambling practices throughout the major cities and central part of the nation.

The Thai lottery system of betting on the last three digits arrived in Burma through Moulmein, apparently at the beginning of the eighties. The city is close to the border and had, at the time, an essential position in the smuggling traffic with Thailand. Illegal lotteries based upon the official lottery draws already exist all over Thailand. The implantation of the illegal Thai lottery betting system was made easier in Burma by the existence in Moulmein (and probably elsewhere) of an earlier system in which bets were placed on the three last digits of the official Burmese lottery and the winner could win a scooter, a rare and coveted thing at that time of "the Burmese way to socialism." Around 1985 U San Lwin became a banker in the new system, and so far it has allowed him to make a comfortable living for himself and his family.

Today, however, Moulmein is an economically stricken town that has not been able to recover from the decline in the volume of smuggled goods trafficked with Thailand at the end of the 1980s. The brief period of euphoria that followed the entry of modernity in the mid-1990s (cars, new buildings, television) in Rangoon and Mandalay largely bypassed Moulmein. The mainly underemployed city population are among the most numerous adherents of the illegal lottery. In many neighborhoods on the morning of the draw, acquaintances greet each other only through the numbers they intend to play. But the economic situation is such that people from Moulmein cannot help but spend less and less money on their bets. Consequently, in the last few years, U San Lwin has had to extend his activities to other cities: first to Mandalay, the northern capital, where he sent a friend to represent him, then to Rangoon, where he's been settled for some time.

Today is a special day. Indeed, the banker usually takes responsibility for financial risks, but not for any personal ones. His participation is completely invisible; he doesn't take any active part in the game procedure. Each of the vendors, the five other persons in the apartment, registers the bets in return for a 25 percent commission. Depending on the case, they either go from house to house or stay in a café, a shop, or in their own apartment; anybody who is in cahoots with a banker can be a vendor, and at every corner of Burmese cities there are betel and cigarette stalls where you can purchase tickets for the illegal lottery.

Vendors keep at least three distinct notebooks or lists up to date. In the first book there is one number per line up to 999, where only betting amounts are written. This book allows the vendor to instantly visualize the total bets on one number, in order to close the betting when the quantity is over the amount the banker can accept and to immediately verify, after the draw, the number of winners and the amounts of money they have won. A second book is used exactly the same way but for bets on only two numbers (up to 99). Finally, in the third notebook or on a separate sheet, they write the names and addresses of the gamblers, as well as the number and the amount of each bet.

The police use these notebooks as proof if, for one reason or another, they decide to take measures against the illegal lottery by arresting vendors. As for the banker, however, he is untouchable; he is never in contact with the gamblers and only receives, from the main vendor, the money collected for each draw, minus the vendors' commissions and amounts due to winners. His passive role and the absence of compromising documents keeps him out of reach of the police. Measures against the illegal lottery however, turn out to be rare; they go against the interests of individual police officers who benefit directly from the illegal lottery system. Senior vendors regularly bribe local police, who in fact reinvest part of the bribe on bets. Fighting illegal lottery practices occurs only in exceptional circumstances and only on the order of high-ranking political authorities.

Such circumstances explain the remarkable meeting today in this Rangoon apartment of the banker and his five vendors. Rangoon police have been hunting vendors following a terrible accident two months ago. The twenty-year-old son of an important military leader was driving fast through the empty capital late as he left a nightclub where he had been celebrating his illegal lottery windfall of 8 million kyat. His huge 4 x 4 hit, at full force, a taxi at a crossroads. The two drivers were killed. The news was not announced officially but traveled around town and was commented upon at length in Rangoon's teashops.

The consequence of this accident has been a wave of repression that has been bearing down upon illegal lottery organizers. U San Lwin's vendors, at the time of the incident, had their own apartment in a Rangoon neighborhood. One person would centralize the bets and the others would go around collecting the money. During a police raid, the surprised female vendor ran to the bathroom to hide the notebooks. In vain. It cost her 200,000 kyat to hush up the affair and be released. Since then the group has left the apartment to assemble, on draw days, in the banker's apartment, for it is unknown to the police. Despite this, everyone remains on guard. Most of the bets are accepted by phone, and the apartment door is padlocked from the inside to give them time to burn the notebooks in the event of a raid.

The vendors are all from Moulmein and are led by two *"commission-za"* (literally "the one who eats the commission") as they are called in Moulmein, or "OG" (for *organizer*) according to Rangoon tradition. The two are women, close to forty, who began their involvement in the illegal lottery about two years ago. One is a former schoolteacher, the other a fruit vendor. Together they pay three employees *(sayay):* a female friend of the same age and two twenty-two-year-old students recruited two months ago during university break, and who seem to want to continue with their involvement. The job is risky, but profitable and not very strenuous.

The whole group still resides in Moulmein but spends most of each month in Rangoon, arriving on the twenty-ninth and leaving on the seventeenth of the following month. Indeed, in addition to the two monthly draws of the Thai lottery (on the first and the sixteenth), there are now illegal bets on the Burmese State lottery draws. The system appeared in Moulmein around 1996 and is all the rage in Rangoon; it could be more successful than the Thai lottery.

The Burmese State lottery *(hti),* founded in 1938 at the end of the colonial period, had been working for fifty years in the same way: there were only six draws annually, the maximum profit was 300,000, and the price of the ticket (2 kyat) never changed during the whole period, which shows how little interest successive regimes had in running the game. In November 1988, just two months after the military coup that ended the "Burmese way to socialism," the new ruling council decided to renovate the institution. The ticket price went from 2 to 5 kyat, the draw became monthly, the maximum profit now reached 500,000 kyat. Later, the system was again modified. This time it was not a simple renovation, but a marked change of speed and volume. Seven monthly draws were instituted, from the third to the ninth of each month (one draw per day), and very significant prizes of several million kyat were offered. The tickets are printed by the Burmese State lottery and are sold for 55 kyat by itinerant merchants and in offices that have proliferated in every city of the country. The winning number comprises one letter of the Burmese alphabet followed by six numbers. The new system of illegal bets that started around 1996, the "two-digit lottery" *(hnalon-hti)*, consists of bets being placed on the two last digits of these official lottery tickets. So there is one chance in a hundred to win, and it is possible to win eighty times the amount placed on the bet. This second system is so popular that U San Lwin now gets most of his profits from the seven monthly Burmese draws. Indeed, many people prefer illegal bets to an official ticket because it allows them to choose the numbers they bet on and to bet exactly as much as they want.

It is 2 p.m. We are getting closer to the draw and the vendors decide to close the betting. The amount of bets seems higher than they had anticipated. On some numbers they have more than the maximum amount U San Lwin accepts. One of his friends agrees (over the phone, from Moulmein) to be the underwriter. At 2:30, everything is arranged and the books are in order. The excitement, that has been high for the last few hours, suddenly falls away. The group of vendors leaves the apartment to eat something while waiting for the draw. They come back around 3:15 and wait, slumped on the sofas. Fifteen minutes later they receive the phone call: 005. One of the "commission eaters" runs to the books to check the number of bets on the various winning combinations.[6] Typical combinations appear in Figure 2.2.

The tension is released and jokes flow from all sides. The profits will obviously be significant, and the group immediately start their calculations. It seems that the total of the bets is over 300,000 kyat. As soon as they finish their business at the banker's apartment, the three employees will collect the amounts bet by phone and will pay what they owe to the winners. Rumors of bankruptcy are numerous, including a case where a careless banker was forced to run away because he couldn't pay a lucky winner.

Two days after the draw, I see Ma Aye again. Contrary to others who gather the different clues they collected in the days before the draw, Ma Aye rarely does any complicated calculations. This time she just played the two numbers, 751 and 761, that the Monk Who Makes the Bankers Run Away wrote in her notebook. She says that the monk had indeed given her the winning number;

---

005 (550 times the bet): a 50 kyat bet;

050 or **500** (*round* in Burmese, 100 times the bet): no bet;

004 or **006** (10 times the bet): five bets for a total of 700 kyat;

05 (15 times the bet): a 100 kyat bet.

Figure 2.2. The Winning Combinations

she just needed to learn how to read his clue. He had underlined only the first two letters of the word "insight meditation" *(wipathana)* and the solution was obvious: 005 (the Burmese letter *"wi"* referring to the double zero, and *"p."* corresponding to Thursday and therefore to the number 5).

Testing Society

July 2002, in the office of a Parisian research lab. We are talking about this bizarre phenomenon that seems to consume Burmese society: the lottery. We are intrigued by one particular fact. Many monks became involved in prediction practices extremely quickly, but spirit mediums, responsible for the cult of the 37 *nat*—the spirit cult that constitutes the second dimension of Burmese religion after Buddhism—seem to have little interest in participating in predictive practices. The shape of this cult should predispose mediums to commit themselves to these kinds of practices. Nat devotees often ask the mediums to intercede with the nat for help regarding business problems and decisions. In fact, such an absence only emphasizes the relation of elective affinity, of adequacy, in the Weberian sense, between the lottery practices and the Buddhist categories that largely structure Burmese society.

A person who decides to buy a lottery ticket usually says that it is going to "test one's karma" *(kan san-de),* in the sense of trying one's luck. In the Buddhist perspective, karma *(kan),* the sum of all the good and bad actions committed in past and present lives, is the fundamental principle that governs destiny. "To have good karma," and therefore to be lucky *(kan kaung-de),* is an expression widely used in many situations. It means to have in reserve many good actions from the past, actions that favor a good rebirth and good material conditions in the present and future lives (such as success, wealth, and good health).

The principles of probability—chance and luck—seem *a priori* to us to define the lottery game. These concepts do exist in Burmese minds, but they are rather subsumed by the notion of karma so that in the end the lottery appears to Burmese to contain an organized logic. Only those with the appropriate karma *(kan kaung-de),* whose karma participates, operates, and contributes *(kan pa-de),* can, according to this logic, find the winning number, even despite whatever indications (sentences or numbers) the monks give. This is not, however, a strictly determinist conception. There is a more complex alchemy at work, since appropriate karma is a necessary, but not a sufficient condition to win at the game: in order to allow the actualization of one's karma, one must still combine a real personal effort *(wiriya)*—which explains long and complex calculations that regular gamblers carry out—with a monk's prediction skills.

For the lay gambler, the possibility of finding the winning number depends in the end on a karmic logic. But for the monk, the possibility of accurately predicting a winning lottery number depends on his personal level of spiritual accomplishment. Becoming a monk—that is, to be able to bear the disciplines and deprivations that the monastic life implies—presupposes that one already has relatively good karma. However, the ultimate goal of the monk is theoretically the end of his positive or negative karma via his accession to Nirvana, the liberation from the cycle of rebirths. The practice of meditation constitutes the main way to reach this goal. The Burmese people, in accordance with this doctrinal vision, consider that meditation, while oriented towards the acquisition of a state of tranquility or mental concentration *(thamadi)*, may at a certain level generate supernormal abilities *(theiddi; eiddi)*, among which is the ability to predict future events or receive premonitions about them. Some monks are thus renowned for their intense practice of concentration meditation associated with living in a forest monastery, and people attribute to them the ability to see, in advance, winning lottery numbers.

Whether asking monastic or lay people about this, the explanation is always the same: "he has good mental concentration" *(thamadi kaung-de)*, meaning a high degree of spiritual accomplishment, and this presupposes that he has gained supernatural abilities or at least that uncommon phenomena occur around him that reveal his spiritual excellence. Such a monk has visions *(a-yon ya-de)* in his dreams or during meditation sessions. His visions give him the substance of his predictions, called *adeik*. This term has several possible meanings (past, sign, or omen) but in these circumstances it stands for a legend or a formula that needs to be interpreted in order to predict the results of a game of chance.

The principle of spiritual accomplishment for the monk and the karmic principle for the laity are not two ideologically and sociologically independent elements. The lottery situation causes a particular relationship between the monk and a layperson to emerge, and this relationship actually shows and reinforces those links that indissolubly tie these two principles and these two characters. On the one hand, the monk is considered to be socially superior to a layperson because of his religious condition and his ultimate goal of extinguishing his karma, but he still needs material support from the lay person to reach this goal. The laity, on the other hand, seeks to ameliorate their karma and to make it productive, and so they need the monk because he is the laity's main "field of merit" (a gift made to a monk is considered to be the best merit producer) and can also provide valuable supernatural assistance to actualize one's good karma.

From a Buddhist perspective, the higher the degree of spiritual accomplishment reached by a monk, the more the gift made to him brings merit to the donor and becomes directly efficient. Considering this fact, much of the structure of the activities and of the future of Burmese society and its members depends on this simple equation: the more the monk's karma is reduced, the more the lay person's karma becomes positive and has a chance to be actualized. And then society, in turn, tends more towards a state of prosperity, justice, and general well-being.

If the lottery situation provides a good illustration of how the bonds of complementary opposition tie monks and laity together, it also inscribes it in new specific terms of exchange that differ from the ordinary mode of reciprocity between the two groups. Indeed, in the lottery situation, the monk usually makes the first gift: the clues he gives to the laity during his sermon (Burmese would say *"dhamma dāna,"* the "Gift of the Doctrine") to help them discern the winning number. In general, a lottery monk will not receive any immediate gift in return. His gift comes later if his hints were productive. While ordinary reciprocity between the monk and the lay person expresses a stable position which each of the two partners enjoys at one given moment in his own community—the amount of gifts a lay person makes reveals his or her position in the laity hierarchy, and the amount of gifts a monk receives makes visible his position in the monastic hierarchy—the lottery form of inverted and delayed reciprocity is, on the contrary, organized by a dynamics of change.

The illegal lottery phenomenon in contemporary Burma is thus characterized by a kind of test of the monk's degree of spiritual accomplishment and of the laity's karma. If the test succeeds, it permits the situation of each partner to evolve positively, and this evolution works according to a mechanism of reciprocal sanctions. The monk renounces the world and remains apart from material and social issues—monastic discipline forbids the monk from holding a paid job and forces him to live on donations. Because his religious authority gives him the status of being a judge of the karma of the individual laity, it thus legitimizes the gambler's profits. These same profits also provide, in the eyes of the Burmese, an empirical, irrefutable demonstration of the monk's "spiritual power" *(dago)*.

If the happy gambler always gives back to the monk a part of the profits, it is not only a remuneration for the service received, but also a way to seal the relationship that articulates the lay person's new social authority—since the individual's favorable karma has just been exposed to all—with the monk's spiritual authority. As for the monk, the gift he gets back helps finance religious buildings that permanently show the veneration he enjoys and his high degree of religious accomplishment. In addition, the hierarchy between the two characters remains distinct. The monk runs the risk of openly making a mistake only if he provides exact numbers, but even then he is never regarded as having truly made a mistake. The responsibility of the failure lies instead with the lack of good karma and sufficient personal effort on the part of the lay gambler. The evidence lies in the gambler's inability to correctly interpret the hints the monk gives in his sermon.

All in all, the lottery situation in Burma may be considered as a specific representation of the mutual dependence, organized into a hierarchy, that characterizes the relationship between monk and laity. Moreover, it implies a testing and confirmation of categories that structure this relationship. In the present situation of economic and political tensions, lottery practices could be an important way to express and convey the strength and current value of these categories and this relationship that are the foundation of the Burmese social structure. The intensification of these practices, taking into account the implied exchanges between monks and laity, are much more than simply the practical consequences of a difficult economic situation, characterized by increasing unemployment. The phenomenon should also be interpreted as a means of reaffirming the system of values and forms of relationship underpinning Burmese social organization and therefore as an efficient way to struggle against the potential negative effects of the present situation. In the continuous circulation of people between forest monasteries, capital cities, and the southern Mon State, it is as if a whole society, doubting, tired, and always on alert, is trying to shore up its foundations. What is really at stake in illegal lottery practices is the very reproduction, the reassuring, of the cultural order.

The effects of this social reproductive mechanism, however, turn out to be ambivalent and paradoxical as betting on the lottery is also the source of certain moral disruptions. Indeed, according to the expression of Ma Aye herself, the gambling faithful come "to create problems" (dokkha pay-de) for monks by demanding lottery numbers from them. The word dokkha used by Ma Aye has several meanings in Burmese. In general, it refers to the idea of a problem or difficulty, as encapsulated in the common expression "to create, to cause problems." Dokkha is also one of the strongest terms in Buddhist terminology: it designates pain or suffering inherent in any life from which the Buddhist monk tries to escape through his quest for spiritual liberation. According to Ma Aye, devotees who chase monks to obtain lottery-number predictions not only disturb the monks with their requests, but they also more fundamentally hinder their quest for spiritual liberation by forcing them to attend closely to earthly matters.

The phenomenon actually raises protests from a minority of monks and laity who believe that giving predictions to gamblers has nothing to do with the monk's vocation and even contravenes the code of monastic discipline (wini). Although there is no rule that explicitly condemns practices such as predicting lottery numbers, critics who condemn it (who may nevertheless benefit themselves from the predictions of monks), state that it goes against the fundamental monastic precept forbidding monks to demonstrate supernatural powers to laity.

More generally, to aid lottery development is to help further a morally reprehensible game that intensifies the desire for material profits. Monks have a central responsibility to the moral future of society and are not supposed to encourage such developments. For these critics, predicting lottery numbers thus represents an unacceptable deterioration of the monastic function and an attack against the ideal behind Burma's moral economy.

Lottery monks understand the argument but defend themselves by contending that their predictions are a kind of necessary evil: to give a sermon for a lottery draw allows them to attract large audiences and therefore to more widely propagate the Buddhist religion, *Sāsana (thathana)*, and, in the case of a successful prediction, to collect donations to finance "religion propagation" operations *(thathana pyu)*. From a Buddhist ideological viewpoint, however, it is also true that the behavior of some individual hermits or forest monks who sit on a main street of the capital city holding signs advertising their lottery number predictions is quite scandalous.[7]

Still, sanctions against monks who predict lottery numbers remain exceptional. Letkhattaung Hsayadaw was sentenced to one month in prison, but this seems to have happened for deeper (but enigmatic) reasons than his prediction practices, which were used as a pretext for the imprisonment. Countless monks all around Burma offer predictions regarding lottery numbers without incurring sanctions or even a warning from monastic institutions. These practices are, if not officially accepted, at least actively tolerated by political authorities and their representatives according to well-understood interests. In fact, the lottery case illustrates in general the way the government uses the *weapon* of monastic discipline, directly or through national monastic institutions, like a Damocles' sword hanging above the monks' heads. At any time, and in quite an arbitrary fashion, it can be used to justify sanctions against a monk or to motivate a purification process *(thantshinyay)* in the monastic community. This is why monks who are regularly consulted by gamblers and who accurately appreciate the limits of their freedom of action remain careful and usually refuse to give numbers directly; they ostentatiously ignore devotees who are taking notes and forbid any photography that could later constitute proof of their activities.

The relationship between lottery monks and political authorities is typical of the way that contemporary Burmese society functions—a society where duplicity and faking are generalized, but where there are functional necessities that proceed according to informal but restrictive rules. To act and to survive in such a system, where one is always on the edge, demands real skills: a sense of game rules, and of cheating rules, can only be mastered with long practice in the system and hence by accepting it and thus reinforcing its general foundations. Contrary to the Burmese society of 1988, Burmese society in the new millennium is comprised of cheaters, "small manufacturers of servitude,"[8] not of game breakers.[9] (See Figure 2.3 for a political lament involving the lottery.)

The Moral of an Immoral Story

The city was quiet, even frozen, stopped in its momentum for so many years now. I had traveled with U Awbatha, whom I met during the birthday celebrations of the most venerated monk in the country, Thamanya Hsayadaw. U Awbatha is a former civil servant from the Department of Health who became a monk upon retirement and spends most of his time on the complicated calculations of obtaining lottery numbers. His chart of the Thai lottery draws, comprising about the last thirty years worth of draws, is covered with esoteric inscriptions.

It was the very beginning of the afternoon, and we decided to visit Winsein Hsayadaw, a forest monk who lives a few kilometers from the city. He became famous all over the country when he began building the world's biggest recumbent Buddha (about 180 meters in length), a monumental

Figure 2.3. The husband says to his wife: "I don't ask to win the lottery, getting democracy would be enough." (Source: *The Aung, Journal La Démocratie,* September 6, 1988 [from Guillard 1990:142])

undertaking for which he was receiving financial support from the highest members of the regime. He was also famous for his lottery predictions. When we arrived, we saw a group of about ten devotees sitting next to him. He was greeting visitors who had come to honor him. Each of the devotees had a notebook and was clumsily attempting to hide it while simultaneously writing down everything the monk was saying and doing. The monk wasn't doing anything to stop them, but was ostentatiously ignoring their presence and their scribbling. As I would learn later, he was himself organizing his own lottery in order to finance his ambitious building project. He was having tickets sold all over the local area, and the prizes were scooters and other articles he had accumulated from donations.

When we returned to the city, my companion invited me to spend the night in his monastery, which is in a popular neighborhood of the city. The next morning the local chief of police came to demand that I go to a hotel. I went to pack my belongings. When I returned to the main room, the chief of police was talking with the hsayadaw. He was sounding him out on his predictions regarding the Thai lottery draw on the following day. Moulmein would stay up late that night.

As I was leaving the city to go to Rangoon and then Paris, I wondered whether what I had seen was a Burmese singularity, explained by circumstances special to one society, one culture, one time? Or should we admit that there is, between the Burmese people and ourselves, no real dissimilarity, but simply a difference of degree? Apart from some nuances, we are also cheaters; don't we depart from our game rules to better manage, or submit to, the order these rules establish? In other words, could the foundation and the dynamics of a social system depend partly on the very contravention of its fundamental values and rules? Could it be possible that the study and comprehension of the production and reproduction of a symbolic order necessarily go through an ethnography of cheating?

The paradox cannot be reduced to simply noticing a difference between theory and practice, to an inevitable distortion between the ideological and the empirical, between the range of ideas and values formulated by a society or some of its members on the one hand and the reality of practices on the other. The Burmese case gives rise to the possibility that some practices accompany, nourish, and even help to create, an ideological system that expresses antithetical ideas and values; the possibility exists that being regularly unfaithful to these ideas and values could be a necessary means of experimenting, testing, and even ultimately supporting the order that these values and ideas promote.

As I sat quietly on the plane, taking comfort in traveling far from such a disruptive country, I could still hear the dying echoes of its disturbing whisper, "What is the point of playing if one cannot cheat?"

Notes

This article was made possible by Monique Skidmore. My thanks for her support, her availability, and her stimulating proofreading. A version of the text was also submitted to the expert eye of Denise Bernot (outstanding professor, Institute National des Langues et Civilisations Orientales, Paris), and to the incisive critique of doctoral students who participated in a writing workshop in ethnology at the University of Paris X—Nanterre: Sophie Bouffart, Vanina Bouté, Claire Chauvet, Rachel Guidoni, Christine Jungen, Alexandra Marois, and Stéphane Rennesson.

1. The expression is from Marshall Sahlins (1976: 211). In some societies, the author explains, it is religion; in others it is kinship, and in others the production of goods that constitutes the main foundation of the cultural schema.

2. Bernard Formoso's work concerning villages in Northeastern Thailand and J. L. Taylor's work on forest monks both mention the common practice of monks' predicting lottery numbers (Formoso 2000:171; Taylor 1993:171, 177). In 2002 I observed the same phenomenon in Laos that Georges Condominas had noted at the beginning of the 1960s (Condominas 1998:48).

3. This term is the Burmese pronunciation of the Thai word for lottery.

4. These institutions were created during the 1980 religious reform period in order to more tightly control the monastic community and enforce the fundamental disciplinary rules (see Schober, this volume). According to the 1995 Ministry of Religious Affairs census, the monastic community is composed of approximately 160,000 monks and 240,000 novices in a national population then estimated to be 46 million. There are also approximately 25,000 nuns who do not belong to the monastic community because they don't receive formal ordination.

5. This deciphering process derives from the system for choosing a personal name in Burmese according to the day of birth—Monday, Tuesday, and so on—that traditionally decides the first letter of the name. The name of a person who was born on a Saturday could then start with any of the following letters: *ta, hta, da, dha,* or *na.* In this system of name choice, the week has eight days because Wednesday is divided into two days, and the deciphering system for the lottery doesn't always take this into account. Regarding the complete correspondence between days of the week and letters of the alphabet, see Shway Yoe (1963:4–5), and also Tosa (this volume).

6. Given possibilities may vary from one place or vendor to another. For example, the possibility to bet on only one number is sometimes offered; if this number appears in the number of the draw, the gambler wins three times the amount of the bet. One can also define the rank (1, 2, or 3) of the number bet on in the winning number. If the ranking is correct, the gambler wins 8 times his bet. In addition, the bet's winnings also vary depending on location, except for the three-digit winning number that pays back 550 times the bet in every way.

7. Monique Skidmore pointed out this practice to me (personal communication

2002). J. L. Taylor tells the story of one Thai forest monk who had put a sign at the entrance of his place to warn visitors that he wasn't predicting lottery numbers (1993: 185).

8. This is Claude Lefort's expression (1976:249).

9. Regarding the game *breaker* character *(spoilsport)*, see Huizinga (1949:11–12) for more detail about a person who refuses to enter the players' world and follow their rules, therefore defying their very legitimacy and threatening the existence of the community they form.

–3–

Women's Practices of Renunciation in the Age of *Sāsana* Revival

Ingrid Jordt

As a matter of fact, whoever wants to develop real Vipassanā-nana [insight knowledge gained through meditation] should first of all discard the notion of I, he, man, woman, i.e. the illusion of I, the illusion of Self to discern that they are merely material aggregates and mental aggregates. Then one has to go on contemplating so as to realise that these aggregates of mind and matter are of the nature impermanence, unsatisfactoriness and insubstantiality. Without differentiation into aggregates of mind and matter, if one were to contemplate on conventional concepts of 'I am anicca [impermanence]; the object of offering is anicca; the recipient is anicca', no real Insight Knowledge would be possible.
—Mingun Sayadaw, *The Great Chronicle of Buddhas*

Periodically in the infinite round of rebirths that is *samsāra*,[1] a buddha by virtue of his extraordinary efforts of purification over incalculable eons of time will discover and proclaim the *dhamma*, the liberating law. The teachings of buddhas are always the same. They illuminate for the world and the heavens the Four Noble Truths: the Noble Truth of suffering, the Noble Truth of the cessation of suffering, the Noble Truth of the causes of suffering, and the Noble Truth of the Eightfold Path leading to the eradication of suffering. The truth of the dhamma, acquired through a buddha's own efforts and culminating in autoenlightenment, blazes brightly in the world for a period of time before the knowledge is forgotten by men, women, and the gods, and the universe is once again cast into ignorance and darkness.

Sāsana (Burmese, *thathana*)[2] is a Pali term denoting both the teachings of a buddha and the period of time during which a buddha's teachings flourish in the world. After the death of a buddha, the *sangha*, the monastic order, protects and perpetuates these teachings. The sangha is invested with the task of assuring that the dhamma is transmitted as accurately as possible to each successive generation. Together with the buddha and dhamma, the sangha comprises the *tiratana*, or triple gem: the Enlightened One, the law proclaimed by him, and the community of holy disciples who live according to the law. The tiratana is the supreme refuge and object of veneration for persons seeking escape from suffering through their own arduous efforts. A buddha cannot save a person. He can only point the way out of the predicament of suffering by expounding upon three immutable truths: that everything changes *(anicca)*, everything is without substance *(anattā)*, and consequently that everything is unsatisfactory *(dukkha)*. It is the task of the sangha to continue pointing the way after a buddha's passing. They adhere to the buddha's code of conduct *(vinaya)*, learn and transmit the canonical teachings of the texts, and practice *satipatthāna-vipassanā* meditation—that they may realize for themselves the goal of the doctrine. While the vocational life of the "world renouncer" offers the most supportive environment for dhamma-striving, the teachings are intended for a universal audience. Yet not everyone has the opportunity to engage in dhamma-striving.

Why some individuals have access and opportunity to renounce the world while others do not is explained in orthodox teachings in terms of merit *(puñña)* and *pāramī* (moral perfections leading cumulatively to insight knowledge and enlightenment). Burmese orthodoxy holds that whereas at the time of Gotama Buddha[3] tens of thousands of individuals had the pāramī to meet with a buddha and realize the dhamma, today, midway through the *sāsana* (predicted to last five thousand years) individuals are bereft of such refined moral perfection. The sāsana is in decline.

Concerns over whom the teachings are for, who the legitimate carriers of the Buddha's message should be, and what opportunities are available for progressing along the Noble Eightfold Path are questions that confront practitioners of every historical period. Practice may be expressed in a wide variety of ways, and legitimation for these practices is to be traced back to the texts. A moral/spiritual hierarchy of purity and purification is reckoned relative to the distinction between ultimate *(paramattha-sacca)* and conventional *(sammuti-sacca)* realities. On the ultimate plane, morality cannot be seen—here one would find *arahat*[ship], or perfect sainthood, and the three lesser stages of sainthood *(sotāpanna, sakadāgāmī, and anāgāmī)*. On the conventional plane, moral purification is evaluated in accordance with visible criteria. This is the nexus where the invisible stores of merit and pāramī are manifest in conventional forms.

The monk, with his 227 rules of conduct (vinaya), stands out as foremost in purity on this plane. Inflections of asceticism—vegetarianism, eating one meal a day from one bowl, sleeping sitting up, meditating in the forest—also demonstrate the purity of a monk and the ripeness of his renunciation (nekkhama) pāramī. Differences in accumulated pāramī cultivation, evident and visible through practices of renunciation, form the basis for comparisons between sangha and laity. Pursuance of theoretical knowledge of the teachings (pariyatti), practice for direct knowledge of the teachings through meditation (paṭipatti), and attainment of enlightenment knowledge (paṭivedha) are suitable endeavors for members of the sangha. By contrast, the laity, because of their attachment to worldly things and the householder's life, are more inclined to make merit through offering materials in support of the order of world renouncers and by adhering to the layman's Five Precepts. On full and dark moon days, the laity may keep eight or sometimes the Ten Precepts as temporary efforts of moral purification.

Maintaining the accuracy of the Buddha's instructions is at the heart of all orthodox concerns over how the Buddha-dhamma should be preserved. Controversies over how to adapt the teachings to new historical circumstances are the basis for persistent sectarian rivalries within the sangha. Orthodox debates endure over how to verify the teachings. Which individuals or divisions (nikāya) in the sangha are the best repositories for the Buddha-dhamma? In Burma, direct knowledge (paṭipatti) and theoretical understanding (pariyatti) are distinctions that are always structurally and dynamically engaged. The ideal of an enlightened sangha, what the Buddha referred to as the ariya sangha—the True Community of Holy Disciples—is held as no longer viable at the midpoint in the predicted 5,000-year span of Gotama Buddha's dispensation. Enlightened beings are rare occurrences and only a buddha is capable of knowing for sure whether an individual has uprooted defilements and experienced the "unconditioned" that is nibbāna. Thus does reliance upon the institution of the sangha and the texts come to be emphasized even while charismatic individuals alleged to have attained enlightenment capture the imagination and veneration of society.

In the 1940s the great monk Mahasi Sayadaw elaborated a precise and detailed technical account of the step-by-step experiences of vipassanā practice (Mahasi Sayadaw 1979). In systematizing the technique leading to insight knowledge and enlightenment, a general warrant, or verification of the Buddha's teachings as set out in the texts was asserted. The systematic approach permitted people from all walks of life to engage en masse in the penultimate training leading to the stages of enlightenment. Paṭipatti, or meditation practice, was no longer seen as the sole purview of the virtuoso vocational monk. The implications this vipassanā movement had for women's practices of renunciation in Burma will be considered in the rest of this chapter.

Lapse of the Bhikkhunī Order and Women's Practices

At the time of the Buddha, a dual monastic order was instituted, with a nuns' *(bhikkhunī)* sangha. According to Theravādin orthodoxy, the dual monastic system lapsed when bhikkhunī failed to maintain the continuity of their order through proper rituals of ordination. Initiation of new members into the order required the presence of at least five bhikkhunī. Eventually the number of bhikkhunī dwindled until there were no longer enough legitimately ordained bhikkhunī to form the quorum necessary for initiating new members and hence continuing the lineage and tradition. From the Theravādin orthodox perspective, once the women's monastic movement died out, no recourse existed for the bhikkhunī lineage's reconstruction.

In contemporary Burma, those who are "inside the sāsana" *(thathana win)* and those who are not conform to a categorical delineation emphasizing authentic membership in the Buddha's sangha. Women are axiomatically excluded from the sāsana since their own monastic lineage was not maintained to the present. Indeed, the span of a sāsana is defined by how long the sangha maintains the order through proper initiation of new members in an unbroken line from the time of the order's inception by a buddha. That women have been relegated to the laity has not, however, discouraged them from striving for comparable opportunities to practice renunciation. Women seeking to renounce the householder's life in pursuit of "noble celibacy"[4] have attempted to create institutions parallel to the sangha with the hopes of reproducing in shadow form the function of the earlier bhikkhunī order.

Women in Burma have not sought renewal of the bhikkhunī order, as happened in Thailand in the 1980s (see Kabilsingh 1991). They have, however, sought to carve out for themselves opportunities for practice that parallel the opportunities for vocational renunciation. They have used their donations to make forceful aspirations or resolves (Pali: *adhiṭṭhāna*, Burmese: *adeik-htan*) that they might be born men in their next lives so they could pursue renunciation and purity of life through wearing the robes (since adherence to the vinaya cultivates purity of mind on the path to Nibbāna).

Visual cues are the first way in which the status of practitioners is identified. The use of colored robes by *thila-shin* (Buddhist nuns) was instituted in the seventeenth century, following a controversy within the sangha over whether or not lay women wishing to undertake the celibate life of a renunciate could distinguish themselves from other lay women by donning colored robes and not the white which marked the lay ten-precept holder (Jordt 1988). The differentiation of the practice of thila-shin from those of ordinary laity was important to the project of distinguishing a dual monastic system. The robes eventually came to include a third, sleeveless piece of material that slipped over the blouse and fell mid-length to the skirt and a thin outer shawl that mimicked the monks' upper robe, worn under the right arm and over the left shoulder. On top of this is often worn another piece of broad cloth, darker in color (brown or ochre), which rests above the left shoulder or in formal situations is worn under the right arm and over the left shoulder. The standardization of the robes, especially the pink robes associated with the lay meditation center of Mahasi (see Figure 3.1), has identified the thila-shin visually as a parallel institution to the sangha.

Unlike men, who have the option to leave lay life and join the sangha, women's spiritual practices tend to keep them tied to the lay householder's life—they are the ones who cook for the monks on their alms rounds, they handle the money in the domestic economy. In short, it is mutually reinforcing, for inasmuch as women handled money and the finances of the household—essentially the production of domestic life and reproduction of the members of the sangha—their role can be viewed as naturally equated to a lower domain or arena of merit production. That women have been associated with the domestic cycle, especially its material sustenance, is mirrored in ideas about the role of women in support of the sangha.

Throughout Burmese history women endeavoring to renounce the householder's life to practice noble celibacy have sought to distinguish themselves from the laity, who are outside the sāsana and therefore situated lower in the hierarchy of moral purity. Plaques dating to thirteenth-century Pagan attest to the fervent desire some women had to be reborn into the proper conditions of a world renouncer. They resolved that, by merit of their generous acts to the sāsana, they might be reborn as a man in their next life, for only as a man could they enter the sangha (Than Tun 1976).

Institutions for vocational nuns have waxed and waned. Controversies raged over the roles women sought for themselves as a parallel order of vocational world renouncers. In the seventeenth century, for example, a long and heated dispute within the sangha eventually resolved in favor of women renunciates wearing colored robes as a sign of their identity as vocational nuns and not merely pious lay devotees (Jordt 1988). House monasteries, or *zayat*, have been one way that women have succeeded in preserving their spiritual practices of renunciation with their families' support and also the support of kings and lay donation societies (see Myo Myint 1984 for a discussion of King Mindon's support of thila-shin). The city of Sagaing is still populated today with these house monasteries as well as other more substantial nuns' institutions (Burmese: *thila-shin kyaung[s]*) that operate very much like *hpongyi kyaung[s]*, monks' monasteries (Kawanami 2000). Some women renouncers, called *yathay*, simply took to the forest with crimson robes and shorn heads. They were characterized by their distinctive practice of plucking the hairs from their head with a beetlenut shell. However, these women hardly represented a

Figure 3.1. Entry Gate to Mahasi Thathana Yeiktha, Yangon (Source: Ingrid Jordt)

movement of any substantial kind, nor did they produce any institutional instantiations.

Kawanami cites the statistics for the number of nuns in contemporary Burma at 30,000, observing that they are "the most numerous among nuns in the Theravada Buddhist world" (2000:159). Explanations for what amounts to a resurgence of women's renunciation practices in twentieth-century Burma and beyond need to be considered in light of broader sāsana revitalization efforts by the state, the sangha, and the laity in the wake of British colonization.

The Mass Lay Meditation Movement

The "mass lay meditation movement" (Jordt 2001) began as a millenarian reaction to the destruction of the Buddhist monarchy at the end of the nineteenth century. Monks such as the famous Ledi Sayadaw advocated that all members of society should strive for Nibbāna before the sāsana disappeared, as had Burmese kingship that was its support. Post-Independence efforts at nation-state building following more than a hundred years of colonialism drew on the incipient meditation movement, growing it to mass proportions through state sponsorship of lay meditation. At the heart of the state's plan to build a common national identity was the revitalization of the Buddha sāsana. Sāsana revitalization after Independence became a social project sponsored by the state as well as civil society. It was directed not only at the sangha but at the thila-shin and the laity as well. Monks for their part were pressured to purify themselves through vinaya adherence. Scholarship and meditation were strongly encouraged.

In the absence of a Buddhist monarch whose authority rested upon his role as protector and promoter of the sāsana, new ideas emerged about how the sāsana could be revitalized. Following Independence, Burma's charismatic first prime minister, U Nu, set out to rebuild a moral citizenry through the societywide project of revitalizing the sāsana. Vipassanā meditation was at the core of this state-building project. Each village was required to send at least one individual to practice meditation in Yangon at the state-sponsored meditation center, Mahasi Thathana Yeiktha, named after the monk who had codified and systematized the practice for common use. The goal was for the practice to spread by word of mouth; it did.

The ideal of universal enlightenment became the central purpose of this movement and the lay meditation center emerged as a new institutional form catering to the spiritual requirements of ordinary householders who undertook temporary renunciation for purposes of "meditation striving" (Burmese: taya a-htok). It is thought traditional for men and women in the last third of their lives to prepare for their next life by undertaking precepts and meditating. Before the mass lay meditation movement it was generally understood that, aside from vocational actors and perhaps the king, who attended now and again to the balance of his merit scale, meditation by the laity was mainly an undertaking for the aged. Concentration *(samatha)* meditation was directed toward the goal of improving circumstances in one's next life. *Satipatthāna-vipassanā* (awareness of mindfulness) meditation, with its goal of attaining Nibbāna,[5] was not the predominant form of practice. Today, meditators come from all age groups, as the immediate goal of practice has transformed from more proximate soteriological goals to the penultimate achievement of enlightenment "in this very life."

In addition to the strong forest-monk tradition and arahat ideal, with its emphasis on the achievement of sainthood by virtuosi monks, the idea of enlightenment here and now was elaborated to include a field populated by virtuosi from all walks of life. The locus of enlightenment shifted from the forest periphery to the urban center. The arahat ideal, while still reserved for monks, was seen as the culmination of a process that could begin as a lay practice, the lay practitioner attaining to one of the earlier stages of enlightenment leading to perfect sainthood while maintaining the householder's life.

Vipassanā meditation emphasized individual enlightenment and, consequent upon enlightenment, establishment within the individual of an unbreakable moral contract with society (that is, adherence to the layman's Five Precepts not to kill, steal, lie, commit adultery, or take intoxicants). This psychic change is understood to have ontological consequences for future rebirths. The first-stage enlightened individual is no longer considered an ordinary worldling *(putthajana),* but an *ariya-puggala,* one who has attained to a stage of holiness. At the Mahasi Thathana Yeiktha meditation center in Yangon, since its opening in 1948, over a million people are said to have attained to one of the stages of insight knowledge or enlightenment.

Prior to the mass enlightenment movement, no elaborate personal habit had been associated with the sotāpanna (first-stage enlightened being). Moreover, the ariya sangha (described in orthodox texts as enlightened and therefore "true sangha" of the Buddha) had never been constructed as a social category for purposes of demonstrating degrees of pāramī (moral perfections required to escape the cycle of rebirths) realization.[6] The ariya, in other words, was conceived as an invisible disposition toward the world and not the social definition of a group. Rank in a spiritual hierarchy, as stated earlier, had been reckoned on two levels: the ultimate *(paramattha)* and conventional *(sammuti)* planes of reality. By the 1950s, however, it was a socially recognized and accepted orthodox assertion that millions of *yogi* (meditation practitioners) were attaining the insight levels of vipassanā meditation and the early stages of enlightenment.

This development had implications for women's practices of renunciation and nuns' institutional arrangements. Simply stated, on the paramattha plane a woman's pāramī could surpass that of a monk. Yet on the conventional plane of reality the sangha's claim (and the laity's recognition) of spiritual superiority was asserted on the basis of membership in the institution of the monkhood itself. The two separate systems for reckoning spiritual hierarchy were thus brought side by side into the public consciousness. Monks, the legitimate members of the sangha, were accorded respect on account of their observation of the vinaya and the sacred task of preserving the Buddha sāsana. At the same time, there was social recognition of a corps of enlightened lay people whose status in penultimate terms marked them as a different class of beings altogether. In Pali, and subsequently in Burmese, the distinction was marked as between putthajana (worldlings) and ariya (enlightened ones).

The articulation of a theory regarding the purity that can be seen (that is, the sangha) and the purity that is invisible (that is, the ariya) corresponded to shifts in political ideology as well. The destruction of eight centuries of classical Burmese Buddhist kingship under colonialism, and the emergence of a new state entity in the form of the modern nation-state after Independence, demanded new explanations for how to interpret the relationship between moral action and present social and political realities. A new paradigm for eremitical life that drew on ideas of the apostolic period of the Buddha came to be emphasized in place of earlier ideas about the relationship and obligations obtaining between sangha, state, and laity in the period of classical kings, the emphasis of which had been on the Asokan-style political organization (Jordt 2001).[7] This harkening back to the time of the Buddha (rather than the time of Buddhist kings) emphasized imagery drawn from the classical texts. At that time men, women, and even gods could become enlightened upon hearing a single phrase uttered by the Buddha.

According to Mahasi Sayadaw, people previously did not possess pāramī in so developed a form. In the present era, however, the very minimum amount of time in which a person can attain enlightenment is seven days if the meditator can achieve continuous and uninterrupted mindfulness. Mahasi Sayadaw asserted that the average amount of time a person with pāramī required to achieve first-stage enlightenment (in the current era) was two months. A painting hanging in the Mahasi Thathana Yeiktha lay meditation center in Yangon expresses in imagery who the main audience for his teachings were. The Buddha sits in front of an enormous crowd of lay people who have gathered to listen to his discourse on the dhamma. To the side, and in far fewer numbers, sit members of the sangha. The central importance given lay people in the picture expresses the idea that the laity are the objects for the penultimate teachings.

The mass lay meditation movement has thus brought about a substantial transformation in monk/lay relations in contemporary Burmese Buddhism. In keeping with long-held convention, the laity still support monks in their role as vocational renunciates. However, and especially with respect to urban monks, it has become a common expectation for monks also to guide the laity on their journey to Nibbāna. The temporary renunciates who move in and out of the meditation center for brief periods of intense meditation are still very much engaged in worldly life. This does not mean that there has been an undermining of the sangha institutions' significance or the laicization of the sangha. On the contrary, the sangha's role as the legitimate purveyors of the teachings has been strengthened, even as it has become the role of lay society to reveal what these are through practice.

Universalizing the penultimate practices has transformed not only lay-monk relations. It has also meant that gender conceptions have undergone changes. The mass lay meditation movement has had the greatest significance for women because it has provided women with an alternative institution for practice, one that permits them access to the highest goals and achievements in the religion while allowing them to keep the status of their social and economic standing garnered in the householder's life.[8] This change in ideas about women's spiritual capabilities had particular consequences for women's monastic institutions after the early 1950s when the state began official sponsorship of women's monastic institutions.

The state's goal to create a citizenry with a national identity took precedence over earlier ideas about the role women occupied in the sāsana. This "citizen laity," which I refer to as the New Laity,[9] had a quite different role to perform vis-à-vis the state. For Burma's first prime minister, U Nu, vipassanā meditation would become the moral foundation for a shared communal experience that would unite the country according to the Dhamma and thereby underwrite a successful democratic nation-state. An enlightened citizenry was viewed as necessary for a successful democratic state capable of ruling itself both by the principles of self-representation and ultimate moral Truth.

Women and the New Laity

Women comprise the majority of vipassanā meditation practitioners. According to the monks who train them in the procedures of vipassanā, women are particularly adept meditators (see Figure 3.2). Yet there is social misrecognition that women are at the forefront of the revitalization of meditation. When I asked monks why there are more female than male yogis, they laughed gently. I interpreted this as good-humored chagrin over a glaring inconsistency in canonical expectations. To make sense of the explanations the monks offered me, however, a few words need to be said about the more general pattern by which monks provide answers to questions requiring "general knowledge," that is, questions not specifically about the texts. In any discussion with sanghas, particularly those monks highly trained in the texts or meditation, the response to conventional problems are typically offered on highly abstract levels of Truth, that is, on the level of ultimate as compared with conventional registers. Aphorisms, social examples drawn from the texts, exhortations by the Buddha, explanations of Abhidhamma principles,[10] and so forth are the typical means by which monks of high training communicate to the laity. For the laity, this mode of communication is itself *dhamma dāna* (gifts of truth), for it puts the laity in the frame of mind of the higher operational Truths of the dhamma as they exist in every conventional truth. In this sense, the monk's discourses, admonitions, and advice (like the sangha institution itself) describe a moral reality with a clearer sense of the dimensions of moral causality. Association with the wise is a necessary condition for pāramī cultivation.

Questions of the sort I asked monks at Mahasi concerning the paradox of women's greater involvement in sāsana activities and the monk's own acknowledgment of their superior performance in practicing meditation were not answered with quotes from the texts. To explain this anomaly monks drew on explanations that emphasized the differences between a man's and a woman's

Figure 3.2. Meditating Monk, Thila-shins, and Lay Yogis at Mahasi Thathana Yeiktha (Source: Ingrid Jordt)

body. What made a woman's body inferior to a man's was precisely what made women in this historical period better practitioners than men. Women simply suffer more than men because of their inferior bodily form.

Specifically, monks responded to my questions saying that a woman's greater interest and success in vipassanā meditation and greater aptitude in realizing the teachings could be understood in terms of two intrinsic features of her embodiment. First, a woman exists in a natural condition of suffering because of her sex. Women suffer more on account of their bodies, for which the endurance of childbirth was given as principal evidence.[11] Said one *na-yaka sayadaw* (chief monk teacher):

> Women suffer more than men do. This is because women must undergo
> the pain of childbirth. Due to past minor sexual misdeeds or because of
> her attachment to being a mother, she is born as a woman in this life and
> so she must suffer more than a man does. On account of this suffering,
> women are more inclined to practice meditation. They have more *samvega*
> [the sense of urgency to get out of the cycle of rebirths].

As in other formulations, having good merit can be an obstacle to achieving Nibbāna, since the enjoyment of one's present status makes one less likely to experience samvega. Thus a woman's suffering is more likely to compel her toward practicing for Nibbāna than a man, who may tarry. This conforms to Burmese folk beliefs about how men, unlike women, possess a special merit quality, *hpon* (Pali: *puñña*), of which the monk is the hpongyi, or great glory/merit.

Second, women are thought to be capable of achieving higher degrees of concentration due to their perceived natural constitution to *endure* pain and life's vicissitudes. That women live longer on average than men was given as evidence of this. By this reckoning, the female embodiment is considered concomitant to the arising of those factors conducive for practice and realization. Sustained concentration *(samādhi)* is an essential factor required for successful meditation. Monks at Mahasi Thathana Yeiktha consider this quality of mind to be a noticeable characteristic of many women yogis.

"Why is someone born a woman?" I asked U Pandita, one of Burma's foremost meditation monks and a learned scholar. U Pandita addressed this from a perspective that I understood was consonant with the Tipitaka, although not explicitly explained in the canonical texts. He speculated that a person is born as a woman for a number of reasons. It depends on *citta*, consciousness. For example, consciousness may become attached to the woman's embodiment out of the sheer momentum of having been a woman in many lives before, or because they are attached to having children. "For example," he said, "the Buddha's mother made a vow during one of the lifetimes of Gotama Buddha that she wanted to be the mother of the Buddha."

This is just a kind of attachment, U Pandita explained, because the first person to whom a buddha preaches his sāsana is his mother. His discourse on the dhamma is given in the heavenly realm where she is reborn after giving birth to him. Other causes for being born as a woman include sexual misconduct in a past life. For example, breaking the precept not to commit adultery can be a cause for men to be reborn as women. Or at the moment of death, when relinking consciousness is taking place, the idea of a woman or the sight of a woman can also be cause for rebirth as a woman. "The desire to be a buddha's mother, to wish for a woman's form, to desire the experience of childbirth is," U Pandita continued, "*moha* (delusion) based on *lobha* (craving)." This is because the aspiration to be a woman forecloses opportunities to strive for Nibbāna (that is, as a man who enters the sangha), and therefore women are closer to being ensnared in the attachments that bond mother to child thereby recapitulating the cycle of entanglement in samsāra.

It is not that women are viewed as the cause for rebirth; however, women are more attached to the reproductive cycle. A woman's thoughts naturally require her to care for her children, whereas men may more readily renounce the world (with a wife's permission). Since women are also involved in handling economic affairs of the household, the option for men to leave the world is made that much more readily available. Moreover, monks are supported in all their necessities by the laity, whereas women who renounce the world in Burma must work for themselves and so endure a less secure institutional existence than do monks.

Occupying the social space of a world renouncer allows the transcendence of social roles and conventionally recognized identification markers eliciting social classification and role demands. One who has renounced the world, who no longer participates in the most fundamental activities of securing a livelihood for material sustenance, but who instead lives off the free-will offerings of society without attachments to family and possessions, achieves a rare and privileged opportunity for dhamma cultivation and realization. Renunciation is therefore the essential condition for spiritual progress.

The thila-shin's struggles to be socially recognized as an ungendered category of persons detached from conventional realities has been greatly helped by the mass lay meditation movement, with its emphasis on penultimate realities. Whereas membership in the sangha overshadows the spiritual value of enlightenment from the point of view of the social recognition of categories of persons, popular discourses about the emptiness of phenomenon and the fact that one of the first insights *(nyanzin)* perceived by a yogi is that all phenomena are either mind or matter *(nāma/rūpa)* have brought into question the rigid exclusion of the thila-shin as persons "inside the sāsana."

The Status of Women as Spiritual Practitioners

As discussed at the outset, Burmese orthodoxy and folk beliefs recognize that women's exclusion from the sangha occurred for historically arbitrary reasons. Nevertheless, because it is believed the bhikkhunī order cannot be reinstated, and because of the monumental disaster that this fact represents for any practitioner desiring to escape worldly life and attain Nibbāna, the status of the feminine gender is universally perceived to be inferior to that of masculine gender. Rebirth as a woman has traditionally been viewed as an obstacle for merit making and the cultivation of pāramī. A monk, by contrast, has leveraged opportunities in just these crucial ways. This schema is considered self-evident enough that even today many women resolve to be born as a man in future lives.[12]

In Burma it has come to be assumed that the *historical* fact limiting a woman's ability to renounce the world in the same way as a man does is also a *phenomenological* fact evidencing a lack in merit in a woman's embodiment. Merit is conceived as both a storehouse for future ontological becomings and the embodied and experienced ontological results of moral actions taken in the past. Present circumstances (such as being a man or a woman, rich or impoverished) represent the moral results for actions taken in prior lives.

Man, Woman, Monk: Third Gender in the Sangha

Burmese gender is compartmentalized into three categories: man, woman, and monk. The monk is the only social category recognized as a penultimate reality. The penultimate reality status of this third gender is defined according to descriptions of reality drawn from the Abhiddhama. Abhiddhama theory emphasizes the relations between mind and matter, matter and matter, and mind and mind as components making up the universe and experience. According to doctrine, man and woman are mere concepts, just as the notion "self" is a concept. The very purpose in studying and practicing the buddhas' teachings is to see through this conventional and shared delusion and to see things as they are—as impermanent, unsatisfactory, and empty of essence (anicca, dukkha, anatta). Monks are asexual beings according to this reckoning, not only because they are "noble celibates" who renounce the world of sexual engagements but also because their materiality is irrelevant to the task of realizing enlightenment consciousness, which does not take biological sex as part of its condition. A distinctive honorific language reserved expressly for monks and entirely free of gender inflections reinforces the idea that monks are not part of worldly conventional life.

As reviewed earlier, the distinction between sangha and laity is perhaps the most fundamental cleavage in the classification of social actors in Burma. The principle that a legitimate sangha order depends upon a continuous lineage connection to the very time of the Buddha is assiduously upheld as the argument for why a bhikkhunī order cannot be resuscitated today. It is held that legitimate institutional forms must be continuous to be authentic and that the transmission process of the teachings relies explicitly upon the teacher-disciple relationship.

When queried about what sorts of alternative procedures might allow for the reinstatement of the bhikkhunī sangha, a learned *dhammācariya* (a monk at Mahasi Thathana Yeiktha) related the following story, which took place in a monastery in upper Burma where the *sayadaw* (monk teacher) was the head monk in residence. It was discovered that one of the resident monks who had been in the robes for more than twenty years was intersexed. Since in Buddhist orthopraxy a hermaphrodite is considered to be a "woman with a pathological disorder" (Jordt 1988:34), the question of whether the monk could legitimately remain in the robes became an issue among the members of the sangha at this temple.

One of the central considerations for deciding whether the monk should be disrobed or not concerned determination of whether the monk had entered the sangha as an intersexed person or whether he had changed after being in the robes. It was determined that the monk's physical transformation had taken place after he had entered the sangha. The preoccupation here was clearly over the question of the legitimacy of ordination. Disqualifying diseases might retroactively be determined as cause for expulsion. However, from the perspective of this sayadaw, the monk had not contracted a disease, he had simply transformed into a woman: "This *bhikkhu* (monk) had become a bhikkhunī (nun)," he said. He added that if five such cases could be produced, it would be possible to reestablish the bhikkhunī order!

While being male is the primary criteria for entering the sangha, taking up the robes is a transformative act in which the individual renounces his or her gendered identity along with worldly life. The term *"tabyi-daw,"* Kawanami observes, is a gender-free term of self-address monks use toward other monks (2001:30–33). *Hsaya-ma* is a term used for schoolteachers, as well as thila-shin. *Hsaya-lay* (small teacher) and, for a very respected thila-shin, *hsaya-gyi* (great teacher), are also gender-free terms emphasizing the role of the thila-shin in teaching and, therefore, recognizing their role in the transmission of the buddha dhamma (ibid).

These words form part of a larger Burmese vocabulary reserved for sangha members. Monks do not "go," "*thwa-de,*" they "*kywa-de.*" Both words mean "go," but the latter can only be used when referring to monks. They do not eat rice, *hsan;* they eat cooked and offered rice *(hsun).* In the honorific language reserved for sangha members, the emphasis is upon the social construction of an asocial being or, rather, a being closer to the *lokuttara* or supermundane dhamma reality.

Kawanami, who conducted her research among thila-shin in Sagaing (the most populous community of women renunciates in Burma), elaborates upon the status of thila-shin in Burma by observing that the language used toward thila-shin demarcates their place in the sāsana order and functions to keep them "outside the sāsana" (Kawanami 2001:30). My own observations at the Mahasi Thathana Yeiktha meditation center indicate that the application of honorific language usually reserved for monks has begun to be employed to thila-shin as well, and this has contributed to the ambiguity of their sacred status. The blurring of social categories of purity, which honorific language is intended to delimit, have made the question of whether thila-shin are "inside" or "outside" the sāsana increasingly ambiguous. A thila-shin's paramattha (ultimate reality) characteristics are far more likely to be emphasized in the context of a meditation center, where practitioners are engaged in the perception and epistemic construction of reality from the point of view of anatta. Alternatively, when conventional roles—formal embodiment in robes and precept holding—are considered, there is a more ready reflex to assign women to a spiritual hierarchy that places them squarely outside the sāsana and not as one of its embodiments.

A woman cannot achieve the status of a world renouncer completely even though from the Burmese perspective her sex does not bar her from its ultimate spiritual achievements. Only monks are socially recognized as individuals who have transcended gender in pursuit of Nibbāna, pāramī cultivation, and sāsana propagation. Only monks merit the support of the laity in the everyday renunciation of social worldly life, thereby creating in the space of their own activities the sacred and transcendent. The laity, for their part, participate in the support and extension of this space of the sacred—the support of the Buddha sāsana—through their charitable acts of dāna and by undertaking to keep morality, or *sīla.* Thus does their merit accumulate and their pāramī incrementally ripen.

The conventional world of man and woman is transcended in the sangha by men who have entered the order and abandoned their engendered identities as members of the lay world. That men can renounce their sex while women cannot does not fully account for the extent of traditional ideas that relate merit to the masculine principle. Melford Spiro (1977:261), in a 1965 study of village life in Upper Burma explains:

> Despite the remarkable extent of sexual equality in Burmese society—
> remarkable not only by contrast with the status of women in Asia, the Mid-
> dle East and traditional Europe, but also with significant segments of the
> contemporary West—it is nevertheless a basic premise of Burmese culture
> that men are *inherently* superior to women. . . . In Burma, the primary rea-
> son offered for male superiority is the belief that men possess that innate,
> inborn quality, known as *hpoun* . . . [U]sually glossed as "glory," *hpoun* . . .
> is a psychospiritual quality, an ineffable essence, which invests its possessor
> with superior moral, spiritual, and intellectual attributes. . . . As a measure
> of their conviction concerning the truth of male superiority, villagers are
> not unwilling to accept its *reductio ad absurdum,* expressed in the proverb "A
> woman is not as noble as a male dog" *(meinmatha hkway-di-lauk mamyat-
> hpu).* This is, of course, a hyperbole but it does convey the intended senti-
> ment—that the masculine is much superior to the feminine. . . . [13] Although
> the spiritual superiority of males is based on their hpoun, its proof, accord-
> ing to the Burmese, is found in a number of Buddhist beliefs and practices.
> Only a male has the Buddhist initiation ceremony (shinpyu), only a male
> can become a monk (which leads to a vicious circle: the male's innate supe-
> riority enables him to become a monk, which in turn increases his already
> pronounced superiority to the female), only a male can become a saint
> (arahat), and most important, only a male can become a Buddha.

Spiro's consideration of village folk understandings of hpon forty years ago, and the subordination of the feminine principle to that of the masculine, needs to be reconsidered for contemporary, especially urban, Burma. The Bur- mese word for monk, *hpongyi,* demonstrates the strength of the idea that it is the spiritual principle of merit that men alone have that is the defining sub- stance of a monk. Etymologically derived from the Pali word *puñña,* its con- ventional usage in Burmese culture locates the psychomaterial phenomena of sentient embodiment in the Burmese Buddhist cosmological theory of the thirty-two planes of existence. In this theory, the causative effect of merit and demerit is played out in the cycle of rebirths. Hpon is associated with an affil- iated cluster of ideas about the implications of this potency for spiritual prac- tice. The hpon concept is profitably viewed as a continuum of ideas regarding merit and pāramī production.

Women do not have hpon, after all, and they cannot become monks. Monks have great merit because they are monks—but not because they are men first. Hpon is a concept of spiritual potential, but this potential can play out in conventional ways in worldly life too. This tautological aspect of the concept—that men, having been born men, have a spiritual advantage over women because they can join the sangha and that their spiritual advantage translates into an advantage of power and authority over women in the conventional world as well—demonstrates the crucial linkage between power and moral authority in the Burmese system. In short, it is precisely the unique merit that men have and can renounce that is the basis of their power in the world.

The application of the merit concept to the male principle describes more than just how merit is transformed into renunciation and realization of a buddha's teachings. Hpon is also the basis of a man's power and influence more generally. The continuum of ideas about merit and potency is to be found in Burmese conceptions about power and its sources, about renunciation, especially about mental defilements *(kilesas)*. The idea of hpon is conceived as a kind of special quality of purity, *potentia*, and power conferred upon a man because of his biological sex.

However, hpon is not conceived as an immutable substance that is the same for all men. Some men may have more hpon than others. Their potency may convert to power in the way that the hpon of monks converts to renunciation and pāramī accumulation. Inherent in these ideas are notions of how potency converts to the renunciation of worldly life, culminating in its penultimate form in buddhahood, or sainthood, on the one hand, and to influence and power culminating in the canonical formulation of the world-conquering king, on the other (see Tambiah 1976 for an analysis of this paradigm's relevance to Buddhist kingship in Southeast Asia). Women do not have a part in hpon and their sex, moreover, is thought to be contaminating and capable of diminishing a man's hpon.

Spiro describes how according to village accounts women are not believed to be capable of achieving enlightenment. This he describes as part of a larger discourse on the embodiment of hpon. I discussed these perceptions from an orthodox perspective with U Pandita. Women, he said, are capable of attaining to the fourth and final stage of enlightenment as evidenced in the canonical texts. In response to my question of why we do not hear much in Burma about alleged women arahat[s], although there is a rather strong tradition of women anāgāmī (third stage enlightened beings), he replied that in the present era we do not find women arahats because of the absence of a bhikkhunī lineage. Without the nuns' order, women can only keep the extended nine or ten precepts devout laypersons keep. Women renunciates do not live off the cooked alms of the laity. They go on alms rounds once monthly to collect dry rice and money. These activities in themselves require a state of mental attachment that an arahat simply does not have. Arahats are said to survive their enlightenment only if they resolve to live out what would have been the natural length of their life. Only compassion can compel an arahat to make such a resolve and someone must request an arahat within seven days of their enlightenment to make such a resolve. Out of compassion arahats extend their lives so that others may benefit from the opportunity to make offerings, venerate, and take guidance from their wisdom.

Having eradicated craving, the arahat can continue to exist only if he is supported in the robes. Lay life requires motivations and actions that an arahat is no longer capable of experiencing in his psychophysical process. Accepting the food and resources of the laity make the extension of his life possible. Women's institutions, however, do not allow full support of this kind, and consequently women arahats have no material institutions that could support them in this embodiment. According to U Pandita, if a woman today attains arahatship, she will take her *parinibbāna* (full Nibbāna) within seven days.

Among the developments in the thila-shin movement of the twentieth century has been the increasing (though controversial) consideration that thila-shin may be viewed as a potential field for lay merit-making. As enlightenment itself is no longer seen as the exclusive purview of the sangha, the merit-fields of extraordinary practitioners, whether man or woman, are reasonably viewed as potent loci for merit-making activities. As one monk reiterated, "The laity are the ones who have the pāramī for paṭipatti (meditation) and paṭivedha (realization). Monks have the pāramī for pariyatti (scholarship) and for nekkhama (renunciation)."

This new conceptualization, in which pāramī is viewed in terms of the monks' role in perpetuating sāsana in contrast to (but not to the exclusion of) enlightenment by a pāramī-ripe laity, stresses the "vocational" aspect of the sangha and their functional role in society by perpetuating the teachings of the Buddha. The sangha is not viewed as the exclusive location where meritorious individuals may strive for Nibbāna. Consequently, the metaphorical social hierarchy in which male gender is viewed as part of a "merit evolution" in spiritual development toward the first stage of enlightenment (sotāpanna) has become untenable. The ideology of gender differences has become engulfed in broader discourses about the potential to attain enlightenment and the degree of pāramī perfection an individual requires for enlightenment. Nowhere in the canonical discussion of pāramī is biological sex discussed as a necessary condition for attaining Nibbāna.

The mass lay meditation movement thus has brought about an accommodation of new ideas about gender and enlightenment and therefore also new ideas of sāsana practice in Burma. These new emphases diverge from traditional roles in precolonial Burma, especially regarding ideas concerning what a woman's greatest source of merit-making may be. In folk tradition the primary means for a woman to achieve the highest merit was through the ordination of her son. The merit of his actions accrued to her since she was his merit base. When a married man wanted to undertake temporary ordination, he needed permission from his wife, and subsequently merit accrued to her. Women therefore accrued merit through providing the sangha with its membership and alms for its members. Female identity was perceived to be the subordinate and supportive basis for the man's hpon and the material support of the sangha.

State Sponsorship

The state has been instrumental in raising the standard of the nuns' order. The first prime minister after Independence, U Nu, tried to nationalize thila-shin lands during the early 1950s. The protest from the thila-shin was so great that he was required to back down and allow the thila-shin to retain "sāsana lands." Burmese classification of sāsana lands, as *sāsanika* property, allowed the thila-shin exemption from taxes on a religious basis. This religious category was distinguished from other sacred tax-exempt lands, referred to in Burmese (from the Pali) as *sanghika* (owned by the sangha), *gaṇika* (owned by a segment within the sangha), and *puggalika* (owned by an individual monk). The legal category of sāsanika is ambiguous. On the one hand, it is used to describe property for universal use and veneration, such as pagodas. But it is also used to cover the land and property of newly emergent institutional forms such as the lay meditation centers. Thila-shin monasteries fell comfortably into this legal classificatory framework. At the same time as women's institutions were set apart as lay institutions, the action nevertheless strengthened the legitimacy of women's claim to their own order as world renouncers and celibates.

During the purification movement of the late 1970s and the Ne Win military regime in the early 1980s, the thila-shin also became a target for purification. State definition for the acceptable boundaries of thila-shin behavior—nuns who begged in the market place, for example, were disrobed on the grounds that they were bringing down the purity of the whole thila-shin order—and state consideration of thila-shin institutions as institutions parallel to those of monks meant that the dual monastic order was reinforced in principle. Through the government's efforts to control nuns' institutions by recognizing their parallel aspect to that of monks, more support for nuns' institutions and activities came to be enhanced. This has strengthened thila-shin claims of parity with the sangha (that is, in every way except the technical one).

Meditation has not been the way that the thila-shin have sought to legitimize their status in their roles. For women who are more interested in dhamma-striving *(taya a-htok)* through vipassanā meditation, I was often told that it was easier to practice as a lay person and temporary renunciate. The vocational requirements in support of the institution occupy too much of a thila-shin's time. Emphasizing their vocational and institutional role as a legitimate source for transmitting the teachings allow the thila-shin to be seen as functioning in the same capacity as monks. Accrual of status to the thila-shin is accorded on the basis of whether they engage in pariyatti training, and the most prestigious nuns' institutions are centers for scriptural training. In this the government supports their role by, for instance, offering them titles for achievement on scholarly exams comparable to those for which monks sit. Although aiming to contain the thila-shin within the fold of their legal scrutiny, each government since Independence has helped support this direction of thila-shin practices. Solidification of the idea of a vocational nun has therefore fastened on other features of their role as renunciates that distinguish them from the laity and put them in a parallel monastic structure to monks.

Double Monastery System

The thila-shin mirror the vocations of the sangha, although in many instances thila-shin become a part of sangha institutions by supporting monks as their "lay" *kappiya,* or attendants. In this sense their support of the sangha is another form of merit-making. Kappiya thila-shin perform the tasks which monks are forbidden to perform, especially the handling of money. Very often the thila-shin work as the cooks and treasurers of temples. For these women, the role of kappiya clearly places them in the position of being lay supporters and not a parallel order for renunciation. Nevertheless, the motivations for renunciation are many and serving the sangha and sāsana in this manner is also a source of merit. An interesting addendum to this form of practice is to note that it is precisely women's position as members of the laity that enables them to function as kappiya. When land or other donations are made to a monk as an individual (puggalika-category property), it is technically held on behalf of the monk by the thila-shin. This is a technicality of sorts because a monk is not allowed to own anything beyond his requisites. Putting property into the hands of a kappiya is, from the point of view of the state, actually making the property the kappiya's. As in the householder's life, women are the ones in charge of handling the profane affairs attached to money and daily maintenance.

Hidden Ariya

Women's practices of renunciation in contemporary Burma have been shaped by ideas about gender that have themselves been shaped by practices of renunciation. The historical loss of the bhikkhunī lineage is held up as explanation and justification for why women must be considered outside the sāsana and for why a double lineage system cannot be reinstated. Vocational nuns' efforts to distinguish themselves from the laity have depended upon demonstrating that their goals and aspirations mirror those of the sangha and not practices of the laity. They have not wanted their vocational renunciation to be that of vocational pious laity supporting sangha institutions—although, this is a prevalent form of practice for many thila-shin in Burma today.[14]

The rise of a mass lay meditation movement has also influenced Burmese ideas about gender identity. The attribution of a third gender identity to monks drew on traditional ideas about the differences between men and women in which men were more likely to have access to a meritorious life as hpongyi. Entanglement with the world through such activities as bearing and raising children, handling money and attending to the economic affairs of the household and business, plus reiteration of the fact that women cannot become sangha members, amount to historical, sociobiological, and cultural assertions of the inferiority of a woman's sex to that of a man's. This construction of female identity was so comprehensive that, at an extreme, villagers could believe that women did not have the capacity to attain enlightenment.

With the mass lay meditation movement, ideas about a woman's capacity to excel in meditation and realize the teachings became an article of truth, as verified by the monks who were their vipassanā guides and teachers. Women who sought temporary refuge and renunciation at lay meditation centers found that they could combine their temporary practices without having to give up the householder's life for the vocational life of a thila-shin. The status of a thila-shin remains low in comparison with monks, since their institutional situations do not afford a woman renunciate opportunity to strive for the dhamma in a conducive setting. Temporary renunciation suits the New Laity of the urban and largely educated middle class.

From an orthodox perspective, the insubstantiality of such essential identities as self, man, or woman was already accepted. Explanations for why women were better achievers than male yogis or monks are explained as inversions of the very same conditions that made a woman inferior in a sociobiological, historical, and conventional cultural sense: because her body caused more suffering, a woman was more motivated to dhamma-strive. That in this moment in history so many people (men and women) should be capable of realizing the supreme teachings is held up as evidence of widespread pāramī and verification of predictions (said to be found in the texts) that at the midpoint in the Buddha-sāsana, a multitude of people would attain to enlightenment.

Emphasis on the universal aspects of the teachings has placed women in a new light, with consequences for women who aspire to renounce the world and live a monastic life. In contemporary urban centers the thila-shin look increasingly like participants in a double monastery system, a perception that has been helped by the actions of the state.[15] As women's activities in penultimate practices qualify them more and more as hidden ariya, thila-shin may increasingly come to be viewed as a viable field of merit. This may lead to more blurring of ideas concerning hpon and gender dimorphism in purity status. As the universal aspect of the teachings continue to be emphasized, women continue to be overrepresented in the lay meditation centers where the penultimate practices of renunciation and enlightenment are now taking place.

Notes

I would like to thank Monique Skidmore for being a patient and supportive editor and colleague. Kalman Applbaum's review of multiple drafts of this chapter are also gratefully acknowledged.

1. All terms are Pali unless otherwise noted.

2. I do not employ the term "Buddhism" as a gloss for sāsana since it does not convey the sense in which practitioners participate in a shared system of meaning.

3. The word "buddha" is capitalized when referring to a specific buddha, such as Gotama Buddha.

4. I borrow this term from Jo Ann Kay McNamara (1996).

5. Nibbāna is the Pali form of the Sanskrit word nirvana. It means literally "blowing out; extinction" (U Sīlananda 1990:226).

6. Enlightenment in each of its stages is not a quality that can be discerned with certainty by an external observer. Moreover, according to paṭipatti (meditation) monks, only a buddha can discern this in a person's mind.

7. In the Asokan model of kingship the king's legitimacy was premised upon his role as protector of the faith. It included ideas about worldly authority, derived from scriptural ideas of the cakkavatti, that emphasized forcible conversion by the king in his quest to convert the world to the Buddha's teachings and establish a universal rule based on Buddhist principles.

8. This is relevant in urban settings where educated, middle-class women have shown particular interest in meditation. However, by no means do I mean to imply that this is only a middle- and upper-class phenomenon.

9. I thank F. K. Lehman for suggesting this term.

10. In the Burma Pitaka Association's *Guide to Tipitaka,* compiled in 1954 at the Sangayana, or Sixth Buddhist Synod, the Abhidhamma is described as follows: "Abhidhamma is mainly concerned with the study of abstract truths in absolute terms. But in describing the dhammas in their various aspects, it is not possible to keep to absolute terms only. Inevitably, conventional terms of every day language have to be employed in order to keep the lines of communication open at all. Abhidhamma states that there are two main types of conventional usage; the first type is concerned with terms which express things that actually exist in reality and the second type describes things which have no existence in reality" (1986:148).

11. While monks formulated the significance of childbirth to women's greater interest in meditation, I did not hear women formulate it in this same way. Women did stress the significance of their insight into suffering in more general terms regarding loss and uncertainty in their life circumstances; however, I did not perceive a strong discourse focusing on the body itself. Furthermore women were keen to point out their very many social freedoms.

12. "Resolves" (Pali: adhiṭṭhāna Burmese: adeik-htan) are aspirations made at the time of a donation or on account of some other wholesome volition or act. By virtue of the wholesome act performed, temporary purification of the mind arises and becomes a forceful mental volition with an especially strong force to take causal effect when the conditions are right at some future time.

13. Spiro's discussion of the belief that the "masculine is much superior to the feminine" as evidenced by the Burmese proverb "A woman is not as noble as a male dog" does not convey the full irony of the statement. What qualifies the statement as humorous hyperbole is not the fact that women and dogs are compared in the sense conveyed by English, that is, that we take dogs derogatorily to mean bitch or a despicable creature. The humor comes from the idea that the gulf between the male and the female principle could be greater even than the gulf separating realms or planes of existence—the human and the animal realm.

14. In Thailand, it is the predominant role women renunciates may have (Jordt 1988).

15. It is a classical feature of all Burmese Buddhist states and rulers to take advantage of world renouncers to further political goals. In the period following Independence, governments have used the moral and social capital of world renouncers for nation-state building and the creation of a moral citizenry (especially 1947–1962) and to control and repress the population (1962–1988 and 1988–2003) (see Jordt 2003).

–4–
The Taungbyon Festival
Locality and Nation-Confronting in
the Cult of the 37 Lords

Bénédicte Brac de la Perrière
TRANSLATED BY ANNABELLE DOLIDON

The village of Taungbyon lies ten kilometers north of Mandalay, the last Burmese royal city. It hosts the best known of the central Burmese festivals honoring the spirits of deceased heroes who are called *nat* and who belong to the Burmese pantheon of the "37 Lords." Among nat festivals, that of Taungbyon is certainly the most important, not only from a quantitative point of view—that of crowds mobilized and volume of monetary and ritual exchanges—but also because it constitutes the model for all the others, a model which is spreading to other festivals whose standardization is an ongoing process.

In modern times the nat festivals forcefully punctuate the life of these regions. They represent important, even vital, economic events for the villages involved and structure economic and social exchanges at the regional level. In addition, they link the local area to the national society, as represented by mediums and their clients who come to the festivals from the principal urban centers, particularly Rangoon. The changes that have occurred in Burma these past fifteen years, particularly those linked to the increasing circulation of money that resulted from the limited reopening of a market economy, have been echoed in the festivals, particularly at Taungbyon, the most important festival, which has seen a noted expansion.

In this chapter I will focus on the changes that have occurred at Taungbyon, the most important festival site, analyzing the complex festival ritual program (that I have already published in French [1992]) and adding observations about other nat festivals made in 1986, 1991, 1995, 1998, and 2000. I will argue that nat festivals set the stage for encounters between spirit mediums, temple guardians, and local communities that reveal power plays and attempts to monopolize and retain the revenue and prestige generated by guardianship and mediumship within the cult and at its festival sites. These repeated confrontations also succeed in differentiating the national society from that of the local communities. These processes, however, are not a new factor created by the contemporary scene; they are inscribed in the ritual setting of the festivals, and they originated in the dynamics of the institutionalization of the Cult of the 37 Lords, in its historical development under the Burmese kings.

The Cult of the 37 Lords

The nat cult is the historical and cultural product of the unification of Ayeyarwadi valley under Burmese kings.[1] The pantheon of the 37 was originally the object of a royal cult and festivals dedicated to one of these figures—or to one group of closely related ones, such as those of the Taungbyon festival—were both a manifestation of the locality and of institutions backed by the king. Today, the nat cult is a complex and varied one that includes different categories of rites which correspond to the units of the cult and to the divisions of Burmese society, namely, the household, the village, the region, and the nation. While festivals addressed to individual or groups of nats retain their importance at the regional level, all 37 together are addressed in private ceremonies *(nat-pwe* or *nat kana-bwe)* in temporary ceremonial pavilions *(kana)* erected for these occasions. They are sponsored mainly by urbanites with economic objectives. These individuals call on the services of "nat spouses" *(nat kadaw),* who are religious specialists of spirit possession.[2] These ceremonies have multiplied in recent times and have given rise to a large corps of mediums.

The 37 Lords are ordered in a list that was fixed by royal decree and has been revised several times, most recently in 1820.[3] The nat currently propitiated in the ceremonies to all 37 do not correspond completely with prior official lists. Only the number of 37 has remained constant.[4] Nor is the hierarchy among the listed nat absolute in the actual ritual performances: certain more important figures emerge from the pantheon, and they give rise to the most renowned nat festivals, including those of Taungbyon.

The legend of the formation of the Burmese pantheon of 37 reveals a reversal in the king's attitude toward the nat. The founder of the first Burmese dynasty, King Anawratha, initially sought to ban the cults that were in force at this time. Unsuccessful, he decided to gather the relevant cultic figures into a pantheon under the authority of Thagya (the Burmese name for Sakka/Sakra, the protector of Buddhism, who corresponds to Indra in Hindu cosmology). This pantheon was embodied in the grouping of statues of the nat around the Shwezigon pagoda (the foundation of which, in Nyaung-U, near the royal city of Pagan, is attributed to Anawratha) to mark its subordination to Buddhism (Htin Aung 1959). Anawratha, prototype of the Burmese kings, emerges in this foundation myth as the founder of a new cult, that of the 37 Lords.

Even though King Anawratha is supposed to have subordinated the nat cult to Buddhism, this has not been enough to allay the suspicion of most orthodox Burmese Buddhists regarding it, even though the cult is observed in a general manner by most Burmese, in parallel with Buddhism, at least insofar as the basic rites are concerned. It is considered indispensable to be Buddhist in order to participate in the cult, and in fact the two practices are closely intertwined. The official ostracism of this cult for the sake of Buddhist orthodoxy can be seen as a continuation of King Anawratha's intent to eradicate the nat.

In the same way the stories of individual nat belonging to the 37 Lords depict them as having imposed themselves on a Burmese king. They are conceived of as the spirits of deceased heroes who died violent deaths because they represented a threat to royal power. Their stories, the more important of which are told in the royal chronicles, describe a necessary transformation from the condition of an inevitably malicious wandering spirit to that of a potentially benevolent nat. This transformation is effected by the king, himself the cause of the heroes' deaths, by the establishment of a local nat cult. The king thus appears, in the majority of the legends of the 37, as a veritable "nat-maker."

The well-known story of the Taungbyon figures—two brothers now known as the "Older and Younger Governors" (Mingyi Minlay)—will serve as an example.[5] It can be summarized as follows.[6] Of Indian origin and renowned for their superhuman abilities, the two brothers served in the army of King Anawratha of Pagan. They had inherited their extraordinary powers from their father, who in turn had gained them by eating the dead body of a hermit. Upon the brothers' return from a campaign in Yunnan, during which they distinguished themselves, they were condemned to death by the king who, according to the *Glass Chronicle* version, "did not trust them." Tradition holds that their negligence in the construction of the Hsutaungbyay pagoda that Anawratha had had built in Taungbyon served as the pretext for their condemnation. This story is corroborated by the absence of two bricks at the top of the vault of the interior niche of the pagoda. Anawratha was preparing to return to Pagan by royal barge when he was stopped by the malicious spirits of the two brothers. On the advice of his astrologers, Anawratha ordered that a palace adjoining the pagoda be built for the brothers, and that the local people pay homage to them. Thus the two brothers became the Taungbyon nat.

There are two moments in the legend when the king finds himself at the mercy of the future nat: before eliminating the threatening live heroes, and before transforming the evil spirits into nat. The king thus establishes the cult of the nat because he finds himself threatened. In addition, the nat are called *min* (translated "lord" after Temple's use [1906], it means king, ruler, governor), who live in "palaces" *(nat-nan)* and rule over the territory the king charged them with protecting in exchange for his homage. The establishment of a cult is thus equivalent to the reinstallation of a conquered, but still threatening, rival power. The transformation may be compared with the incorporation into the royal domain of a territory where the former rival keeps his sovereignty, in exchange for his allegiance to the victor.

The stories concerning both the foundation of the pantheon of the 37 Lords and the origin of the figures belonging to this pantheon underscore a confrontation between monarchical authority and local powers. The processes may be more aptly qualified, however, as allowing the differentiation of locality and central authority. By depicting the nat as an initially evil influence that imposes itself on the king who then transforms it into a tutelary spirit of a locality that has submitted to the Buddhist kingship, these stories describe a process of hierarchization.

Nat Festivals

As a ritual category, nat festivals are framed by the local setting: they are addressed to a single nat—or a closely related group of nat—in the territory where its cult originated. These annual ceremonies are designated by the name of the city or village where they are held, followed by the term for "festival" (for example, Taungbyon *bwe*). Both the commemorative rites of these ceremonies and the obligations incurred by the local population may be explained by the legendary biographies of the nat. But festivals do not come solely from local communities; they are also linked to royal institutions.

Each particular nat festival was originally linked to the local area and community, having been entrusted to its protection by royal decree. The domain of the nat of Taungbyon was thus delimited in administrative texts of the eighteenth century, where the territory was called *djosi* (Searle 1928). The obligations of the local population, today transmitted orally, were formerly also defined in official reports, along with other obligations to the king and his representatives. In its territory the nat has a sanctuary called the nat palace *(nat-nan)*, within which it is represented by a statue called a "royal form" *(pondaw)*. Although the setting of the festivals is local, they seem to emanate from the kingship.

Furthermore the Burmese court traditionally sent its representatives to some of the festivals to pay homage to the nat. Today, although the celebration of nat festivals remains a customary obligation for the inhabitants of a given territory, it also involves a much larger population. All those who feel linked to the nat by the intermediary of possession also come to pay homage to the nat, notably the mediums from all over Burma for whom the festivals present the opportunity to recharge the spiritual power of the nat. Although the mediums say they are "maintained" by the nat—the profits made during the ceremonies they conduct in their ordinary practice come from the nat—they make the opposite statement about their taking part in the nat festivals, arguing that it costs them money because they come to entertain the nat through their dance. While the economic reality of these festivals is, on analysis, more complex, this discourse indicates that festivals are perceived as a tribute due to the nat by those possessed by it as well as those who live in its territory.

These festivals surpass the local dimension not only because they mobilize the mediums of the general cult of the 37, but also because they link each nat to the other ones. The festivals in honor of the principal cultic figures form a vast ritual cycle of three festival periods each year. In hurrying from festival to festival, the crowd of pilgrims and mediums goes with the sun: in March, they are in the west of the Ayeyarwadi valley going from south to north, and in August in the eastern valley, from north to south (see Map 2). The ordering of the ceremonies thus traces a circumambulation of central Burma, a ritual arrangement of which its enactors are not conscious, and the planning of which is unknown (Brac de la Perrière 1998c).

Moreover, the spatial distribution of the festivals is meaningful: they are all celebrated in central Burma, the region where Burmese power has flourished since the tenth century. More characteristic still is the appearance or enlargement of certain festivals upon the establishment of a royal city nearby. A formerly prominent nat festival was that of Mount Popa, a spiritual center since at least the Pagan kingdom's apogee. In the second half of the nineteenth century the Popa festival vanished, while the Taungbyon festival gained new significance. As attested by royal edicts, the Taungbyon festival was long patronized by the king, but it became the most significant festival because of its proximity to Mandalay when it was established as a royal city. A new nat palace was then built that reportedly replicates a throne room. A hierarchy similar to the one of the Burmese court was established in the assembly of mediums who take part in the festival. In short, the ceremony was designed to mimic that of the Burmese court.

Traditions among the community of mediums attribute a central role to King Mindon, who founded Mandalay in 1857, in establishing the importance of the Taungbyon festival. They credit Mindon, known to be a very pious Buddhist, with the same initial refusal that is attributed to Anawratha in the cult foundation myth. But according to these oral traditions, the nat, and particularly the Taungbyon nat, imposed themselves on King Mindon, as they had imposed themselves previously on King Anawratha, in such a way that he not only had to revert to the cult but also to restore its institutions. The building of the nat palace and the offering of the nat statues are thus attributed to Mindon.

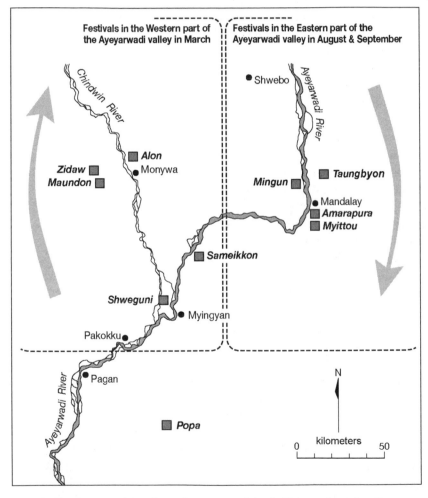

Map 2. The Tripartite Annual Ritual Nat Festival Cycle (Source: Bénédicte Brac de la Perrière)

As for the hierarchy of ritual functions within the nat cult, it seems that it was actually the last Burmese monarch, King Thibaw (1875–1885) who instituted it by appointing the main master of the ritual. But the confusion between the two kings is significant because it ties the restoration of the cult to one of the kingdom. The history of nat festivals and their institutionalization is thus directly tied to that of the royalty and to the ritualization of its relations with local communities.

The Domains of the Taungbyon Festival

Three annual ceremonies are celebrated in the village of Taungbyon to honor the Taungbyon Brothers. They commemorate their departure for the war (December), their return (March), and their disappearance (August). The last one is most significant and will be analyzed here. The festival takes place for five days during the lunar month of Wagaung, from the tenth day of the rising moon to the full moon.

Except during the festivals, Taungbyon is a dusty village. During the festival, however, the village is transformed, all free space being taken over by the temporary festival infrastructure. Apart from the section of the audience that is replaced each day, the other participants settle in for the whole festival before it starts. They are the fairground people and, above all, the mediums who arrive with members of their group and clients and settle into temporary bamboo camps.

Such a crowd requires great organization. Lodging, water, and electricity must be provided to the many mediums and nat devotees. This organization falls within two main domains: the pagoda (or more precisely the two pagodas celebrated at the same time as the nat) and the palace of the nat belonging to its guardians (see Map 3).

The two pagodas, Hsutaungbyay and the later-built Hsutaungya, are located north of the nat palace and facing east. They are managed by a pagoda association, formed in April 1991, that brings together the religious authorities of Madaya (a small town north of Taungbyon) and Taungbyon's seven monasteries. It replaced the religious association of Mandalay that previously managed the pagodas. This move means that the control of the festival has been taken over by government-backed institutions from politically engaged religious associations. The services of fourteen official departments and organizations during the festival also come from Madaya, including the police, the Myanmar Red Cross, and the immigration services. The pagoda association controls sites in the "big" and "little" markets, shows and movie theaters, and the pagoda space itself, where vendors have their stalls. Stalls are sold one

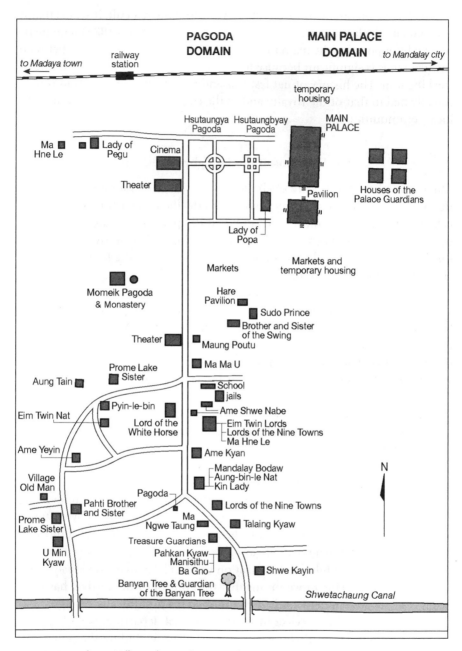

Map 3. Taungbyon Village during the Annual Nat-pwe (Source: Bénédicte Brac de la Perrière)

month before by auction. Contracts are let for the rights to provide water and electricity for the whole village and for the installation of showers. The profits from these concessions are used for the maintenance of the pagoda.

Adjacent to the pagoda territory, the palace of the nat is surrounded by a large open space. The palace is composed of two pavilions, both facing to the west and the village, contrary to the pagoda, an orientation which connotes their submission to Buddhism. In the first pavilion, the nats, that is their statues, stay all year. These statues include the two Brothers, the Infant of the Oboe (a very popular female nat child called Ma Ne-lay), and the royal secretary who pleaded the cause of the two brothers to the king. A ritual showering of the statues takes place in the second pavilion.

The nat palaces and domains are owned by palace guardians (nan-dein), a hereditary position. Their ritual function is to provide the nat with appropriate worshipping. In Taungbyon, guardians say that they descended from the two Chinese princesses whom Anawratha charged with guarding the palace. They can prove their descent from the beginning of the nineteenth century, when King Bodawpaya, who was reigning in Amarapura, gave a paddy field to their grandmother, Amei Khwei. Succession is said to have been matrilineal until the last generation, although the guardians' profits are actually held jointly by members of the same generation. Indeed, in 1961 Spiro (1967:116) noted that there were only two guardians, matrilineally related, who shared the position: one at the palace and one for the statues. A medium estimated that by 1991 there were thirty-seven guardians. Since then, several brothers at the core of this group have given their position to their descendants, who are fewer in number. It is difficult to decide whether this joint ownership system was favored by the recent growth of the festival.

This family thus manages the whole domain of the nat. They rent bamboo camps around the palace to mediums. In contradistinction to the pagoda association, guardians supervise the organization of the festival themselves and distribute space according to "tradition" (yo-ya). This means each year allocating the same spaces to the same mediums (and upon their deaths to their successors), who have to pay a rent that is regularly increased. Guardians also collect offerings to the nat from local villagers, according to customary agreements. But above all, they collect offerings from mediums on the occasion of the performance of dances in the main palace, according to a program whose importance will be discussed below.

Members of the guardians' families are thus the main beneficiaries of the festival incomes in Taungbyon. They maintain their heritage by jealously protecting their monopoly on the festival organization. However, this monopoly on the main palace is counterbalanced not only by the multiplication of secondary palaces, as we will see, but also by the hierarchy of titled mediums having a ritual position in Taungbyon.

The Titles of the Mediums

According to the mediums, King Thibaw, who succeeded Mindon, created the actual hierarchy of ritual positions by appointing U San Hla nat chieftain for the seventy-three princely houses of Mandalay. His main duty was to maintain the cult at the palace of the nat attached to the royal city and to pay tribute to the nat of Taungbyon in the name of the king by presenting his offerings for him. After the collapse of the monarchy, the nat chieftain still presided over the ritual of tribute to the nat of Taungbyon, but no longer represented the king. The position became autonomous. The position still exists, and it is the only one that involves a hereditary right in the hierarchy of mediums.

U San Hla, who trained many mediums, had no son, so he passed on his position as nat chieftain to his nephew and his position as guardian of the palace of the royal city to his main female disciple. These two appointments thus became separate. The nephew died at the beginning of the 1980s and was replaced by his grandson. In 1984 the grandson, who was twenty-four years old, was propelled into the role of nat chieftain because he was the only one in his family of rice growers to accept the role. His possession dances still showed his inexperience. However, he was supported by the profession, and he now leads the ritual without any particular difficulty, although without any virtuosity either. He has been criticized for his lack of authority in front of the palace guardians and in particular for his management of the mediums' ritual positions.

The nat chieftain is assisted by mediums, men and women who have the titles—"one who has the *baung* (hat worn by ministers in the time of the Burmese kingship)" *(baung-zaung)* and "queen who has the *tho* (hat worn by Burmese queens)" *(tho-zaung mibaya)*—that liken them to ministers and queens. The duties accompanying these ritual positions consist of opening the festival along with the nat chieftain and performing the rituals that recall the Brothers' legend. They also act as masters of ceremony for all the other mediums during their dance at the main palace, and as such they are entitled to a portion of the offerings presented by the mediums at these occasions. Like the palace guardians, they take advantage of the ceremonial system and act thus as an interface between guardians and ordinary mediums.

The duties of the ministers and queens are passed on (it is a rule of transmission) to one of the deceased's disciples who is chosen by a ritual of appointment among the disciples or by indications of a preferred successor given while the person was alive. However, the oldest dignitaries mention an "election" by the nat, through a dream, for example, and tell how people have come to them because they had been elected by the nat and how they resisted as long as they could. The responsibility is heavy, and if they are not the nat's "chosen," then they face death. Moreover, a long resistance when the nat chooses someone leads to all sorts of misfortunes such as the incapacity of that person to be a medium. These misfortunes are in turn interpreted as signs of election, and they are finally what encourages these senior mediums, according to their statements, to accept the responsibility.

Four queens and one minister were originally the highest dignitaries. After the Second World War and until 1988 there were eight dignitaries, four ministers and four queens. This number doubled in 1991 and rose to eighteen in 1995. The leader of the palace guardians, who has control over the dignitaries' ritual positions, explained that some members of the old guard became too old to "turn"—to complete some of the commemorative rituals—and younger ones had to act as substitutes.

It is common knowledge, however, that positions have been sold and this has given rise to a general reprobation among the community of mediums. We can measure this disapproval by looking at the dignitaries list that accompanied the mediums' dances in 1991: only seven of the sixteen dignitaries on duty were on the list and among these it was the seniors who are mentioned several times, especially the oldest one, who despite being eighty-nine years old, danced with almost no interruption during the whole festival. It is also significant that the recent deaths of dignitaries, except for the oldest pair, were interpreted as punishments from the nat. In addition to the opprobrium attached to buying their position, some dignitaries were criticized because they broke the often-cited rule that ministers need to be "men," not transvestites (mein-masha). Increasingly numerous among mediums, the transvestites have in recent times gained popularity as ritual performers and that has favored their accession to the position of dignitary.

After 1995 the number of dignitaries started to decrease because of two factors: the deaths of the oldest members and a change in the management of the palace guardians who, after some difficulties, stopped making appointments in exchange for money. Little by little, the new dignitaries have started to accompany, in their dance turn, the mediums with whom they are closest. The renewal of the titled members of Taungbyon has thus been ensured, although by means considered as nontraditional.

Taungbyon's dignitaries also open most other nat festivals so their hierarchy stands as the general reference. In Taungbyon, however, the small number of "chosen" mediums, compared to the growing number of ordinary mediums, forces those not directly attached to the dignitaries' network to find lodging outside of the domain of the main palace, and this has stimulated the emergence of secondary dances as the profession of spirit mediumship becomes more complex.

Secondary Palaces

For many years the palace domain has been too small to accommodate all the participants. Villagers rent temporary camps in their yards to house the mediums having no "traditional" place. In the mid-1980s mediums even started to build secondary palaces. By 1986 there were twenty-five secondary nat palaces in Taungbyon and thirty-one in 1991 as the rate of palace construction began to decrease. Among the secondary palaces, nine are situated along the road that leads to the canal and the river. They are considered traditional because they are dedicated to secondary characters in the Taungbyon Brothers' legend and play a part in the ritual in honor of the main nat.

This is not the case for the other secondary palaces. They developed after the 1980s with the increasing number of mediums who do not have the right to dance in the main palace. They are dedicated to other nat among the 37. In the cult logic, there cannot be more than one palace for each nat in the festival villages or it casts doubt on the presence of the nat. Confronted with the disorganized multiplication of palaces in Taungbyon, Madaya township authorities felt compelled to ask the mediums in charge of these buildings to justify their foundation.

For each of these palaces, there is a system of dances similar to that at the central palace. Taungbyon is the only festival site where dances are performed in secondary palaces. In Shweguni, to "stop the drum," which means to celebrate any other ceremony, is explicitly banned. During the festival of its main nat, "the Famous," secondary nat can visit only in temporary shelters and there can be no dancing associated with them.

The banning of dances in secondary palaces ensures the monopoly of the main palace. However, conflicts have developed in other local communities around festival management and have led to the duplication of the main palace in villages such as Maundon (Brac de la Perrière 1998c). Amarapura's case, where there are no less than three main palaces, is again different. Each of these palaces was built at different times for contextual reasons and claims to be the authentic palace of the Lady of Popa, who is the mother of the Taungbyon Brothers and is celebrated there one week after her sons. Even in Shweguni, a palace guardian built, in 1998, a second structure dedicated to the hero of the festival in order to accommodate more dances.

These processes of duplication of the main palace stand in contrast with the monopoly that the Taungbyon guardians' family managed to keep over custodianship of the Brothers' palace. This placed great pressure on the mediums' community and intensified their demand for ritual space which necessitated the development of the secondary palaces. The Taungbyon festival has thus expanded beyond its initial celebration of the Taungbyon Brothers, with guardianship of the secondary palaces going to either mediums or villagers.

The creation of new palaces obviously gives more "spaces" to the festival. It allows internal articulations of the profession to occur. In this matter, the interests of ordinary mediums come close to those of the villagers and stand against the monopoly of the guardians' family and, to a lesser extent, against the dignitaries. Nat festivals are thus being adapted in different ways according to contextual power struggles between mediums, palace guardians, and villagers.

Tributes to the Brothers in the Main Palace

A complex ritual program actually shapes the encounter of mediums, palace guardians, and the local population. Nat festivals follow a similar ritual pattern all over central Burma. They are principally structured by a series of double tributes in the main palace: the presentation of offerings by locals and the mediums' dances that last the whole festival. In addition to tributes paid to the tutelary spirit of the domain, the ritual includes a recalling of how that particular nat was made. This aspect imbues each festival with its specific character. In Taungbyon the specific events are the "meeting of the royal council," performed on the tenth day of the lunar month, the "ritual shower" on the following morning, the "hunting of the hares" on the fourteenth day, the "felling of the trees" on the fourteenth and the fifteenth days, and finally the gilding of the statues. We will see that tributes and commemorative rituals allow contrasting forms of confrontation between mediums, palace guardians, and the local population.

The Taungbyon Brothers draw a continuous influx of devotees who press forward in front of the nat. Their tributes take different forms depending on the category of pilgrim. The program begins with tributes paid to the Buddha, after which pilgrims buy flowers and bouquets of leaves at the entrance of the main palace that are displayed to the nat and then kept by the purchaser as objects invested with the protection of the nat.

A more significant tribute can be paid by offering a tray *(bwe)* containing a whole coconut and a hand of bananas (which can be considered the basic offering for any ritual in Burma). In Taungbyon the tray holds two hands of bananas, "because there are two brothers." Mediums offer their first tribute tray within a day of their arrival. They buy it from wholesalers who come for the festival. Local villagers pay tribute according to the days prescribed by the custom of each village. Every household sends a representative, most often the housewife. Lines of women arriving with trays prepared at their home and loaded on their heads are one of the most memorable images of the nat festivals.

Trays are presented in the palace in three different ways: the palace may keep the whole offering (*kadaw-bwe* or "tribute tray"); the palace may keep half and give the remaining half of the offering back to the donor (*way-bwe* or "divided tray"), or the palace may give the entire offering back to the donor increased with more hands of bananas after it has been presented to the nat (*htat-pwe* or "increased tray"). At the back of the palace, behind the altar of the nat, fruits are piled up in a storage room. During the rituals, when people cannot reach the altar, they go directly to the storage room to make their offering.

In addition to the trays mediums offer to the palace and those they only show *(pya-bwe)* before putting them on their own altar in front of their nat statues, they pay tribute when they are possessed by the nat and dance for them. This kind of tribute is the *tet-pwe* ("the offering to go up" or "the offering that goes up" to the palace). These dances take place in the palace apart from the other rituals. They start the day of the official opening of the festival, the night of the tenth day of the rising moon and continue to the last day, the full moon, from the middle of the day until late into the night.

The Opening Ritual and the System of Dances

In Taungbyon the opening ceremony is called the "meeting of the royal council." Elsewhere, the festival begins with the "royal shower" dance. The crowd grows in the afternoon. The orchestra settles down at the end of the main palace and the dance floor; the space that separates them from the altars is enclosed by a wire grid. After a collection for the pagoda, the ceremony begins with the "call of the big nat," an evocation of the main nat figures, collectively executed by all the dignitaries, as well as the "dance of the five *pa*," which succinctly embodies five of the main nat by their specific steps.

Each dignitary then performs accompanied by one of his peers, according to a scenario that is the same for all the tributary dances of the ordinary mediums. The first dance, with a dignitary acting as master of ceremonies, is known as the "hare hunt" and recalls the Brothers' taste for the hunt. In a ritual that is connected to the Shweguni nat, the Famous, the medium then performs solo the "bets on the cock fights" three times. This ritual consists of passing a cup around the audience until a fixed minimum amount is collected. With the full cup in his right hand and a cock figurine in his left hand, the medium dances and spins the cup without anything falling out; this little *tour de force* proves the presence of the nat. The content of the first cup goes to the orchestra, while the others are shared between the guardians and the dignitaries. As each medium ends the dance of his "bets," his followers leave the room and are replaced by the followers of the next medium. Mediums follow one another until four in the morning of the following day.

Because of the increasing number of mediums, the guardians' family limits the dance to twenty minutes. There were 336 dances in the main palace during the festival in 1991, and mediums need to reserve their turn with the palace guardians. A medium keeps the order number obtained the first time the medium did a tet-pwe from one year to the other, and it is passed on from master to disciple, along with the space that was rented in the domain of the palace. If a medium is absent more than twice, this position is forfeited. Such a system requires mediums involved to participate, but its rigidity is not compatible with the dynamism of the cult and the growing number of mediums, since only the most important mediums, or disciples of those who used to be important, have their turn in the palace. A consequence, as we have seen, is the multiplication of secondary palaces.

To go up to the palace, mediums have to pay an amount that is revised every year; it rose from 1,000 to 55,000 kyat between 1991 and 2002.[7] They also have to bring a *pahso* (a male ceremonial *longyi*), scarves, and "royal banquets" *(sa-daw-sa)*. The palace guardians set the rules regarding the components of the banquet and the quality of the offerings. Omissions of these requisites are mentioned in the book where mediums' order numbers are written down. It is impossible to say how much money the festival generates but it is without a doubt a considerable amount for Burma: the rights, for the dance only, generated 336,000 *kyat* in 1991, to which should be added the monetary offerings the mediums solicit during their dances.

Mediums' dances are a major element of the festival. The medium makes it a point of honor to have his or her performance noticed. And in order for his or her clients to receive the full attention of the nat and be specially protected, the medium's dance needs to surpass that of other mediums, to represent a moment of exception. Strategies differ, but the most typical seems to consist in taking particularly good care of the staging, the costumes, and the dance steps. Some mediums even make their younger and best-looking disciples dance; this is how young male transvestites *(mein-masha),* usually good dancers, come to be increasingly present in greater numbers among the groups of mediums. Others prefer to put their emphasis on respect for "tradition." For all of them, however, the dance is the height of the festival.

The dances are salient because they demonstrate the relation of possession between the medium and the nat. Even though the explicit goal of the dance is to entertain the nat, and even though dances are presented like a show, mediums are considered possessed: mediums dance for the nat, but at the same time the nat dance through the mediums. When an outsider sees the extreme mastery of the dance, the steps and the figures that embody the nat, he or she could think that the performance is more about theater than possession. But this is not at all the case. The dance, with the mastery of the body that is implied, is the mark of the possessed in Burma.

Because of the "bets on cock fights," these dances are also the most profitable part of the rituals for the guardians. Very often the amount of the "bets" quickly climbs, since the medium's followers regard it as the ideal way to get in touch with the nat. In addition, money can also be given directly to the possessed medium, who then scatters it like rain around the room. Mediums throwing coins (and wads of bills since the beginning of the 1990s) have always been part of the ceremonies in which the nat are embodied. The action shows the nat's satisfaction and demonstrates that the ritual was well accomplished. It is also a technique that makes real the link established by the medium between the audience and the nat. The Burmese people believe that money given by nat will multiply, and mediums throwing money around creates the picture of a nat giving away riches, which justifies the nat's cult.

But throwing bills takes on additional significance during the nat festival. The growing audience for the mediums' dances prompted the guardians to enclose the dance floor to ensure the management of the dance sequences. Since that time mediums' comments before and after their performance show that, for them, throwing bills permits them to favor their clients rather than the palace guardians in the process of redistribution. The closed space in which mediums now embody the nat in Taungbyon results in their clients and close relatives benefiting from this windfall.

The closed dance floor isolates the mediums' tributes from the population's tributes and gives the impression that there are two parallel festivals. (This system already existed in 1986 in Taungbyon and is becoming standard in all nat festivals.) It has increased the tension between the villagers and the urban community of mediums and their clients who manipulate huge amounts of money for themselves, even though the mediums complain about the greediness of palace guardians. At the same time the image of abundance that the mediums seek to project helps reinforce the nat position as wealth providers.

The Ritual Shower

The "royal shower," in which the nat effigies are washed, is celebrated the following morning, the eleventh day of the lunar month. The procedure varies depending on the festival, but it always includes removing of the statues from

the palace, a move which marks a change of state from their reactivation during the festival due to the "arrival" of the nat.

At one time the Taungbyon Brothers' effigies were transported to the river.
Nowadays, they are taken from the main palace to the secondary pavilion
where the ritual takes place. They are carried on a royal palanquin *(waw-daw)*
by men of the guardian militia, in a procession led by the nat chieftain, the
dignitaries, gong players, and lines of guards dressed with the red velvet uniform of the armies of the Burmese kings (see Figure 4.1). This line of armed
men recalls the fact that the two Brothers belonged to Anawratha's army.
Nearby villagers perform the roles by customary obligation and pass their costumes on to each other.

The palanquin is left at the entrance of the pavilion and the statues are
placed on altars where the guardians "shower" them, dry them, change their
clothes, and wash the betel cups and boxes. These ritual showers recall the
libation of the royal person that was a remarkable sequence of the monarchy
rituals, not only at the king's enthronement, but also at periodic tribute rituals (Brac de la Perrière 2005). Even now it remains a striking feature of standard respect paid to monks and elders at Burmese New Year occasions. Dur-

Figure 4.1. Taungbyon *nat-pwe:* the Brothers' procession leaving the palace and
circumambulating the pavilion where the images will be given their ritual shower
(Source: Bénédicte Brac de la Perrière)

ing the festivals, the ritual shower of the nat statues actually opens the tribute rituals and consecrates the transition from the usual state of the nat in its residence, to its state as ruler, ready to accept offerings. This is further marked by the homage the nat pays to the Buddha that is performed on the way back from taking the effigies to the main palace through the rocking of the palanquin *(U taik-)* in the direction of the pagoda.

Hunting Hares

During the following days mediums succeed each other, dancing in front of the nat until the celebration of the "hunting of the hares" ritual, on the fourteenth day. A young man whose family comes from the village of Natywakon has been in charge of this ceremony since 1989 told me about the tradition of the hunt.

> The two Brothers used to stop in my ancestor's village to quench their thirst and eat when they were hare hunting. As we know, they liked this kind of hunt. When they went to war, we didn't see them again, of course. Upon their return, they came again, and since they had become wealthy, my ancestors blamed them for not paying for the meals they were having in the village. They died shortly after this episode. They became spirits (*luzein*, wild or "green" men), and they went back to drink at an old woman's house in the village who asked them why they couldn't be seen. After they left, the old woman discovered they had left gold in the pot of palm beer she had served them. We never saw them again until they became *nat.*
> Then they asked the villagers to bring hares to their palace in Taungbyon. As the villagers couldn't find their way, the *nat* sent dignitaries to welcome them and give them golden tamarind fruit. That's why now we go seven times around the palace and we are given bananas!

The day of the ritual, the young man leads a group of young villagers from Natywakon to present two hares to the palace. Starting from a specific pavilion in Taungbyon, they follow a long ritual route to the palace and walk around it seven times, keeping it on their left. An assembly of Natywakon villagers accompanies the procession, hurling such obscenities that some mediums prefer to close their doors when they pass by. Only Natywakons can join this group, and in 1991 they severely beat a group of young people who attempted to join in.

The group's shouts portray the danger that these heroes, and then their spirits, were for the king and the order he represents before their transformation into nat. Indeed, the provocation is explicitly for the festival's institutions:

the staged royal order, the palace, the nat, as masters of a domain, and their court. It also demonstrates why they had to be transformed into nat through the institution of their cult and the attribution of a domain: they had to be pacified. It is significant that it is local people who perform the rebellious side of the two Brothers.

The hares are then delivered to the pavilion dignitaries, who present them to the nat in the main palace. They are later prepared as a salad and eaten by the dignitaries. The ingestion of the hare represents the acquisition of the subversive aspects of the Taungbyon Brothers and corresponds, for the dignitaries, to acquisition of spiritual powers similar to those of the Brothers.

Felling Trees

The presentation of the hares is immediately followed by the "felling" of two "trees," or, more precisely, two branches, erected to the north and west of the palace, one for each Brother. These two fellings are seen as trials (*da san*, "to try the knife"). They are repeated twice the day after, the last day of the rising moon, at the end of the afternoon. A previous felling was performed on the thirteenth day in one of the traditional secondary palaces standing on the way to the river, that of the Lord of the Nine Cities. It is said that the trees cut down this way represent the spirit responsible for the death of Anawratha, the Pagan dynasty's founder, and also the king responsible for the death of the two Brothers and the Lord of the Nine Cities. The story told by the *Glass Palace Chronicle* can be summarized as follows:

> Anawratha was coming back to Pagan. He heard the news that a furious buffalo was devastating a nearby village. On his elephant, he went to the village to charge the buffalo. But the buffalo was not of the natural kind and Anawratha's karma was exhausted. The buffalo charged the elephant and gored Anawratha, causing his death. This buffalo was an enemy in a previous life and became the spirit of a *lein* tree. Since the spirit had not honored Anawratha when he was passing by, the king had the tree struck with the scepter given to him by Sakra until the spirit came down from his tree and paid him homage. Since then, he had been looking for revenge.

The mediums tell the story almost exactly like this to their audience. Only the tree species is different: the one they use for the ritual is *htein*. As far as I know, tree-felling takes place only in Taungbyon, Myittou, and Taunthaman, for those characters whose death is attributed to Anawratha. The ritual thus links the revenge of the tree spirit to the possible revenge of the nat.

The felling is preceded by a ritual of circumambulation by dignitaries between the nat statue inside the palace and the tree's spirit outside (see Figure 4.2). They go out seven times and turn three times around the branch placed in front of the entrance, keeping it on their left. The queens cross the swords they are holding over the offerings that have been placed on the ground around the branch. The trees are considered to be the nat's trees, and it is known that the spirits of deceased heroes find refuge in trees before they eventually transform into nat.

The final time that the procession goes around the branch the nat chieftain stands alone and uses a sword to cut a piece of the branch that he brings back, running, to the palace. He leaves the remains of the branch to young villagers who jump on it and fight to get a piece of it. In a matter of seconds, the branch is torn apart. For the local community the significance of the ritual lies in this tearing apart of the tree branch, pieces of which are then buried in the fields to ensure good harvests.

The procession of dignitaries carries the spirit of the "tree" into a statue and transforms it into a nat by going back and forth between the branch planted outside the spirit's home and the nat statues inside. It transforms a spirit into a nat by the very act of installing it in a statue. From this point of view, it is logical that the nat chieftain who used to be in charge of the nat royal

Figure 4.2. Taungbyon *nat-pwe:* dignitaries circumambulating the "tree" during the "felling of the trees" ritual (Source: Bénédicte Brac de la Perrière)

cult cuts the tree down and takes a remnant into the palace; this ritual resembles an actualization of the spirit's transformation into a nat by the king. The nat chieftain here becomes the king who renews the efficacy of the ritual object, the statue. Moreover, the ritual actualizes a more fundamental transformation that occurs in the background, that of spirit cult into nat cult.

This rite is, however, mostly seen as an evocation of Anawratha's killing by the tree spirit. The *Chronicle* says that this killing becomes possible only when Anawratha's karma is exhausted, and the king's sovereignty depends on his karma. His sovereignty has been given to him by Thagya—in the chronicle it is Sakra, guardian of Buddhism—in the form of attributes like the scepter that allows him to control the spirits. As soon as his positive karma is exhausted, revengeful spirits' threats return as the balance of power is reversed. In relation to this, it is significant that the rite of the presentation of the hares—which recalls the Brothers as individuals who do not obey norms and are therefore endowed with maximum efficacy—is associated with the felling of the tree under which the group stops: both are reminiscent of the same aspect of the nat, rebellious spirits who threaten the order that the king is trying to impose.

In the end, the Burmese interpretation of the felling and the one to which the ritual's analysis leads, involve only two aspects of the king-nat relationship: the threat that spirits represent and the king's pacification technique. We can also say that one is the local version, different from the norm, and the other is a national or pan-Buddhist version of unification in action. Even if the ritual reasserts the king's obtaining submission of the divergent and local rival forces that the nat represent, the threat nonetheless remains present in the festival. The shadow of the king's negative karma is always a reminder that his sovereignty is finite. A synthesis of Buddhism, the cult of the nat, and the monarchy occurs, with the Buddhist aspects encompassing the two others and defining their relationship. In Burma, it is ultimately only the adoption of Buddhist values that makes possible sovereignty over powerful local forces.

Enfolding the Local within Buddhist Society

The mediums start packing as soon as the last tree is felled. The following morning the last ritual is accomplished: it involves gilding of the statues the expense of which is borne entirely by the palace guardians. The gilding is performed in the palace when the village is already almost deserted by the mediums. The festival thus ends suddenly, with the mediums leaving as quickly as possible.

Nat festivals are the local rituals of the Burmese cult of the 37, caught in a dialectical relationship. Nat receive the tributes, surrounded by dignitaries, in their palace. They hold a dual position: they are the domain's masters as well as spiritual masters acting through possession. Sovereignty over a domain and possession are linked by the ritual like two aspects of the same relationship that expresses itself on different levels of practice: the local level (sovereignty) and the general level (the cult of possession). Festivals articulate both levels, and they follow each other in central Burma, in the palaces of the main nat or groups of nat so that we have the image of a court that moves, each time honoring a different ruler, as if the nat hierarchy is rotating (see Map 2).

In addition to tributes paid to the tutelary spirit of a domain, the ritual also includes recalling the nat-making legend. These very developed and evocative rituals have extremely abstract and stereotypical versions that are performed during ceremonies of the 37. These later rituals are so formalized that they lose the original meanings infused in the developed ritual versions of the specific nat festivals. The participation of the mediums in the festivals thus allows them to invest their day-to-day and urban performances with meanings drawn from local and specific traditions.

These specific rituals also set the articulation of the nat cult with the broader Burmese Theravāda Buddhist society, in a symbolic way that takes the shape of a vivid tension. The local represents the dangerous, nonstandard force that is not yet transformed. In Taungbyon villagers shout obscenities, hunt hares, and grow restless around the palace, in a fashion similar to the two Brothers. The center is occupied by the transformed and potentially beneficial forces of the nat and the cult that is the instrument of their transformation. The nat chieftain, with the medium dignitaries, carries the tree spirit's force inside, into the nat statue. He, like the mediums, represent sovereignty and the authority of Burmese kingship made manifest throughout the populations of Burma.

The tension between the local and the national manifests itself through different values given to the ritual: the tree-felling is a fertility rite for local people, a reactivation of the main statues for the mediums. But this tension should not be understood as a simple juxtaposition of two levels at which the cult is operative. It is necessary and central to the ritual as a whole and permits the identification of the local and the national levels and their confrontation. Indeed, beyond the transformation of the spirit into a nat, the foundations of Burmese identity are reproduced.

It is significant that the values attributed to locality in the festival emerge so strongly as divergent from Burmese-Buddhist morality. During the festival the most condemned behaviors are necessary: sexual provocation, eating hare, and violence are all staged in specific rituals with the crowd's approval. They are necessary because they are the basis of the power the heroes used to compel the king to reinstall them by instituting their cult.

These demonstrations occur outside of the palace. The palace is where the Brothers of Taungbyon reside as nat, transformed by the cult. Inside the palace they acknowledge their allegiance to the Buddhist monarchy. They pay tribute to the pagoda and even have a meditation cell. It would be simplistic to simply speak of antagonism existing between the cult of the nat and Buddhism. It is more the encysting of the former within the latter.

In these festivals that ritually stage forms of integration of the local into the kingdom, the cult of the nat is an agent of Burmese construction. This dynamic is still active nowadays in the power struggles between mediums, palace guardians, and village communities and is expressed through the ritual system of tributes, the dances. The dances are crucial for the festival economy and may have been created by mediums to replace royal patronage after the British deposed the last Burmese king at the end of the nineteenth century.

The medium profession developed rapidly with growing demands for ritual specialists that paralleled the economic liberalization of sectors of the Burmese economy in the 1990s. These developments placed enormous pressure on the ritual system and led to a multiplication of dances and dignitaries. The expansion of the capacity of the ritual system is in everybody's interest: as a source of legitimacy for mediums and as a source of revenue for villages in proportions previously unknown to them. Adaptations have occurred differently, depending on particular power struggles between village communities and palace guardians on one hand and mediums and dignitaries on the other. The logic of the cult has not changed, but spirit mediumship has become the vehicle for an increasing standardization of the festivals. This is a dialogical process: mediums are both bringing standardization in the local rituals by their participation and infusing their standardized urban practice with local traditions.

The confrontation between the local and the broader Burmese Buddhist society in these festivals is ongoing, as it has been for centuries, although it has been accelerated by the move from socialism to capitalism in the past decade. The confrontation between local ritual institutions and their link with the general cult can only be understood as a succession of confrontations that grow more frequent in time. The festivals allow the symbolic elaboration of an autochthonous principle through staging of local forces confronting the royal order, even though the monarchy disappeared in 1885. Central Burma's unity as the kings had achieved it remains, and the cult of the nat paradoxically holds a unifying and hierarchializing value for a centralizing power that places itself under the authority and protection of Buddhism.

Notes

I wish to thank Monique Skidmore, who convinced me to rework the essay for this volume and, through her dedicated reading of an overly long draft, helped me a lot in getting it right.

1. This cult is known through the folklorist description that was written by Temple (1906), a work which many later Burmese authors have used to support their own accounts (among them, see Bha Nyunt 1981, Khin Maung Than 2001, and Pho Kya 1973). Well-known analysis from anthropologists include those by Bekker (1989), June Nash (1966), and Spiro (1967). My own approach departs from Spiro's, my purpose being the analysis of the ritual system and its sociological grounding. My terminology differs as well: I call the ritual specialists "spirit mediums" rather than "shamans" as their practice involves possession, that is to say, the entering of the spirit into its medium (Brac de la Perrière 1989:52, 91–119).

2. Spirit mediums say they are first "called" by one *nat* of the pantheon. This calling takes the form of some sort of misfortune that is interpreted as the expression of the nat's desire. The newly "called" have to accept the possession and honor the *nat* through participation in the cult in order for the *nat*'s influence to become beneficial. Their link to the calling *nat* is then consecrated through an initiation ritual described as a "marriage" to the *nat*. This explains why the term "*nat*-wife" is used to denote mediums, even though the vocation involves as many men as women (Brac de la Perrière 1998b). The new medium does not become a specialist of the cult until completing an apprenticeship during which he or she masters possession by all of the *nat* of the pantheon.

3. This list was established to update the previous one, which dated back to 1805, through an inquiry conducted by the then crown prince, the Myawadi Myoza, to the musicians performing for the rituals. The result was the *Mahagita Medani Kyan*, a compilation of ritual songs that is still prevalent.

4. The number 37 probably is an indirect borrowing from the 32 members of the Tavatimsa, the abode of the Hindu gods ruled by Indra. One has still to add the four *lokapâla* (the guardians of the four directions) and Indra to get the 37 (32 + 4 + 1). The prevalent hypothesis is that the Burmese got this cosmological ordering from the Pyu and the Mon (Brac de la Perrière, 1989:31–32, Shorto 1967, Mendelson 1963).

5. Because Anawratha is said to have offered a jar of gold at their birth, they are noted in official lists as the Elder of Pure Gold and the Younger of Pure Gold (Shwehpyingyi and Shwehpyinnge). Later in this text they will be referred as the Taungbyon Brothers. This is a correction for the expression *Frères musulmans* that I used in my 1992 essay. The brothers are never explicitly called Muslims in Burmese but rather Kala (Indians or foreigners), although ritual specificities—such as pork avoidance and *fez* headdress—strongly suggest this religious origin.

6. Traditions dealing with the nat come from different sources. Although biographies of a number of nat are found in the Burmese royal chronicles, different stories are told or depicted in rituals, either through local traditions or by spirit mediums. Concerning the Taungbyon Brothers, the summary presented here combines what is usually told by devotees and what is related in the *Glass Palace Chronicle* (Luce and Pe Maung Tin 1956:83–84).

7. The official value of kyat is fixed at 7 kyat for US $1. On the black market, however, this value is highly volatile. During the summer of 1991 it varied around 100 kyat per dollar and had reached over 1,000 kyat in 2004.

—5—
Respected Grandfather, Bless This Nissan

Benevolent and Politically Neutral Bo Bo Gyi

Mandy Sadan

Visitors to the southwest corner of the Shwedagon pagoda platform will come across a statue of a rather portly gentleman who is getting on in years and is holding on tightly to a staff, his face looking down on homage-payers with the gentle smile of a dear grandfather or favorite uncle. The Burmese people who come before this figure are typically seeking assistance from him with the more mundane aspects of their lives, rather than the spiritual. They want amelioration of a grave economic situation, protection from the dangers of a modern urban lifestyle (including motor accidents), or success in education in order to rise out of poverty and create a financial hedge against the ever-rising inflation. Although lacking physical strength, this old man has seen a great deal in the millennia of his life. It is through longevity that this figure has acquired the qualities of wisdom and benevolence that homage-payers are seeking to invoke on their own behalf. This is the Bo Bo Gyi spirit—*bo bo* meaning "grandfather," or "elder/ancestor" in its more general sense, and *gyi* meaning "great" or "respected."

The fact that the term Bo Bo Gyi has associations with the broader notion of "grandfather" or "ancestor" has given rise to the suggestion that this spirit recalls a vestige of ancient and now-forgotten ancestor worship (Rodrigue 1992:9). That the Bo Bo Gyi may have originated as a village guardian spirit, the spirit's emplacement confirming human habitation in a locality is another, possibly related, line of argument. However, the contemporary understanding of the term is increasingly related to a "type" and this type has a standardized figurative expression found not at the entrance to the village, but at the pagoda.

The spirit Bo Bo Gyi has been brought within the pagoda physically, as represented in the plastic arts, but also metaphorically, as an ally and supporter of orthodox Buddhism, despite its possibly animist or ancestor-worshipping origins.

Yet within the pagoda compound the guardian spirit is not the only figure referred to as Bo Bo Gyi. One may hear talk of both living and dead human Bo Bo Gyi, nonhuman and superhuman figures, all of which share this title. Some of the associations these other figures carry in relation to longevity, benevolence, and wisdom also shed light on broader understandings and applications of the term. In this chapter we journey in search of the archetypal Bo Bo Gyi. Such a search highlights not only the contemporary dimensions of belief and homage in the syncretic Burmese religious system, but also the ongoing politicization of even the most faded and aging plaster statues in contemporary Burma.

In Search of an Archetype

One Sunday, finding myself with some free time for letter writing, and reluctant to give up my attachment to the very un-Burmese concept of "the weekend," I pinned a notice to my door. "Do not disturb unless in case of emergency" it stated, reflecting the victory of hope over experience. Within minutes the note was torn down. Thet Way and Choe Nwe Soe stood on my doorstep declaring that they had emergency information about Bo Bo Gyi. This was something of a revelation, as Thet Way had on previous occasions made quite clear to me his antipathy to all discussions of Burma's pantheon of spirits. Any talk of *nat* and his eyes roll and glaze over. But, wonder of wonders, Thet Way, nat-phobe, is a Bo Bo Gyi-phile.

Thet Way: I really want to tell you about my experience with Bo Bo Gyi! Before my matriculation exam,[1] I made a solemn promise that for every distinction I received, I would give him a *kadaw-bwe*.[2] I also promised that if I got a distinction in Burmese language, I would give him a shawl.

Mandy Sadan: So why did you decide to make this promise to the Bo Bo Gyi?

Thet Way: Because "bo bo" is like a grandfather and "gyi" is very old and respected, so it's like a great ancestor or grandfather.

MS: Can you have old and respected grandmothers?

Thet Way: No. Well, Medaw is a respected female. Like the Chinese Kwanyin. Medaw, the goddess of mercy. But she's not Burmese, you know . . . . Medaw is not a term that should be used for a nat. A nat is a very cheap thing with all their silly dancing and alcohol and cigarettes and all those gay guys. A Bo Bo Gyi *is* very pure and sublime. There's no Bo Bo Gyi-*pwe* (festival). You don't get alcohol and gays around a Bo Bo Gyi. I pay homage to three things: the Buddha, my parents and my teachers (they're like one thing), and the Sule Paya Bo Bo Gyi.

MS: Why do you pay homage to the Sule Bo Bo Gyi?

Thet Way: Because it's near my house. Actually, it's also the oldest one, but that isn't the reason for me. It's just nearby.

MS: How long have you been paying homage?

Thet Way: Just one year, because of my matriculation. Well, I paid respect in the past but not regularly. For two months before my exam I paid respect once each week. Then, after my exams, I went every night for three months.

MS: How did you ask him to help you? Is there a set phrase?

Thet Way: No. Well, maybe, but I don't know it. I just said in a simple way "Please help me to get high marks." There are special leaves in the hand of the Sule Bo Bo Gyi and one of the wardens gives you some of them. First you tell him which day you were born on and then he'll tell the Bo Bo Gyi in a loud voice and will hit the flat gong at the side.

MS: What exactly does he say?

Thet Way: It's something like: "Monday-born son is paying respect to you. Please help him and make him prosperous and distinguished and let him be one who can spread the *sāsana*."

MS: And how do you pay homage?

Thet Way: Just in the normal, quick way, like I do to you, you know [i.e., kneeling with feet raised on toes, forehead and hands lowered to touch the ground three times]. There's supposed to be a special way where you touch the ground in five places, but it's too difficult so I don't bother. I put them [the leaves] into my chemistry, physics, and biology textbooks because they are the hardest subjects. After the exam I threw them away. I didn't miss a single day.

MS: Why did you choose three months?

Thet Way: Because it isn't a very long time. When the results came out, I kept my promise and gave him four kadaw-bwe and a scarf on a Monday. I know this sounds silly, but I'm sure he smiled at me when I gave them to him.

MS: What about since then?

Thet Way: I haven't been back, but he's always on my mind. The Bo Bo Gyi is for my education. That's because he's the brightest and most intelligent of the heavenly beings. But he's not a nat. I don't worship nat.

MS: So, what about Bo Bo Gyi in general?

Thet Way: If you make a statue of a Bo Bo Gyi, you make a Bo Bo Gyi. . . . At Shwedagon the story is that Thagya-min was put in charge of building the pagoda and nat helped him. Because there's supposed to be a hair relic in the pagoda, they needed someone to protect it. They chose the Bo Bo Gyi because it had to be someone old, wise, and pure. Do you want to see Bo Bo Gyi?

MS: Yes, I'm going to go next weekend to have a look at Sule Bo Bo Gyi and some others.

Thet Way: Why don't you take us, then we can all get some merit!

MS: What? Like a Bo Bo Gyi crawl?

Thet Way: Yes! Great! A Bo Bo Gyi crawl! Look, I'm really sorry if I've said something wrong, you know. I don't know much about it, but I just wanted to tell you about my experience. It was an emergency!

Shwedagon Bo Bo Gyi

Our first stop on the Bo Bo Gyi crawl was the Shwedagon pagoda. The positioning of the Shwedagon Bo Bo Gyi statue inside a glass case gives the shrine a rather less dynamic feel than that which Thet Way had described at Sule. Thagya-min stands to the right of Bo Bo Gyi, the two being linked at the Shwedagon because although the Bo Bo Gyi protects the pagoda, Thagya-min was responsible for building it. Impressions of this Bo Bo Gyi statue were that it was disappointing. Po Kyar and Min Kyaw had visited previously and had complained that the figure looked "rather ugly" because of the quantity of cloth that it was draped in and also the appearance of the face, which did not look old. When they had visited, a Rakhine *pahso*[3] had been wrapped around the statue's waist on top of many other skirtcloths. On the day of our visit, however, the silk pahso had been covered with an ordinary cotton one, although the Rakhine cloth was visible underneath, showing that donations had been made in the intervening period. This superpadded appearance prompted both Thet Way and Choe Nwe Soe to declare with some distaste, "Shwedagon Bo Bo Gyi is very fat!"

Po Kyar and Min Kyaw remarked that the figure simply did not evoke the feelings of respect that they were expecting, and nobody had paid homage when they had visited. On our visit also there was no one before the Bo Bo Gyi pavilion, but paving slabs were being relaid at the time, which made access difficult. There was no warden on hand to accept donations as there is at the Sule pagoda, suggesting that personal, rather than mediated homage is the order of the day, and to this end there was a stone before the figure so that homage-payers could find out if the Bo Bo Gyi would grant their wish. One must decide before lifting the stone whether it will feel heavy or light and, if correct, the request will be fulfilled.

It was evident that none of them—Po Kyar, Min Kyaw, Thet Way, or Choe Nwe Soe—had really taken much interest in the Shwedagon Bo Bo Gyi before, hence their surprise at its appearance. When we left, Thet Way told me that "Sule Bo Bo Gyi is much better, you'll see; this one doesn't *look* like a Bo Bo Gyi."

Sule Bo Bo Gyi

A very different atmosphere prevails around the Bo Bo Gyi figure at the Sule pagoda. The statue has its own shrine room, which is reasonably spacious, and is assigned its own warden, whose job it is to take donations from people calling on the Bo Bo Gyi for help or else thanking him for deeds done. This warden does not have any special powers as of a medium, but is simply an employee of the pagoda. His job is to control the flow of donations, although he does call on the Bo Bo Gyi on behalf of homage-payers. Kadaw-bwe, scarves, and pahso that had been donated were placed to the side so that they did not swamp the figure. A steady stream of people came in to pay homage, and some remained and meditated with beads in front of the statue.

Of the appearance of this Bo Bo Gyi, Thet Way said, "You see, he looks *old,* doesn't he?" The Bo Bo Gyi did look old in a slightly caricatured way. The application of lines as wrinkles, of protruding veins on the arms and feet, and the slight puffiness of the jowls all combined to give the impression that the figure depicted a spirit of great age (see Figure 5.1). The close association of Bo Bo Gyi with benevolent action was symbolized by a mouth slightly upturned in a gentle smile—quite a difficult effect to achieve successfully. However, the figure was full of character in comparison with much modern statuary in pagodas, and looking at the Sule Bo Bo Gyi, it was easy to see how Thet Way had thought that the statue had smiled at him when he had handed over his offerings for his matriculation successes.

Yet I was struck immediately by certain aspects of the statue's visual vocabulary, aspects that Thet Way apparently preferred to ignore. The Sule Bo Bo Gyi wore a hat commonly seen worn by the category of nat known as *deva.* Deva is a Sanskrit term usually translated as "celestial being." They are believed to be forever youthful and to reside in luxurious palaces in the celestial heavens. They do not intervene in human affairs, although some contend that they can grant wishes. In Burma they are frequently represented in pagoda murals as supporters of Thagya-min—indeed, such a mural adorns the wall of the Sule Bo Bo Gyi pavilion. However, around this hat, scarves had been tied in the same way as those of nat dancers paying homage to the 37 Lords. When I later showed the photograph of Sule Bo Bo Gyi to Po Kyar and Min Kyaw, they also objected strongly to the pahso that the figure was wearing. This kind of pahso is similar to that worn by nat mediums, who drape the extended piece of cloth over their shoulders. Po Kyar and Min Kyaw disliked what they saw as the cheapening of the figure by visual correspondence with the Cult of the 37 Nat.

This representation produced a visual ambiguity as to whether or not Bo Bo Gyi was more closely associated with the kind of nat known as deva or with the Cult of the 37 Nat. For those who are looking for a little more support from the spirits than orthodox Theravādan practices might allow, yet who dislike or fear the rituals of homage to the 37 Nat, theosophical gray areas such as this provide the necessary room for manoeuvre. Through these intellectual spaces it becomes possible for people to rationalize their occasionally idiosyncratic personal beliefs and claim that they are justified within the framework of orthodox Buddhism—in this case by asserting the connection of Bo Bo Gyi with "higher" nat such as deva. They claim that they are not paying homage to beings lower than humans in the celestial hierarchy, which is forbidden.

Bo Bo Gyi also has another card up its sleeve. Justification of homage-paying may also have nationalist overtones. There is an often-repeated assertion that Bo Bo Gyi is a wholly Burmese spirit that transcends the ethnic syncretism of many other nat. I have yet to hear the logic of this fully explicated, but it may be that this is a contemporary remythologization of what originally might have been a genre of territorially bounded ancestor spirits. Certainly in contemporary nat festivals we see the integration of non-Burmans into the

Figure 5.1. Sule Pagoda Bo Bo Gyi, Yangon: the pagoda guardian archetype sculpted to portray wisdom, benevolence, and longevity (Source: Mandy Sadan)

broader Burmese Buddhist society via the rituals of the cult (Brac de la Per-rière 1998a), and Brac de la Perrière in this volume charts the transformation of local spirits into national figures during the tripartite annual ritual cycle of nat festivals in central Burma.

I was concerned that the effect of my inquiries might be to throw some doubt into Thet Way's mind concerning his homage to Bo Bo Gyi, and I there-fore refrained from mentioning the statue's obvious nat attire. In his desire not to be a nat worshipper, which in his mind meant the 37 Lords, Thet Way had dissociated his Bo Bo Gyi from all things nat. We focused instead on the aspects of the statue that made it appear old. "Look at its face. It looks really old," he and Choe Nwe Soe said.

Botahtaung Bo Bo Gyi

We battled traffic towards the Botahtaung Bo Bo Gyi. This was the first time that Thet Way and Choe Nwe Soe had seen the statue there apart from in my photographs. By this time they were fed up with Bo Bo Gyi and had started planning their evening at a nightclub. Questions of mine like, "Why have so many clocks been donated to the Bo Bo Gyi? Is it because they are associated with time and long life?" were given short shrift with answers such as, "No, it's because people like clocks." I realized that the day would shortly have to end, and they clearly hoped so. However, they thought the Botahtaung Bo Bo Gyi looked old and had a "good face." Po Kyar and Min Kyaw had also liked the figure, but from their reactions, this figure clearly lacked the prestige of the Sule Bo Bo Gyi, even though it is the most carefully crafted and best executed of the three we had seen so far.

The Botahtaung figure, as a relatively modern sculpting, can teach us much about the ideal visual representation of the archetypal Bo Bo Gyi. The Botahtaung Bo Bo Gyi has an exceptionally high quality of crafting to the facial features, especially in the application of age lines and the sculpting of wrinkles. It appears old, yet benevolent, with a gentle smile, a walking stick, prayer beads, and holding Eugenia leaves (see Figure 5.2). Reasons for the superior crafting of the Botahtaung pagoda Bo Bo Gyi lie in the pagoda's recent history. The "original" Botahtaung pagoda was almost completely destroyed in the Second World War and was rebuilt between 1948 and 1953. There is, however, no guarantee that any new religious construction will have instant popularity in the Burmese social landscape, despite this being "the land of pagodas." This was demonstrated most recently by the huge degree of popular cynicism accompanying the construction of the Tooth Relic pagoda on the outskirts of Rangoon, which was completed in 1997 and which seldom seems to have more than a handful of visitors (Schober 1997).

Likewise with the almost deserted compound of the Maha-wizaya pagoda built by Ne Win adjacent to the Shwedagon pagoda. A complex interaction of place, myth, and very often politics determines the degree of popular authenticity afforded to any site and thus also the number of ordinary Burmese merit-seekers who will visit to make voluntary donations. It is therefore not uncommon for some less popular sites to attempt to replicate successful features found at others in an attempt to increase the degree of popular "draw" that they have. The presence of a popular figure like a Bo Bo Gyi can act to "pull people in," as can be seen at Sule. In cases where the convergence of myth and place may appear contrived, the artistic qualities of the site and its statuary become more important in helping to raise the status and appeal of the claims.

A further attempt to increase the popular appeal of the Botahtaung Bo Bo Gyi is by making it part of a trio. The statue is flanked on the right by Thagyamin and by Thura-thadi on the left. As Thet Way stated, many pay homage to Thura-thadi for education, so the figures together form a complementary

Figure 5.2. Botahtaung Pagoda Bo Bo Gyi, Yangon: a pagoda guardian statue with an exceptionally high quality of crafting, but lacking mythic resonance and hence popular appeal (Source: Mandy Sadan)

threesome, which is more attractive to homage-makers and donors. Yet despite this linkage and the statue's artistic quality, the Botahtaung Bo Bo Gyi suffers from comparison with that at Sule because it lacks mythic resonance [see below]. Even U Aung Su, one of the Botahtaung pagoda trustees, appeared rather less interested in the Botahtaung figure than that of Sule pagoda and told us to concentrate our enquiries there.

Thus despite Thet Way's comment, "If you make a statue of a Bo Bo Gyi, you make a Bo Bo Gyi," this is clearly not the whole story. Artistic value is of much less importance than authentication of place through myth when it comes to the popular appeal of some Bo Bo Gyi over others. This also constrains the degree to which pagoda trustees or the politicized religious establishment may successfully manipulate popular attachment to such figures. At this point, therefore, it is necessary to outline the Bo Bo Gyi myth that creates a preeminent status for the Sule Bo Bo Gyi as a pagoda guardian archetype.

The Myth of the Sule Bo Bo Gyi

Thet Way, Choe Nwe Soe, and I had previously engaged in a brief conversation with U Tha Yin, one of the Sule pagoda trustees who is also interested in the Bo Bo Gyi and is collecting stories about them. He told us that there were maybe ten or eleven popular Bo Bo Gyi in the Rangoon area, of which the most important were at the Sule, Shwedagon, Botahtaung, Kyaikkahsan, Kyaik-hkauk, and Hmawbi pagodas. The Sule Bo Bo Gyi is the oldest or earliest or all of these, a point which is commonly repeated. U Aung Su, a trustee at Botahtaung pagoda, told me that the Bo Bo Gyi belief started in the hills and then gave this a Buddhist slant by stating that, ideally, pagodas are built on hills. The spirits of the hills are considered older than any other—those of rivers or forests, for example—because hills and mountains are themselves the oldest features of the earth. The spirit of that place knows everything that has happened there because "we consider it as old as the mountain." When a pagoda is built, it is the duty of this spirit to guard it. Clearly this is protection by an animist spirit over a territory in which it already resides, rather than the descent into a territory of a spirit from a higher plane.

In the legend of the Sule Bo Bo Gyi that U Tha Yin related, long before the time of Gotama Buddha, this spirit was a demon that ate elephant meat. This is considered a most heinous act in orthodox Buddhism. However, the demon met one of the buddhas and was reborn as a high-level nat as a result. Later, in the time of Gotama Buddha, the merchant brothers Tapussa and Bhallika brought the hair relics to Burma. King Okkalapa allowed the eight relics to remain at the Botahtaung pagoda, where they had been brought ashore, for six months. One relic subsequently remained at Botahtaung, but the others were to be enshrined elsewhere. The duty of enshrining them and building a pagoda went to Thagya-min, but the relics were only to be enshrined on the same site as relics from the previous buddhas. Thagya-min searched and searched for the correct place but could not find it. In the end he had to ask the Sule Bo Bo Gyi because this nat had been in existence the longest. It knew where the previous relics had been enshrined because it was so old that it had seen them. The Bo Bo Gyi pointed to Theingottara Hill, upon which the Shwedagon pagoda was to be built as a result, and told Thagya-min that that was the place he was looking for. In memory of this, the statues of Sule (and Botahtaung) point towards the Hill.

In this story, that links the foundation of the three main city pagodas— Shwedagon, Sule, and Botahtaung—it is significant that there is no particular role for the Botahtaung Bo Bo Gyi, and the statue is rather an emulation of the Sule figure in its gesture of pointing. It is the Sule figure that functions as the archetypal pagoda Bo Bo Gyi, and it is his popularity that other figures such as that at Botahtaung and Mandalay Hill [see below] are seeking to emulate.

Respected Grandfather, Bless This Nissan

The importance that authenticities of place and myth have over mere figuration and emplacement of the Bo Bo Gyi statues is further demonstrated by considering the Shwe Nyaung Bin Bo Bo Gyi. One Sunday Po Kyar, Min Kyaw, and Mai Dwe decided to take me to see a Bo Bo Gyi figure out on the road past Mingaladon airport at Shwe Nyaung Bin. I had seen many cars and trucks around Rangoon with flowers and leaves attached to their front bumper because, I was informed, the owners had paid homage to a Bo Bo Gyi. Later Po Kyar told me he had discussed the matter with a friend, and they had decided that the Shwe Nyaung Bin statue represents a nat and was not really a Bo Bo Gyi. It was the first time Po Kyar had been to the site since childhood, and he seemed quite shocked upon arrival that he had associated this site with a "true" Bo Bo Gyi. The shrine, however, had "Bo Bo Gyi" marked clearly above it, and Po Kyar, Min Kyaw, and Mai Dwe used this to stress further that the term is an honorific that can be applied to any spirit that is very old and respected, if people wish to do so. The donors of the shrines obviously believed the spirits there to be Bo Bo Gyi, or else they hoped to persuade others of this fact to encourage them to come.

The shrine was very busy on this Sunday morning. Cars were queuing to be blessed. Upon donating 300, a kadaw-bwe was placed on the hood (on a cloth to protect the paintwork of these newly bought vehicles) and a warden chanted a blessing and sprinkled water on the car. In response, the vehicles had to pass a kind of spiritual driving test by performing a reverse-forward maneuver three times in homage. That all drivers managed to do this without once using their horns shows a degree of constraint rarely witnessed in Burma. The warden then tied a bunch of leaves and flowers to the bumper in a manner similar to that in which we had received leaves from the Sule Bo Bo Gyi.

When Po Kyar, Min Kyaw, and Mai Dwe looked at the shrine, they saw a row of wooden figures that were of the same size and type as the generic nat figures of household shrines or at mobile, privately funded *nat pwe* (nat spirit festivals), and were so surprised that they had to check with one of the vendors that we were in the right place. "But they don't look like Bo Bo Gyi; they look just like ordinary nat," they said. There was an attempt to make the figures look old by giving them a slightly jowly appearance, and the mouths were turned up in benevolent smiles, but the overall effect was of badly crafted ventriloquists' dummies. All the figures carried walking sticks. We were informed that the figure second from the left was the original. Despite the drawbacks in artistry, the site was clearly popular; a constant stream of cars arrived and a lengthy queue formed. Next to the shrine was an enormous, lush banyan tree. Po Kyar told me that he could remember his mother saying that when she had traveled this road as a girl, it had a reputation for being very dangerous. Apparently that reputation still lingers. At the time of our visit the road was in the process of being widened and was busy with much fast-moving traffic.

We drove away from the shrine, but a few hundred yards down the road we came upon another. "This must be the real Bo Bo Gyi," they said, "It looks like a Bo Bo Gyi." Mai Dwe and I carefully examined this much newer shrine, and Mai Dwe said that she believed that the shrine had been built more recently, but that the figure was far superior. Later they all admitted to me that if they had had to choose one to be the "real" Bo Bo Gyi, they would have chosen this one. The standing statue was almost lifesize, with a skillfully crafted face which gave the correct attitude of age, wisdom, and benevolence; furthermore, it was golden, a sign of royalty. This figure was clearly emulating the archetypal Bo Bo Gyi figure to be found at pagodas despite the fact that it was in a simple roadside shrine, the Buddhist orthodoxy of which is highly contentious.

The truly striking thing, however, was that this shrine, just a few hundred yards down the road from where a queue of homage-payers was developing, was completely deserted. And it was also despite the fact that this figure was surrounded by affiliates, in this case a range of popular nat figures and others—Nan Karaing, Ko Myo Shin, Bo Min Gaung, and Shin Ubagok. It stood next to a dying banyan tree. This Bo Bo Gyi, despite its artistry, clearly lacked popular authenticity.

As we returned home, we called in at the monastery of Ya-gyaw Hsaya-daw. While looking around the monastery compound, we came across a *yok-khazo* (tree spirit) effigy in a tree shrine. For the first time I was struck by the fact that it was holding a walking stick. The representation was the choice of the donor, but some people like to represent this disembodied spirit as a figure wearing white and carrying a stick.

Po Kyar: What is your idea?

MS: Is it possible that the shrines at Shwe Nyaung Bin could have started as a yokkhazo spirit shrine, like this, and then, because of the age of the tree and the particularly dangerous stretch of road, it could have gradually become known as a Bo Bo Gyi shrine?

Po Kyar: Now you're starting to understand!

Longevity and Wisdom: Figuring an Archetype

From the journey so far, the following conclusions can be drawn about the archetypal pagoda guardian Bo Bo Gyi. This kind of spirit is considered to be the oldest nat or spirit in the locality. There are, however, many other, more powerful spirits in the Burmese spirit world than the Bo Bo Gyi. What distinguishes it is its greater wisdom, which is a consequence of its longevity. It is generally felt in Burma that it is the responsibility of elders to act as guides for the younger generation and here one sees this social obligation being reflected in the spiritual realm.

Another product of its longevity is that the Bo Bo Gyi performs only benevolent acts. A pagoda Bo Bo Gyi is involved in the human sphere most directly through the granting of wishes, but it will grant only those wishes that are clearly benevolent both to the homage-payer and others who might be affected by them. If one wishes to make a request to a pagoda Bo Bo Gyi, its assistance is easy to call upon, as it is not striving to become known in, or to operate through, the human plane via the medium *(nat kadaw),* as are some other spirits. If one breaks a commitment made to a Bo Bo Gyi, such as not giving a donation of a scarf or a kadaw-bwe despite one's wish being fulfilled, it could be within the spirit's power to cause harm, but the reality is more akin to the feeling one might have after letting one's grandfather down rather badly —it would be difficult to look him in the eye again. Great age, it is believed, tends to negate the potential for malevolent action.

The pagoda guardian Bo Bo Gyi archetype has a standardized visual vocabulary. The carved figures are large, often of near-human size. They are standing and wear long flowing robes. Most wear a pointed hat, commonly associated with the celestial spirits, and scarves may be tied about the head as with other nat images. The pagoda guardian Bo Bo Gyi is a nat according to the general definition of the term, and homage is therefore nat homage; yet many who abhor the activities associated with paying homage to the 37 Nat are completely at ease in calling upon these figures for assistance. This is because the myth of the pagoda archetype frames this figure as an adherent and supporter of orthodox Buddhism.

However, there are clearly suggestions of animist origins in the historical evolution of the pagoda Bo Bo Gyi archetype, developing as it probably did from a nature spirit or "ancestor" spirit to become an associate of a deva. The importance of place as a vestige of this still seems significant even today, especially in the popular authentication of statuary. The pagoda Bo Bo Gyi is still primarily a territorial nat, with statues being effective territorial markers that homage-payers visit *in situ*.

Certain qualities possessed by the pagoda guardian Bo Bo Gyi, such as territorial authority, wisdom, benevolence towards supporters, and longevity as a means of having seen past buddhas or of awaiting those to come, indicate that the pagoda Bo Bo Gyi type does not have a monopoly on these attributes. This fact is demonstrated at a symbolic level by considering the iconography and visual vocabulary of the Bo Bo Gyi guardian spirit statues. For example, many hold a walking staff as a sign of age. Some monks have staffs of this kind (especially the famous "walking stick monk" who cures people at his regular Rangoon clinic several times per year), but the character most famous for using one is the medicine *zawgyi*. These figures are popular in Burmese folk tradition and their dance with a red stick is easily recognized and mimicked by most Burmese. The stick is used for digging out and grinding medicinal plants by which the zawgyi attains his special powers. In contrast to the Bo Bo Gyi, however, a goal of all kinds of zawgyi is the acquisition of longevity through the attainment of eternal youth (Pranke 1995).

Other visual signs, such as the holding of prayer beads or the wearing of a ring containing an alchemist's (philosopher's) stone *(dat-lon)*, which are also associated with the attainment of suprahuman longevity, suggest cognitive connections with other figures from Burma's complex religious landscape, especially *bodaw* and *weikza*.[4] Indeed it became obvious early on in my journey that most of the lay Burmese people I asked for an interpretation of Bo Bo Gyi considered it less as an archetype than a conceptual category that can be applied to a host of figures, nonhuman and nonhistorical figures alike. This produces the dichotomy that on the one hand there is an archetypal figure, *the Bo Bo Gyi*, but there is also a range of figures who are referred to as Bo Bo Gyi but who are not of the same type as the pagoda guardian. It is also apparent that these other figures, sometimes referred to as Bo Bo Gyi, have a potentially subversive sociopolitical potency. The pagoda Bo Bo Gyi archetype is distinct from them in that it is politically neutral in comparison. That is not to say that it is apolitical because the contention that it is a wholly Burmese spirit clearly layers the modern Burmese state across the ethnopolitical geography of pre-history, but rather that today it appears devoid of subversive sociopolitical potential—it is a "safe" spirit to which one can pay homage.

Bo Bo Gyi, Bodaw, and Weikza

The concept of Bo Bo Gyi as an honorific, rather than the term as it relates to a genre of nat, is best explained by considering it in relation to two other terms which in conversation were frequently juxtaposed or conflated with it—bodaw and weikza. Two figures also found in pagoda compounds that help to clarify the distinctions between Bo Bo Gyi as an honorific and Bo Bo Gyi as a genre of nat, as well as the relation of this term to bodaw and weikza, are Bo Bo Aung and Bo Min Gaung.

Bo Bo Aung, and the more modern but equally esteemed figure of Bo Min Gaung, are humans believed to have exceeded the ordinary spiritual development of laity, and indeed of many monks, by the practice of Buddhist *samatha* techniques such as concentration (which may, for example, be developed through the use of water, flames, and prayer beads) and non-Buddhist techniques that use *lawkī pyinnya,* as Tosa delineates in this volume. Attaining such power enables them to escape an ordinary death. Instead, it is popularly believed, they merely gave up their bodily forms to enter a separate plane, that of the weikza, from which they retain contact with the human sphere to act benevolently for all humans in their struggle to break out of the cycle of rebirths that causes suffering (Schober 1988; Tosa 2000). Unlike the homage-payers of the pagoda guardian Bo Bo Gyi, certain followers may be chosen as channels for the continued expression of their powers from this separate celestial level, but they may also be contacted by anyone who develops the correct powers of concentration. They therefore clearly have more in common with Mahayana than Theravāda Buddhism.

Burmese people may refer to Bo Bo Aung and Bo Min Gaung as Bo Bo Gyi, bodaw, or weikza, but these titles are not completely coterminous. Bo Bo Gyi may be used in reference to both human and nonhuman figures, but this is not generally the case with bodaw and weikza. These two terms imply the attainment of special powers by human beings. Although Ferguson and Mendelson (1981) make no mention of the term bodaw when writing about weikza, both terms are widely used, and many people have difficulty defining the difference between them, and often conclude that there is none, except that a weikza might be slightly "higher." The consequence of this is that weikza, a Pali term, tends to be reserved for certain kinds of monks. However, this is not a rigid distinction and the use of one title or another largely reflects the degree of respect given to the figure.

Figures such as Bo Bo Aung and Bo Min Gaung are politicized in the sense that both are associated with narratives of opposition to political authority. Bo Min Gaung in particular became associated with Burmese nationalist, anti-colonial movements at the beginning of the twentieth century. Because of their capacity to make themselves known through the bodies of chosen followers, Bo Bo Aung and Bo Min Gaung have a continuing potential to mobilize popular sentiment through charismatic leaders—something of which the present regime is fully cognizant. Clearly personages of this type can pose a considerable threat to political authority as they exemplify the potential power of the populace, as Houtman discusses in this volume. In this respect they also have more in common with some of the territorial nat Bo Bo Gyi that have not been brought within the pagoda compound, rather than with the pagoda guardian spirit. For example, a very powerful spirit, sometimes referred to as Bo Bo Gyi, has its territory in the environs of the home village of former dictator Ne Win. This Bo Bo Gyi is believed to be of a millenarian type that will one day appear and lead a powerful rebellion similar to the Saya San Rebellion of the 1930s (Herbert 1982). Anyone who could convincingly claim to be the channel of a powerful local territorial spirit such as this might expect to accrue much local popular support, which could be readily politicized.

While the authenticity of the special powers of figures such as Bo Bo Aung and Bo Min Gaung is popularly accepted, the military regime and police authorities are keen to differentiate them from other contemporary lay figures who claim similar powers. Such lay practitioners of both samatha and lawkī pyinnya techniques are typically referred to as bodaw and are regularly the target of negative publicity and campaigns to suppress their activities. Popular culture in Burma, particularly in the form of rumor, very often functions as an alternative social commentary, as Tosa discusses in this volume. Contemporary Burmese rumors frequently attribute supernaturalism as the cause for particular political events and as instrumental in the rise to power of certain charismatic individuals. At a popular level, therefore, the ability of a belief in supernaturalism to function as a tool for political mobilization is real.

The military regime remains vigilant regarding the potential contained in the prevalent belief in supernaturalism as an active agent of political events. In March 1997, for example, persistent and violent disturbances were sparked off in Mandalay by damage done to the Buddha image at the Mahamuni pagoda. Rumors abounded that one of the causes of these disturbances was a philosopher's stone *(dat-lon)* concealed in the statue. The rumor contended that a crack had been made in the Buddha image so that the military council could remove the stone in the hope that they could be made invincible by possession of it. This rumor spread with great speed, and seemed to be readily integrated into popular discourse on this issue as a reasonable interpretation of the tense political situation. For this reason, anti-bodaw campaigns that claim to protect the public from unscrupulous fraudsters also provide a check against the emergence of popular messianic figures claiming to have superhuman abilities.

As a result of these campaigns in "security" journals such as *Hmugin,* just as Bo Bo Gyi is being confirmed as a type, so too does it seem that the bodaw is being interpreted in a negative sense as a magician or ascetic of Indian heritage. The bodaw was frequently explained to me as being like an Indian *sadhu,* and to some extent the bodaw has taken on what Ferguson and Mendelson (1981:65) euphemistically call an antiyogic sentiment but which in reality relates to entrenched anti-Indian sentiment that continues to be pervasive in Burma. In 1997 the regime conducted a strong anti-bodaw campaign in the Mandalay region. In addition to entrenched anti-Indian feeling, such attacks draw significant support when they appeal to orthodox Buddhists who historically conduct regular purges of fringe Buddhist elements. In the light of claims that Burma is both a modern and devoutly Buddhist state, such campaigns also aim to reduce popular attachment to those aspects of Burmese popular religious and folk traditions that are deemed open to scorn and ridicule by "outsiders." In early 1997 this was of particular concern because of the "Visit Myanmar Year" campaign and the push to attract tourists.

Although, as Tosa points out in this volume, the 1979 law banning the formation of *gaing* (groups) around weikza suppressed much weikza activity for two decades, official differentiation between acceptable and unacceptable practitioners is rather more difficult in the case of the monk weikza. In contemporary Burma, revered hsayadaws who head monasteries and monk weikza with extraordinary powers are extremely important and may, as with the late Thamanya Hsayadaw, present considerable moral challenges to the military council. Thamanya Hsayadaw was one of the most highly respected figures in contemporary Burma and had authority over a large territory around his monastery near Pa-an. He insisted unflinchingly on upholding Buddhist precepts within this area, in particular that no meat be consumed and, most problematically for the authorities, that no guns be carried (Rozenberg 2002; Tosa 2002). It was a demand with which they were largely forced to comply for fear of appearing un-Buddhist. Those monk weikza who practice less orthodox techniques than meditation are more open to criticism, but, given that they are monks and that they have a clear Buddhist goal for the acquisition of such powers, the authorities must be circumspect in how they deal with them.

A popular example is Bo Pauk Sein, whose shrine is situated in the north of Rangoon. He is believed to have given up his bodily form and is now residing in the celestial level of the weikza. He is also believed to have had a spiritual connection with Bo Bo Aung and Bo Min Gaung. Bo Pauk Sein's particular power and act of benevolence since his "going out" (Schober 1988) is that of wish fulfilment. Hundreds of pieces of paper with wishes of all types are placed upon the railings around the pagoda in the main shrine building. Those who cannot afford to make a donation may take a money box that has been painted to resemble a zawgyi that they return when it has been filled. The zawgyi figure plays a supporting role at the site, again highlighting the interconnectedness of Burmese figures from both monastic and popular religion. My informants occasionally referred to Bo Pauk Sein as being "like a Bo Bo Gyi, but better."

Apportioning the Supernatural Terrain

Some of the similarities between the various figures in and around the pagoda compound that are referred to as Bo Bo Gyi are as follows. They all make wishes come true and have existed, or will exist, for millennia, during which time their involvement in the human sphere will be benevolent. Homage is easy to perform and of a personal nature. They grant only those wishes that uphold the Five Buddhist Precepts expected of lay Buddhists. The statuary of these figures shares a common iconographic vocabulary for qualities of age, wisdom, benevolence, and the development of supernatural powers. However, the term Bo Bo Gyi, with its grandfatherly connotations of protection and guardianship, denotes a figure too warm in its attachment to the world to be appropriately applied to monks. The aim of a monk weikza is meant to be dispassionate detachment from the human sphere. There is also an inhibition against addressing the popular arahat[5] figures of Shin Thiwali and Shin Ubagok as Bo Bo Gyi, despite their benevolence and protection of homage-payers. Their role is considered neither local nor national but as transcending such boundaries.

While there are similarities between Bo Bo Aung, Bo Bo Gyi, and pagoda guardians, such as longevity, wisdom, and benevolence with a local or a national focus, there are also important differences. First, Bo Bo Aung's longevity, and that of other weikza, is a projection into the future, awaiting the time of the future Buddha; it is Mahayanist in origin. The longevity of the pagoda Bo Bo Gyi, in contrast, is a projection back in time, of a life lived through to old age. Furthermore, the longevity of the weikza is a result of his attaining special powers, not a cause of them, while the Bo Bo Gyi has relatively minor powers and they have arisen through his longevity.

One final contrast should be made concerning a figure like Bo Bo Aung and the Bo Bo Gyi. It is perfectly acceptable to have a small figure of Bo Bo Aung, a figure or photograph of Bo Min Gaung, or a photograph or item of paraphernalia of a monk weikza at one's household shrine. Yet despite there being a standardized visual representation for the Bo Bo Gyi, one could not have a small pagoda "type" figure either near the shrine or in or outside the home. If one seeks the help of a Bo Bo Gyi, one must go to them, to the marker point of their territory in the pagoda. It is this earthbound territoriality that marks the pagoda Bo Bo Gyi as one of the lower spirits.

Transitioning from Spirits to Bo Bo Gyi: Mingun and Mandalay

There are some spirits outside the pagoda, as has been seen at Shwe Nyaung Bin, which may be referred to as Bo Bo Gyi. This use of the term is often made in relation to named spirits who are believed to have a strong local territorial power, such as U Shin Gyi, who is often referred to as a Bo Bo Gyi in the delta region. Recalling the propaganda against fraudulent bodaw, Maung Zin showed me a notice in a local paper warning people in a small delta town to beware of bogus donation seekers after a "U Shin Gyi Novitiation" scam. Because of his importance as a guardian spirit of the waterways in the delta region, as well as the fact that he is assumed to do only good deeds, U Shin Gyi has become known as a Bo Bo Gyi. To authenticate this, Maung Zin puts great emphasis on the fact that the chanted invocation calls on "Bo Bo" U Shin Gyi. Important local spirits such as that at Alon, near Monywa, at Mingun, and Myin-byu-shin (the "Lord of the White Horse"), may all be referred to as Bo Bo Gyi by their adherents.

There does seem, however, to be an attempt to authenticate the Sule Bo Bo Gyi as the principal legitimate archetype, making the Bo Bo Gyi a spirit genre rather than an honorific concept. As stated, the military regime's ongoing concern about the political and socioreligious potential of spirits, mediums, and those claiming suprahuman powers seems to have been influential in effecting this transition. In 1997 this was the conclusion that could be drawn from the transitions relating to the term Bo Bo Gyi that were taking place in the Mandalay region.

The village of Mingun is best known for the huge pagoda base built by King Bodawpaya. It was intended to be the foundation of the biggest pagoda in the world before an earthquake split it down the middle. I was initially drawn to Mingun because of the story of the "Brother and Sister of the Teak Tree," who were reported as being swung in front of the local Bo Bo Gyi at the time of their pwe.[6] Boats and boxing were the main topics of conversation on the boat ride to Mingun, but the following Bo Bo Gyi revelation was unexpected.

MS: Is there a Bo Bo Gyi statue around here?

Tin Oo: Bo Bo Gyi! No, there's no Bo Bo Gyi. Show your business card at the jetty and you won't have to pay $3. Do you want to go to the pagoda first?

MS: Are you sure there's no Bo Bo Gyi?

Tin Oo: I don't know of any Bo Bo Gyi. This is like a different religion. I am only interested in Buddhism. Do you want to climb the pagoda? Take off your shoes.

MS: Do you know if there used to be a Bo Bo Gyi?

Tin Oo: No. Look, I think there's a small statue somewhere but I don't know where. You're really interested, aren't you?

Eventually we located two shrines we had walked past previously, lying between the remains of the two huge *chinthay* (guardian lion) figures at the river's edge that would have protected the pagoda. Only one of the shrines had a statue inside, and this had few of the characteristics of the Bo Bo Gyi archetype except for a clock behind the figure on the back wall. The statue was also accompanied by a white horse. The image was seated and was flanked by two Shan knives. There was no stick and no attempt to give the statue an appearance of great age. It was not wearing a nat hat but instead had a headband wrapped about it. Above the shrine there was a sign stating "Bo Daw Gyi." To all intents and purposes, this was the Bo Bo Gyi.

MS: It doesn't look like a Bo Bo Gyi. There's no walking stick.

Tin Oo: Look, it has two knives.

MS: What about the horse?

Tin Oo: This is for the Bo Bo Gyi, you know? This nat can only do good things.

MS: But you say that this is only a small statue. Where is the big one?

Tin Oo: I don't know. . . . Do you want to go to the nat shrine? It's best if we walk.

When we entered the shrine, the nat guardian was fast asleep in the midafternoon heat. Initially she did not appreciate being awakened, but then she warmed to us a little. I took the opportunity to ask about the Bo Bo Gyi and whether or not the Brother and Sister of the Teak Tree were swung in front of a Bo Bo Gyi statue during the festival in Wagaung.

Tin Oo: She says that the big Bo Bo Gyi statue was moved about two years ago. It used to be by the big pagoda, you know. We walked right past the place! Between that and the bell. . . . She says it was moved to Mandalay. If you want to see it, you must go to Mandalay.

MS: So it's in Mandalay? Is it a different statue than the Mandalay Bo Bo Gyi?

Tin Oo: No! It's the same. There's only one Bo Bo Gyi. . . . The one here was taken to Mandalay so now you can see the Bo Bo Gyi in Mandalay.

MS: So the one I'll see in Mandalay looks the same as the one that was here?

Tin Oo: Yes. Exactly the same. . . . It's on Mandalay Hill. Everyone knows it.

When I arrived back at the jetty and asked a gathering crowd of trishaw drivers for someone to take me to see the Bo Bo Gyi on Mandalay Hill, the subsequent conversation revealed that not one of them knew where it was on the hill. When eventually the correct entrance stairway was found, it turned out that there was no visual resemblance to the small Bo Daw Gyi statue at all. The Mandalay Bo Bo Gyi is exactly what you would expect a Bo Bo Gyi to look like—a standing figure with an old-looking but benevolent face, a walking stick, prayer beads, a nat hat, and shawls. The situation resembles that for the Sule Bo Bo Gyi in that a warden is responsible for taking donations, chanting requests and invocations, and making offerings. Eugenia leaves are given to homage-payers and the front of the shrine is full of kadaw-bwe offerings. The statue has its own spacious room. On the left as one enters the room, there is also a separate shrine to the locally popular Myin-byu-shin.

The Bo Bo Gyi which is figured on Mandalay Hill is a relatively recent addition to the site, and local informants perceived that the positioning of the Bo Bo Gyi statue is an attempt to recreate some of the benevolent and powerful aura attached to more established Bo Bo Gyi sites in Rangoon, most notably that of the Sule pagoda Bo Bo Gyi. Some also stated that this was an attempt to bring a popular figure to the site, as many have criticized the redevelopment of the hill in recent years. The convergence of myth and place was thus contrived in this instance and the figure lacks authenticity.

Thinking again about the figure at Mingun, the removal of the old statue was likely an attempt to erase traces of nat homage from the central pagoda area at Mingun, a promoted tourist site. This accords with other government policies towards nat propitiation and the sensitivity of the subject, especially where foreigners are concerned. Nat, nat kadaws, and nat pwes are felt to be inappropriate to the public image the new Union of Myanmar wishes to project.

The removal of the Mingun statue coincided with the erection of a fine bronze lifesize standing statue of the highly revered Momeik Hsayadaw, who died in 1994. This hsayadaw was one of the most respected religious figures in contemporary Burma and is highly venerated. His statue now occupies the shrine room between the pagoda and the bell from which the Bodaw Gyi/Bo Bo Gyi was removed, and a clear hierarchy of religious status is thus confirmed in this tourist site. The hsayadaw is promoted as the true reflection of the dignity and power of Burmese Buddhism, and the local significance of the Mingun Bo Bo Gyi, which is associated with both the bodaw and nat spiritism, has been reduced. The Bo Bo Gyi as pagoda guardian "type" is consolidated, and attachment through it to the less-orthodox elements of Burmese popular religion, is thereby reduced.

Personal and Politically Neutral Belief

Bodaw literature abounds as individuals make claims trying to win supporters. Notices are placed in local newspapers and magazines warn readers of these characters, in particular of their assertions that they can double your money or the quantity of your jewelry. Many of them claim to be able to survive burial underground for extended periods, but pictures in magazines show tunnels supposedly providing for their escape. As stated earlier, the bodaws have been targeted as "undesirable elements" in the Mandalay region where the bodaw figure has a strong presence, including the Mingun Bo Daw Gyi, the Mandalay Bo Daw, who is one of the 37 Nat, and the Ahlone Bo Daw Gyi, who is another "big" Bo Bo Gyi figure in Central Burma. In addition, U Khanti, who "built up" Mandalay Hill, is associated with such figures. All of this demonstrates that these aspects of Burmese popular religious culture are alive and even flourishing in the current uncertain economic and political climate, but they have come under increasing pressure. This only makes more difficult the protection of oneself against the many hazards of contemporary life, and the half-smile of the Burmese Bo Bo Gyi promises a grandfatherly care in troubled times.

The regime's suspicion of the subversive and revolutionary potential of contemporary mystic leaders has resulted in many Burmese people turning to the representations of kindly benevolence in the statues of the Bo Bo Gyi as a powerful, hopeful, and politically neutral spirit. However, in consolidating an archetype as a genre, important cognitive shifts are being undertaken in relation to the complex understandings of the term Bo Bo Gyi as an honorific and a concept. These shifts have also produced a transformation in the way that Buddhist cosmology is represented in the social landscape of contemporary Burma. However, despite this transformation, there is still a primary need for authentication of spirits, and without the correct convergence of myth and place, such transformations have limited popular appeal. Only time will tell whether many of Burma's powerful and protective spirits will be transformed into benevolent Bo Bo Gyi to whom homage may be paid at an iconographically generic statue placed in the outer corners of a pagoda.

Notes

Research for this essay was carried out during 1996–1997. Thanks are due Dr. Elizabeth Moore, SOAS, who first raised my interest in the subject of Bo Bo Gyi, and Anna Allott, for reading a very early draft. Special thanks are due Monique Skidmore for encouraging me to publish my work and for her efforts in shaping it editorially. Most of all my thanks go to numerous friends and colleagues in Burma who were so intrigued by my interest in this subject and who went to such lengths to help satisfy my curiosity.

1. Matriculation exams are taken at the end of the Tenth Standard, when students are usually about sixteen years old. Although nine subjects are examined, they are grouped such that it is possible to get five distinctions.

2. The four kadaw-bwe cost him 1,000 kyat, and they were bought at the pagoda.

3. Rakhine *pahsoes* and *htamein* (men's and women's skirt-cloths respectively) have the reputation of being some of the best quality of all those made in the country. Rakhine pahsoes are considered appropriate dress for men on all formal occasions.

4. These are two related terms, weikza being derived from Pali and bodaw Burmese. They are used for figures who may practice alchemy or advanced meditation techniques or both to attain eternal youth. In a Buddhist context this youthfulness is supposed to ensure that they will live long enough to see the coming buddha. However, the superhuman abilities they acquire in addition to this in the process, such as the ability to make themselves disappear or fly through the air, also connects them with popular religious practices and beliefs.

5. Arahat means the "perfected one" and is used in relation to those who are finally freed from the suffering of existence in the cycle of birth and death, and attain Nirvana.

6. The story is related in "Nat Pwe" (Rodrigue 1992: 69–71). The nat pwe dates are wrong, however, the festival takes place in Wagaung (August), not Tabaung (March). In a nutshell, the two tragic children were swept adrift on a teak log after running away from their governess. The local Bo Bo Gyi told them that they had been transformed into nat, and they took up residence in a teak tree on the shore, where they became powerful river guardians (see Brac de la Perrière, this volume, and 2002).

−6−
Buddhist Visions of Moral Authority and Modernity in Burma

Juliane Schober

Since the popular uprising in 1988, the confrontation between the military regime and the pro-democracy forces has ground to a seemingly unchanging stalemate with no foreseeable solution to the political impasse. The change of government to representatives of the National League for Democracy (NLD), promised by elections in 1990, has not occurred. The national convention to draft a new constitution abandoned its work following the NLD's boycott in the mid-1990s. At present, Burma is governed by the State Peace and Development Council (SPDC), which represents a continuation of the military regime that functioned as the State Law and Order Restoration Council (SLORC) since 1988. Aung San Suu Kyi, Burma's pro-democracy leader and 1991 Nobel Peace Prize Laureate, is again confined to house arrest at her home on University Avenue, near Inya Lake, in Rangoon, while her and her party's activities are closely monitored and frequently curtailed by agents of the regime.

This chapter examines modern forms of Buddhism, politics, and civil society in Burma. Acknowledging the range of contemporary Buddhist practices and interpretations one finds in Burma today, the essay specifically looks at two very different interpretations of modern Buddhism that uphold competing claims about moral authority, political legitimacy, and national community. These two distinctly modern visions of moral authority and civil society emerged in Burmese Buddhism in the aftermath of the 1988 pro-democracy uprising and the subsequent rule of the military councils. One is the nationalist, centralized, and ritualistic patronage of Buddhism by the State Peace and Development Council (SPDC), and the other is the socially engaged Buddhism advocated by Aung San Suu Kyi that emphasizes personal, social engagement, ethics, and meditation. The former employs large-scale rituals to legitimate a political hierarchy of the state, while the latter advocates meditation, individual empowerment, and social ethics to resist spiritual and material exploitation by the state. Both visions of moral authority are rationalist interpretations of power for which one may find justification in references to the Theravāda textual tradition.[1] Both of these forms of modern Buddhism intersect with Euro-American political traditions derived from post-Enlightenment thought. And both employ modern technologies of communication and mobilization in order to engage a broader public in national and international contexts.[2] They appeal to modern Buddhism to imagine their respective visions of the nation's future and use that vision to justify their respective political claims.

This chapter's central claim, therefore, is that among modern Buddhist communities in Burma, specific religious interpretations and practices entail corresponding visions of moral authority and are closely tied to particular social and political visions of the modern Burmese nation-state and national community. These forms of modern Theravāda Buddhism express issues central to modern politics and public life, such as national identity, ethnicity, national territory, and control over or potential fragmentation of the political center. Contemporary Buddhism in Burma is at once polarized and coopted by the need for legitimation among the prevailing power structures. In the absence of secular means of legitimation—for instance, a national constitution, a parliamentary process, and independent civic institutions—there is a great need for public legitimation to sanction moral and political authority. At the same time there is a need to strengthen the role of civil society and secularism to ensure continuity for any political system in Burma. The need for public space given to the secular is especially pressing in a nation-state that is at once engulfed by a struggle for moral and political authority in a multiethnic context and is, at the same time, challenged by the political omissions of the past. A final concern addressed here is, therefore, the place of civil society and the secular in envisioning the future of the Burmese nation-state.

Theravāda Buddhism and Modernity

In Buddhist Southeast Asia, encounters with modernity generally were part of a broader confrontation of traditional polities with the knowledge, political forms, and extensive economic networks of the colonizing West. British and French colonial expansion shaped modern forms of knowledge and social formations and caused a crisis of political and moral authority (Keyes 1993, Keyes, Kendall, and Hardacre 1994, Pollak 1979, Swearer 1992, Tanabe 2002). Responding to the threat of colonization, the Burmese monarch, Mindon (r. 1853–1878), like his Thai counterpart, Mongkut (r. 1851–1868), introduced social, political, and legal reforms. He has been credited with reforming and rationalizing politics and religion, while fostering a renaissance of traditional Burman culture.

Religious reforms, begun in Thailand in 1851, commenced in Burma in 1872. They were far-reaching and involved revisions of religious texts, laws, monastic education, practice, and so on. They centralized the *sangha* (monastic order) as an institution and attempted to rationalize religious practice and beliefs. They sought to establish a modern Buddhist culture stripped of much of its traditional, mythic, cosmological, and ritual elements. Three Anglo-Burmese wars (1824–1826,1852–1853,1885), followed by successive colonial expansion, overwhelmed the Konbaun dynasty and its traditionalist culture in 1885. The British plundered the cosmic center, the Mandalay palace, and turned it into a garrison, Fort Dufferin, moving the Burmese consummate symbol of royal power, the Lion Throne, to a museum in Calcutta. Rangoon flourished as the colony's administrative and economic center.

The Burmese experience of modernity thus commenced with colonialism eclipsing traditional cultural values, institutions, and life ways (Thant Myint 2001). This encounter with modernity was hastened by the restructuring of Burmese society through colonial forms of knowledge and classification (Cohn 1996, Furnivall 1948), dislodging secular power from the religious worldview in which it had previously been embedded. In separating the secular power from its Buddhist foundations, the British followed a deliberate policy of non-involvement in the religious affairs of the colony. The lack of religious legitimacy given to the colonial authorities and the widespread desecration of Buddhist sacred sites by colonial agents fueled Burmese resistance and nationalism (Maung Maung 1980, Ni Ni Myint 1983).

While Mindon's religious reforms after the Fifth Buddhist Synod in 1871 opened the door to modernist Buddhist developments, a diversity of modern Buddhist practices and institutional forms emerged subsequently in reaction to the cultural and religious disjunctures created by colonial rule (Schober 1996, 1997, 2004). Reformed Buddhist rationalism allowed for the questioning of the received wisdom of traditional Buddhist authority in a variety of ways. It engendered Buddhist responses to modernity ranging from cosmologically inspired resistance against colonial domination (Sarkisyanz 1965; Herbert 1982) to fundamentalist retreats in reaction to modern social realities (Schober 1993; Matthews 1993). The general decline of Buddhist monastic authority was

matched by an increased laicization of religious authority through meditation. New public debates developed about the moral and ethical authority of
the state, monks, and the laity after independence. The ensuing ideological
struggle for a civic religious community (see Reynolds 1977) reflects, and is
informed by, recent political, social, and economic developments and their
continuing importance in the determination of Burma's future as a nation.[3]

Civil and religious practices are also significant forces in resolving the present ideological struggle for modernity. They will likely also inform the intellectual and religious legitimation of the modern Burmese state in the future.
In contrast to traditional polities that employ an ideology rooted in cosmological Buddhism (Reynolds and Reynolds 1982), competing visions of authority
characteristic of modern nation-states often challenge traditional orders and
provide alternate avenues for legitimation (Keyes et al. 1994). Our understanding of present religious developments, monastic reforms, popular piety, and
public morality must be set against the historical developments of the Theravāda tradition in Burma (see Mendelson 1975), against the complexity of its
social, cultural, and economic landscape (Silverstein 1980; Steinberg 1991,
1981, 1982; Taylor 1987), and within the context of Burma's position among
other rapidly modernizing Southeast Asian nations.

Some scholars have argued that the contemporary Burmese state represents a continuation of colonial structures. British colonial rule in Burma
created secular, parallel power structures that endure in the present (Gravers
1999). Following Furnivall, Gravers argues that colonial society in Burma was
organized in a hierarchy according to ethnic categories (that is, English, Burmans, and minority groups), in which members interacted within one another
and not across ethnic boundaries. Power was brokered through membership
in "clubs" that demanded ethnic homogeneity and unquestioning loyalty
from members. Gravers sees in this configuration the basis for both Burmese
ethnic nationalism and xenophobia. A characterization of the military elite as
members of "Ne Win's Club" was particularly apt well into the 1990s. Another
example is the "Tuesday Club" hosted by Brigadier General Abel, the former
minister of national planning and economic development. Some dissenters
even characterize the current regime as a form of internal colonialism, claiming that "they" are as bad as the British, and Aung San Suu Kyi has described
the current democracy movement as the second struggle for independence
(Marshall 2003). Several factors impede the emergence of postcolonial social
formations in Burma, most notably, the state's control over civil society, the
processes of political representation, media outlets, access to the global flows
of information, and access to higher education. Many of these modern social
formations are yet to be institutionalized or routinized,[4] and any discussion of

modern Buddhism here must acknowledge the fragmentation of civil society and religion in the contemporary Burmese nation.

Buddhist Culture and Authority in the Modern State

The relationship between the current Burmese state and Theravāda Buddhism is a modern variation on a traditional paradigm. It also reveals an ongoing struggle among modernist, traditional, and fundamentalist Buddhist communities and their supporters.[5] Since independence, the state under U Nu in the 1950s, under Ne Win in the 1980s, and again under the SLORC in the 1990s, sought to reshape Buddhist piety and social morality in the image of political ideologies in order to legitimate its rule. The present religious reforms seek to institute a scripturalist, otherworldly, nonpolitical, and centralized sangha that can be entrusted with legitimating the fundamentalist religion promoted by the state. This vision combines the traditional paradigm of state-sangha relations and popular piety with a socialist ideology of the state's religious agency (Bechert 1973, 1988; Schober 1984; Tin Maung Maung Than 1988).

Since it assumed power in 1988, the State Law and Order Restoration Council (SLORC) and its successor regime, the State Peace and Development Council (SPDC), implemented a comprehensive reorganization of monastic and lay Buddhist practice. Since the protracted negotiations of the national convention failed to formulate a new constitution, the state's promotion of Buddhism has become a primary source of political legitimation, enhancing the prestige of a class of the military, technocrats, and civil servants. Current state patronage of Buddhism focuses on public merit-making at national monuments and local pagodas, instilling the regime's vision of Buddhism among the laity and citizenry, and missionizing among non-Buddhist and minority groups on the nation's periphery. The regime's agenda encompasses control over monastic institutions and mobilizing the general population for Buddhist and nationalist causes. It has silenced the sangha through various procedural reforms, reorganizing monastic protocols and revising the required training to become a *sayadaw* (abbot). The state seeks to instill among its citizens and within the sangha its own brand of Buddhist nationalism. The military regime's patronage of Buddhist relics and Burmese dynastic history creates alternate sources of legitimation and popularizes the perceived splendor of Burma's traditional past. It aims to integrate the current regime within a historical lineage of Burmese Buddhist rulers to create a political and cultural identity for itself that is a continuation of past dynastic splendor. Finally, it attempts to transform a political and national community into a ritual community to ensure stability and prosperity for the nation-state.

Perhaps to diminish the sangha's voice in interpreting Buddhist texts and doctrines, the regime actively promotes large-scale rituals and mobilizes the Buddhist public to participate in them. These rituals bind the periphery to the center through merit-making in which participants incur social obligations to ritual sponsors. In this way, civil groups and social classes become ritually indebted to the political elites that epitomize the state's power. These mass rituals turn national communities into religious communities and celebrate the restoration and new construction of sites that enshrine a ritual presence of the Buddha and of the Burmese kings. General (and now deposed Prime Minister) Khin Nyunt expressed these religio-nationalist sentiments while accepting donations for the renovation of Ngadatgyi pagoda in Bahan township in Rangoon. He stated, "During the time of the State Law and Order Restoration Council, religious structures such as pagodas, stupas, monasteries and lakes are renovated or constructed. . . . Those who will donate cash for general renovation will thus gain merit" (*New Light of Myanmar* 1994a).

The regime's objectives in propagating Buddhism are reflected in the cultural, political, and economic contexts of the national veneration of the Buddha's Sacred Tooth relic in early 1994 (Schober 1997). These rituals were marked by the politics of giving. They engendered massive donation drives, creating patterns of patronage in which ritual clients incurred obligations toward the center. Membership in select groups of donors profiled economic and political elites whose names were listed daily in national and local newspapers and other media. Important donors were also depicted in photographs as they participated in merit dedication ceremonies held at Kaba Aye. While generous giving entitles donors to privileges, it also entails continuing obligations to the patronage of a political elite. The public portrayals of generosity *(dāna)* and loving kindness *(mettā)* in support of the Burmese national ethos imply competition among donors for political recognition.

The state's administrative agency is particularly evident in the agendas and activities of the Ministry of Religious Affairs and the Ministry of Culture. Each plays an important role in the implementation of mutually reinforcing objectives and hegemonic structures. The Ministry of Religious Affairs is responsible for three related areas—the sangha, the Buddhist laity, and non-Buddhist minorities. It works closely with the National Sangha Mahanayaka Council to regulate the sangha through a centralized administration that extends from the center to the local level. Since its inception in 1980, the Sangha Mahanayaka Council has been responsible for supervising the affairs of all nine officially recognized ordination lineages, registration of individual monks, monastic education, and leadership training programs for sayadaws. Its administration is housed at Kaba Aye, adjacent to the ministerial offices.

Like the mandatory reshuffling of civil service positions, monastic representatives to the central Mahanayaka Council rotate every few months. This prevents power bases from forming among senior sangha members, renders their presence on the Council largely ceremonial, and brings the Council's agenda under the control of the ministry. The regime rewards, materially and with prestigious titles, senior monks who advocate political disengagement within the sangha, promote scripturalist interpretations of Buddhist texts, and restrain junior monks who may sympathize with the pro-democracy movement.[6] Since 1996 members of the NLD have been prohibited from seeking ordination in an effort to discourage the party's popularity among monks. This prohibition prevents members of the opposition from becoming sources of merit for the citizenry in general and denies proponents of the democracy movement access to monastic practice sponsored by the state.

In economic terms, the state has gained control over the influx of all significant donations to the sangha and closely monitors monastic finances, religious construction, and social welfare projects through several venues. The seemingly ubiquitous presence of lay assistants to members of the sangha enables effective oversight of monastic activities and the direct involvement in the personal affairs of individual monks, which includes managing their personal finances, travel plans, and interactions with lay supporters. State agencies collect and make significant financial contributions to Buddhist causes and social welfare programs, such as hospitals and homes for the elderly. These donations are encouraged from private individuals, state collectives, and even foreign dignitaries.[7] They further finance extensive construction projects of religious monuments, the restoration of *stupas* (reliquary monuments) and of royal palace grounds, and other merit-making rituals.

Missionizing among the national and international Buddhist community complements these efforts. Within the ministry, the Department for the Propagation and Promotion of the Sāsana (the Buddhist dispensation or religion), established in the early 1990s, promotes Buddhism through lay associations among Burmese Buddhists. Among civil servants and other elites at government offices, lay associations are also dedicated to religious instruction and the recitation of prayers and *suttas* (discourses delivered by the Buddha). Several million "trainees" have passed the Buddhist Culture Courses offered at lay meditation centers and in association with government agencies. In his opening address to an Advanced Course on Buddhist Culture in North Okkalapa township where the most violent antigovernment riots occurred in 1988, Minister of Religious Affairs Lt. Gen. Myo Nyunt was reported as stating, ". . . each of the trainees is to help preserve national culture through religious education and [he] stressed the need to safeguard the nation against the threat of extinction of race and culture" (*New Light of Myanmar* 1994d). Most government bodies sponsor affiliated lay meditation or recitation societies and hold temporary ordinations for their staff. Throughout the country, selected monasteries once again provide basic formal education in secular and religious subjects to children and youths.

Missionization among religious minorities is an equally significant, though less publicized function of the religious ministry. Its stated purpose is to assure the independent and orderly activities of the Christian, Muslim, and Hindu communities. However, their activities are closely monitored and often curtailed. In collaboration with the Sangha Mahanayaka Council, the Department for the Propagation of Sāsana also oversees Buddhist missionary activities among Christian and animist tribal minorities on the nation's periphery, where forced conversion to Buddhism has been reported. While Buddhist missionization at the nation's center is described as an effort of national and ethnic integration, it is seen on the periphery as an attempt to extend the central government's control and infrastructure into territories of ethnic and religious minorities.[8]

The Ministry of Culture and its campaign, since the mid-1990s, to instill a correct view of Burmese national culture in many ways echoes the state's involvement in religious affairs. Its objectives include the preservation of Myanmar culture and history by providing an umbrella structure for historical research, archeology, fine arts, the National Museum, and a new Institute of Culture. The Ministry's website states its mission as follows:

> To educate the public to be fully imbued with the prevalent ideas; to help develop the unity, nationalistic spirit and patriotism among the people; to help the elimination of decadent culture; to support the promotion of the morale and morality of the public; to help develop the union spirit in exposing culture, [and] to make endeavors in promoting the development and standard of culture.

Faced with a plethora of modern values, ways of life, and patterns of consumption, particularly among young members of the elite, the ministry's role is pivotal in defining, limiting, and regulating the interpretation and expression of Burmese culture. In his address to the First Buddhist Culture Course held at Kyaikkahsan Dhammapiya Meditation Center, Myo Nyunt reminded the trainees "'. . . not to let what is alien to Myanmar eclipse our views and our economy.' He also stressed the need to preserve culture, religion, and Myanmar traditions as Tatmadaw [military] joining hands with people safeguards the independence" (*New Light of Myanmar* 1994b).

Significant in this regard are archeological excavations and restorations of historical sites, especially royal palaces at Mandalay, Shwebo, Pagan, Siriketra, Mrauk-U, and Kogun Cave in Kayin State. Comprising both reconstructed royal palace grounds and religious monuments, they represent the regime's vision of a glorious dynastic past. Government officials continually inspect the progress of work at these sites and officiate at ceremonies and rituals held there. Concurrent with the reconstruction of Burmese cultural sites is their public display as national treasures in the media. Several museums have been built in recent years at sites of religio-national significance. Foremost among these efforts is the renewed attention given to the National Museum which houses archeological items, regalia of past dynasties, Buddha images, and other materials that represent the visual and performing arts and the cultures of minority groups (see Anderson 1991, Reynolds 1977).

The state's vision of Buddhism and nationalist culture blurs distinctions in the public sphere between religious restoration and the restoration of important sites in Burmese dynastic history. Extensive construction at Buddhist and dynastic sites resembles a modern state cult (Schober 1997). The deliberate blurring of religious and political authority is also expressed in a statement by an eminent monk, the Mahasi Ovadacariya Pathein Sayadaw Agga Maha Kammathanacariya Bhaddanta Acikkhana, who addressed a Buddhist Culture Course at the Mahasi Meditation Center in Rangoon in this way: "[O]nly glorious persons have the opportunity of contributing to the promotion of the Sasana, and the State Law and Order Restoration Council, unlike previous governments, has such [an] opportunity [for] renovating and constructing religious monuments and buildings and carrying out affairs for the flourishing of the sasana" (*New Light of Myanmar* 1994c). Among its most prominent religio-cultural projects are two recently constructed pagodas in Rangoon and Mandalay to commemorate the arrival of the Chinese Tooth Relic to Burma in 1994.[9] In April 1999 the regime hoisted a new diamond-studded pivot (*hti,* lit. umbrella) onto the Shwedagon pagoda in Rangoon, a national shrine that is believed to house a hair relic of the Buddha. Grand preparations have also been mounted by state agencies to further the construction of the Maha-wizaya pagoda sponsored by the former dictator, Ne Win.[10]

The regime's patronage of religious and historical sites is integral to the construction of a national community, "Myanmar" culture, history, and religion. Such patronage represents the most far-reaching effort in modern Buddhism to create a ritual state cult aimed at a national community in which the military and other agents of the state facilitate access to religious merit and social prestige. A modern technocratic elite employs traditional ritual patronage to consolidate its hegemony and enjoin a large segment of its population into participation in the state's veneration of Buddhist relics. Participation in these rituals affirms one's place within a socially and ritually differentiated hegemony within which power relations are negotiated. It is intended to legitimate political hegemonies, mobilize large, diverse communities, and promote political integration and a cultural ethos in an imagined modern nation-state.[11] Its elaborate ritual theater draws on precolonial forms of royal patronage and its contemporary celebration epitomizes issues at the interface of history, culture, and politics.[12] Social, religious, and political contexts of these state rituals highlight the ways in which patronage of a religious past legitimates political institutions and facilitates pragmatic agendas of the regime.[13]

The regime's modern imagination of national community, religion, and history is informed by the traditional Asokan model of righteous rulers and by the patronage of Buddhism's material manifestations *(rūpakāya)*.[14] From the vantage of traditional cosmological Buddhism, the veneration of the Buddha's relics localizes his presence in cosmological, social, and political domains and generates merit to aid eventual transcendence of this world *(samsāra)* and the attainment of enlightenment *(nibbāna)*.[15] The recent activities described here differ from traditional examples in that their religio-nationalist character is a reaction to the contested realities of modern secular and political pluralism. The cosmological symbolism of the state's rūpakāya cult notwithstanding, the pragmatic objectives of the state's cult likely arose from the rational constraints of modern politics. The regime's political authority does not depend on Buddhist symbols of just rule to enforce its policies. It further differs from traditional forms of relic veneration in that ritual patronage of the Buddha's remains accrues not to an individual, the traditional just ruler *(dhammarāja)*, but to a corporate class of civil and military elites that constitute the governing body of a nation-state that otherwise conceives of its purpose in modern political and pragmatic terms.

The state's modern use of cosmological symbols creates a national culture, community, territory, and history that are "essentially" Burmese and "essentially" Buddhist. The ethos of the regime's support for Buddhism is therefore integral to the kind of cultural nationalism, history, and community the state envisions for its citizens. It seeks to project, to its citizens and to outside observers, a vision of Buddhism in which the state, sangha, and laity, speak in a single voice, emphasizing righteousness, scripturalism, and morality *(sīla)*. In this way the regime uses state sponsorship of Buddhism as a means for bringing about a new religious synthesis. The regime is promoting a vision of Burmese Buddhist nationalism as cultural and political ideology to legitimate its contested rule. The administrative policies implemented in support of these ideological claims are far-reaching. They include the organization of state rituals and the construction of religious monuments, restructuring the lay and monastic domains, and missionizing Buddhism among minority groups in the nation's periphery. The regime's interactions with Burmese transnational and international communities similarly echo this Buddhist nationalist tenor.

The state's Buddhism shares with Western political theories an emphasis on functional rationality and bureaucratic efficiency. The state promises social stability and economic prosperity as a result of Buddhist merit-making. In this way, the modern nation-state attributes political significance to the religious sentiments of many Burmese Buddhists.

Aung San Suu Kyi and Socially Engaged Buddhism

Aung San Suu Kyi's emergence in national and international public spheres proceeded under Burmese political auspices and national sentiments. She had returned to Burma just prior to the popular uprising in 1988 and conducted a successful electoral campaign for her party, the National League for Democracy, which she serves as secretary general. She lived abroad most of her adult life. She was educated at Oxford University in Great Britain where she also raised a family. She became an articulate spokesperson for a generation of Burmese who felt deeply the social and intellectual isolation Burma had endured since the mid-1970s. Her struggle for democracy has been recognized with numerous honors. In 1991 she received the Nobel Peace Prize, with which she has established a health and education trust for Burmese people. She is the recipient of the 2002 Al Neuharth Free Spirit of the Year Award given by The Freedom Forum, an American organization that promotes democracy and freedom of speech around the world for "her spirited, nonviolent struggle for human rights and democracy" (Freedom Forum 2003). As the daughter of Burma's national independence movement leader, Aung San, she enjoys charismatic appeal among Burmese, Buddhists, and secular supporters in the West. Her impact as a symbol for the Burmese desire for democratic rights and Buddhist values is heightened by her uncompromising resolve to uphold her beliefs and goals in the face of political pressures and personal adversity. Her public demeanor is marked by charm, wittiness, and a simple lifestyle. She has stated that she is guided by the political goals of Mahatma Gandhi and his struggle for Indian independence from British colonial rule.

Her commitment to nonviolent civil resistance and the spiritual counsel she seeks from Buddhist teachers have become hallmarks of her political activism. In exile at home, Aung San Suu Kyi lives the life of a modern world renouncer. She submitted herself with discipline and perseverance to hunger strikes and prolonged house arrest imposed by a military regime that refused to hand over government to her victorious party. Reflecting on the solitude of six years' of house arrest (1989–1995), she remarked, "Like many of my Buddhist colleagues, I decided to put my time under detention to good use by practicing meditation. . . . In my political work, I have been helped and strengthened by the teachings of members of the sangha" (1997:160).

Aung San Suu Kyi has frequently commented on the spiritual strengths she found in the practice of meditation as a strategy for nonviolent resistance. Her inspirational message emphasizes inner strength as preparation for political action and social change. Along with right speech and truthfulness, she continually urges the practice of mindfulness *(sati)*, faith *(saddha)*, energy *(viriya)*, concentration *(samādhi)*, and wisdom *(paññā)* (1997:159), all of which derive from spiritual cultivation. Like her, many of her Burmese supporters find refuge in meditation, where silent practice and freedom of thought are protected by a secluded community built on spiritual cultivation and trust. This shields her supporters to some extent from an ever-present government scrutiny of civil and religious life. Like Gandhi's ashram, Burmese meditation centers are separate, if not utopian, communities engaged in a spiritual and social resistance against an oppressor. Given a government policy that excludes pro-democracy supporters from monastic ordination and other forms of religious practice, meditation thus becomes an alternate site of religiosity that is often synonymous with political resistance.

Two of her essays in particular reflect on religious motivation, discipline, and self-sacrifice. Recalling her religious teachers, she invokes the spiritual guidance Buddhists derive from practicing the Eightfold Path. One teacher reminds her of the well-known Jataka story of the hermit Sumadha, the future buddha, "who sacrificed the possibility of early liberation for himself and underwent many lives of striving that he might save others from suffering" (Aung San Suu Kyi 1996). For most Burmese this narrative evokes a common Theravāda interpretation that focuses on the prophesy of the future buddha's spiritual enlightenment. Aung San Suu Kyi gives the story a moral justification that stresses a socially engaged Buddhist interpretation, inspired by a Mahayana emphasis on the social involvement of the future buddha in the life of his community. The implied multivocality may allude to her spiritual aspirations and social commitment.

About another teacher, Aung San Suu Kyi (1997:161) writes that "he sketched out for me how it would be to work for democracy in Burma. 'You will be attacked and reviled for engaging in honest politics,' pronounced the teacher, 'but you must persevere. Lay down an investment in suffering *(duk-kha)* and you will gain bliss *(sukha)*.'" The passage suggests interferences in her activities by the regime and the slanderous treatment she received in editorials of the *New Light of Myanmar* which referred to her as "Mrs. Michael Aris," implying that she lost her Burmese identity and nationality through marriage to a British citizen. Elsewhere (1996) she invites analogies with her personal circumstances and the story of Padasari, a woman whose tragic loss of family makes her "the epitome of the consuming fire of extreme grief" until the Buddha's teachings bring her peace of mind and "the joy of victory over the self." One is reminded of the separation from her own family that she chose in order to further the causes of the Burmese democratic movement. Her statements on current events and developments in Burma are often grounded in ethical considerations of the greater common good and the nature of the moral responsibility of the state. Her speeches, essays, and letters evoke a vision of a modern, rational Buddhist ethic in which the moral conduct of the state, social justice, and the material and spiritual welfare of individuals and families are closely linked to issues of participatory democracy, human rights, and dignity. In one of her essays, "In Quest for Democracy" (1991:168–169), she places the Burmese movement for democracy during the late 1980s into this Buddhist framework.

> Members of the Buddhist sangha in their customary role as mentors have led the way in articulating popular expectations by drawing on classical learning to illustrate timeless values. But the conscious effort to make traditional knowledge relevant to contemporary needs was not confined to any particular circle—it went right through Burmese society from urban intellectuals and small shopkeepers to doughty village grandmothers. . . . The Burmese people, who have no access to sophisticated academic material, go to the heart of the matter by turning to the words of the Buddha on the four causes of decline and decay: failure to recover that which has been lost, omission to repair that which has been damaged, disregard for the need for reasonable economy, and the elevation to leadership of men without morality or learning. Translated into contemporary terms, when democratic rights had been lost to the military dictatorship, sufficient efforts had not been made to regain them, moral and political values had been allowed to deteriorate without concerted attempts to save the situation, the economy had been badly damaged, and the country had been ruled by men without integrity or wisdom.

Her writings alternate between explicit critiques of Burmese political failures and her allegorical use of Buddhist narratives, symbols, and virtues to contest prevailing political realities. For instance, she elaborates on traditional Buddhist visions of governance: the Seven Safeguards against Decline, the Four Kinds of Assistance to the People, and the Ten Duties of Kings: liberality, morality, self-sacrifice, integrity, kindness, austerity, non-anger, nonviolence, forbearance, and nonopposition to the will of the people. She sees such traditional Burmese virtues as drawing on

> time-honored values to reinforce the validity of political reforms they consider necessary. It is a strong argument . . . for democracy that governments

regulated by principles of accountability, respect for public opinion and the
supremacy of just laws are more likely than an all-powerful ruler or ruling
class, uninhibited by the need to honor the will of the people, to observe
the traditional duties of Buddhist kingship. Traditional values serve both
to justify and to decipher popular expectations of democratic government.
(1991:173)

Reminiscent of Martin Luther King, Jr.'s "Letter from Birmingham Jail,"
Aung San Suu Kyi's *Letters from Burma* contain her eloquent comments on
social, cultural, and political themes.[16] The series commences with an extended
recollection of a pilgrimage she undertook to a mountain monastery, Thamanya, near Pa-an in southern Burma, shortly after her release from house arrest.
In the course of this journey, she facetiously comments on poor road conditions along the way and recalls the moral integrity of the imprisoned King
Manuha and his defiance of Anawratha, his captor and founder of the Pagan
empire. She describes an ideal community of monks, female ascetics, villagers,
and pilgrims who enjoy the generous benefactions of the charismatic monk U
Vinaya who resided there until his death in 2003. Through his work, he had
founded this community, marked by seemingly idyllic harmony and economic
security. Her description stresses especially the extensive education and school-
ing that enrolled at the time nearly 400 children. In her conclusions (1997:17),
she notes

> People will contribute both hard work and money cheerfully if they are
> handled with kindness and care and if they are convinced that their contri-
> butions will truly benefit the public. The works of the Hsayadaw are upheld
> by the donations of devotees who know beyond the shadow of a doubt that
> everything that is given to him will be used for the good of others. How fine
> it would be if such a spirit of service were to spread across the land. Some
> have questioned the appropriateness of talking about such matters as *metta*
> (loving kindness) and *thissa* (truth) in the political context. But politics is
> about people and what we have seen in Thamanya proved that love and
> truth can move people more strongly than any form of coercion.

Her interpretation suggests that an ideal society is based on voluntary
work contributed by its members and on benign and mindful governance
upheld by Buddhist values. In her weekly letters Aung San Suu Kyi offers cogent
observations from a Buddhist perspective on social injustice and its causes. She
takes up corruption among civil servants, health-care providers, and teachers;
the shortsighted, profit-oriented immorality of foreign investments under the
military council; the misrule of arbitrary laws; political repression and the

threat to safety; imprisonment of members of the resistance; the political agenda of the National League for Democracy; the courageous spirit of those who struggle for democracy; the preemption of NLD members from performing merit-making rituals and from joining the sangha; the plight of young children and hope for their future; and celebrations of national and religious holidays, of ethnic diversity, and the strength of national unity.

Her political activism and social ideologies are grounded in the modern ethics of socially engaged Buddhism. From this premise of an enlightened, modern Buddhist ethic, Aung San Suu Kyi has articulated an encompassing Buddhist vision of moral authority, social justice, and political empowerment. It is not surprising, therefore, that her discussion takes up the election of the mythic first king of Buddhism, Mahasammata, who restored peace and justice to a society plunged into moral decay and social chaos. This is a familiar theme in the discourse of socially engaged Buddhists that has also been taken up by contemporary Thai intellectuals as well.[17]

Aung San Suu Kyi's Buddhism shares with other socially engaged Buddhists, and advocates of "liberation theologies" generally, the premise that religion is a positive force in social life that ameliorates social, economic, and political injustice and spiritually empowers popular resistance against the state's coercion.[18] Such modern religious interpretations emphasize the improvement of basic social services such as health care, education, and human rights. Socially engaged Buddhism thus emerges from the intersection of traditional religious values and Western post-Enlightenment thought that empathizes universal human rights and a participatory political process. This intersection of Western political theory and modern Buddhist thought affirms the universality each system of ideas claims, enhancing the appeal of her message on a global level. In her address to the World Commission on Culture and Development, Aung San Suu Kyi (1994) writes that

The true development of human beings involves much more than mere economic growth. At its heart there must be a sense of empowerment and inner fulfillment. This alone will ensure that human and cultural values remain paramount in a world where political leadership is often synonymous with tyranny and the rule of a narrow elite. People's participation in social and political transformation is the central issue of our time. This can only be achieved through the establishment of societies which place human worth above power, and liberation above control. In this paradigm, development requires democracy, the genuine empowerment of the people. When this is achieved, culture and development will naturally coalesce to create an environment in which all are valued, and every kind of human potential can be realized.

An unequivocal and consistent advocate of democratic reforms grounded in a modern Buddhist ethic, Aung San Suu Kyi's voice is joined by others who share her vision. In addition to certain Burmese monks and lay people engaged in meditation, socially engaged Buddhists are prominently represented in Thailand by Bhikkhu Buddhadasa and Sulak Sivaraksa, by the Vietnamese monk Thich Nhat Hanh, and by the Dalai Lama, who focuses the world's attention on the plight of Tibet and the Tibetan Buddhist diaspora.

Western converts to Buddhism are already acquainted with other messages of Buddhist universalism. Their familiarity with Aung San Suu Kyi likely focuses on her religious charisma and only to a lesser degree on her political agenda or on the political realities of the contemporary Burmese state and its Buddhist citizens. The further removed from the context of daily life in Burma that the interviewer appears, the greater the likelihood that the reporting will emphasize religious aspects and Aung San Suu Kyi's charisma over her politics. The portrait presented to Buddhists around the world is usually one in which a modern world renouncer engages in the politics of resistance against a centralized state on the basis of Buddhist timeless values. Resistance against oppression and injustice are thus justified by recourse to Buddhist moral authority. Particularly through the agency of organizations like the Buddhist Peace Fellowship and features in magazines like the *Shambala Sun,* Western Buddhists have come to know Aung San Suu Kyi first and foremost as a socially engaged Buddhist, a social activist, and charismatic figure of "the Orient." Many of Aung San Suu Kyi's Buddhist sympathizers in the West may be characterized as an "audience cult," inspired largely by Western definitions of Buddhist virtues (see, for example, Nattier 1996 and Tweed 1992). Few among Aung San Suu Kyi's Buddhist supporters in the West have independent knowledge of Burma's social and cultural contexts. Her most vocal supporters in the West, however, are secular, political activists who may also be motivated by a belief in the universality of human rights, and some of them may even favor a modern, metareligious ethic articulated by contemporary "saints," many of whom have been previous recipients of the Nobel Peace Prize.[19]

Buddhist Modernities and the Problem of the Secular

The two modes of modern Buddhism outlined here characterize poles at either end of a continuum of Buddhist belief and practice in Burma today, and not all contemporary Buddhist practice is encompassed by them. The disparity between them indicates a broad range of possible intersections of modern Buddhism and Western political thought. Nevertheless, both types of Buddhism serve as ideological justification for their respective visions of society, moral authority, and the state. They differ in the ways each constructs its own

Buddhist understanding of moral authority in a modern context. They also differ in the ability to implement their respective visions. In the present context, the socially engaged, ethical Buddhism of Aung San Suu Kyi and her supporters lends moral authority to resistance against the regime. Aung San Suu Kyi's political and religious message shares certain affinities with values, such as human rights and the empowerment of individuals, deemed universal in the West. Conversely, in the absence of a national constitution, the regime represents a centralized military state based on bureaucratic rationalism and legitimated by a nationalist vision of Buddhism that affirms the center's authority over differentiated levels of social and political power. The reality of the present, however, makes clear that the legitimation of civil authority remains entrenched in political divisions of the day and in Buddhist and cultural institutions unlikely to fade soon.

These two modern forms of Buddhism may be seen in some ways as unwittingly or unwillingly coopted by the politics of the day. And, conversely, lacking secular means of legitimation, the politics of the state depends on the moral authority of Buddhist communities. The preceding discussion shows that, even in a modern context, political legitimation in Burma continues to depend, in significant ways, on Buddhist sources of authority. This kind of understanding of political authority keeps the secular domain beholden to religious ethics and preempts full participation by ethnic minorities in the national project. Finally, greater roles for secular power and knowledge in the public domain may lessen polarization among religious communities. Repeated collective violence between Buddhists and Muslims in recent years demonstrates the need to strengthen the public role of secularism and pluralism. One can readily imagine numerous developments in Burma that will foster a modern civil society and sustain political, economic, social, and religious pluralism. It will be the work of future generations to conceptualize, establish, and institutionalize this kind of postcolonial project in Burma.

Notes

I presented versions of this essay at Harvard University, the University of California at Berkeley, Arizona State University, and at a meeting of the Association for Asian Studies. I gratefully acknowledge the many insightful comments I received from various scholars in these contexts. Their observations enhanced this essay in numerous ways. All mistakes and omissions are my own.

1. The *Sigalovada Suttanta* (Rhys-Davids 1991) expounds lay ethics and can be viewed as a textual basis for the socially engaged Buddhism Aung San Suu Kyi represents and advocates. The *Mahaparinibbana Suttanta* (Rhys-Davids 1968) tells the story

of venerating and enshrining the Buddha's relics and may be seen as providing the conceptual paradigm for the ritualistic, nationalist Buddhism practiced by the military regime.

2. In his reflections on imagined communities and nationalism, Anderson (1991) observes the significant role "print capitalism" plays in the development of national histories and ideologies of modern nation-states. See also Leehey, this volume.

3. The types of religious practice described here may appear to a Burmese observer to be historical continuations of religio-political polarities that had already emerged during Mindon's reign between those who in xenophobic and unrealistic ways advocated military battle to combat encroaching colonial networks, while others within the court, most notably the Kinwun Mingyi (Thant Myint 2001:158), argued for an open engagement of the precolonial "other." The history of the Anglo-Burmese wars and of the subsequent colonization of Burma tells us how this dynamic unfolded. A renewed attempt to overcome cultural, political, and economic isolation must begin with institutionalizing civil society in a postcolonial context.

4. Both examples of Buddhist modernism described here are hybrid forms that emerged from the intersection of two distinct global systems, namely, Buddhism and Western post-Enlightenment political thought. Theories about such intersections of religion, society, and politics often ignore the fact that the concept of the secular derives ultimately from a Judeo-Christian worldview, and a presumed separation of religious and secular domains in other cultures will be shaped by religious values and hybrid social forms that remain embedded in local dynamics.

5. For a description of fundamentalist trends in Burmese Buddhism, see Schober 1993, and also Keyes et al. 1994.

6. The SLORC-SPDC has silenced within its national boundaries voices that speak for alternate visions of Buddhism, political hegemony, and moral legitimation. Since the state controls social discourse about ritual and the hegemonic constructs it envisions for the nation, alternate voices must be gleaned from silence, in absence from ritual participation, and in the counter texts of expatriate communities beyond Burma's national boundaries.

7. The systematic collection of private donations for religious and social welfare supports a range of projects in contemporary Myanmar. While collections on behalf of the Tooth Relic pagodas produced very high returns within a short time, they are part of a pattern whereby the state increasingly seeks to finance religion, social welfare, and monuments of national culture through private contributions.

8. Since the mid-1990s, repeated violent clashes between Buddhists and Muslims have occurred. Muslims have generally been targeted by rioting mobs, led not infrequently by individuals wearing Buddhist monastic robes. Yet it seems unlikely that monks who normally reside in strictly controlled monasteries would be free to engage in social and political activities that, amidst the general social tensions in Burma, might easily spill into larger demonstrations of social discontent. Some senior monks have

publicly distanced themselves and the sangha as an institution from the persecution of Muslims in Burma. Others have alleged that riots and violence were instigated by agents of the regime disguised in Buddhist monastic robes to command the authority normally granted to monks by the Burmese Buddhist majority (see reports in Burmanet News, April 22,1997a, 1997 b).

9. Elsewhere I discuss the state's veneration of the Buddha's Tooth relic and similar rituals as a modern transformation of cosmological Buddhism (Schober 1997).

10. See Schober 2001, for an exploration of the role of relics, stupas, and Buddha images in Burmese negotiations of power.

11. I follow Anderson (1991) in my treatment of nationalism as a cultural form.

12. My use of ritual theater and the dramaturgy of power follows Geertz's discussions of these concepts (1980:136). To this characterization of premodern state ritual as an apt description of the regime's hegemonic intent, I would only add that the modern theater state appears to be a self-consciously constructed legitimation of its hegemony.

13. A just ruler does so within the ritual and social structures of an economy of merit. Homage and generosity *(dāna)* toward the Buddha's spiritual and material remains are seen as indications of religiosity, social status, and political legitimacy. Concerning the role of relics in Buddhist polities, such as the Kandyian Tooth relic in precolonial Sri Lanka, John Strong (2003:280) writes, ". . . possession of the Buddha's tooth was seen as an indispensable attribute of kingship. Its cult was the privilege and duty of the legitimate ruler and was thought to ensure social harmony, regular rainfall, bountiful crops, and righteous rule. Its possession meant power."

14. Veneration of the Buddha's relics is a central aspect of the material extensions *(rūpakāya)* of the dispensation (Schober 2001, 2004). It represents a cosmological strand of Theravāda Buddhism (Reynolds and Reynolds 1982; Keyes et al.1994) and the galactic polity (Tambiah 1985). This form of Theravāda Buddhist practice has characterized the history of traditional polities since the time of Asoka (Strong 1983). Accordingly, a just ruler *(dhammarāja)* has the prerogative and obligation to act as the ritual patron of some of the tradition's most evocative root metaphors.

15. See Schober 2004.

16. Initially, in 1995–1996, her letters appeared each week over the course of a year in the Japanese publication *Mainichi Daily News*. In early 1997 they were compiled and published by Penguin as *Letters from Burma*.

17. See, for example, Peter Jackson's essay on contemporary Thai political discussions of King Ruang's Three Worlds in Ling (1993). The reader is also referred to Sivaraksa (1981) for discussions that similarly justify democracy as a desired political ideology that is grounded in Buddhist ethical precepts.

18. Swearer (1995) and Queen and King (1996) discuss Aung San Suu Kyi and her politics of resistance as grounded in the liberation theologies of the modern Buddhist Asia.

19. Western sympathies with modern Buddhism have complex historical roots. In

the mid-nineteenth century, Western intellectuals discovered their affinities to, and made a selective appropriation of, Buddhist beliefs and philosophies. This has engendered a romantic fascination with Buddhist "mysticism" and other "spiritual truths of the Orient." The back pages of magazines such as *Tricycle* and the *Shambala Sun* advertise Buddhist financial investment services and compassionate marriage counseling. Such kaleidoscopic and culturally disembedded Buddhist articulations have been heightened by novel ecumenical encounters of disparate Asian Buddhist genealogies in Western contexts.

−7−
Sacralizing or Demonizing Democracy?

Aung San Suu Kyi's "Personality Cult"

Gustaaf Houtman

The May 1990 elections in Burma resulted in a decisive victory for the National League for Democracy (NLD), largely as the result of the popularity of Aung San Suu Kyi, the daughter of the popular national hero Aung San. Over time, however, the NLD has been unable to make actual its victory against an army that is giving little or no ground. Though confirming that the roadmap's final destination will be a democracy of sorts, the regime has not been in any haste to complete its national convention and is yet to permit full-scale party political activity. The chief criticism the regime levels at Aung San Suu Kyi and her NLD colleagues, and party politicians more generally, is that they and the people who support them practice "personality politics." Here I seek to understand some of the underlying ramifications of this accusation as set in a Burmese political context.

The Parameters of Personality Politics

The accusation that party politics equates with personality politics is not dissociated, of course, from the army's own desire to gain and retain control over the entire country without testing their own unpopularity with another vote. In this sense the regime clearly fears popular, often charismatic, political leaders. The regime's unpopularity is compounded, of course, by the many unpopular things any government has to do; it is further compounded by not having been elected to do these unpopular things. Nevertheless, their principal worry, insofar as they state one formally, is that party politics (read "personality politics") leads to disunity and leaves the country vulnerable to the same kind of foreign exploitation that took place during the colonial period.

The regime's formal reasons for disqualifying political parties (including the NLD) from a formal political role has to do with personality politics. On the Burmese regime's official website it defines "Union Spirit" as "the established notion of regarding the entire Union as a family or a household." As part of its Union Spirit preamble, the military council states that

> It is necessary to dissociate oneself from a narrow racial outlook, a strong attachment to one's own region, strong attachment to one's own party, personality cult, bigotry and extremism. At a time when priority is to be given to the interests of the Union and the entire national people . . . [a]ll need to seriously take into account the historical event that among the conflicts which arose due to racialism, a strong attachment to the region, bigotry and extremism, the people of Union suffered misery and hardships. (SPDC 2002)

If selfish behavior goes with party politics, then something has to stand against this as "correct" behavior. The conclusion to this very same document says that "all the people of the Union should seriously keep in the[ir] hearts that the Union Spirit will flourish and propagate only if it is based on goodwill, magnanimity, forgiveness, equality and farsightedness while avoiding sheer racial and regional outlook and the extremes of party cult, ideological cult and personality cult." This suggests that good politics is about kindness and higher moral and spiritual behavior.

Some Political Concepts

The military and the NLD position themselves conceptually against one another in terms of what amounts to a local Burmese debate about a hierarchy of "good" concepts and personalities. The regime presents political rights or wrongs not in terms of authority conveyed by the electorate, but in terms of a historical all-encompassing patronage role it claims for itself ("the army is father, the army is mother"). In this role, personalities—whether that of Aung San, the founder of the army and father of Aung San Suu Kyi, or of the now deceased and disgraced Ne Win—are highly problematic. Just as the monetary notes *(kyat)* were depersonalized by introducing the lion to replace the image of Aung San, so too a depersonalization of power has taken place in Burmese politics in a movement away from historical personalities towards the world of impersonal objects. This depersonalization goes well beyond Ne Win's attempts to depersonalize Burmese politics.

The Pondaung fossils, the new museums, and the reconstruction of the royal palaces have gradually come to convey an alternative form of legitimation to the personality cult. Legitimation is based not on the personal charisma of the nation's leaders but upon the claim to be a member of a historical institution, the army, that keeps the country out of foreign hands and unifies it.

This objectification of the mythical source of political power by the regime is symptomatic of more than just that; it is designed as a way to keep influential civilians out of positions of authority in government and to obfuscate the electoral ineligibility of the army. It is also accompanied by a polarization of "authority" *(a-na)* and "influence" *(awza)*. In short, an "a-na system" is a dictatorship, suggesting that it does not cope with influence *(awza)* by means of incorporation, but rather by means of exclusion. However, the more the regime emphasizes authoritarian rule *(a-na)*, the more influential *(awza)* and charismatic figures spring from obscurity onto the national political stage. These figures, unlike the comparatively impersonal army personnel, appear like circles drawn by the mythical wizard *(weikza)* Bo Bo Aung, who challenged the king to wipe out a series of circles he then multiplied endlessly with his magical powers.

Having lost the elections in 1990, the regime is today frightened of a democratic vote for personalities who are possessed of awza, that is, influence and charisma. In a press conference Gen. Khin Nyunt (1989) justified the employment of the authoritarian instruments of state against the NLD by saying that the Communists "decided to fully exploit the propensity of the Myanmar masses to be enthused with personality cults and the sudden rising popularity of Daw Aung San Suu Kyi." The army, used to holding the reins of power since 1962, knows that their authoritarian *(a-na)* instruments have failed to create enduring structures of state, and they now fear the invisible, fluid, and unbounded trickling throughout the country of influential *(awza)* and popular personalities who are electorally more eligible than the army. They fear these individuals might just succeed in snatching away their privileges.

From the rise of the charismatic leader Saya San in the 1930s under British colonial rule, to the pre-Independence Wunthanu movement and the Freedom Bloc, Burmese history is replete with charismatic figures emerging in an authoritarian environment. This fact tells us much about Burmese political culture and how the populace has in the past responded to dissatisfaction with authoritarian governments. Burmese leaders and the Buddhist populace in crisis situations cultivate and privilege personal perfection through *mental culture,* by which I mean the numerous techniques of mind purification and mind control summed up as *bhāvana,* including concentration meditation (*samatha,* which also encompasses the four "social" meditations or *byamazo taya*) and insight contemplation (*vipassanā*). This gradually shades off into forms of "secular" or worldly knowledge (*lawkī pyinnya*), such as magic, numerology, and cabbalism. The paradox that I describe here is that while the military complains about personality cults destroying Burmese politics, it is precisely its own authoritarian form of governance that produces these personality cults it so intensely dislikes.

Undoubtedly the most influential of such personalities alive in Burma today is Aung San Suu Kyi, the daughter of *a-za-ni* (martyr, in the Buddhist sense), Gen. Aung San. Aung San had great charisma and influence with the public and is credited with having brought national independence to Burma as a civilian. Leaving Oxford, England, Aung San Suu Kyi's visit to Burma in March 1988 to nurse her mother, the very month when the protests began, prompted one observer to refer to her as "truly an accidental tourist politician" as she became drawn into national politics at a crucial historical moment. Many other daughters and widows in South and Southeast Asia have also been drawn into national politics in this way, whether it be in Pakistan, Bangladesh, Indonesia, or the Philippines. Aung San Suu Kyi challenged the use by the Tatmadaw (armed forces) of her father's legacy for its own legitimization, and in the process of demanding a return to democracy, she exposed sufficient ambiguities in Aung San's political heritage to undermine his use as a figurehead to support military rule.

After criticizing Ne Win in July 1989, Aung San Suu Kyi was placed under severe constraints, including long periods of house arrest. The 1990 elections demonstrated that the National League for Democracy, which she cofounded, was by far the preferred political party. Aung San Suu Kyi was declared free from house arrest in 2000. The following three years saw the death of Ne Win, his relatives jailed for treachery against the state, and a supposed series of "confidence-building" negotiations being held between the NLD and the State Peace and Development Council (SPDC). The political situation remained in an effective stalemate until the massacre of members of the NLD motorcade on 30 May 2003 led to further bloodshed and another round of imprisonment, including this time Aung San Suu Kyi herself.

Although Burmese people may feel uncertain about the future, in their hearts it seems that most support Aung San Suu Kyi and hope that the generals will eventually concede ground. Until they incorporate her awza, and that of other respected civilians, into a national government, however, it is unlikely that there will be an end to personality cults and conspiracies.

A Contemporary Awza Leader

In the absence of access to instruments of government, Aung San Suu Kyi's approach (Aung San Suu Kyi et al. 1997:7–8,111–112; Aung San Suu Kyi [henceforth ASSK] and Aris 1995:18–19) has been to emphasize spiritual dimensions to the political process and to incorporate Buddhist qualities into her leadership qualifications. Indeed, she has said that there is no conflict between Buddhist and political pursuits, and that "politics is about people, and [that] you can't separate people from their spiritual values." The result is that her political aspirations have become linked, in the public eye, to her spiritual aspirations. During the time of her house arrest she began to take an interest in the practice of vipassanā contemplation as taught by U Pandita, the well-known teacher in the Mahasi tradition who came to prominence under the sponsorship of Prime Minister U Nu in the early 1950s. In this sense she followed her senior colleagues, the cofounders of the National League for Democracy, U Tin Oo and U Kyi Maung, both vipassanā practitioners (Tin Oo in the same Mahasi tradition, but Kyi Maung, now deceased, in the U Ba Khin tradition). The circumstances of house arrest and imprisonment have meant for her and her colleagues a renewed interest in vipassanā (Aung San Suu Kyi et al. 1997:9, 215–218, 224, 228), much along the lines of such insubordinate ministers as U Hpo Hlaing, who in the nineteenth century under King Mindon also dedicated himself to vipassanā while exiled or placed under house arrest (Houtman 1999:198–202).

This aspect is clearly put by Aung San Suu Kyi (1997:162) when she says

> . . . one seeks greatness through taming one's passions. And isn't there a saying that "it is far more difficult to conquer yourself than to conquer the rest of the world?" So, I think the taming of one's own passions, in the Buddhist way of thinking, is the chief way to greatness, no matter what the circumstances may be. For example, a lot of our people [political prisoners] meditate when they're in prison, partly because they have the time, and partly because it's a very sensible thing to do. That is to say that if you have no contact with the outside world, and you can't do anything for it, then you do what you can with the world inside you in order to bring it under proper control.

Facing a corrupt and repressive military regime that endeavors to expose her as corrupted by reputed negative and amoral personality characteristics and a treasonous acceptance of foreign money, Aung San Suu Kyi has consistently emphasized a more spiritual and ethical approach to political leadership. However, in proclaiming that liberation of the country can be found through what amounts to a personal spiritual quest, and in criticizing the regime for not reforming in terms of their own personal Buddhist practice, she also further raises the spiritual capital invested in her by her supporters.

She makes reference to Buddhist concepts and practices used for decades in the political fight for national independence and the post-Independence period, and even during royal governments in the centuries before. Employing ideas such as *byamazo taya, mettā, karuṇā, pāramī, samatha, sati, vipassanā, nibbāna, yahanda,* and *bodhi* in the fight for democracy raises the stakes. For example, she believes that her role is to be involved in engaged Buddhism, which is "active compassion or active metta" (1995:247), and that: "the dream of a society ruled by loving kindness, reason and justice is a dream as old as civilized man. Does it have to be an impossible dream? . . . We are so much in need of a brighter world which will offer adequate refuge to all its inhabitants" (1993). She has also written that

> Paradise on earth is a concept which is outmoded and few people believe in it any more. But we can certainly seek to make our planet a better, happier home for all of us by constructing the heavenly abodes of love and compassion in our hearts. Beginning with this inner development we can go on to the development of the external world with courage and wisdom. (1998b)

In addition,

> We want a better democracy, a fuller democracy with compassion and loving kindness. . . . We should not be ashamed about talking about loving kindness and compassion in political terms. Values like love and compassion should be part of politics because justice must always be tempered by mercy. We prefer the word "compassion." That is warmer and more tender than "mercy." (Aung San Suu Kyi, cited in Stewart 1997:118)

With these ideas she attacks the greed and corruption that she feels characterizes the military regime. Rather than placing these in a sociological or political context, however, she associates corruption with the mind, and in particular with the defilements of the mind *(kilesa),* and the *arahant* (worthy one) as the only one to have been elevated from this through emancipation of the mind, by attaining perfect purity of mind through meditation. She thus argues that

> when one says that he wishes to be pure, you have to first discover what he means by purity. Like truth, it's a very large concept. It's something towards

which you aspire and struggle all the time. If anybody says, "I have achieved purity," he or she is probably not that pure. I doubt that anybody who is not an *arahant* could actually say, "There's no impurity in me." But I think that if you are in search of purity, you've got to know what impurity means. For people brought up in Buddhism, I don't think it's so difficult, because we have our concepts of greed, hatred and ignorance which create impurity. So anything that you can trace to ill-will and greed, that is impure. And anything that you can trace to ignorance, now that's a problem. How do you know that you are ignorant, if you are ignorant? (1997)

This quest for purity is also the quest her father clearly marked as the political ideal. Since politics is a "mundane" affair that, unlike the issues of nibbāna, does not excite the Burmese people, what we discover in Aung San's speeches is a struggle to find respectability for politics in the Burmese system of thought. He takes as his reference two indigenous models for political behavior. Though he views politics as being about *loka* (the mundane sphere) or *samsara* (cycle of rebirths), the most revolutionary and the highest politics are historically practiced by the politician who personally aspires to perfection in the here and now. In the Buddhist system this would normally mean a person who is, at the minimum, uprooting the mental defilements *(kilesa)* and pursuing the perfections *(pāramī)* with a view to attainment of nibbāna. Historically, politicians would also maintain the value of perfection in society through support of the sangha, or monastic order, and by commemorating its attainment through such actions as building pagodas. This is based on the view that if mental defilements are reduced throughout the country, then people will prosper and there will be no disasters. The second is the lawkī pyinnya path, which is based on low and "dirty" opportunist practices of astrology, magic, and wizardry, that leave the selfish mind intact with its defilements.

Aung San, in his schoolboy politics, attempted the second model. Towards the end of his university days and in his early Thakhin period,[1] he abandoned this to find a synthesis with Marxism. By the end of his life, just prior to national independence, he synthesized a redefinition of Burmese "secularism," incorporating democracy and socialism as an extended path centering on the ideal of byamazo taya as a "social" meditation. Aung San concluded that Gotama, before attaining enlightenment, sought out and encountered for six years various erroneous views, only to change his mind. The Burmese political terminology Aung San used has its roots in Buddhist spiritual practices. Indeed, the path to nibbāna was relevant to the desire royalty expressed in their prayers to attain nibbāna after their great acts of merit, as recorded in the stone inscriptions and in their building of pagodas as commemorations of the Buddha's enlightenment.

Angel or Female Bodhisattva?

If the foregoing indicates that Aung San Suu Kyi in a sense, through her choice of practices, use of language, and expression of higher political ideals, contributed to a personality cult from which, like her father, she finds it difficult to extract herself, below are some concrete ways in which this gained form.

The 37 *nats* are a pantheon of Burmese spirits associated with particular regions formally instituted at the Shwezigon pagoda in Pagan by King Anawratha (1044–1077), who founded the Pagan dynasty and also adopted and first instituted Theravāda Buddhist kingship. The Nat pantheon was instituted in subordination to Buddhism at the bottom of the pagoda platform. This involves the incorporation of local powerful supernatural beings feared or respected for their powers in particular regions into a single system (Brac de la Perrière 1989). Their biographies indicate that they were either greatly loved or greatly pitied by the people, before they met their violent deaths, often at the hands of the authorities.

One difference between a nat and an a-za-ni, such as Aung San, is that the latter is worshipped as a hero by government also, and not just propitiated by a select, factionalized public. In addition, unlike the concept of the nat, which is generally placed lower in the Buddhist hierarchy, an a-za-ni partakes of the higher Buddhist realm to which monks and Buddhists aspire. The concept is also commonly used for monks successful in passing scriptural learning exams but more particularly in meditation.

Aung San Suu Kyi has been referred to by her followers as the "Angel [Nat] of University Avenue" and as a "female bodhisattva" (ASSK 1997:9–10). Some intellectuals have suggested to me that she is the "Angel [Nat] of Democracy." Others have referred to her as: "a heroine like the mythical mother goddess of the earth [Vasundra] who [through her extensive past meritorious acts] can free them from the enslavement of the evil military captors" (Mya Maung 1992:163).

Sacralizing Democracy

Many people in rural Burma regarded Aung San as a universal king and a manifestation of Bo Bo Aung, and he denied this (Houtman 1999:251–54). Similar supernatural phenomena are attributed to Aung San Suu Kyi. The previous incarnation of the military council, the State Law and Order Restoration Council (SLORC), refused to hand over power in August and September 1990, following their loss to the NLD party in the 1990 elections. As cofounder of the NLD, Aung San Suu Kyi was closely associated with its political victory. The regime took many unpopular measures before and after the election. As

Kei Nemoto (1996a) has described, during his visit to Burma just two and a half months after the general election, Burmese people interpreted the swelling of the left breast of Buddha statues and the bleeding of the eyes as indicating Aung San Suu Kyi's imminent rise to power—the swelling of the left breast indicating Aung San Suu Kyi's nurturing characteristics.

It may have been "true" that the image's left chest was thicker than the right because of the way the Buddha's robe folds across the left shoulder, leaving the right shoulder bare. A thickness of the left chest would likely have been sculpted that way originally. However, I am more interested in the prevalent interpretation of this as a good omen relating to Aung San Suu Kyi. The people who visited the image said that her power would continue to grow in order to save Burmese people from their suffering. The interpretation of the phenomenon varied a little, but a typical interpretation was by a young graduate of Mandalay University. "This phenomenon and its interpretations spread throughout the country up to September the same year. It is likely that [this] . . . gave an impetus to many Buddhist monks to take part in the protests with the NLD supporters between September and October against SLORC's neglect of the results of the 1990 elections" (Nemoto 1996b:26–27).

Debunking the Cult

These positive characterizations of Aung San Suu Kyi's supernatural power contrast with the negative characterizations by her adversaries. They call her the spirit "Mother of the West" (Anauk Medaw) (see Figure 7.1), as we can see in the following excerpt from the state media (Thanlyet 1996).

> Your Mrs. Michael Aris, called Anauk Medawgyi, is just following the
> course of Thakin Than Tun, her aunt's husband. As I have [had] experi-
> ences, past and present, I can see her steps well. Both of them are of the
> same mentality. They are [the] same in having great aims and thinking
> highly of themselves in arrogance. They are [the] same in marching along
> the path towards their wishful goal.

The state media also refers to Aung San Suu Kyi as the head of the Byama (Brahma), after she supposedly contributed to ruining economic progress after her release in 1995.

> Persons who are called the Byamma's Head always get angry as soon as they
> know their nickname. . . . I can't be certain whether Mrs. Aris would be
> angry or take pride if she were called the Byamma's Head. But she has surely
> become the terribly hot Byamma's Head right after the restriction was

revoked. . . . Even though you are being held by golden hands, your terrible heat will melt them down as you are the Byamma's Head. So, you'd better leave this nation. As citizens, we are demanding deportation of Mrs. Aris. The only word we have to say to you is "Get out." (Thant Ein Hmu 1998)

The Byama's Head refers to the myth underlying the Thingyan New Year festival, when Athi Brahma's head was cut off after he lost a bet with Sakka over a mathematical problem. His supernatural powers meant that his head was too hot to handle by ordinary mortals, and the day the head changes hands is New Year, with all its symbolism of cooling water.

The vilification of Aung San Suu Kyi in the state media is particularly

Figure 7.1. Anauk Medaw, also known as the Western Queen (Anauk Mibaya), seated on a lotus throne, nursing her baby (Source: Temple 1906)

interesting because it is not aimed at denying the supernatural characteristics attributed to her. They do not portray her simply as an ordinary person with political aspirations. If the supernatural qualities the Burmese military regime attribute to her are generally debased and based on negative roles, people are evidently more generous.

The fact that supernatural powers are not denied here also suggests that political power more generally is conceived, even legitimated by, a conjoining with certain cosmological events and supernatural powers. Its reverse—the appropriation of supernatural powers by the military—is clearly seen in the recent case of Gen. Khin Nyunt's "discovery" of several white elephants and his "successful" renovation of the Shwedagon pagoda, no doubt both clearly affirmations of his royal aspirations.

The Buddha could have become a universal king; indeed kings are conceived of as bodhisattva. Nat also have many of the powers of royalty, but they are of a lower order and subject to royal authority. To turn Aung San Suu Kyi into a nat suggests that the military regime, which after all conceives of itself in terms of the role of kingship, should be able to command her. This would not quite be the case if she were considered a bodhisattva. So it is in their interest not to have her perceived as some entity they do not control.

Some of the publications written about Aung San Suu Kyi by foreign media and aimed at foreign audiences have been equally extreme, also playing on themes such as spiritism, spirituality, and fate. For example, in *Vanity Fair* she has been characterized as "Burma's Saint Joan" (ASSK 1997:9). She is also referred to as "Burma's Woman of Destiny." Although Buddhist writer Alan Clements has asked many interesting questions, he does sometimes excessively overemphasize her, and her father's, spiritual side, such as when he suggests that Aung San was a "spiritual seeker" (ASSK 1997:1) or when he asks whether she turned her house arrest into a "monastic-like life" (ASSK 1997:104).

Barbara Victor (1998:222) argues that Aung San Suu Kyi's supporters are responsible for creating her supernatural image. Foreign media often see this as problematic for a political leader, and journalists sometimes complain that she does not distinguish her personal identity from her political image. Clearly the "spiritual" aspects of Aung San Suu Kyi's political *modus operandi* sit uneasily with Western commentators who view politics as an inherently secular domain and who have little or no understanding of alternative models, even if these have been in place for a very long time.

> According to several journalists, *The Lady* (as she is popularly known) takes umbrage if she is challenged on any specific issue or position. She becomes haughty, they say, retreating behind an academic snobbism that tends to intimidate and discourage people from approaching her. A journalist from

Time magazine recalls that when she asked a question that Aung San Suu Kyi perceived to be challenging, her response was to rise and exit. "One of her aides came in and just announced that The Lady had a previous appointment," the journalist says, "and the interview was over." (ibid.)

Some journalists have been antagonized by this cocktail of holy imagery. For example, Lintner (1997) wrote that

> [Aung San] Suu Kyi's almost mystical streak makes her writings, and books about her, different from those about and by other democratic leaders who have spent time in prison, such as Nelson Mandela, Vaclav Havel or Mahatma Gandhi, who was but a saint and a shrewd politician. . . . These three books show that Suu Kyi is indeed a good saint but . . .

Lintner goes on to criticize Aung San Suu Kyi's lack of detailed economic planning for action in Burma and argues that this "may fail to prevent more martyrs being made by the kangaroo courts of Burma." In other words, playing her saintly role leads her to neglect the hands-on style of leadership required for a good politician.

This critique of Burmese political leaders from the West is not uncommon. It echoes the criticism that Burma's only democratically elected prime minister, U Nu, received when in government in the late 1950s and early 1960. Maung Maung (1963:65–66), for example, represented U Nu's Buddhist and Nat spirit beliefs and rhetoric as constituting evidence of "a Gandhi without Gandhi's predilection for politics."

Her followers are unwilling to allow the "deconstruction" of Aung San Suu Kyi herself, and permit only engagement of the junta's criticism. Supporters argue that the military regime makes use of the slightest criticism of Aung San Suu Kyi for its own ends and thus are critical of negative reports about Aung San Suu Kyi's political style that appear in the foreign media. The regime, on the other hand, pretends that *any* criticism of its actions is "foreign"-instigated and an illegitimate form of interference. Democracy is only acceptable when it is "Myanmar democracy" that conforms to "Asian values," and the arbiters of these values are the army commanders.

Religious Rhetoric as Political Method

Aung San Suu Kyi (1995:174, 237–238) herself has not been without input into what effectively has become a personality cult around her leadership; it cannot be simply dismissed as solely a creation of her situation or her commentators. She views the human condition as "trying to gain enlightenment and to use the wisdom gained to help others," and that "while we can't all be Buddhas, I feel a responsibility to do as much as I can to realize enlightenment to the degree that I can, and to use it to relieve the suffering of others" (1997: 148). Her highest personal goal is "purity" in a "spiritual" sense (1997:28), which is related to the purity of an arahant (1997:31). Though she has denied being a "female bodhisattva" (1997:9–10), she greatly emphasizes the development of mettā, one of the Ten Perfections *(pāramī)* practiced by bodhisattva, and she admits to meditating. Aspiring to mental perfection, and believing that only incessant self-perfection permits a political leader to be worthy of respect, she has used the concept of saint for herself, though in a metaphorical sense, as part of the neverending struggle for perfection that musicians and artists strive for in an imperfect world (1997:61).

Aung San Suu Kyi (1998a) evidently realizes that a cult has grown around her and that she has had some hand in its growth. She is aware of the attitude of much of the foreign media to the infusion of the political with the religious and supernatural in Burma, and she has responded to the regime's personal attacks on her by saying she finds them "less disconcerting than articles or speeches that attribute me with vaguely saintlike qualities." Such practice, she contends, runs counter to democracy. Quoting one of the drafters of the Constitution of India, she makes the argument that "hero worship is a sure road to degradation and to eventual dictatorship," and, in her own words, she says that "there is no room for hero-worship in a true political struggle made up of human beings grappling with human problems." But in this very same article in which she seeks to moderate the public image of her spirituality, she cannot avoid using the metaphor "dark nights of the political soul," an evident play on St. Teresa of Avila's contemplative experiences of the *Night of the Soul.*

> When I am asked what sustains me in the dark nights of the political soul,
> I am inclined to answer: "understanding, compassion, friendship." This is
> perhaps not the kind of answer the questioners want. Perhaps they would
> rather hear about mysterious inner resources, some wonderful inspiration,
> some memorable experience that gives us the strength to withstand the
> hardships of the human lot. But our powers of endurance are slowly and
> painfully developed through repeated encounters with adversity.

Mettā and Thamanya

Mettā, or "loving-kindness," is the most important form of meditation in Aung San Suu Kyi's thought, and she has used it persistently throughout her writing since her house arrest (1997:ix, 3, 11, 17, 133; 1997b 3–5,17, 21, 32, 56,

66, 90, 118, 122, 133–134, 143). Karuna, or "compassion," comes close second in frequency (1997:3, 17–18, 56, 238–239). Mettā is also the most important quality of Burmese culture that Aung San Suu Kyi wishes to see preserved in the future (1997:56), and in that respect she is not alone, for in the book *The history of Burmese culture* it is argued that this is the foundation of Burmese culture as influenced by Buddhism (Theikpan Sòyin 1976:148).

The emphasis placed on mettā by Aung San Suu Kyi, and indeed the NLD leadership as a whole, is not some liberal ideal, but a part of mental culture. It is a strong political concept with rich local cultural connotations and historical precedents that Burmese find easy to understand. As Aung San Suu Kyi (1997:143–144) has put it, "Some people might think it is either idealistic or naïve to talk about mettā in terms of politics, but to me it makes a lot of practical good sense."

The most successful role model of mettā held up by Aung San Suu Kyi is described in the first four chapters of *Letters from Burma*. These deal with her 4 October 1995 visit to U Vinaya, better known as Thamanya Sayadaw, who lived at first on Thamanya mountain in Pa-an, but until his demise in November 2003 lived at the foot of this mountain. This was the first visit Aung San Suu Kyi made outside her home immediately after her release from house arrest. Another visit was made shortly after her second release. Thamanya Sayadaw is of some significance to the "spiritual warfare" occurring between the junta and the NLD. Having almost 4,000 Karen refugees living around him, and living in an area that has not been under full government control since 1948, he publicly criticized the military council and openly expressed support for Aung San Suu Kyi.

The Thamanya Sayadaw was a Pa-o monk held in great regard by the Burmese, as described in U Sandima's (1993a) *Events in the life of Thamanya Mountain Hsayadaw*. The history of the mountain resort where he lived is described in *Serene pinnacle of Thamanya Mountain* (1993b). I myself briefly visited the Thamanya in early July 1998, taking the bus from Rangoon in the early evening and arriving at Pa-an early the next morning. From there the Thamanya mountain resort was an hour's bus ride. During my visit some of the Thamanya's attendants took me around the projects, including two schools, the many monasteries and retreats on top of the mountain, and the monasteries below. The grounds owned by the sayadaw cover a three-mile radius around the mountain, where about 7,000 families live. The sayadaw owns twenty-two vehicles, including heavy-duty trucks used for various construction projects, the building and maintenance of roads, and various communal utilities.

Thamanya's most distinctive emphasis is on mettā. It is said that people originally came mainly to receive the sayadaw's mettā, but in recent years people mostly came because of poverty in the on-going financial crisis. Increasingly wealthy business people—both women and men—have come over the last year. This suggests that mettā is becoming more commercialized as the free market takes hold of Burma. When I asked him about this, the sayadaw did not emphasize the donors, but said that it was a single monk for whom this entire empire was built up.

The Thamanya Sayadaw, however, was clearly himself also a product of the political and economic situation. He is viewed as a monk who contributed to the well-being of all those who visited him, and to their businesses. In this sense pilgrims viewed him as a "productive" monk. This explains why he collected such enormous wealth, which he redistributed to the destitute. I met several young children there, for example, who had either run away from home or whose parents had abandoned them. In addition to receiving mettā, they get as much free food as they like, the financing for which comes from the wealthy. This is clearly a mechanism for redistribution in difficult times.

The military regime relies on approximately twenty monks whom they cultivate for their powers and occasionally invite to Rangoon. However, the greater the geographical distance between the monks and Rangoon, the more difficult it is to keep these monks tied to their patronage. On the other hand, the further away these monks are, the more useful they are to gain control over far-flung regions. The military was very keen on fostering a close relationship with the Thamanya Sayadaw, but he responded to their overtures by daring to criticize them quite openly. The stories about his powers are legion. Some have alleged he is a *yahanda* (worthy one), which would put him in the same category as Shin Arahant, the monk who assisted the Buddhist king Anawratha in his reform. During my visit, some of the Thamanya's attendants said he was "more than a weikza and more than a yahanda," suggesting that he is a kind of minor buddha.

Like many monks who practice samatha, Thamanya was a vegetarian. His power is readily conveyed through pictures distributed to pilgrims visiting him. For example, in Rangoon and Mandalay, the majority of taxi drivers have his picture or that of some other renowned samatha monk fixed against their windscreen for safety.

The sayadaw's mettā extended to his environment and shaped the community around Thamanya mountain, for today the people of Thamanya town eat only vegetarian food and only vegetarian food is sold in the food stalls. Visiting pilgrims eat vegetarian food for several days prior to their departure. I was accompanied by five people, all of whom were vegetarian for the duration of the trip. One had already spent a year eating vegetarian food according to the instructions of this same sayadaw. They do so in sympathy with the monk's emphasis on mettā (of which vegetarianism is part, since it is about avoiding the killing of sentient beings). His mettā was so great that he fed all who came to see him, without fail.

As Aung San Suu Kyi (1997:13) has noted, the people at Thamanya live in "a sanctuary ruled by the mettā of the Hsayadaw" and in "a domain of loving-kindness and peace." In criticizing the regime, she remarks how bad the roads become when one leaves Rangoon, yet how good they are in Thamanya Sayadaw's hands, "far superior to many a highway to be found in Rangoon." She describes the situation where the junta forces people to contribute labor to build roads, whereas the sayadaw achieved his works by voluntary contributions from the people. At Thamanya, "whenever the Hsayadaw goes through his domain people sink down on their knees in obeisance, their faces bright with joy."

At the two schools surrounding Thamanya Sayadaw's monastery, 375 children are taught by 13 teachers, without basic resources such as books. Aung San Suu Kyi (ibid.) concludes that the monk's works "are upheld by the donations of devotees who know beyond the shadow of a doubt that everything that is given to him will be used for the good of others. How fine it would be if such a spirit of service were to spread across the land." Her conclusion to this piece sums up her interest in mettā:

> Some have questioned the appropriateness of talking about such matters as *metta* (loving-kindness) and *thissa* (truth) in the political context. But politics is about people and what we had seen in Thamanya proved that love and truth can move people more strongly than any form of coercion.

This suggests an important criticism of the regime, which can only pretend to have mettā in their slogans. It also suggests that wherever the destitute look for refuge in mettā, monks who partake of this quality, such as the Thamanya Sayadaw, become extremely powerful figures. That most taxi drivers have photos of Thamanya Sayadaw in their cabs, but not of the Burmese generals, suggests that if the military want to extend their influence, they must come to terms with such compassionate monks. The result of such popularity is the devotion of an enormous amount of resources to these monks and the pledging of voluntary labor, which has significant political value, particularly when contrasted to the regime's use of forced labor.

Aung San Suu Kyi's initial intention appeared to have been to visit a monk greatly respected by both the people and members of the regime, with the aim of working towards reconciliation. Some even speculated that she met with some high-ranking military officials at Thamanya in preparation for future dialogue. A senior advisor close to her father supposedly even suggested she pay her respects to Ne Win. The idea was that although they may not be able to reconcile formally, they might be able to arrange a Buddhist ceremony where they could meet informally. Soon after returning from her visit, Aung San Suu Kyi held a ceremony to mark Buddhist Lent day, and included among the invited guests was General Ne Win, though he did not attend (Aung Zaw 1995).

The many informal stories of the meeting between Aung San Suu Kyi and Thamanya Sayadaw have turned her into something of a heroine in opposition to the regime, and these stories are still recounted by Burmese people today, even years later. Though many of the stories are obviously mythical, they invariably demonstrate Aung San Suu Kyi's spiritual upper hand over the now-deposed Prime Minister Khin Nyunt. Such stories include the following:

1. The sayadaw manages, through his superior *jhānas,* to enter her compound despite all of the guards and is able to talk freely to Aung San Suu Kyi, and although Khin Nyunt has repeatedly invited the sayadaw to Rangoon, he refused to come.
2. Khin Nyunt visited U Thamanya shortly after Aung San Suu Kyi did. U Thamanya came down the mountain to meet Aung San Suu Kyi and later invited her to come back and visit again. In contrast, Khin Nyunt had to walk up the mountain by himself, and he was not invited back. He tried to give U Thamanya a van, but U Thamanya said that monks don't need vans, and told him to take it back.
3. The sayadaw spoke out openly in support of Aung San Suu Kyi's efforts when they met; he openly reprimanded Khin Nyunt.
4. The sayadaw permitted his picture to be taken with Aung San Suu Kyi but not with Khin Nyunt.
5. Khin Nyunt was only given a brief audience with the sayadaw, but Aung San Suu Kyi was given over an hour.
6. When Khin Nyunt tried to start his car as he was leaving, he couldn't. He had to go back up to Thamanya Sayadaw and ask for help. The sayadaw told him that when he stopped being angry, his car would start. Finally, after a period, Khin Nyunt was able to start the car. Such an incident did not happen to Aung San Suu Kyi during her visit.

Aung San Suu Kyi's (1997:134) emphasis on mettā and her involvement with samatha practice is clearly significant in her image as a powerful politician with the Burmese people. Since they have renounced violence, it can only be mettā that remains for the democracy movement and the NLD to hold itself together:

Our League may be a democratic one but we are not an organization that is unjust or repressive to others. If there are any grudges that stem from the past between our party members and the people, we will resolve them. At this time, as I have said, our party is thriving on Metta. We have no power, we have no weapons. We also don't have much money. There is also the matter of that eighty thousand dollars . . . (laughter). What are our foundations? It is Metta. Rest assured that if we should lose this Metta, the whole democratic party would disintegrate. Metta is not only to be applied to those that are connected with you. It should also be applied [to] those who are against you. Metta means sympathy for others. Not doing unto others what one does not want done to oneself. It means not obstructing the responsibilities of those [who have] Metta. It not only means not wanting harm to befall one's own family, but also not wanting harm to befall the families of others. So our League does [not] wish to harm anyone. Let me be frank. We don't even want to harm SLORC. But SLORC also doesn't want to harm us. Our Congress has come this far because we have managed to reach a degree of understanding with the authorities. I would like to say from here that I thank the authorities for making things possible since this morning. We do not find it a burden to give thanks where thanks are due. Not is it a burden to give credit where credit is due. So it is not true that we do not give thanks or credit where it is due. There will be thanks where thanks is due, credit where credit is due . . . so be good. One is never over-cautious. This is a Buddhist philosophy.

We are not working solely for the benefit of our party. We are not working to gain power. It is true, we are working for the development of democracy. Because we believe that it is only a democratic government that could benefit the country. Let me make it clear that it is not because we want to be the government. And also because we believe that it is only the people that have the right to elect a government. That is why we asked that the government be made up of people that were elected by the people. Not because we want power. Power only gives stress. Power comes with responsibility and I believe that anyone who understands that cannot be power-crazy. I know how much responsibility goes with a democracy. That is why we are not power-crazy people. We are only an organization that wants to do its utmost for the people and the country. We are an organization that is free from grudge and puts Metta to the fore.

Aung San Suu Kyi gives the regime a choice of fulfilling one of two roles. They can be a Devadatta, the ever-scheming detractor of Buddha who does not respond to or generate mettā, who is unwilling to listen to advice, and who is incapable of attaining enlightenment until the time of death. Or they can be an Angulimala, the fearsome killer and mutilator, who, while attempting to kill the Buddha, is transformed by mettā and achieves enlightenment at that very moment, and who ends up making a constructive contribution to the monastic community of which he became part, even attaining arahatship (see Figure 7.2). This is an important element in the "revolution of the spirit."

Reaffirming Party Politics

Aung San Suu Kyi has repeatedly sought to minimize her designation as a "big leader" *(gaungzaunggyi)* or an "extraordinary" person (1997:62), or as a saint or female bodhisattva (1997:9). She tells her followers (1997:212–213) not to "... think that I will be able to give you democracy. I will tell you frankly, I am not a magician. I do not possess any special power that will allow me to bring you democracy. I can say frankly that democracy will be achieved only by you, by all of you." Her party colleagues have also regularly denied that she is, or indeed pretends to be, a saint (Aung San Suu Kyi 1995:270). In interviews, she has frequently and very strongly suggested that democratic change should involve the democracy movement as a whole, and not involve her as the per-

Figure 7.2. The power of *mettā* can be seen when the Buddha overcomes the killer Angulimala with his *mettā*. Angulimala cut off his victims' fingers, which are shown around his neck. (Source: Temple 1906)

sonality representing it (ASSK 1995:249). When described as representing Burma in interviews, Aung San Suu Kyi (1995:255) clearly stated that "we must not emphasize this personality business."

It was evident from the party resolutions of the NLD conference held between 27–29 September 1997, how the NLD was internally concerned about the image projected and was working towards avoiding personality cults, in part as a response to such accusations. Such action is reminiscent of her father, Aung San. He wanted to discourage the popular perception, encouraged by writers such as Thakhin Kodawhmaing, which attributed to him the role of concentration meditation wizard, the mental cultivator *cum* universal ruler. He said in his first Anti-Fascist People's Freedom League (AFPFL) conference speech that everyone should "take proper care that we do not make a fetish of this cult of hero-worship" (Aung San 1971:25). And nine months later, in a 1 September 1946 speech, he said that ". . . at this time I am a person who is very popular with the public. But I am neither a god, wizard or magician. Only a man. Not a heavenly being, I can only have the powers of a man (Aung San 1971:140, cited in Aung San Suu Kyi 1991:28).

Despite being satisfied about the working of political parties after the AFPFL victory in the Constituent Assembly election on 17 April 1947, Aung San stated that "the masses have supported the AFPFL on an organizational basis and not on [a] personalities basis" and that "the standard of Burma politics has risen" (Silverstein 1993). There is no doubt, though, that Aung San's personality was as crucial an element in the vote for the AFPFL as was Aung San Suu Kyi's in the vote for the NLD. Indeed, Aung San Suu Kyi, whose popularity rests on Aung San's political personality, inherited the very "personality problem" her father encountered and the dangers of martyrdom.

To understand the issue of legitimation and electoral eligibility in politics, we need to understand a great deal more than just the technicalities of human rights discourse and of political representation. We need to delve into the way in which Burmese politics does not usually resemble the kind of secular politics as we might recognize, one that is unaffected by cosmology and supernatural forces. Secularity, and emancipation from secularity on the path to perfection of the person, is an extremely important dimension of Burmese politics. As we can see, there is clearly an attempt to sacralize and demonize democracy at one and the same time, and various kinds of supernatural forces are portrayed as bearing witness, or taking sides, in a battle over where the country should go from here.

The regime may have employed the Anauk Medaw image as one of "secularity" in an attempt to taint Aung San Suu Kyi's image. However, Anauk Medaw is usually portrayed as a queen compassionately nourishing a child in one of the early royal dynasties. Though subject to the authority of the king, such a nurturing image can only add to the perception many Burmese proclaim of the swollen left breast of the Buddha image. This overlaying of imagery suggests electoral eligibility of a woman in power, much in the way that eleven other women—including in Indonesia, the largest Muslim nation in the world—have come into the presidency and premiership since the Second World War in South and Southeast Asia as daughters and wives of national heroes.

Note

1. Young Burman nationalists started to use "thakin" (master) in 1928 in front of their names in response to the way English colonialists were referred to. This became a political movement that Aung San joined in the late 1930s.

-8-

The Chicken and the Scorpion

Rumor, Counternarratives, and the Political Uses of Buddhism

Keiko Tosa

In this chapter I analyze the meaning and content of rumors current in Burma at the beginning of the 1990s. Several years after its defeat in a general election, the military regime began to look to Buddhism as a form of moral legitimacy in order to retain political power. The period from 1990 until Aung San Suu Kyi's release from house arrest in July 1995 was one of ascendancy for the military regime (Fink 2001:78). In conditions of military repression, opinions about the regime are likely to be expressed in rumor. Skidmore (2003a: 13) has pointed out that rumor in urban Burmese spaces has become a form of broader discourse. I propose that rumors constitute "popular resistance" under the strict control of speech censorship and that they decode the moral legitimacy of the regime by the folk rubric of *lawkī pyinnya* (lit. "this-worldly knowledge").

Historically, a great many rumors regarding the successive military regimes[1] have existed in the public sphere, a prevalent one being that former Gen. Ne Win's absorption in astrology was such that the economic fortunes of the country lay in the hands of fortunetellers during the Burma Socialist Programme Party (BSPP) period (1962–1988). These kinds of rumors have not, however, been regarded as reliable resources for research, especially in the fields of political science and economics. On the other hand, many anthropologists collect village rumors and use them as legitimate informant discourse.[2] Such ethnography has largely been conducted in relatively small communities where rumors can be easily confirmed, and it is not difficult to identify those transmitting rumors. In urban areas, however, it is difficult, if not impossible, to know the origin and extent of a rumor.

Rumor has been an object of study in sociology and as a form of urban folklore.[3] Morin, for example, defines rumor as a false story. He bases his argument on an analysis of Jewish trafficking of women in New Orleans as a story without any real basis (Morin 1980). Kapferer defines rumor more broadly as "the emergence and circulation in society of information which is not publicly confirmed by official sources or denied by them" (Kapferer 1990:13). He denies that an absolute reality exists in any society, emphasizing instead that truth-value is not of primary import for rumors and that reality is essentially social and exists in the place where it obtains the greatest social consensus. In this sense the creation and dissemination of Burmese rumor is truly a social act, one in which reality is contested and daily remade in the public domain.

The rumors examined here were collected in Rangoon in 1991–1992, when I was conducting research on the religious practices of *gaing* membership and belief. Gaing is a term referring to a group of people organized around a founder who is known as a *weikza* (see below). Street rumors were commonly being discussed not only within my group of informants but also by the people around them, and it became clear that rumor was playing an important role for urban people. I checked on the veracity and circulation of the rumors in the central Kamayut township where I lived, and in the Ye Kyaw ward of distant Mingala Taung Nyun township where I conducted research. I asked about these rumors among a diverse range of informants including civil servants, office workers, merchants, shopkeepers, publishers, and also among people regarded as having expertise in lawkī pyinnya. I did not discuss rumors that I had heard, but instead waited for my informants to volunteer specific rumors.

Among the many topics of Burmese rumors, in this chapter I focus upon a significant and prevalent kind of counterpolitical rumor that combines resistance to the regime with "traditional" folk knowledge and techniques such as astrology, omens, and *yadaya* (a technique for manipulating the results of astrology or portents). These forms of knowledge and practice have been documented in previous Burmese studies and in the ethnographic record.[4] Astrology is consistently mentioned in these rumors concerning political power, particularly those rumors involving members of the ruling military council. Folk knowledge such as astrology is included in the broad category of lawkī pyinnya in Burma, but very little attention has been paid to this category of knowledge. This is not owing to an omission by scholars but is rather a reflection of the fact that it is rarely spoken of in daily life.

This said, however, in locales where Buddhist ideology is dominant, Burmese people admit to a particular distinction between the everyday reality of the mundane world *(lawkī)* and *lawkottara,* otherworldly or "more Buddhist" events and issues. When people engage in practices focused upon lawkī, that is, the affairs of this world, they do so on the assumption that it is not the same as, and exists in contrast with, Buddhist praxis, which is oriented toward otherworldly aims. In the remainder of this chapter, I explain the content of lawkī pyinnya (and the lawkī/lawkottara dichotomy) before turning to an analysis of the political rumors of the 1990s. The rumors I examine here centrally involve lawkī pyinnya, and they show how delicate resistance is encapsulated in this particular fusion of Burmese discourses.

Tea Circles: The Location of Rumor

Katsumi Tamura (1997:122), in a discussion of human relations in a village of Upper Burma, describes the *lahpet waing,* or "tea circle," where villagers gather and talk while drinking Burmese tea. When farmers finish working in their fields for the day and in the evenings after dinner, individual groups of men, women, and some mixed sex groupings of the same generation meet together. The tea circles are the locations in which villagers exchange information such as future farming plans and news heard on the radio as well as current village rumors.

In Rangoon similar tea circles exist in teashops, markets, and workplaces. Markets are always crowded and full of people from early in the morning to late afternoon, and most of the customers are women. They call in at their regular shops and meet shopkeepers, friends, and neighbors, with whom they converse and gossip. Such exchanges are usually marked by brevity as they occur in the space between market transactions. Teashops, in contrast, are places to sit and talk for long periods. People seem to enjoy the conversation much more than the drinking of tea and coffee. Teashops have traditionally been male spaces, and it is only since the latter half of the 1980s that women have increasingly frequented teashops.

Within urban teashops there are a series of unspoken rules that guide political discussion and the exchange of rumors regarding the regime. These rules are based upon the well-known fact that military intelligence personnel are present in teashops. Burmese people are understandably nervous when talking about politics in public. The discussion of political rumors that cautiously began to occur in tea circles in the early 1990s corresponded with the beginning of arrests of members of the National League for Democracy (NLD) and the coercion of remaining members to denounce the party. Even those people with no direct relation to the NLD were extremely careful when talking about politics and did so in lowered voices. Individual members of tea circles surreptitiously checked the membership of their own circle and the teashop in general, before turning to delicate topics. Tea circle members usually associate only with members of their own group except on occasions when word is received about new or important emerging events. During my field-work, rumors about the regime and senior military officers constituted one of the dominant teashop discourses. The political rumors tended to involve moral dichotomies such as the military versus the pro-democracy movement.

Rumor and State Media

There is a considerable distance between the information-oriented societies that are the subject of most sociology and the society that I discuss here. In Burma, access to information has been strictly controlled for more than forty years. There is a relationship in any society between the degree of media free-dom and pluralism and the prevalence of rumor. Following the 1962 coup of Gen. Ne Win, an attempt was made to control all publications within Burma. At the time, there were a variety of renowned newspaper publishing compa-nies such as *Hantha-wadi, Kyemon,* and the *New Light of Burma.* These com-panies were nationalized after 1964 and the Ne Win regime, known as the Burma Socialist Programme Party (BSPP), established strict censorship laws under the Department of Information. Television broadcasting began in 1980 and was managed by a single, state-run station. News of domestic policies and the outside world became very limited and coincided with a dramatic eco-nomic downturn that made printed material very scarce.

At the peak of the Democracy Summer of 1988, a number of journals and papers, exercising freedom of speech, were published without official permis-sion. However, with the formation of the State Law and Order Restoration Council (SLORC) following the repression of the pro-democracy uprising, all private publications were banned. Later the regime was to issue one single printing permit to the *Loktha Pyithu Nayzin* (The working people's daily news).[5] There remained only one official television and radio broadcasting station.[6]

The restrictions upon international news have ultimately failed, as when the Nobel Committee announced the awarding of a Nobel Peace Prize to Aung San Suu Kyi in 1991. The state media carried no mention of this news, but one day after the announcement, most Burmese people were aware of the award. A great many people were illegally listening to shortwave radio broadcasts from abroad, particularly the British Broadcasting Company (BBC) and the Voice of America (VOA). Those people who did not listen to the radio person-ally heard the news from neighbors and friends. In the early 1990s the most reliable sources of information were undoubtedly the foreign radio broad-casts, and the subsequent rumors were conveyed orally.

Rumor is, of course, a political tool that can be employed by any side, and the military regime has used its media monopoly to deny political rumors or to put a different spin on them. In January 1992 a rumor began to spread throughout Upper Burma that a frog had gobbled up a snake. This occurrence is contrary to Burmese laws of nature and is traditionally interpreted as a bad omen, most especially as an omen predicting a revolution or an uprising against the ruling class. The interpretation of this omen comes originally from an episode of *Mahasupita Jataka* (J77: The dream of King Kosala), one of the stories of the former lives of the Buddha. King Kosala had sixteen strange dreams and asked a wise Brahmin to interpret them. "A frog gobbling up a snake" constituted the subject matter of the fourteenth dream. Most Buddhists know about the episode and its interpretation, even if not many people know the particular Jataka in much detail. The rumor gradually spread to Lower Burma. Finally, *Loktha Pyithu,* the only newspaper at that time, published the rumor as news on January 21. It inserted a photograph with the caption: "A frog swallowed whole a thumb-sized snake at the house of U Kyaw in Twe Kyaw, Sein Pan, Mandalay Anauk Daung Township, on November 30, in 1991." The following day the newspaper printed an enlarged photograph of the frog with the same caption. In addition, however, the paper also inserted a *mawgun*[7] poem, supposedly from a reader named Aung Zeyya. In his poem Aung Zeyya argues that as the frog was a Burmese variety, it is a good omen and signals the prosperity of the nation and the increased potential for Burmese people to make merit.

These kinds of "readers' contributions" now regularly appear in state media. Most readers do not think that they are real contributions, but believe instead that they are simply a more sophisticated form of propaganda designed to convey the regime's ideology in a roundabout way. The day after the poem appeared, many people were talking about this news and insisting that they never heard the interpretation made by Aung Zeyya and that the right interpretation should be the reverse instead. The great mass of public opinion was that a state-controlled newspaper had been used to reject the rumor and establish the "correct" interpretation of the event. This example shows not only that political rumors have considerable power and compete with the outpourings from the official media, but also that through the media the military council concede the power of rumor under censorship.

Lawkī Pyinnya

The frog gobbling up the snake is an example of the many prominent political rumors that have challenged the regime's moral legitimacy and which in turn have been manipulated by the military regime through the state press. In the remainder of the chapter, I describe and analyze five political rumors. To understand them however, it is necessary to understand the most common way in which Burmese people order their world, through the concept of lawkī pyinnya. Lawkī pyinnya means the following kinds of knowledge: (1) the interpretation of predictions (including *tabaung, sane, bawaw,* and *thaiksa*), omens or signs *(ateik, nameik),* and dreams *(einmet);* (2) cabbalistic squares or runes *(in, aing),* amulets *(let hpwe),* mantras *(mandaya),* and Pali verses *(ga-hta);* (3) astrology *(bedin);* (4) alchemy *(eggiyat);* and (5) indigenous or traditional medicine *(tain-yin hsay).*

All of these are considered "this-worldly knowledge," forms of knowledge that contrast with "otherworldly knowledge" or lawkottara pyinnya (Pali: *lokuttara pañña).* In Theravādan societies the dichotomy between lawkī (this world) and lawkottara (other world) is of vital importance. Lawkottara pyinnya is knowledge necessary for attaining Nirvana and the learning of Buddhist scripture, while lawkī pyinnya is knowledge that can be used to obtain power in this earthly realm. In this sense, modern (Western) education and technical knowledge falls under the rubric of lawkī pyinnya.

Specialists such as astrologers *(bedin hsaya)* and alchemists *(eggiyat hsaya)* practice and transmit lawkī pyinnya. Gaing members and monks also convey lawkī pyinnya, although they do not necessarily study a particular branch of folk knowledge as an occupational specialty. Gaing are people organized around a *weikza* (Pali: *vijja),* a term that originally meant "knowledge," or "the person who holds knowledge," and referred to an expert in a particular branch of lawkī pyinnya, such as astrology, alchemy, or healing. A gaing is thus an organization that initiates its members into the world of lawkī pyinnya. Following initiation, new gaing members are introduced by a teacher to the secret knowledge conveyed by the founder. Not all founders are still alive and in fact, many gaings perpetuate the knowledge of a particular weikza or *htwetyat pauk,* who has "gone out."[8]

One of the largest gaing, Shwe Yin Kyaw, rapidly expanded in the 1970s and its membership included army and civil service personnel. In 1979 Ne Win outlawed gaing activities and gaing were shut down, at least publicly. However, many gaing continue to exist and convey lawkī pyinnya knowledge, including knowledge of cabbalistic squares, alchemy, magical healing, and particular ritual methods by which gaing members believe they will eventually become weikza.

Much of the knowledge that is lawkī pyinnya resides with monks, although orthodox monks distance themselves from knowledge of this-worldly affairs as much as possible. Theoretically, the sangha (monastic order) should be concerned only with lawkottara, not with lawkī pyinnya.[9] Lawkī knowledge seems to be more common among monks belonging to the Thudhamma sect than among those belonging to the more orthodox Shwegyin sect. Many monks have acquired this knowledge, but most are unwilling to make this public because of the religious norm.[10]

To increase the power of their techniques, many gaing hsaya use such Buddhist practices as meditation and chanting sutras and call these practices the "lawkottara way." They sometimes criticize rival gaing as being too involved with affairs of lawkī, compared with their own practices. On the other hand, most gaing hsaya define themselves as being intimately associated with lawkī compared with the more "lawkottara way" that constitutes the practices of monks.[11] In everyday usage, individual techniques included under the lawkī pyinnya rubric exist separately and are seldom regarded as one encompassing category or field of knowledge. However, it emerges as a particular category of knowledge and practice when it is necessary to make distinctions about the relationship that a practitioner or adherent has with Buddhism.

Even though they are rarely seen as fitting together in a unified system of knowledge, the techniques of lawkī pyinnya do possess common features and specialists of individual techniques insist that connections exist between many of the techniques. Indigenous medical practitioners, for example, are required not only to learn about medicinal herbs but also to understand astrology and alchemy in order to become outstanding healers.

Three phases are contained within the term lawkī pyinnya.[12] They are: to "grasp a basic law," to "interpret" based upon the law, and to "operate" the result of such an interpretation.[13] Each technique within the lawkī pyinnya framework involves two or three of these processes. For example, alchemy is based upon the law that every metal corresponds with an element *(dat)* and a planet, and that through a certain manipulation based on the rules existing between the elements, a metal or other physical objects can also be reconfigured. In Burma, alchemists most often strive to transmute metals into different substances such as gold, usually with the ultimate aim of producing a dat-lon with supernatural power (a philosopher's stone). The result of "operating" upon the connections that exist between metals, elements, and planets is the *dat-lon* and, like amulets and charms, it can change the future by eliminating disease or changing fortune.

The use of cabbalistic charms *(in)* is based upon the same law. There are various kinds of in, but one of the more orthodox forms consists of a piece of paper divided into squares on which various kinds of cabbalistic symbols are written, usually in the Burmese alphabet. The alphabet, converted to planets and elements, is arranged in a form to keep all dat, (that is, the basic elements) in the most stable form. The arrangement is flexible, and it is possible to write a charm to strengthen a specific element, if needed. This is a way to "operate" dat. There is not only a clear connection between these techniques, but there is a common orientation toward, or recognition of, the basic properties of the Burmese universe, even though individual practitioners may manipulate different aspects of lawkī pyinnya. Underlying this common mode of manipulation of elements, cosmology, and portents, is a belief central to lawkī pyinnya —no events occur in this world without there being a reason for that occurrence. The reason an event occurs, and the event itself, are mutually constituted; the particular reason for an event is what gives the event its visible manifestation in the world. This is a temporal feedback loop where the occurrence of the present or the future is presaged in a certain form in the present event. Astrology is a form of knowledge that relies on macrocosms, on particular events in the present in which astrologers can read the shape of the future. It is based on a series of formulations that causally relate the changing configuration of the stars and planetary bodies to the existence and well-being of animate and inanimate objects on the earth. Interpreting omens or signs is similarly a form of knowledge manipulation that relies on the relation of events that occur on the earth, such as a frog eating a snake, or a figure occurring to a person in a dream, or the existence of a prophetic rumor. In each of these portents, there is a recognition that the shape of the future is discernible in the connections between events and the reason for those connections to occur.

On the other hand, all things in the world are constituted by the most basic material of existence (dat). All things will continue to exist in their present form, in an unchanging way, as long as the basic elements (themselves constituted by dat) are maintained in perfect harmony. Usually four elements (four dat: wind, fire, earth, and water) are emphasized as the basic elements. Before constructing large or public buildings such as pagodas or hospitals, the ritual to place symbolically all four basic elements on the ground *(ok-myit cha bwe)* is requested as the necessary process of construction. Dat is not just the stuff from which animate or inanimate bodies are made: it also constitutes the nature of the relationships between elements and larger structures, such as bodies, and complex events that are made from the elements.

Rumor and Lawkī Pyinnya

The majority of the Burmese people understand these basic formulations of the way the mundane world works and the causal relationships central to this logic. J. G. Scott (Shway Yoe 1989[1910]:8–9), also known as Shway Yoe, resided in Burma at the end of the nineteenth century as a schoolmaster at St. John's College, Rangoon. He documented the following rhyme and noted that it was one of the first things boys learned in monastic schools: "Monday's number, I ween, is always fifteen; the tiger's the beast, and its place is the East." The rhyme is a mnemonic for understanding and remembering connections between the days of the week, the ten planetary bodies,[14] the guardian animals, the years when particular planets have influence over worldly affairs, and the points of the compass or the bearing that the planet occupies (called the "direction"). Even in the twentieth century the rhyme was commonly taught by monastic schools, but it is not taught under the present education system. The content of this rhyme, and many others like it, however, still exist as shared folk knowledge in oral memory.[15]

If an astrologer, for example, orders a client to make an offering "at the corner of Monday," most Burmese would understand what this means. In the larger Burmese pagodas, the eight corners of the pagoda base correspond to the eight days of the Burmese week (in the Burmese astrology, Wednesday is divided into two days, with Wednesday afternoon being Rahu), and also to eight bearings. The guardian animal of that day is sometimes also located at each corner. Thus as one circles the pagoda, each corner of the pagoda base visually depicts the connections that pertain between the days of the week, the planets, the bearings, and the guardian animals. There is another important technique, *kein* (lit. "number"), to convert a letter of the alphabet into a number, and by this means any entity known to the Burmese can be assigned to a numerological index and then to the other components (see Figure 8.1).

One of the most important oral traditions involves the connections that pertain between this system and the consonants of the Burmese alphabet. These consonants are grouped together into mnemonics that indicate the way in which Burmese infants should be named. Most Burmese name their child after the day on which they were born, according to this rule in which every letter of the alphabet corresponds to a particular day of the week. This means that when a Burmese person is introduced to someone, both parties can immediately tell the day of the week on which the other person was born. A Mon-

Number	1	2	3	4	5	6	7	8	9
Week	Sun	Mon	Tue	Wed	Thu	Fri	Sat	Yahu	Ketu
Planet	Sun	Moon	Mars	Mercury	Jupiter	Venus	Saturn	—	—
Element	Fire	Earth	Air	Water	Earth	Water	Fire	Air	
Guardian Animal	Garuda	Tiger	Lion	Tusked Elephant	Rat	Guinea Pig	Naga	Tuskless Elephant	
Year	6	15	8	17	19	21	10	12	
Direction	NE	E	SE	S	W	N	SW	NW	
Alphabet	Vowels	k, hk, g, hg, ng	s, hs, z, hz, ny	l, w, y	p, hp, b, hb, m	th, h	t, ht, d, hd, n	y, r	

Source: Tosa 2000:56

Figure 8.1. Connections between Numbers, Days of the Week, Planets, and Other Symbols

day-born person, for example, will have a name that begins with one of the following consonants: k, hk, g, hg, ng, and receive in his or her naming ceremony *(kin-bun tat)* a name such as Hkin Kyi or Ngwe Aung. Even people who know only the barest outline of the lawkī pyinnya system nevertheless have as part of their "common sense" view of how the world works the foundations of lawkī pyinnya. This process, where lawkī pyinnya knowledge has become reified as tacit knowledge, occurs throughout many domains of Burmese life.

This commonsense knowledge of how the Burmese world works, affects the diffusion and increases the potency of the political rumors described below. It is not necessary to be a lawkī pyinnya expert in order to find such rumors plausible; they are generated within a common cultural knowledge framework. It is this acceptance of political rumors because of their congruence with the logic of lawkī pyinnya that the military regime recognizes as the primary danger associated with the spread of such rumors.

The Chicken and the Scorpion

In September 1988 the military, led by Gen. Saw Maung, established a new government called the State Law and Order Restoration Council (SLORC) and appointed Brig. Gen. Khin Nyunt, the head of Military Intelligence, as the first secretary (S1). Many rumors and jokes began to spread about the new regime. One rumor suggested that the military regime was using the technique of "dat exchange" to change the political situation. This was the rumor: "With the National League for Democracy (NLD), led by Aung San Suu Kyi, becoming increasingly popular, the new regime appointed Khin Nyunt as S1. This was the regime's attempt to nullify the charismatic power of Aung San Suu Kyi through the technique of dat-exchange between the chicken and the scorpion."

Although it may initially sound nonsensical, this rumor made sense to most Burmese people in their various tea circle discussions. The parts of the name Suu Kyi begin with the consonants "s" and "k." "Suu" is a name derived from Tuesday's group that includes all names beginning with the consonants hs, s, z, hz, and ny, and "Kyi" is a name derived from Monday's group that must begin with k, hk, g, hg, or ng. Each consonant is synonymous with a particular celestial body, and the name Suu Kyi corresponds with Mars and Moon through the kein technique. Dat then works like simple arithmetic, or the basic rules of polarity, where a negative element can cancel out a positive element. The rumor implies that the appointment of Khin Nyunt strengthened the power of the regime against Suu Kyi because his name equates to Moon and Mars (the *k* is part of the Monday cluster and *n* belongs to the Tuesday cluster). The appointment of Khin Nyunt was thus aimed, according to the rumor, at neutralizing the power of Aung San Suu Kyi, and this does indeed constitute a plausible reading of the political situation throughout the early 1990s.

This rumor was the most prominent of a family of political rumors that used the same logic of dat translation to provide reasons for particular actions of the major political players. For example, in translating the names of generals such as Ne Win, the future course of that figure's relationship with the public, and with history in general, can be discerned. Ne Win translates, in the system converting the alphabet into a planet, to Saturn and Venus: Ne is involved in the Saturday group, which begin with the consonants of t, ht, d, hd, and n. Win falls under the influence of Wednesday, which has the consonants l, y, and w. "The public" *(ludu)* is translated as Venus and Saturn. This rumor implies that it was inevitable that the people would rise up against the dictatorship of Ne Win and that eventually his power would be neutralized. Again, this situation is believed to have come to pass as Ne Win was forced to resign in the aftermath of the Democracy Summer, but the people were not victorious either, as a new generation of dictators replaced him. A subsidiary rumor also circulated, which recast the suppression of the uprising by the feared riot police *(lon htein)*, for Lon Htein, like ludu, also corresponds to Venus and Saturn.

This exchange and method of accentuating or canceling out the effects of dat is known as *dat-yaik dat-hsin*. In this technique the names of objects are transferred into days of the week, then into planetary bodies, and finally into the most basic elements of dat. These elements of dat are then manipulated according to the laws that govern the elements. There are complicated formulas for the calculation of the correct time to manipulate the elemental combinations and for ascertaining the "friendly" *(meik-dat)*, versus "enemy" *(yan-dat)* elemental combinations.

The particular technique of dat-exchange used in these rumors is known as the "chicken and scorpion" *(kyet-kin dat pyaing)* technique. This does not pitch friendly elements against enemy elements but instead uses the same elements in an opposite fashion. The chicken *(kyet)* and the scorpion *(kin)* come under the influence of the same planetary body, the moon. Whichever of the two animals embarks upon a course of action first, that animal is believed to become the eventual winner. Implicit in the political rumors is the belief that the military strategists are using the chicken-and-scorpion technique.

In Burma there is no distinction made between first and last names. "Aung San Suu Kyi" is simply a name; it cannot be broken into constituent parts and have only some of the parts analyzed. The rumor does not explain why "Suu Kyi" was chosen as the elements to manipulate via the dat system. What is certain, however, is that once the interpretation was established as following the logic of the kyet-kin dat pyaing system, it gained plausibility and circulated widely.

Khin Nyunt's Female Impersonation

The following rumor circulated widely in 1991: "Some fortunetellers predicted that a woman would take a position of leadership. Then Maj. Gen. Khin Nyunt dressed up like a female actor and climbed along a hilltop. His subordinates called out three times to him, 'Ma Ma Nyunt' (elder sister Nyunt), to which he replied, 'Shin?' (lit. "you," which is a female term for reply), before turning around three times."

Most Burmese people believe that the regime performs yadaya.[16] When an astrologer determines that a negative event will happen in the future, yadaya is the name given to actions designed to change the future predicted by astrology, omens, or portents, and hence to change one's fortune. Yadaya is conducted under the auspices of the various lawkī pyinnya specialists. There are two kinds of yadaya: *bokda yadaya,* a manipulation of fate within a Buddhist idiom, and *lawkī yadaya,* a this-worldly manipulation of events to change the future. The former involves improving one's karma by acts of Buddhist merit-making such as the building of pagodas or monasteries, and through donations to the sangha and for the perpetuation of the *sāsana* (Buddha's teachings). The latter involves non-Buddhist methodologies.

Lawkī yadaya is either of the "evasion" or "invitation" variety. There are several forms of evasion. *Kein chay,* for example, creates an artificial replica of the foretold negative situation, and the prediction is realized through its imitation. Another method of evading foretold consequences is to "kill" an object that is comprised of the element of one's enemy (yan-dat, or kyet-kin dat). In this way the simulation works to fulfill the prediction, and in both of these cases the dangerous future that had been predicted is avoided. By contrast, invitation involves *yadaya hsin,* which is an attempt to invite a positive future event by imitating that which people hope will happen. In the dat system this is conceptualized as attracting the desirable future by luring it into the present using "friendly" elements.

The bizarre rumor about Khin Nyunt's female impersonation implies that the military regime is using the kein chay yadaya technique. By impersonating a woman, Khin Nyunt was attempting to create an artificial appearance of the prediction and thus, through imitating the prediction, to stop a "real" female leader from taking power. The actions described in the rumor were thus interpreted by the Burmese people as originating in the fear that the military junta has of the revolutionary leadership potential of Aung San Suu Kyi when she appeared on the political scene in 1988, and their need to use lawkī techniques to ensure that she would not come to national or enduring political prominence.

Pagoda-Building and Repair

In the wake of the 1990 general elections, many people were concerned about how the regime would respond to its loss in the elections and what shape its new policies would take. The SLORC did not announce its intentions and made no comment as to when, or if, they would hand power over to the democratically elected members of parliament. The media instead reported on an enormous quantity of donations by members of the military council to the sangha. In 1991 a prolific period of pagoda-building began. A Committee for Pagoda-Building and Repairing was established and it began to repair several famous pagodas.[17] The Committee invited donations from Buddhists to finance the reconstruction projects. The restoration process and the donation rituals, attended by monks and senior military officers, were reported daily in the state media. A rumor began to circulate that the Golden Façade project (a project of rebuilding urban locales and pagodas) was a form of yadaya conducted by the military council in order to strengthen its base of political power.

The building of pagodas is, for Theravādan Buddhists, an important method for gaining merit. Among the Theravāda societies, the people of Burma seem to lavish especial attention on pagoda-building. Like the Burmese dynasties of the Pagan period and later, kings, Independence heroes, and democracy leaders have all attached a special significance to pagoda-building. Burma's first and only democratically elected prime minister, U Nu, for example, built the World Peace pagoda, and Gen. Ne Win built the Maha-wizaya pagoda adjacent to the Shwedagon pagoda. The pagoda beautification project of the SLORC-SPDC follows in the same nation-building tradition. It establishes a claim to political legitimacy through moral (Buddhist) legitimacy as the state supports the perpetuation of the sāsana.

"Buddhist practice" is, however, a delicate concept. A practice seemingly based on Buddhism may be perceived as yadaya in another situation. For example, ordination as a monk is a crucial first step in order for men to attain Nirvana. However, for the great majority of men, who do not believe that full-time monastic life is for them, a temporary stay as a monk, such as when a boy is first ordained during a *shinbyu* ceremony, constitutes one of the best opportunities to make merit for a better rebirth. Crucially, this is also an opportunity for a man to transfer merit, made by becoming a monk, to his mother, thus creating an even greater store of merit, for giving away merit is even more meritorious than making the merit in the first place. In addition, by temporarily becoming a monk, a man is able to change his fate, especially if he suffers from bad fortune or is in bad health. In this case, his ordination is construed as a form of yadaya.

Gen. Ne Win's construction of the Maha-wizaya pagoda generated an enormous amount of public attention. The majority view was that this was not a Buddhist act, but an act of yadaya designed to allow Ne Win to remain in political power and have great longevity.[18] His death in late 2002, at age ninety-one, supports this interpretation, and the rumors that circulate about the motives behind the contemporary Golden Façade project use the same reasoning.

Saw Maung's Yadaya

Pagoda pilgrimages are similarly interpreted as yadaya rather than the propitiation of Buddhism. In 1991 Gen. Saw Maung, chairman of the SLORC, undertook a pilgrimage to sites of historical Buddhist significance, such as Mandalay and Pagan, visiting several pagodas with his family from December 1991 to January 1992. His journey was prominently reported in the state media each day.

A rumor circulated at the time that identified a possible motivation for the much-publicized pilgrimage and Saw Maung's fascination with the figure of King Kyanzittha Min to the point where he identified himself with the king. He was seen praying to the image of King Kyanzittha Min that sits beside a variety of Buddhist images at Pagan. Using the same chicken-and-scorpion logic as before, Saw Maung's actions were interpreted as a form of yadaya. Saw Maung was attempting to accentuate his own chance of success, and those of the military government in particular, by bringing together two elements with the same dat properties. That is, a soldier, a member of the military *(sittha)* who wishes to survive or remain *(kyan)*, is associating himself with a particular king *(kyanzittha)*. Saw Maung's travels throughout the country meant that he was the subject of a wide range of political rumors.

Another rumor involved his visit to the National Broadcasting Station (Myanmar Athan-hlwint Yon) on January 30, 1992. He greeted the station managers and while he was shaking hands, he was noticed to be holding Buddhist prayer beads. It is unusual to see military officials carrying prayer beads, especially when shaking hands at official functions. This fact was widely reported in the state media and caused a buzz of confusion and discussion in the Rangoon teashops. Shortly after the incident, a rumor spread throughout the city that black magic (*auk lan:* lit. the "lower road") had been applied to the prayer beads so that the journalists with whom Saw Maung shook hands would be compelled to become his allies and present news about him in a positive manner.

Chanting Sutta in a Helicopter

On that same day, January 30, many people noticed that a helicopter was repeatedly flying at a very low altitude over Rangoon. The following day, *Loktha Pyithu Nayzin* reported that several members of the most important sangha committees, including presidents and vice presidents of state, Rangoon division, and township division Sangha Maha Nayaka committees, had inspected Rangoon City by helicopter and that they had chanted the *Mangala sutta* (Blessing Discourse).[19] This sutta is a comprehensive summary of Buddha's teachings containing the thirty-eight rules for a beautiful life and is well known as one of the eleven *parittas* (protective sutta) which have great power, if chanted and listened to in the correct way, and can ward off dangers or harm.

The helicopter was seen by a great many urban residents, and there was no unified or even dominant view expressed through rumor as to the significance of the event. Many people told me that it is highly unusual for Buddhist monks to ride in helicopters and to be made to recite sutta in the air. One of my informants interpreted the event as a form of yadaya to change the future, because an earlier rumor had suggested that a prediction existed concerning a negative event that would shortly occur in Rangoon. The chanting monks may have been a way that the military council was seeking to avert the prophesied negative future of the city.

Rumor, Politics, and Religion

In the early 1990s it was thus an important matter as to how the Buddhist activities of ruling council members should be interpreted. Steinberg (2001: 44–46) argues that five foci have been used to legitimate various Burmese governments: nationalism, Buddhism, socialism, the military, and elections. After the pro-democracy uprising, it became clear that the socialist experiment had failed, and this was further emphasized by the clear victory of democratic forces in the 1990 election. The military turned to nationalism and Buddhism to strengthen its political and moral legitimacy.

The aim of Ne Win's religious policy was the unification of the various sangha sects, and this was attempted by hosting the Congregation of the Sangha of All Orders for Purification, Perpetuation, and Propagation of the

Sāsana in 1980. The government in the BSPP period seldom appealed to orthodox Buddhists via media coverage of the Buddhist actions of military leaders. But from the 1989 inception of the SLORC, the media has been used to give extensive coverage of Buddhist deeds by members of the military council and their wives. This includes donations to monks and their attendance at pagoda construction and opening ceremonies. The regime ordered the construction of Tooth Relic pagodas in Rangoon and Mandalay, and the Chinese Buddha's Tooth Relic was temporarily housed in the pagodas. In addition, the military council conferred titles upon members of the sangha at elaborate ceremonies.

Many Buddhists are embarrassed and feel ambivalent about this ostentatious military merit-making. On the one hand, they remember how the military fired upon an unarmed citizenry during the 1988 uprising, a violence that violates basic Buddhist tenets. On the other hand, the same military organization has begun performing meritorious Buddhist works.[20] Burmese people commonly argue about the possibility of lay people attaining merit from these military Buddhist deeds and about the feasibility of the military decreasing its collective karmic debt through these actions. Even though many people remain skeptical, there is no doubting the strength of the state media. The renewed state emphasis upon making merit and upon Buddhist practice has resulted in a general strengthening of Buddhist ideology throughout the country.

It was also at this time that a certain form of political satire appeared. Jokes such as "the television is full of yellow and green" and "the television might be broken because only yellow and green comes out," were common. A similar sentiment is expressed in the joke where a disgruntled customer complains to the shopkeeper where he bought his TV that "this is supposed to be a multicolored TV, but all I ever see is green and yellow" (Fink 2001:218). These jokes refer to the monotonous appearance of the khaki green of the Tatmadaw alongside yellow monks' robes in the state media.

Many people often clearly express the view that Buddhist works portrayed in the media are not really merit-making activities but rather are practices based upon lawkī pyinnya principles. The rumors occurred at a time when lawkī pyinnya practitioners were not being criticized, and it was considered normal for all sectors of the populace to draw upon lawkī pyinnya to create favorable circumstances. The Astrology Council continues to choose auspicious times for the staging of national events, and many generals routinely attend official occasions where lawkī pyinnya is necessary to the success of the event. The most common of these are the pagoda umbrella-hoisting ceremonies *(hti tin bwe)* and the cornerstone placement ritual *(ok-myit cha bwe)* for official and Buddhist buildings. Several gaing saya and lawkī pyinnya specialists are invited to these occasions. The relationships between the Astrology Council and the state, and between individual astrologers and members of the SPDC, remain strong.

Lawkī pyinnya was not the target of the political rumors of the early 1990s. Those rumors constituted an attempt to deconstruct the political uses of Buddhist ideology by seeing if the events recorded in the rumors could plausibly be explained by an alternate reading of the facts. This reading utilized lawkī pyinnya to test the common hypothesis that the rumored events were motivated by a quest for this-worldy political goals rather than other-worldy Buddhist ambitions.

Pagoda construction and repair are practices that accumulate great merit, but the rumors suggested that when seen through the lens of lawkī pyinnya logic, these activities constituted instead a form of yadaya. Secular political aims were suggested in each of the political rumors I have discussed. Saw Maung's visit to the broadcasting station was interpreted, in the rumors, to be an act of black magic, and requiring monks to recite sutta over Rangoon was also interpreted as the pretext of Buddhist practice while yadaya was being performed.

Even among a population that is 90 percent Buddhist, there was an attempt in tea circles to diversify the readings of apparent truth and motivational analysis so heavily censored by the regime and promoted in propaganda and other state media. It is difficult to know the psychological background of each individual who conveyed the rumors. However, we can guess that if a person conveys the rumors under the strong suppression of freedom of speech, he or she might do so because it seems plausible. Rumor is an important facet and method of conveying public opinion. Moreover it can be said to be a conscious form of resistance.

We should not think of lawkī pyinnya as simply magic, or another occult practice, but rather as a key conceptual framework by which the great majority of the Burmese people order, understand, and act upon the world. These rumors are not primarily about lawkī pyinnya, nor even about resistance. Fundamentally, these political rumors express the outrage that a predominantly orthodox Buddhist population feels towards the political use of Buddhist ideology. This outrage sits uneasily beside the knowledge that the kinds of Buddhist practices repeatedly displayed in the state media are the primary means by which Theravāda Buddhists follow the Path to Enlightenment.

The Burmese people may occasionally succeed in decoding the regime's uses of Buddhist ideology, and in doing so they may somewhat weaken the regime's power when it relies on moral legitimation gained through patronage of Buddhism. Those rumors that imply the regime is manipulating aspects of lawkī pyinnya, however, give rise to the suggestion that the regime is being protected through harnessing a power originating in lawkī pyinnya practice. In the final analysis, then, rumor is an ambivalent and weak weapon because in focusing upon and interpreting these political activities, the Burmese people cannot but help admit that the regime are masters of power.

Notes

I would like to thank Monique Skidmore for her perfect encouragement and significant suggestions on my draft. She also improved my English. I wish to thank Junko Koizumi for her helpful suggestions and careful reading of my Japanese draft.

1. Several other scholars have written about rumors in Burma. For example, Steinberg mentions the rumors about Ne Win and astrology (Steinberg 2001:5, 30), and Fink (2001) describes several political rumors in detail.

2. There have been descriptions of witches *(son, sonma)* in the ethnography of Burma (Nash 1965:177–180, Spiro 1967:24–28), and most of the information has depended on rumors or the narratives of villagers.

3. See, for example, Brunvand 1981; Ikeda, Oshima, et al. 1996; Kapferer 1990; and Morin 1980.

4. Nash (1965:177–182, 192–201) treated these categories of knowledge separately. Nash did not treat omens as a separate item. He explained the cabbalistic charms used by *auk-lan* (lower road) and *ahtet-lan* (higher road) *hsayas* (masters) under the heading of "witchcraft." Astrology and alchemy were placed under the rubric of "predictive and divinatory systems," and indigenous medicine was separately designated under the umbrella of "curing systems." Spiro (1967:25, 35–36) also attempted to categorize the same system. He does not mention omens and explains cabbalistic charms under the heading of *auk-lan hsaya* and *ahtet-lan hsaya*. He makes passing mention that "most astrologers are of Hindu origin"(1968:148) and only mentions alchemy through *dat-lon* (1968:35,183). There are other independent works on astrology (such as Schober 1980 and Shorto 1978), tabaung (Old 1914), and cabbalistic charms (Brown 1916, Clark 1932).

5. The publication of *Kyemon* (Miller) was later resumed. *The Working People's Daily News* resumed publishing in April 1993 as *Myanma Alin* (The new light of Myanmar).

6. Myawaddy TV station was commissioned into service as an act of commemorating Golden Jubilee Armed Forces Day, 1995.

7. *Mawgun* refers to a category of poetry composed to record significant events so that knowledge of them will be retained in the collective public memory.

8. Most famous weikza are believed to become htwetyat pauk. This means literally "to break or to open the place of exit" or "to have gone out." There are many interpretations of htwetyat pauk, but one of the basic understandings is that it means saints

who have acquired supernatural powers through meditation and practices of lawkī and have transcended this world.

9. Close examination of the historical documents such as the *Sāsana Vamsa*, the *Thathana Lankara Sadan*, chronicles, and royal orders leads us to speculate that for the most part the people who conveyed such knowledge were probably monks (see Tosa 2000). The norm that orthodox monks should not concern themselves with lawkī pyinnya seems to have been established or reaffirmed through the successive purifications of the sangha.

10. Nash (1965:175–180) reports a case in which a monk engaged in medical treatment as an ahtet-lan hsaya (lit. "higher-road master") in Nandwin village. He explains that ahtet-lan hsaya contrasts with auk-lan hsaya (lit. "lower-road master"), who use evil medicine obtained from dead bodies, and who "operate" upon the world by producing cabbalistic charms (*in*).

11. For a detailed discussion of the dichotomy of lawkī and lawkottara, see Tosa (1996).

12. The following description is based on accounts given by medico-religious specialists (such as indigenous medicine healers, astrologers, and alchemists) and by members of the Athanadiya and Manawmaheiddi Gaing. I include also my experiences of learning the basics of astrology and the writing of cabbalistic charms (*in*) under the guidance of astrologers and gaing hsaya.

13. When "operation" is used in anthropological studies of divination, it often indicates that the fortuneteller or diviner arbitrarily changes or "operates" the interpretation when face-to-face with clients. However, I use it here to mean the technique of "changing the result" through the act of interpretation.

14. "Planet" is used as the translation of the Burmese *gyo* (Pali: *grah*) indicating the following planetary bodies: the sun, the moon, Mars, Mercury, Jupiter, Venus, Saturn, Yahu (Rahu), and Keik (Ketu). Rahu originally indicated the "ascending node" of the moon, but in Burmese astrology, the time from noon Wednesday until midnight is called Rahu. Ketu refers to the moon's "descending node" and does not relate to a particular day of the week, nor with the alphabet or a certain direction, although it is counted as the ninth planet.

15. In order to verify that the particular mnemonics in question have not changed over time, I interviewed a Brahmin astrologer in Mandalay, and a Rangoon monk famous for *dat-yaik dat-hsin*, and compared their knowledge with that contained in published works about *Inga Weikza* (Sein Hsan 1991). The Burmese texts assert that Taungdwingyi Hsayadaw established the basics of the technique (known as dat-yaik dat-hsin) in its present form in the eighteenth century. The verse contained in the hsayadaw's text (Taungdwin 1988) and the verse taught by astrologers and monks at present are identical.

16. The original meaning of yadaya is to "reform a thing."

17. Covington (2002) points out that the activity of the Committee caused a world-heritage disaster at Pagan when they repaired and reconstructed historic and artistically significant pagodas in a shoddy fashion.

18. This rumor was widely circulated in the BSPP period. Spiro (1970:258) points out that building a pagoda is the most effective defense against and means of averting the dangers caused by negative planetary influences and terrestrial omens.

19. The *Mangala sutta* is found in Pitakas as follows: Kuddakapath, 3–4: Sutta Nipata, 308–309.

20. The lavish donations to the sangha also constitute the carrot part of the carrot-and-stick approach. Many young monks support the pro-democracy forces and abhor the violence routinely committed by the regime. Although conscious that monks should in general not concern themselves with this-worldly affairs, after August 27, 1990, many Mandalay monks turned their alms bowls upside down and thus refused to allow members of the military to make merit by donating to the sangha. This caused an enormous loss of face for the SLORC, who responded by arresting, imprisoning, and disrobing the monks (Fink 2001:214–15).

–9–

Writing in a Crazy Way

Literary Life in Contemporary Urban Burma

Jennifer Leehey

The publishing industry in Burma has been quite vibrant during the years of SLORC-SPDC rule in spite of the regime's notorious opposition to press freedom. The publishing district is in the heart of Yangon (Rangoon) from Thirtieth to Fortieth streets. In these narrow roads, mostly in crumbling, colonial-era buildings, one finds numerous small offices for different magazines, journals, and publishing houses. Here also are the printing presses, desktop publishing (DTP) services, stationery shops, bookstores, and secondhand booksellers' stalls, as well as countless teashops and simple restaurants.

Writers and editors meet in teashops to discuss manuscripts and exchange payment. Assistants stop in on their way to and from errands as they shuttle copy proofs from the DTPs or from the censorship office. Magazine cover designers display sketches of their ideas, and everyone exchanges the daily gossip as they perch on low stools drinking tiny cups of strong sweet tea. Later, as the heat of the day subsides, the restaurants that serve alcohol become more crowded. Editors, writers, and poets meet over bottles of beer and rum to drink away the frustrations of the day. The frustrations are many and often as much a product of petty practical difficulties, such as power failures that delay printing, as they are a result of overt state repression. But direct censorship is always a concern.

I was talking with a writer for a business magazine in a restaurant one evening in 1999 during my most recent visit to Burma. He had conducted research for an article about hospitals and health care and then had written the piece in two segments. In the first segment he wrote about a badly run hospital where someone had died because of unsterile conditions; in the second, he wrote more positively about a hospital that was doing good work, but he included some critical observations as well. Only the second part passed Burma's official censorship body. "This is how we write," he said. "We must always think: How can we pass the censors? We write without writing clearly." He filled his glass. "Writing in a crazy way" *(yu-thalo paw-thalo yay-de).*

In Burma today, aggressive state censorship works in concert with techniques of surveillance and intimidation to stifle political debate and suppress criticism of government policies. At the same time a relentless rhetoric pervades the state-owned news media promoting an official vision of the "Myanmar" nation. The ruling military authorities seek extensive control over public discourse. Yet there is still a variety of semi-independent producers of popular, journalistic, and literary works that this chapter explores.

My focus is on new forms of literary experimentation in Burma, the so-called new-style *(han-thit)* literature. New style is not a large movement, and it is controversial among Burmese intellectuals, but it is significant. New style, I will argue, is an indicator of current conditions for meaning-making in Burma today. The movement is both an expression of disillusion with the literary realism of the 1960s and 1970s and a response to the byzantine workings of the press regulatory and censorship system. The new style is interesting for what it reveals about the subjective experience of everyday life under military rule. This literature has emerged out of, and in its own way represents (or, better put, *indexes*), the peculiar material and semiotic conditions that obtain in Burma today.

Before discussing new-style literature, however, I will review the history of press regulation and censorship in Burma and describe the conditions for writing and publishing that have emerged in the SLORC-SPDC period.

Censorship in the BSPP Era

Some form of the present-day censorship apparatus has been in place in Burma for over four decades. The main legal instrument of censorship, the Printers' and Publishers' Registration Law, was promulgated in 1962, shortly after the military coup that brought Gen. Ne Win to power. Before Ne Win, during the parliamentary era in the 1950s, Burma had one of the freest presses in Asia. There were more than thirty daily newspapers in several languages, published in several cities, with editorial positions reflecting a broad range of political opinion. Prime Minister U Nu did maintain a Press Review Department, but it only monitored and did not directly censor publications.

After 1962 conditions for publishing changed markedly. By 1963 the media were under attack: several newspapers were closed down, including the influential English-language daily *The Nation* edited by U Law Yone. Several editors and journalists were arrested, apparently for printing criticism of government policy. Gen. Ne Win's Revolutionary Council began producing an official state newspaper, *Loktha Pyithu Nayzin*, with an English version called *The Working People's Daily*. Then in 1964 all private newspapers were nationalized and brought under the direct control of the Ministry of Information where, it was proclaimed, they would have "full freedom of expression within the accepted limits of the Burmese Way to Socialism" (*Guardian* magazine October 1964, quoted in Allott 1981:18). Burma's newspapers, along with the other mass media such as radio (and later television), became mouthpieces of the Burma Socialist Programme Party (BSPP) government, presenting directives, exhortations, and information issued by the official Burma News Agency (BNA).[1]

Private publishing of books and non-news periodicals continued, but under a strict new regulatory framework. The 1962 Printers' and Publishers' Law established a Press Scrutiny Board (PSB) *(sa-pay si-zit-yay ahpwe)* to police the ideological content of books and periodicals.[2] Unlike U Nu's Press Review Department, which had simply monitored publications, the PSB was vested with extensive power to prohibit the distribution of any material it deemed unacceptable. The board not only supervised the language and contents of all printed works but also determined the number of copies that could be legally printed. During the BSPP period, the government exercised control over publishers in part by limiting the allocation of state-subsidized paper, an especially effective mechanism, as paper was in short supply under the centralized socialist economy.[3]

The 1962 Printers' and Publishers' Law has been amended several times, mostly to expand its scope. In practice, the procedures of the PSB have encouraged self-censorship. Through the 1960s and into the 1970s, most books and all magazines were presented for scrutiny *after* they had been printed but before distribution. Book-length works on politics, economics, and religion were exceptions: they had to be submitted before printing in typed-manuscript form. The assumption underlying this system was that most texts would be swiftly vetted, but in practice the PSB often required changes or deletions which then had to be carried out on already printed and bound work at the publisher's expense. Pages had to be removed and offending words and paragraphs laboriously covered over in indelible ink. If a work was banned, the entire print run had to be destroyed. Few publishers could afford to take many risks, especially given the prohibitive cost of paper.

In the mid-1970s writers and publishers were raising objections to the system. In a rhetorical maneuver no doubt intended to elicit official sympathy, one writer spoke before a meeting of the Hlutdaw (People's Parliament) and drew attention to the terrible waste of paper for which the state was expending its scarce foreign exchange (Allott 1981:24). In 1977 the government instituted new *pre*publication scrutiny procedures shortly after the publication of *Hpaung-ga-za Maung Maung*, a book with antigovernment themes (Allott 1981:34, n37). Under the new instructions, all book-length texts had to be submitted as manuscripts in twenty typed copies. (Magazines were still permitted to submit for scrutiny after printing.) Prepublication censorship entailed new hardships: writers had to contend personally with the board's many demands for alterations, and it could take months, even years, to receive final approval to publish.

One of the most vexatious problems for writers and publishers in the BSPP period (and still today) was determining *what* the PSB would reject. Its decisions often seemed quite arbitrary. In 1975 the Ministry of Home and Religious Affairs issued a memorandum laying out ten principles for the censorship board to follow, but the guidelines were vague and sweeping (prohibiting, for example, "anything detrimental to the Burma Socialist Program") and did little to reduce uncertainty.[4] Virtually any piece of writing could be objected to under one or another of the principles, depending on the whim of a particular censor (Allott 1993:7).

Censorship had multiple effects on literary life in the BSPP era. Because no independent news reporting was permitted, and because of the difficulties involved in publishing book-length works, monthly literary magazines became an especially important venue for serious writing in the 1970s and 1980s.[5] These magazines featured short stories, serialized novels, general interest and foreign news features, cartoons, and poems. Short stories and articles were relatively easy to remove from a bound magazine if so required. Small book-rental shops run from the front rooms of private houses also became widespread in this period because of the high cost and general scarcity of reading materials. These shops, where patrons borrow books and magazines for a small daily fee, are still common today.

In early 1988 there were indications that restrictions on the press might be easing. A number of magazine articles critical of the government and economy were allowed to appear. It also became possible for private individuals and organizations to obtain licenses to publish new magazines on topics such as film, pop music, family life, religion, science, and foreign affairs. Then when antigovernment demonstrations swept the country in August 1988, dozens of *un*licensed publications sprang up, carrying reports of the protests and interviews with opposition leaders. Even the state-run newspapers seemed to be printing accurate information without intervention. The brief period of press freedom came to a rapid close, however, when Gen. Saw Maung seized power in September. The unauthorized publications disappeared overnight. For a few days all the national newspapers were closed down as well and then *Loktha Pyithu Nayzin* (The working people's daily) was allowed to resume publication, again under strict state control. The paper was subsequently renamed *Myanma Alin* or *New Light of Myanmar*.[6] A great many dissident writers and journalists were arrested and imprisoned[7] and a blacklist of "subversive" authors, whose work could not be published—indeed whose names could not even appear in print—was drawn up by Military Intelligence and supplied to the Press Scrutiny Board.

Under the new State Law and Order Restoration Council (SLORC), censorship mechanisms were swiftly reinstituted. Although the Burma Socialist Programme Party had dissolved, the 1975 censorship guidelines were retained with the references to "socialism" simply deleted.[8] The Printers' and Publishers' Registration Law was amended in 1989, increasing the maximum penalty for violations to seven years in prison (Venkateswaran 1996:41). New topics became off limits for nongovernment publications, including democracy, human rights, the events of 1988, the previous BSPP government, and the military. Nongovernment media were not permitted to make reference to senior government officials or opposition figures, especially Daw Aung San Suu Kyi. Despite this unquestionably effective suppression, the PSB became particularly suspicious of *hidden* ideological messages, as I will discuss below.

Truth and Censorship under the SLORC-SPDC

Even more than its BSPP predecessor, the current regime attempts to make itself the center of authority and truth. Through control of the media, and through billboard campaigns and public spectacles of various kinds, the military rulers construct and impose on the populace a particular interpretation of Burma's past, present, and future reality. Control of the public sphere works on two levels: negatively, by silencing alternative, potentially oppositional, discourses through censorship and intimidation; and positively, by *filling up* the discursive space so that alternative perspectives and visions are all but drowned out.

Under the BSPP, socialism was the central rationale of the state and the military was portrayed as leading the country to a glorious socialist future. While the SLORC-SPDC has made moves toward a more open economic system, encouraging both the internal private sector and external investment, no overarching principle of "capitalism" as such has been embraced. The ideology of the current regime is a nationalistic adulation of the military itself, its activities, and plans for the people. State rhetoric revolves around a few key themes: the threat to national unity, progress toward economic development, the preservation and "uplift" of national culture and morale, and, above all, the need for military leadership to accomplish national goals—defined, of course, by the military itself. In official discourse, the Tatmadaw (Defense Services) is hard at work, sacrificing "blood and sweat" to hold the country together in the face of terrible threats from both neocolonial outsiders and internal traitors. The military leaders guard authentic Myanmar culture and tradition while providing the order and discipline necessary for economic development and progress.

A 1999 cartoon (see Figure 9.1) from the news daily *Myanma Alin* gives a visual example of this rhetoric. On the horizon is a vision of Myanmar modernity, a "developed, progressive nation," combining images of skyscrapers and Buddhist regalia. On the right, Myanmar citizens ("the people") are marching in a disciplined way toward this bright future, while beside the road, motley members of the National League for Democracy, including a snaggle-toothed Aung San Suu Kyi, receive dark glasses from apparently Western "neocolonialists." (The disembodied arm reaching down wears a Western-style suit jacket and has a hairy hand.) In the cartoon, the people march by, rejecting the NLD

"The ones who look at everything through dark glasses—how can they see the truth?"

Figure 9.1. "Modern, Developed, Progressive Nation" cartoon (Source: *Myanma Alin* 1999)

and their "dark view" of the future. The opposition party is portrayed as deluded, unable to perceive self-evident truth.

Much of state propaganda is devoted to informing the people of their "desires" and "national objectives" and presenting current conditions in the country in the rosiest of terms. Newspaper articles with headlines such as "Yangon full of activities" paint a picture of bustling economic vitality and good feeling in the nation's capital that belies the actual widespread struggle for subsistence. Bad news in general is subject to censorship even when it concerns events that we would not usually consider a failure of government, such as floods, accidents, and even losing soccer matches. Indeed, I remember one cheerful article in the *New Light of Myanmar* in 1999 describing a bright clear day in Yangon when in fact it had rained. Such examples, which could be multiplied, display the conceit of a regime not content to manipulate the truth, but instead claiming a remarkable degree of direct control over the fabric of reality. As in the cartoon, understandings of reality that contradict the state-sanctioned vision are simply designated falsehoods.[9]

Within this general framework of state control over "truth," private or (more accurately) "semi-independent" publishing has nonetheless continued. In fact, there has been an *expansion* of the publishing industry under SLORC-SPDC rule. With the liberalization of certain sectors of the economy in the 1990s, more print-quality paper became available and opportunities for small-scale entrepreneurial ventures in publishing opened up. New publishing houses were established and an array of new periodicals appeared, including monthly magazines and small weekly and biweekly papers called *"gya-neh"* (from English "journal").

The quality varies considerably among these fifty or so independent publications. Many are cheap tabloids printing true-crime stories or movie-star gossip often drawn from B-grade English-language media. There are popular weeklies and monthlies concerned with astrology, numerology, and the supernatural, topics of perennial fascination in Burma that were prohibited from print in the socialist period. The 1990s also saw the introduction of several substantive private magazines specializing in "open-market economics" and local and international business, with titles like *Dana* (Wealth), *Myanma Dana*, and *Living Color*. While some of the articles in these magazines are translations from foreign periodicals like *Time, Newsweek,* or the Singapore paper *The Straits Times,* the features or cover stories draw on investigative research conducted by Burmese journalists on business-related issues inside the country's borders. The business magazines are primarily nonfiction, but one also finds fictionalized accounts as a genre of "literary nonfiction" has emerged largely in response to censorship (as I discuss below). The formula of cover stories, foreign news, tips on management and export opportunities, interspersed with cartoons and short literary pieces has been well received by an information-hungry country.

With this growth in the publishing industry and with periodicals finding niches that did not exist before, one might get the impression of a new latitude in Burma's public sphere. But writers, editors, and publishers I interviewed asserted without hesitation that working conditions are *more*, not less, restrictive under the current regime. Censorship has grown more complex, capricious, and burdensome. The guidelines delimiting acceptable discourse are vague and shifting, while penalties for violation of the Printers' and Publishers' Law can be severe—as I've noted, up to seven years' imprisonment. The regulatory system is rife with corruption, and this has spawned a new level of bureaucracy and costs in the form of private brokers who manage the process. For someone attempting to make a livelihood in the publishing arena, there are multiple practical inducements to self-censor and keep one's publication well within the narrow confines of the SPDC vision.

The state intervenes directly in "private" publishing at many junctures. Every book and periodical is obliged to carry on its first or second page a series of government slogans: the Three National Causes, the Twelve National Objectives (including the Four Political Goals, Four Economic Goals, and Four Social Goals), and other mottos. Editors of private magazines and weeklies are regularly encouraged to attend press conferences at various state ministries and report on what was said. Occasionally the PSB will instruct editors to publish a particular article issued by the government, promoting patriotism, for example, or attacking the opposition party or some other matter of "national interest." This request must be met or the publication will not receive its distribution permit.

In general, private publications are expected to follow the government's lead. Editors, publishers, and government censors are instructed to keep abreast of speeches and announcements in the official newspapers so as to avoid publishing any items that do not "accord with the times." (PSB guideline #7 prohibits "any descriptions which, though factually correct, are unsuitable because of the time or the circumstances of their writing.") For example, if Gen. Than Shwe gives a speech on appropriate attire for young people, private publications must either repeat his message or avoid the topic of teen fashions altogether. This is perhaps the most insidious requirement of the censorship system, rendering editors unable to set objectives for their periodicals. One editor interviewed by Tin Maung Than in 1995 spoke of being obliged to pursue "a policy-less policy" with his magazine, while another described publishing as "dancing to the tune of the censors" (Tin Maung Than 1996).

The state bureaucracy and the publishing industry are particularly intertwined in the area of licensing. In the early 1990s the authorities issued a number of new publishing licenses to government departments and agencies so that these offices could develop sources of revenue to subsidize employees' low salaries. In many cases, government departments have chosen to raise funds by *leasing* their licenses to private individuals who then produce a magazine or (more commonly) a weekly "journal" for profit. Typically in such arrangements, the licenseholder, be it the Ministry of Cooperatives or the Drug Control Board or the Office of Military Intelligence, does not exercise editorial control, although there is a vague understanding that the department that owns the license may be held responsible for the publication if some serious problem occurs.[10]

Another common method for would-be publishers to enter the field is to purchase the title of an older magazine or weekly that has gone defunct. The publisher must then pay a bribe to the PSB via a broker for permission to change the periodical's "theme" (subtitle) and editor. Since only the *title* of the periodical can be transferred, and not, strictly speaking, the publishing *license* (which has been issued by the state to a particular entity), the periodical with its new subtitle is not completely legal. The publisher may have an understanding with the PSB and may operate for years under such an agreement, but he or she knows the essentially *un*licensed publication can be shut down at any time.[11] What we find in these various arrangements is a complex alignment of interests among private publishers, brokers, and government bureaucrats that blurs distinctions between the state and private sector and works to keep publications in line.

A significant development in 2000 was the licensing of a new weekly periodical, *The Myanmar Times and Business Review,* with an Australian national, Ross Dunkley, as editor-in-chief. Owned by the Myanmar Consolidated Media Co. Ltd., *Myanmar Times* was copublished by Dunkley and Sonny Swe, the son of Col. Thein Swe, who headed the Office of Strategic Studies (OSS), a think-tank established by the department of Military Intelligence Services (MIS). The weekly is expensive by local standards, but it is attractively produced and has proven a reliable source of timely information on select domestic news, business, and international affairs. It now boasts a print run of 7,000 for the English-language edition, and 50,000 for the Burmese, and has become an obvious alternative to the dreary and largely uninformative state-produced news dailies.[12]

Since its appearance, *Myanmar Times* has been allowed somewhat greater latitude in its reporting than most news-oriented private publications in Burma. Operating under the aegis of the powerful OSS and MIS, the weekly has not been subject to the same scrutiny procedures that most publications face. As a result, *Myanmar Times* writers are often able to "scoop" their competitor's stories—a source of continuous irritation for many independent-minded journalists in the country. *Myanmar Times* operates under the *guise* of free competition, apparently validated by forces of "open-market" capitalism rather than the asserted authority of the state, yet the paper represents just another *kind* of extension of state power into Burma's "private" publishing world, from a different section of the government.[13]

For most private producers of books and periodicals excluding the *Myanmar Times,* publishing involves daily interaction with the grinding mechanisms of the censorship bureaucracy. As I discussed in the previous section, scrutiny procedures have developed since their inception in 1962, mostly expanding in scope. Through the 1990s and into the twenty-first century, the trajectory has continued toward mechanisms that promote self-censorship, and in general those that render censorship invisible to readers and observers.

Currently in Burma, all serious journalism is *pre*censored, that is, submitted to the PSB for initial scrutiny before printing. This procedure, known colloquially as *tin-htok* ("submit-print"), has been the requirement for all *books* since the 1977 amendment to the Printers' and Publishers' Law (reiterated in 1989). Technically magazines and other periodicals are still considered exempt: most editors are permitted to print an edition first and then submit copies to the board for approval. This latter system, called *htok-tin* ("print-submit"), has become increasingly onerous, however, especially for the more substantive magazines concerned with business and social affairs that are often required to make extensive revisions before distribution.

Until the mid-1990s, under the htok-tin ("print-submit") system, editors covered up rejected passages with indelible black or silver ink and removed or glued together censored pages. Then in 1996 the PSB issued new instructions that such alterations had to be made in a less obvious fashion. The board was responding in part to an argument put forward by certain writers that blackened-over passages in magazines would create a bad impression on foreign visitors during the government's heavily promoted "Visit Myanmar Year."[14] Rather than relaxing press restrictions, as presumably these critics had hoped, the PSB concluded that censorship should be disguised. Now if a censor objects to even one sentence, the entire page must be removed and replaced with acceptable material. Changes must be as seamless as possible, with pages renumbered and sentences rephrased so gaps in the text are not apparent. Because such extensive alterations are difficult and costly to carry out on already printed material, prepublication scrutiny has become the only practical option for many editors.

Changes in printing and publishing technology in Burma, specifically the introduction of computers in the 1990s, have made precensorship more feasible.[15] Editors who use computers to do their layout will give the PSB a sample printout for inspection. Any changes ordered by the board are then made invisibly on the computer, usually by expanding advertisements to fill in space. Of course, copies of the magazine or weekly must still be submitted *after* printing for final approval, and there is always the possibility of additional last-minute objections from the censor board. If the publication has gone through precensorship, however, there is a greater likelihood that the distribution permit will be issued efficiently, allowing editors to meet their distribution deadlines.[16] Currently, a few confident magazines or weeklies still use the old htok-tin ("print-submit") procedures if their material is quite uncontroversial and certain to pass the censors. For many periodicals, however, prepublication scrutiny has become the norm, compelled by both PSB requirements for seamless alteration and editors' very practical concerns to meet deadlines and return a profit.

As PSB regulations work in tandem with economic pressures, there are also various penalties built into the system to ensure compliance. If an editor distributes a magazine or weekly without making required revisions, he or she faces losing the publishing license for several months or permanently. If a particular publication repeatedly runs afoul of the censors or submits an article that contains too much unacceptable material, the censor board will refer future decisions on that publication to higher authorities, either the office of the deputy minister of Home Affairs or the Office of Military Intelligence. In such instances, permission to distribute is delayed, and the periodical probably falls behind in its publication cycle, incurring serious financial losses.

In certain cases, the process can be quite punitive, even vindictive. At the end of 1995 the general-interest monthly magazine *Thint Bawa* (Your life) had 58 of 160 pages censored from one issue. It was one of the crudest examples of censorship seen in Burma since 1989. The issue was devoted to the topic of education, in honor of the seventy-fifth anniversary of the founding of Rangoon University, and the cover story was a comparison of Burma's colonial and national education systems. Censors understood the story as a veiled critique of the current educational environment. Subsequent issues of *Thint Bawa* came under heightened scrutiny, and the March 1996 number had 72 pages removed—one-third of the magazine. Censors began rejecting words, passages, and articles for no logical or ideological reason (Allott 1996). The intention clearly was to punish the editors for daring to test limits and intimidate them into greater self-censorship.

For most editors and publishing houses, self-censorship is a pragmatic strategy for staying in business. Meanwhile, as I have discussed, prepublication scrutiny has become an everyday way to "dance to the tune of the censors." The net effect of various developments in the publishing industry has been the *erasure* of the marks of censorship so that the practices by which the regime polices public discourse have become less visible, even as they have become more thoroughly restrictive.

So how do writers, editors, and publishers in Burma's literary world *(sa-pay lawka)* manage under these conditions? There are a variety of editorial strategies and responses. Certainly for some, state regulation and censorship are accepted as normal. One writer for a weekly paper told me he had no difficulty with the censor board because he knew what was appropriate to publish. "I do not criticize my country," he explained. For such people, censorship is a bureaucratic problem, a set of procedures to follow in the course of a workday, but the process does not create any special psychic tension, at least as far as I could discern in interview.

Others find the procedures of scrutiny and revision fundamentally degrading but submit to the requirements of the bureaucracy because they need to earn an income. One editor for a small weekly described his experience. "There is the part of me that does my work, what I have to do. Then there is the part that keeps separate. I try to stay free," he said. Some older writers who remember better times simply refuse to take part in publishing under the current regime. One gentleman told me that he was asked to contribute an article to a friend's magazine, but had declined. "I am too old," he explained: "My knees are no good," meaning that he would not kneel in submission to the authorities.

Compromise strategies are common. An editor or publisher might comply with the system to a certain extent, producing an innocuous weekly to make money, for example, while seeking occasional opportunities to produce work of greater social significance. A friend proudly showed me a book he had recently published, a collection of essays by the late great writer and translator Mya Than Tint. It had taken years to pass censors and had cost more to produce than he would probably recover through sales, but he was pleased, explaining, "This I do for my dignity."

Some independent-minded writers and editors will continually struggle with the system, feeling a responsibility to keep at least the *principle* of an independent press alive. They try to counter the official monopoly on public discourse by insinuating veiled social or political commentary into their articles and stories. One technique I mentioned above is the use of fictionalized accounts. Sometimes in the business magazines critical reflections on social conditions are incorporated into stories with dialogue and characters so the commentary is less threatening to official sensibilities.[17] Through the 1990s *Thint Bawa* explored social issues of great concern in Burma—including education, AIDS, the role of the media in a democracy, methods of negotiation, and the social effects of fear—while steering clear of explicit political commentary. Writers would approach topics in a general way, discussing the negotiation techniques used by the African National Congress in South Africa, for example, and hinting to readers to transpose the analysis to the Burmese situation.

None of this is easy, however. Articles that involve great labor are frequently rejected and over time the effort to maintain a space for alternative discourse can be exhausting. Writers, editors, and publishers who take too many risks face financial failure, arrest, or exile. *Thint Bawa*, for example, was eventually closed down and its editors, Tin Maung Than and Maung Thit Sin, now live in the United States.[18]

For everyone, the pressure to self-censor is constant. Tin Maung Than (1996) described to an audience of journalism students at Carleton University in Ottawa, Ontario, the experience of a Burmese writer struggling with what he calls "the power that determines the shape of a writer's work."

> [This] power is not only external but also internal—exercised by the writer himself or herself both consciously and unconsciously. While he writes, he enjoys his effort or his creation (if it is fiction), but at the same time he disgusts the system and loathes himself because he has to betray partially or totally, his conscience, his theme and his own words that he chooses, that he loves. Unable to bear the inner torment, the writer sometimes no longer tries the possible presentation and aborts the idea, the plot, the scene and the voices in silent tears.

In the ongoing struggle with censorship, it is common for Burmese writers and journalists to lose their sense of purpose. The endless obstacles and penalties sap initiative and numb creativity. Many intellectuals in Burma become exhausted and stop writing and publishing altogether. I turn now to the new-style literature, which presents an alternate strategy for creative intellectual production under these conditions.

New-Style Literature

An intriguing and possibly hopeful development in the literary world during these years of SLORC-SPDC rule has been the rise of so-called new-style literature. The term "new style" *(han-thit)*, taken from a magazine of the same name, is used in Burma in reference to various forms of contemporary literary experimentation. Other terms circulate: *mawdan* (modern), *pos-mawdan* (postmodern), and *khit-paw* (contemporary). There is much murky debate in

Rangoon teashops about what these different words mean, whose writing belongs in what category, and so on. I use "new style" here as an umbrella term for convenience.

The movement is associated with certain writers including Thissa Ni, Nay Myo, Kyu Nit, Zaya Lin, Taryar Min Wai, and Min Khaike Soe San. There are many poets including Aung Cheint, Maung Kyaw Nweh, Aung Way, Hla Than, Htun Way Myint, Min Htet Maung, and Myint Moe Aung.[19] Zaw Zaw Aung, whom I discuss below, is an influential writer and an essayist on literary theory in his mid-sixties. While some new-style writers like Zaw Zaw Aung have inhabited Burma's literary world for decades, a great many are young, in their teens, twenties, and early thirties, and the movement is often associated with the generation that came of age in the post-1988 period. The most enthusiastic readership for new-style prose and poetry draws from the younger set, especially urban-dwelling high school and university students, according to editors I interviewed.

Particular magazines are known for promoting this literature. In *Han-thit* (New style) magazine, currently edited by Tin Ko Aung, one finds experimental stories and poetry as well as essays by writers like Zaw Zaw Aung introducing readers to notions of "postmodernity." The magazine, which has a circulation of about 3,000 copies, began in the late 1980s and has been influential since the mid-1990s, although it has struggled to stay in business. In 1996 a staff editor at *Han-thit,* Aung Zin Min was arrested and imprisoned for supporting the large student demonstrations of that year in his articles and poems. In 1998 *Han-thit* closed down temporarily for economic reasons as continual difficulties with the censorship board had resulted in heavy publication costs. It was shut down by the authorities in October 2002 for one month as punishment for printing an indirect reference to a "blacklisted" writer.[20]

Somewhat more conservative than *Han-thit, Dagon* magazine has a mission to "promote a modern sensibility" in Burma, according to editor Myat Thit, whom I interviewed in 1999.[21] *Dagon* publishes so-called "modern" writing by Burmese authors and poets as well as the works of "modern masters" in translation, such as Simone de Beauvoir, Albert Camus, John-Paul Sartre, James Joyce, Franz Kafka, and Virginia Woolf. Many excellent translations of modern world literature were produced in earlier decades, especially the 1970s, and *Dagon* republishes them to inspire new writers and audiences. *Tharahpu,* edited by Min Htet Maung, is a smaller literary magazine also associated with the new style. In addition, there are popular nonliterary magazines devoted to fashion or movies which will include new-style stories and poems on occasion, such as *Mahaythi, Yok-shin Tay-kabya, Yanant-thit, Kalya,* and *Beauty.* Some of these have quite large circulations.[22]

Two small-scale *unauthorized* publications linked to the new-style movement deserve special mention. Between 1993 and 1996 a student-founded poetry magazine called *Ya-zu-thit Myit-kyin* (River narrows of a new century) was published without PSB knowledge. It was inexpensive, and circulated quietly. After the demonstrations in late 1996 many of the writers involved with the magazine were arrested or had to go underground because of their political activities and the magazine ceased publication. In July 2002 students from several Rangoon universities began publishing another such magazine, *The Universities Literary Journal,* under the auspices of the University Students Literary Association. A key figure in the group was Thaw Thaw Myo Han, a Rangoon University of Technology student who was also a contributor to *Han-thit* magazine. He and two other students were detained by the authorities for several weeks in August 2002 for political activities.

So what is this new style in Burmese literature? In general, the writing is marked by heightened attention to textual form over content. It is subjectivist: the poems and prose explore internal psychic experiences and play with fantastic or magical imagery. There are often references to foreign places or objects that the writer has never seen except in imagination, through foreign literature or movies on video. New-style poetry is always "free verse" (*ka-yan-me,* lit. "without rhyme"), and the prose tends toward "stream of consciousness" *(atway-asin).* The most radical pos-mawdan prose eschews plot, character, and diachronic sequence of any kind. The writing often defies coherent interpretation. Some say it is intentionally chaotic and obtuse.

Literary experimentation is certainly not "new" in Burma and a brief review of previous developments in the literary world will help to situate the current movement as well as the controversy it has engendered. In the 1930s there was the *khitsan* (lit. "age test") movement, pioneered by Rangoon University students who sought to "test the age" with literature that fused Western and Burmese styles. Khitsan prose and poetry was relatively simple, without the ornate embellishments of traditional Burmese literary forms. In the late 1940s the left-wing writer and editor Dagon Taya promoted what he called "new literature" *(sa-pay-thit)* in his magazine *Ta-ya* (Star). Dagon Taya's style was renowned for unusual word choices and artful simile, and he attended to social issues like the struggles of poor workers and peasants. One of the writers who published in *Ta-ya* magazine, Kyi Aye, was an existentialist, influenced by the writings of Camus and Sartre. She introduced stream-of-consciousness writing to Burmese audiences along with the notion of "art for art's sake."

In the 1950s writers were joining different political factions—there were socialist, pro-Soviet communist, and pro-Chinese communist groups—and literary criticism became highly politicized. The role of literature in society was a prominent debate, one that continues in teashops today. While some argued that literature was fundamentally about individual self-expression, supporters of "socialist realism" argued that writing should be politically committed, that it should "serve the people" and help to bring about social change. In the 1960s and 1970s, under General Ne Win's military-socialist government, there was official endorsement of this principle. Writers, known as "literary workers," were encouraged to produce "literature of benefit to the people" *(pyi-thu akyo-byu sa-pay)* and support the government's nation-building aims (Allott 1981:24).

Stylistic innovation continued within the dominant paradigm of "realism." In the mid-1960s, the Burmese scholar Minn Latt wrote a thesis proposing that formal, literary Burmese should be abandoned in favor of a new, modern standard: a written style more closely linked to the language as it is spoken. The idea was promoted by the Upper Burma Writers' Association, a left-wing literary clique centered in Mandalay, whose members began writing all prose, including dialogue, narrative, and exposition, in a colloquial style. Their campaign was opposed by the literary establishment in Rangoon. The writing was perceived as "communist" in inspiration.[23] In the 1970s was also the "free-verse" movement: Burmese poets began experimenting with non-rhyming forms of versification.[24] Two books about international poetry published in the early 1970s were influential: *Poetry, Rhythm and Image* by Win Pe (pen name: Mya Zin); and *Shade of a Palm Tree,* a compendium of world poetry in translation by Maung Tha Noe. The Upper Burma Writers' Association published the first collection of free-verse Burmese poetry. *Up-country Poems* was edited by (Ludu) Sein Win and Kyi Aung and printed at Ludu press in Mandalay.

Also during the 1970s *Mo-way* magazine rose to prominence as a voice for dissident youth culture. It was published in Rangoon, and contributors were writers from both major cities, Mandalay and Rangoon. *Mo-way* focused on international socialism and modern literature with articles about events in China, Vietnam, and Cuba; satirical essays; short stories; free-verse poetry; and works of world literature in translation. The magazine continued into the 1980s under editors Nat Nweh and Maung Thwe Thit. Many of today's new-style writers published their first pieces in *Mo-way,* and it is considered a precursor to magazines like *Han-thit* and *Dagon.*

So what distinguishes new style from earlier literary movements? Most emphatically, new style is *not* socialist. Through the 1960s and 1970s in Burma, notions of the "modern" were intimately linked with left-wing ideologies. In the 1980s, however, there was growing disillusion with socialism and communism as intellectuals confronted the gap between fine Marxist ideals and the hateful dictatorial practices of centralized governments. As leftist ideals faltered, young Burmese writers and intellectuals began seeking new ways to be "progressive." The new-style turn toward subjectivism can be seen as a rejection of the socialist-realist principle that literature should be for and about "the people." Attending to textual form, new-style writers reject the idea that writing should carry an ideological message.

Stylistically, the movement has antecedents in Dagon Taya's unusual verbal associations, Kyi Aye's stream-of-consciousness, free-verse poetry, and so on, but new-style writers take language play to new levels. According to poet and editor Min Htet Maung, images in the free-verse poetry of the 1970s were "clear and stable," while images in new-style poems are more complex. An example is Aung Way's "Beethoven Moonshine-liquor," an early new-style poem published in 1984, in which allusions to classical Western music mingle with images of Burmese village life. New-style prose is similarly multilayered with elements that don't cohere. In "Winner Takes All," Zaw Zaw Aung's first experimental short story written in the mid-1980s, there are apparently two characters, "I" and another, but as the story proceeds, it seems the two may be one person after all. The story involves a search for missing bars of gold, but the characters, the setting, and the sequence of events are not clear. The plot, such as it is, does not resolve. Previously Zaw Zaw Aung had written popular detective stories that were considered somewhat low-brow by literary authorities, but the critique of "Winner Takes All" was sharper: well-respected critic Aung Thin called it incoherent and irrational (*akyo-akyaung manyi-nyut-hpu*, lit. "cause-effect not-accord.")

Writers and critics in Burma distinguish two broad literary genres: "realism" (*bawa-thayok-hpaw sa-pay*, lit. "life-portray-literature") and "romance" (*seik-ku-yin sa-pay*, lit. "imagination literature"), which includes love stories, mysteries, thrillers, and adventure stories. Romantic writing is marketable, but usually considered less respectable. In the 1980s and 1990s, new-style writers were exploring the potential of the romantic literary forms and blurring genre boundaries. Ju, the pen name of Dr. Tin Tin Win, is an especially popular fiction writer whose work defies easy categorization. Her style is "modernist," with simple sentences and dreamlike narrative. She writes about love and relationships and explores with poetic euphemism such scandalous topics as premarital sex, women who love more than one man, and suicide. She is often called a "romance" writer, while her harshest critics call her work "poisonous" and "indecent" (*nyit-nyan-de*). Yet I have heard her fans (men and women) assert that her writing is "realistic" because "she shows the true feelings and ideas that women have." Ever since her first best-selling novel, *Remembrance (Ahmat-taya)*, was published in the mid-1980s, debates about Ju have raged among Burmese intellectuals.[25] Her challenge to traditional constructions of Burmese femininity has clearly struck a vital nerve.

Short-story writer Maung Tin Sint describes his mawdan writing as "inner thoughts, external conversations, foreign news in the paper, strange events and coincidences, all mixed together and written down in one place." In the early 1980s he wrote socialist realism, but grew tired of that style and began to experiment, inspired in part by insights he had gained into the workings of his mind through his meditation practice. In the 1990s he became known for stories about ghosts, spirits, and magical power, topics that were prohibited during the BSPP period as contrary to the values of socialism. Some have called him Burma's first "magical realist." [26]

Without question, state censorship and the increasingly restrictive conditions for writers in the post-1988 period have been major factors in the development of the new style. Simply put, realism in the tradition of Dagon Taya is difficult to publish. A literary work concerned with the everyday struggles of ordinary people will probably not pass censors if it draws attention to such realities as declining educational standards, government corruption, prostitution, or the HIV/AIDS epidemic. Since 1962 creative writers have represented social conditions in their literary pieces using oblique imagery, irony, or allegory. Anna Allott's 1993 collection of Burmese short stories in translation gives many fine examples of such writing produced in the late 1980s and early 1990s by writers including Ne Win Myint, Nu Nu Yii, Nyi Pu Lay, San San Nweh and Win Pe.[27] However, literature with strong social or political message has become more difficult to produce under the SLORC-SPDC, as censors have become more suspicious of hidden meaning. The PSB now demands that writers or their editors provide written explanations of stories and poems, making all literary allusions explicit. As one frustrated writer said to me: "People are not allowed to say and write what they think. In the past, in the *ma-sa-la* time [BSPP-era], you could say things if you were creative, careful. But now is the worst time. Everything is silenced—except what *they* say."

Of course, realism still has a place in Burma's publishing scene: indeed, as I have mentioned, works of realistic fiction sometimes appear in *non*literary contexts such as business magazines as journalists seek to soften the impact of the information they wish to convey. There are also creative writers who still produce fine realistic stories. But it is unquestionably a problematic genre because of censorship and the related issue of marketability. One popular magazine editor put it bluntly: "The people hate realism: there are no readers for it. Life today is more difficult than what can be portrayed in a novel. Readers like romance, fantasy, something new. They want to free their minds of worry."

Rejecting socialist realism for philosophical and practical reasons, new-style writers have sought fresh philosophical orientation and many have become interested in theories of postmodernism. Burmese intellectuals have had some exposure, albeit limited and fragmented, to contemporary Western literary criticism in recent years. Zaw Zaw Aung (the author of "Winner Takes All" mentioned above) has been an important relay. His 1998 *Primer on Literary Theory (Sa-pay thabaw-taya achay-gan kyan)*, which drew heavily on Brian McHale's 1987 text *Postmodernist Fiction,* familiarized Burmese readers with such French poststructuralist thinkers as Ferdinand de Saussure, Roland Barthes, Jacques Derrida, Jean Baudrillard, Jean-François Lyotard, and Michel Foucault. In the space of a dozen pages, these names are attached to tantalizing hints about complex new bodies of thought. Zaw Zaw Aung has also published several long essays and articles about modernism and postmodernism in magazines like *Han-thit.*

It is difficult to tell how much purchase these ideas have gained. In teashop discussions, questions are raised about whether Burma can have a pos-mawdan literature if the country hasn't become mawdan yet. One writer I interviewed asserted, "Here in Burma we have 'modernism' and 'post-modernism' at the same time. It's all mixed up. It's all hybrid." Barthes' (1970) concept of a "writerly" *(scriptible)* text has been well received. People are interested in this notion of indeterminate texts, where there are no settled "signifieds" (meanings), but a play of diffuse and shifting "signifiers" (material elements). Barthes' point that readers are active *producers,* rather than mere consumers, of the meaning of a text is not a difficult concept for Burmese writers, with their decades of experience writing under censorship and relying on readers to infer meanings from oblique references.

Following are some examples of new-style writing that are particularly influenced by the new literary theory. First is a poem by Taryar Min Wai, a writer in his early thirties. He was a student activist in the late 1980s and early 1990s and spent five years in prison. He was released under the condition that he would not be involved in politics but has been permitted to write. He is one of the most popular and successful of the new-style writers.

One Who Is Possessed by a *Nat* [28]

blown away
how many cities of monsoon has it been?
one who doesn't return the call,
even though he's heard the telephone ring.

O papa!
into the great rain cloud

> I want to fall in exhaustion and "sleep"
> It's so tiring
> to try to "straighten" the sky.
> Taryar Min Wai
> *Mahaythi* magazine June 1997
> (translated by Jennifer Leehey)

This poem is in "free verse," without rhyme or alliteration in the original Burmese. There is a collage of images: a storm, a telephone call, a plaintive cry to a parent. There is little cohesion between the lines. Even basic rules of syntax are violated. For example, the poet asks "how many cities of monsoon?" using "cities" as the classifier (counting word) in a thoroughly idiosyncratic fashion. (A grammatical question would be: "How many monsoon *seasons* has it been?") There are quotation marks around certain words, suggesting ironic disengagement, but it is not at all clear why these words should get any special consideration.

I interviewed the poet at some length about this poem, but he coyly declined to explain it, assuring me that I was free to understand it however I pleased. "In socialist realism there is only one perspective, one correct way to understand. The meaning is very clear," he said. "In modernist writing, there are multiple points of view, so there are many possible meanings. The meaning is not decided. What is 'sky'? What is 'straighten'? What will the character do? What should he do? This is not clear."

The poem did not pass the censors initially. Originally it read "O mama!" and the Press Scrutiny Board, assuming this was a reference to Aung San Suu Kyi, demanded alteration. This is one of the curious paradoxes of censorship in Burma: political messages are "found" by the system when arguably none are intended by the author. The indeterminancy of a poem like Taryar Min Wai's intensifies the irony. Sometimes new-style poets will discuss literary theory in their explanations to the Press Scrutiny Board, in the manner of "This is a writerly text. Don't you know Roland Barthes?" In this case the poet simply made the requested change.

Next is an example of pos-mawdan prose, an excerpt from a longer piece written by Zaw Zaw Aung in December 1997. It did not pass the PSB.

Nameless Prose No. 12 *(excerpt)*

Watering and cleaning the small lawn. I can't take on this responsibility, so I give it to my best friend, Miss Rose. She will handle it. If something is wrong, look to tomorrow. The present can be found there. Upon the lake, the moonlight establishes a castle of laughter. Don't let the wicked men come.

Cultivate ten thousand flower plants. My lady-friend will open the flower festival. There is no tear, no soldier in the festival. Just the songs. There are so many times of tears for our beloved one. Cultivate the yellow rose. Among the smells at the ten thousand flowers festival, we will meet again.

Have no idea to throw out the old distorted conservatism. Do you want to step outside of the mainstream? Do you want to show your own idea just once? Don't disturb the smell of flowers. Allow to spread lightly, freely. When one thinks about thinking, the matter one thinks becomes an idea. This sentence is not good. Erase it.

> Zaw Zaw Aung
> December 1997, unpublished
> (translated by Aung Soe Minn)

Again, there are multiple images. Meanings are suggested but they are unstable. In the final lines of this excerpt, the author begins to conceptualize his experience ("when one thinks about thinking"), but then he stops himself and the reader is drawn up short. The text resists being read at anything but the most surface level. In semiotic terms, these are signs that draw attention to their own arbitrariness.

In contrast to Taryar Min Wai, Zaw Zaw Aung refuses to make changes in his writing to please the censors. For him, a work of art is the product of a particular moment, a particular movement of the mind. The moment cannot be repeated, and the piece cannot be altered without losing something essential. If the Press Scrutiny Board asks for changes in his writing, he just withdraws the piece.

New-style literature has enthusiastic readers among the younger urban population who are excited by innovation, but many writers in the sa-pay lawka don't like it. The late Tekkatho Bhone Naing, a scholar of Burmese literature, formerly the rector at Moulmein University, told me in 1999 that he saw in the new style evidence of the deterioration of Burma's intellectual life. The younger students, he said, lack a clear understanding of both Burma's classic traditions and Western literature. "These young people, because they want the future, they want to throw all tradition into the trashbin of history. They try to borrow ideas from the West, but they only borrow surface appearances." He criticized free-verse poetry for its lack of structure, calling it "chopped-up, exalted prose." While he approved of experimentation, fresh images, and symbolism, he said, "if you move too much into symbolism and imagism then the writing becomes incomprehensible."

New style is often criticized as self-indulgent and solipsistic, and many question the young writers' apparent fascination with the West. Nu Nu Yii, a realist writer put it, "[These new-style writers] want to write freely, but no one can understand. Even they do not know what they write. Princess Diana, Leonardo da Vinci. They write these names, they write about other countries, places they do not know, just because it is foreign. They like the sound of the words, that's all." Old guard socialist realist writers in the sa-pay lawka frequently criticize the new style for being antisocial and nihilistic. They think the writing lacks political value. "This is not art-for-art's sake. This is not art for the people's sake," one writer said to me. "This is art-for-nothing's sake. It is nothing."

Ludu Sein Win, a well-respected veteran journalist, is a prominent critic of the new style, especially its more radical pos-mawdan manifestations. Ludu Sein Win is a Marxist and a modernist. He was a key member of the Upper Burma Writers' Association and an early promoter of free-verse poetry. (He was the editor of *Up-country Poems* mentioned above.) He welcomes literary experimentation and recognizes that young people will always seek new ways to express themselves. However, he denounces Zaw Zaw Aung, whom he perceives as an intellectual showman trying to impress young audiences with superficially "new" theories. He fears Zaw Zaw Aung is teaching young people passivity in the face of Burma's very real social and political problems. "I don't like this so-called new modernism or post-modernism," he said to me. "It is aloof from society, it is just escapism. They say 'realism' is not possible anymore, but it is. We have to be careful, but we can write the truth and have it published. We must try. Society needs realism."

The rivalry between Ludu Sein Win and Zaw Zaw Aung is personal and longstanding. In the 1970s, when Ludu Sein Win was promoting "modernism," Zaw Zaw Aung was a tutor in the Burmese department at Rangoon University, part of the literary establishment defending the neoclassical khitsan tradition. Both were left-wing at the time, but belonged to different factions. Now Zaw Zaw Aung has rejected socialism and taken up postmodernism, a shift that Ludu Sein Win perceives as insincere, a chameleon-like transformation of appearances. Younger writers in Burma observe the ongoing antagonism between these two older intellectuals with some dismay. "They are our teachers," one writer in his mid-twenties said to me. "They have education, they know English and we do not. But they have old jealousies. Red flag, white flag: these are old quarrels. We want new ways to think." [29]

In the literary world there is general frustration over the pettiness of everyday practical and interpersonal struggles, and many wonder whether the debates over literary theory that occupy them truly have any bearing on the country's larger social and political situation. The following poem by Maung

Linn Yone, an old-school writer, captures the spirit of the ongoing controversy over new style as well as the sense of isolation and impotence so many intellectuals feel. The title "Wuthering Heights" (in Burmese: *lay-htan-gon*) refers to a teashop on Thirty-Third Street in downtown Rangoon favored by writers and editors. The teashop was nicknamed after the well-known English novel because of all the "wind" that blows back and forth there between the intellectuals.

Wuthering Heights

Outside our haven "Wuthering Heights"
Still in full force, the thunderstorm's might.
Whilst, inside, ceaselessly we endeavor,
to make ends meet at home, as ever, we
try to squeeze cash from our publisher.
Bitterly criticizing each other.
Chattering loudly about works big and small
of "Modernism" "Existentialism" "Stream of Consciousness" and all
"Oh, I know best" and "I'm the best"
These "I" dramas we boisterously act.
"I" "me" and "mine" are the words loudest.
Arguing for hours, in non-stop debate we engage,
Still the thunderstorm outside is in full rage.

Maung Linn Yone (Shan State)
Cherry magazine, Feb. 1999

One notes that unlike the free-verse new-style poems given above, this poem rhymes, even in the English translation (which the poet produced himself.) Curiously, the poem passed the Press Scrutiny Board. Apparently the censors did not read political meaning into the poet's concern for the "thunderstorm."

River Narrows of a New Century

It is a legitimate question whether new-style writing has social and political value given that the philosophical orientation of these writers is to reject political ideology. Writing that dwells on internal psychological experiences and writing that only plays with texted surfaces, it would seem, could scarcely influence a reader's social and political awareness. Socialist realists believe in the liberating potential of telling the "truth." From their perspective, this new-style writing cannot contribute in any meaningful way to positive social change in Burma.

What critics of the new style fail to recognize, however, is that this writing is, in its own way, an active response to current conditions in the country. First, new style is a rejection of the state-sanctioned vision of Myanmar modernity. The movement reaches for a more expansive, global vision of the modern than that proffered by the state. New style seeks to be more modern than other forms of modernity: it is so modern that it is pos-mawdan. Drawing inspiration from international literature and poststructuralist literary theory and playing with foreign imagery, the new style gestures beyond the boundaries of Myanmar to a larger global society.

In the new style, meanings shift and are elusive, but that very shifting captures something important about the subjective experience of everyday life under military rule. This literature is fundamentally about the struggle for creative expression, the struggle to create meaning in a society where the authorities assert a monopoly on signification. The regime seeks to arbitrate "truth," so the response of the new-style movement is to reject "truth," or rather to bracket "truth" off and play in a realm where truth-claims are not pertinent.

At the same time, however, new style *does* communicate. It has attraction because it gives aesthetic expression to aspects of contemporary experience: feelings of frustration, exhaustion, recklessness, and yearning. Consider, for example, the name of the student poetry magazine produced in the mid-1990s that I mentioned above: *River Narrows of a New Century*. The image evoked is of water rushing between steep banks where a river narrows. The new style is like this swiftly moving river: constricted, chaotic, dangerous, and moving into the future.

The more radical new-style writing with its hyper-attention to surface form draws attention to the material conditions within which meaning in Burma is produced, specifically the censorship system. The Press Scrutiny Board insists on meaning, on clear links between what is said (the signifier) and what is meant (the signified.) New-style writers consciously detach signifier from signified, concede the territory of meaning, and reach for the ineffable. In this way, new-style writing engages and effectively indexes the mechanisms of censorship. The writing draws attention to the forces and practices that delimit the realm of the utterable. This is crucial, given the regime's current efforts to erase the signs of censorship.

Both supporters and critics of the new-style movement will assert that this writing is not "realistic." The question becomes: what is realism within the contemporary context? Given the contorted conditions for meaning-making in Burma today and the inevitability of "writing in a crazy way," it may be that

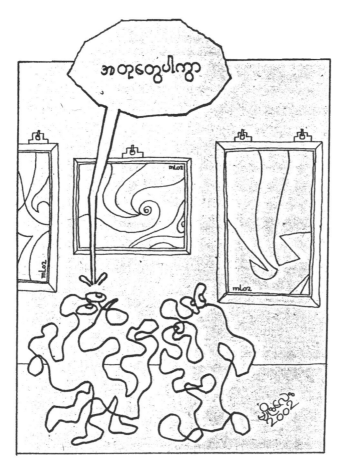

Figure 9.2. "A Replica!" (Source: *Han-thit* magazine
April 2002)

new style is not so "unrealistic" after all. Consider the cartoon (Figure 9.2)
from *Han-thit* magazine with its ironic portrayal of "modern art." The cartoon suggests a universe where nonrepresentational art can be perfect mime-
sis: "a replica!" Art is imitating life, the cartoon tells us. But life itself is distorted, twisted, unreal.

It seems the new style has some radical potential. Reaching for a free space
for the mind is an act of defiance and an act of self-liberation under extraordinary circumstances. The following poem by the late Maung Kyaw Nweh
alludes to this hopeful possibility:

Fish

For almost all my life, I have been fishing.
Catching not even one of those fish.
Look! What I finally caught—
it was the whole universe.
When I pulled it up
My fishing pole bent
And became a rainbow
Which was fishing for me.

Maung Kyaw Nweh
Sa-pay Gya-neh, June 1997

Notes

1. By the mid-1970s there were only seven daily papers remaining in Burma, all government-owned and publishing in either Burmese or English. (Licenses for Chinese and Indian-language papers were discontinued in 1966.) All but one were published in Rangoon. The titles were: *Loktha Pyithu Nayzin, Kyemon, Myanma Alin, Botahtaung, The Working People's Daily,* and *Guardian,* from Rangoon, and *Hantha-wadi* published in Mandalay. In 1978 *Hantha-wadi,* edited by Win Tin, was ordered to close, and Burma's second largest city was left without its own newspaper for several decades (Allott 1981:20, 33; n.28, 29).

2. Scrutiny mechanisms were also established for film- (and later video-) scripts, song lyrics, paintings, book covers, posters, and calendars.

3. Each registered publisher was allowed to purchase a monthly allocation of controlled-price paper from the state-owned Paper and Printing Corporation. Government agencies producing official publications had priority for paper. State-produced books or periodicals were printed in large numbers and in some cases distributed for free, while private publishers were permitted only small print editions (for example 2,000–3,000 copies for a magazine) that barely covered the cost of typesetting. Some independent publishers circumvented regulations by purchasing paper on the black market and printing larger editions than legally permitted, but the high cost of black-market paper kept profit margins slim (see Allott 1981:20, 25–26).

4. According to a 1975 memorandum issued by the Printers' and Publishers' Central Registration Board under the Ministry of Home and Religious Affairs, texts would be scrutinized by the PSB to determine whether or not they contained:

1. anything detrimental to the Burma Socialist Program;
2. anything detrimental to the ideology of the state;

3. anything detrimental to the socialist economy;

4. anything which might be harmful to national solidarity and unity;

5. anything which might be harmful to security, the rule of law, peace, and public order;

6. any incorrect ideas and opinions which do not accord with the times;

7. any descriptions which, though factually correct, are unsuitable because of the time or the circumstances of their writing;

8. any obscene (pornographic) writing;

9. any writing which would encourage crimes and unnatural cruelty and violence;

10. any criticism of a nonconstructive type of the work of government departments and any libel or slander of any individual (quoted in Allott 1981:29–30).

5. Literary magazines have been an important part of Burma's literary scene since World War II. In the 1970s there were several popular titles including: *Shu-mawa* (which began in 1947), *Thway-thauk, Sanda,* and *Mo-way.* By the mid-1980s there were some twenty to thirty monthly fiction magazines. Most were privately owned, although the army's publishing house produced two popular magazines as well: *Mya-wadi* and *Ngway-ta-yi* (see Allott 1981:22–23; Smith 1991:22).

6. The name change was part of the regime's effort to disassociate itself from socialism and recuperate an older nationalist tradition. *Myanma Alin* was a leading nationalist newspaper in the 1920s and 1930s. The new *Myanma Alin,* which issued its first number in April 1993, bears on its masthead the statement "Established 1914."

7. Among the leading writers and journalists jailed in the late 1980s for their political activities were Ba Thaw (pen name, Maung Thawka) and Win Tin. Maung Thawka, beloved novelist and translator of Shakespeare, also a former naval commander, was arrested in connection with a letter he wrote to a Tatmadaw (armed forces) commander. He was sentenced to twenty years hard labor and died in detention in 1991 at the age of sixty-seven. Win Tin, former editor of *Hantha-wadi* news daily and a close advisor to Aung San Suu Kyi, was arrested in 1989 at the age of sixty-one. He was sentenced to three years and then an additional ten years hard labor. In 1996 the sentence was extended yet another seven years because of his activities, along with twenty-one others, producing clandestine publications while in prison—including a report to the U.N. Special Rapporteur on Human Rights about conditions in Rangoon's Insein Prison. He is in poor health, suffering from a number of serious ailments. Reportedly he has refused to sign a letter promising to give up political activities as a condition of release.

Numerous writers and journalists have been imprisoned during the SLORC-SPDC era. While certain notable figures have been released in recent years, there are at least fifteen writers and journalists still languishing in Burmese prisons at the end of 2003, according to reliable sources inside the country. Human rights advocacy organizations estimate that there are some 1,300 or more political prisoners in Burma at the end of 2003 (see also reports on Burma on the Committee to Protect Journalists [CPJ] website, [www.cpj.org]; Reporters Without Borders [Reporters sans Frontières, or RSF] website, [www.rsf.fr]). As of this writing (October 2004), there is a new report that Win Tin may soon be released along with a number of other political prisoners.

8. Guidelines #1 and #3 were changed to read: 1. anything detrimental to the "sovereignty of the state" (previously "Burma Socialist Programme"); 3. anything detrimental to the "objectives of the state" (previously "socialist economy") (Tin Maung Than 1996).

9. The SLORC-SPDC's claim to arbitrate truth is most apparent in their rhetoric against foreign media and agencies that monitor events in Burma. Shortly after assuming power, the SLORC vociferously denounced the BBC (British Broadcasting Company) and VOA (Voice of America) broadcast services in a tract famously entitled "A Sky Full of Lies." In April 2000 the SPDC attacked a report on imprisoned journalists and political activists in Burma produced by Reporters Without Borders (Reporters sans Frontières). The Office of Strategic Studies (OSS) under the Myanmar Ministry of Defense published a vehement denial: a small, neatly produced book, in English, entitled "The Truth."

10. At this writing, October 2004, a major crackdown against independent publishing is underway, directed at publications associated with the once powerful Office of Military Intelligence Services (MIS). In the aftermath of the purge of MIS chief and Prime Minister Gen. Khin Nyunt, some thirty publications have been suspended or banned, including several news-oriented magazines and weeklies with wide readership, among them: *Living Color, New Gazette, First Eleven, 7-Days, Myanmar Interview, Idea, International News Journal,* and *Kumudra* (The lotus). The popular monthly *Living Color* was licensed to Ye Naing Win, Gen. Khin Nyunt's son, although it operated under independent management. Other recently closed publications had publishing licenses hired from MIS officials or Khin Nyunt's associates. The closure of these publications, along with the removal of the reform-leaning prime minister, signals the ascendance of hard-liners within the military leadership and indicates that the Burmese semiprivate press is headed into a particularly restrictive phase.

11. In December 2002 the PSB announced that individuals could apply for a new kind of license, a so-called "personal publication" *(ko-yay ko-htok)* license. There was a brief fifteen-day window for filing the necessary forms. The sudden announcement prompted speculation among publishers that the quasi-legal agreements involving transferred titles were about to be shut down. In fact, nothing came of the surprise announcement: no new licenses were issued to those who applied, and the anticipated crackdown against independents did not occur at that time.

12. There are several newspapers supervised by the Myanmar News and Periodicals Enterprise (MNPE), a branch of the Ministry of Information. In addition to *Myanma Alin* and *New Light of Myanmar,* there is *Kyemon* (Mirror) and *Myodaw Thadin* (City news) published in Rangoon, and *Yadana-bon* (Treasure) and *Mandalay*

Nayzin (Mandalay daily) published in Mandalay. In November 1998 a Chinese-language news weekly was launched for the benefit of the Chinese community in Burma. Called *Mian Dien Huo Bao* (Burmese morning post), it is the first Chinese-language newspaper in the country in over thirty years. Reportedly its style and tone is similar to other Burmese newspapers.

13. At this writing (October 2004), publication of the *Myanmar Times* has also been suspended as part of the sweep of media linked to Khin Nyunt, his associates, and the Office of Military Intelligence Services (see note 10 above).

14. A delegation of writers and magazine editors approached the PSB in January 1995 and made this tactful argument against censorship, appealing to official concerns about Myanmar's international image. One notes a parallel with the complaints about censorship voiced by writers in the mid-1970s. The writer (U Pu Htwei) who spoke before the Hlutdaw addressed the then-pressing concern about conserving paper and foreign exchange (Allott 1981:24). In neither case did the carefully worded appeal achieve its intended goal of easing controls on the press. Instead, both times, the situation got worse. The lesson for members of the literary world, it would seem, is not to complain.

15. The introduction of computer technology into Burma's publishing scene has been gradual. In 1995 most magazine editors were still computer illiterate, according to a survey conducted by Tin Maung Than. Computers were used only for typesetting and for color separation. Among ninety-two magazines, only five had their own computers and only two used computers in design, layout, and management. In 2002 in-house computer layout has become much more widespread but still not universal.

16. It takes three to four days for a weekly and one to three weeks for a monthly to clear the system. Bribes make the process run more smoothly and editors typically turn over 10 to 20 percent of a print run to the censor board, which sells the publication on the street for profit.

17. For example, in the mid-1990s a writer for a business magazine constructed a cover story on tourism, a sensitive issue for the government in the run up to the 1996 "Visit Myanmar Year." The author created two fictional characters, a man and a woman, both tour guides, and wrote the article as a love story, mixing dialogue between the characters and descriptions of tour scenery with the real facts of the business. The dialogue between the characters included some moderate criticism of the government's tourism policy. Discussing the story, Tin Maung Than points out that the article was perceived as legitimate journalism in Burma: no one called it "fiction." He suggests that such writing "goes beyond new journalism and probably beyond even literary non-fiction" (Tin Maung Than 1996). It seems this curious genre of quasi fiction is less challenging to the official monopoly on "truth."

18. The cover story that had been censored from the December 1995/January 1996 *Thint Bawa* magazine was published and distributed without Tin Maung Than's knowledge by expatriate Burmese dissidents. In 2000 the booklet called "Slave Educa-

tion versus Freeman Education" was intercepted by Military Intelligence officers and Tin Maung Than came under scrutiny. Later that year he was detained along with another publisher and interrogated for five days about a handful of photocopies he had made of a speech by the former deputy minister for economic development, Brig. Gen Zaw Tun, on Burma's economic difficulties. Expecting to be arrested, Tin Maung Than and his family fled to Thailand and are now residing in the United States. Coeditor Maung Thit Sin has also received political asylum in the United States. *Thint Bawa* magazine continued for a brief time under new editors but then was closed down.

19. These names were collected in conversations with editors and writers. The list is certainly not comprehensive: one notes that these are all men, even though a sizeable percentage of writers in Burma are women. Ju, probably Burma's most popular writer today, is a woman, but there is debate about whether she can be designated as a "new style" writer.

20. Specifically: the magazine quoted from a poem by Maung Kyaw Nweh, who died in September 2002. His poem referred to *another* writer, Ko Lay, who is blacklisted because of his political activities with the NLD. It is unlawful to publish even the *name* of a blacklisted writer (Reporters Without Borders [RSF] website, Burma Bulletin 10.30.2002).

21. In the 1930s and early 1940s there was an influential magazine of the same name published and edited by Thakin Kodawhmaing, a revered figure in Burmese letters. *Dagon* in its current incarnation has been publishing since 1985. Myat Thit became the editor in 1991.

22. *Mahaythi* and *Yok-shin Tay-kabya* boast circulations of 18,000 and 10,000 copies respectively. Circulation figures are always approximated. The official print allotment, posted per PSB regulation on the inside page of every magazine, is always less than the number actually printed and sold.

23. Today the issue is no longer contentious. Colloquial-style written Burmese has become widely accepted in print. Literary style has not disappeared, but has incorporated colloquial elements.

24. Burmese is a mostly monosyllabic tonal language, so rhyme, including "rhyming" tone, was long considered absolutely intrinsic to poetry. In the resources of the language, there is nothing comparable to English stress or vowel length with which to create aesthetic rhythm. Classic Burmese poetry was composed in lines of four syllables (*lay-lon-zat*, "four-word verse") with a complex internal rhyme scheme. Khitsan and "new literature" poets introduced new rhyme patterns but generally maintained the traditional four-syllable-per-line structure. The idea of free-verse (nonrhyming) poetry was radical indeed.

25. A Bangkok-based democracy activist once told me, probably with some hyperbole, that debate over Ju "nearly split the NLD."

26. The term "magical realism" was first applied to Maung Tin Sint's 1989 short story "A Horse," in which the narrative flows from the animal's point of view. Maung

Phan Khet, whom I understand is a professor of Asian literature at Tokyo University in Japan, used the term in a review. The story was translated into Japanese and published in a collection sponsored by the Tokyo Foundation. Maung Tin Sint told me he was surprised by the review. "I thought I was writing symbolism!" he said. Burmese writers are curious about "magical realism," but they have had little exposure. Mya Than Tint's translation of Gabriel Garcia Marquez's *One Hundred Years of Solitude* was just published in 1998 after many years of delay by the censors.

27. Many of these writers, it should be noted, were imprisoned for extended periods in the 1990s, including Nyi Pu Lay (from 1990 to 1999) and San San Nweh (from 1994 to 2001). The writer Win Pe went into exile in the early 1990s.

28. Nat refers to a celestial being or spirit (see Brac de la Perrière, this volume).

29. Red flag and white flag refer to two distinct branches of the Communist Party of Burma (CPB), which became an underground insurgent organization in the late 1940s but had above-ground supporters. In the 1960s and 1970s Zaw Zaw Aung was ideologically aligned with the red flag faction and Sein Win with the white flags. The CPB collapsed in 1989.

–10–
"But Princes Jump!"
Performing Masculinity in Mandalay

Ward Keeler

The male star of a Burmese theatrical troupe is called a "prince" *(min-tha)* and in certain portions of such troupes' night-long performances he takes on the dress and demeanor of an idealized Burmese male aristocrat. But it is difficult for an American observer, and I suspect this would be true for most Westerners, to look at images of a Burmese theater troupe's star in his princely mode without drawing certain inferences about his sexual orientation. To put it bluntly, a Burmese theater prince looks to us like a drag queen. And drag queens, most Westerners assume, are men who have sex with men. These inferences about Burmese troupes' stars are for the most part beside the point— and probably for the most part wrong.[1] Yet the question of how gender roles, appearances, and performing arts mesh in Burma's all-night popular theater *(zat-pwe)* performances is not beside the point at all. On the contrary, it is very much at the heart of these performances, and, too, at the heart of why performance practices have developed in the ways they have over the past forty to fifty years.

If outsiders jump to the conclusion that min-tha are "gay,"[2] it is not simply due to the yards and yards of brightly colored fabrics, multiple necklaces, diamond stud earrings, and brilliant red lipstick and nail polish that they wear—although all of these elements of the princely costume would likely help plant the notion in some people's minds. There is in addition the matter of style: hand gestures (delicate, mannered) and even facial expressions (fey and dreamy) that in the princely mode take on what might be seen as an effeminate cast. But that this reading of the princely style is something of a red herring was brought home to me when I spoke with a group of Burmese friends about the matter of style and gender in a prince's performance. When I commented that, as an American, I had trouble not seeing a certain effeminacy in the princely style, they looked surprised and said, "But they jump!" Indeed, princes do jump: a prince's dances always include at least a few athletic leaps, whereas a princess would never jump.[3] In addition, my friends pointed out, a prince's costume is obviously very different from a princess's costume. The princes' garments imitate—embellish, yes, but still imitate—the aristocratic dress of Burma's male erstwhile royalty. No one familiar with those styles would confuse a prince's attire with that of a princess.

So to confuse the princely style with an American drag queen's is a particularly piquant illustration of an anthropological truism: that people tend to misread other people's behavior in light of their own cultural conditioning. Yet the underlying question, and the more interesting one, is how people conceive of masculine style, or styles, in contemporary Burma, and why, in performances at least, they are so preoccupied with that issue—while feminine styles seem to matter much less.

The short answer as to why Burmese theater princes dress and carry themselves in the way that they do is that they thereby enact not a transvestite impulse but rather a specifically masculine refinement. Derived from aristocratic traditions, this style still enjoys some prestige in Burma, despite the disappearance of the aristocracy since the British takeover of Upper Burma in the late nineteenth century. But what I wish to show in what follows is how other constructions of masculinity have come to supplement, or largely supplant, that particular idealized conception of masculine behavior. My evidence stems primarily from all-night popular theater (zat-pwe) performances I saw in Mandalay in the rainy season of 2002, along with conversations I had with performers and other friends in Mandalay at that time.

Performing Gender

Performances are particularly fruitful places to look to in order to see how people think about gender because, as Judith Butler (1990) has argued, gender is always a performance. Butler means by this that there is no given, absolute "femaleness" or "maleness." Male and female, and so masculinity and femininity, can be defined only relationally. How that contrast gets set up and modified varies culturally and through time. But the contrast, or, really, sets of contrasts—however unconsciously acquired, assumed, and acted upon—exist and persist only by virtue of the fact that all of us perform them all of the time. We may think of masculine and feminine styles as "natural," but that is only because we constantly affirm them in the way we ourselves act and in the ways we read other people's actions. Inasmuch as these actions are not naturally given but rather culturally and historically variable, one cannot *"be* a man" but only *"act like* a man." Male and female are roles we take on—that is, ones we perform, and gender is a performance.

It follows from this simple assertion that when people go to see performances in the strict sense of the word, gender is likely to enter into their thoughts as they observe the performers. It also follows that when performers wish to engage an audience's attention, they will often play on gender roles by entangling masculine and feminine identities in the course of performances. A moment's reflection about Western genres, whether of elite or popular arts—*Twelfth Night, The Marriage of Figaro, The Milton Berle Show, Some Like It Hot*—will confirm the ubiquity of such a move's undying effectiveness in a great many different places, genres, and times.

A Performance of Zat-pwe

By the same token, it is worth considering how gender matters in contemporary zat-pwe performances. To begin with, I describe a performance given in July 2002, by the troupe whose star is named Ko Naw We. The performance took place near Amarapura in a field in front of a monastery. The monks from this monastery sponsored the performance to mark the passing of an old abbot a couple of years before, and also to celebrate the success of several monks in passing the state-sponsored Pali exams.

The Opening

The performance took place on a stage erected specifically for this purpose, and started at 9:15 in the evening. The curtain opened to reveal a conventional portrait of the Buddha, and a tableau vivant of a monk, an ogre, and a woman, all making obeisance to the portrait. Following this, a woman dancer—she later turned out to be the troupe's principal female star, Ma Thida—performed a dance in homage to the *nat* (spirits). A tray she carried with the standard sorts of offerings made to these beings showed that this was the import of the dance. But all Burmese performances start with some sort of gesture of respect to the spirits. The tableau vivant is a recent innovation, one in keeping with a reformist spirit in Burmese Buddhism, to make paying reverence to the Buddha precede the proffering of respect to the spirits.

At 9:30, with the curtain closed, several performers gathered on stage and began singing, accompanied by both Burmese and electronic instruments, the music including a heavy drum beat and an electric organ. When the curtain opened, three women started dancing, shifting suddenly several times between

Burmese movements and ones associated with Burmese and Western pop music. They were then joined by the star of the troupe, Ko Naw We, dressed in the princely style, with layer upon layer of brilliantly colored cloth, his long hair piled on top of his head, and wearing lots of jewelry and makeup. He took a microphone and started singing a light Burmese song, then danced briefly, and sang some more.

At 9:45, the first of a series of performers appeared on stage, a young man dressed in a silk *longyi* (traditional sarong-like garment) and Burmese jacket over a Burmese-style shirt. The audience applauded him, clearly recognizing him, and he smiled and waved. This was Ko Bali, a talented young actor, singer, and comic, who performed in all parts of the performance. At this point he sang a couple of Burmese pop songs, accompanied by both Burmese and electronic instruments. He was followed by a number of other performers, including two women. But each singer appeared singly on stage, and like Ko Bali, each was dressed in costly Burmese clothes and sang Burmese pop songs dating as far back as the 1960s.

The Opera

The section of the performance called the "opera" started at 10:30. This is a brief play that recounts a tale with some sort of moral lesson. It usually takes place in the relatively distant Burmese past, or in a legendary place. In this case it concerned three young men—played by the troupe's star, Ko Naw We, Ko Bali, and a third young man—who are returning home after studying at the "university," where they have acquired skills, respectively, in sculpting, painting, and infusing life into objects. This play was performed in "classical" dress (Ko Naw We in his princely garb, Ko Bali and the third student in comics' outfits); the language was contemporary conversational Burmese; and, unusually for present-day Burmese performances, it was accompanied by nonelectronic Burmese instruments only. It was played primarily for laughs. Its moral intent was at the same time clear: that one must never deny one's indebtedness to one's benefactors. This point receives frequent expression in the Burmese arts, and indeed in Burmese conversation as well.

The Stage Show

The opera ended at around midnight, and after a short pause the section of the performance called the "stage show" started. A stage show consists of what Burmese call "heavy" rock songs, ones accompanied by electric guitars, electric organ, and a drum set, with a very heavy bass beat. Once again Ko Bali was the first to perform, and he and each of the people that followed him sang two songs. Almost all the singers were male, although Ma Thida did appear, wearing Bermuda shorts and a long shirt, to sing two songs. Finally Ko Naw We appeared and sang a long set, often with other males performing as backup singers or as breakdancers.

Ko Naw We performed first in tight blue jeans, with his long hair loose. He modified his outfit constantly, such as adding a baseball cap (often turned backwards), changing muscle shirts (always branded), and putting on sunglasses. He strutted about the stage, shook his long hair violently, snarled and looked fierce while singing at the top of his lungs. For the most part, the stage show implied anger and violence just as contemporary Western hip-hop and other forms of rock music do, although this was occasionally undercut by Ko Bali's comic moves. The decibel level was extremely high, and the energy level on stage similarly so. It went on until 2:30 in the morning. The audience watched it all intently, although people do not clap at the ends of songs in Burma, so the otherwise remarkable resemblance to a Western rock concert was undermined in the odd silence that followed the concluding chords of each song. The players of the Burmese orchestra, jammed together with their instruments to the side of the stage, slept through it all.

The Straight Play

The straight play *(pya-zat)* followed. It concerned a man, played by Ko Naw We, and his wife, played by Ma Thida, whose marriage is destroyed when a rich neighbor gets the woman drunk and persuades her to run off with him. The daughter of the original couple dies when an agent of the lover tries to kidnap her to join her mother; her mother kills her lover for this; and the husband kills his wife whom he holds responsible for their daughter's death. Finally, the police come to take the husband away to prison. The play gave Ko Naw We the opportunity to embark on long moralizing and melodramatic speeches. (The play is scripted, but he told me in conversation later that he often elaborates spontaneously on the speeches during his performance.) Throughout the straight play, the electric keyboard provided a musical accompaniment, giving the proceedings the feel of a melodramatic movie, or a soap opera on television.

The Duet

The final portion of the performance, called the "duet" *(hnapa-thwa)*, consisted of first one male dancer dressed as a prince coming on stage and singing pop songs and dancing, and then another. A group of six women sat or danced in a semicircle behind them, and three male comics (including Ko Bali) stood at the edges as the princes' retainers. As each prince sang, he held a microphone, then gave it to someone else on stage when he was about to dance. At several points, the comics intervened, sometimes letting a prince stand back and rest a moment, sometimes engaging him in comic banter. The first prince was not a very effective singer and was subjected to some kidding on Ko Bali's part. The second prince was an older man, probably in his forties. He had appeared singing pop songs early in the evening and had sung again in the stage show (dressed at that point in a flashy black-and-white outfit, with a long dangly earring and dark glasses). But now he was dressed, and he danced, as a prince. Finally, Ko Naw We appeared, dressed in yet a different princely costume, this one a brilliant red.

Ko Naw We danced briefly, both gracefully and energetically. He didn't, however, engage with the other people on stage very much, and he left the stage soon after. By this time it was after five in the morning, and the crowd had thinned considerably. The older prince gave a final speech to the audience, and then, after the curtain came down at close to 5:30, he led the rest of the company who had gathered on the stage (excepting Ko Naw We) in a long Pali chant. The sun had risen shortly after five and it was now bright; the performance area was littered with hundreds of plastic bags and other trash.

The Significance of Costumes

In the West, and in much of the rest of the world, the stage costume of male rock stars differs only in degree, if at all, from the clothes young men wear much of the time: young men have come to emulate the clothes of rock stars in a great many settings. Muscle shirts, torn jeans or knee-length shorts, and running shoes or boots: all of these conventionalized accoutrements of the young man on stage now pervade men's everyday dress the world over. But in Burma these clothes are still very highly marked. It is a general impression among Burmans[4] that the government looks askance at any grown male wearing trousers instead of longyi (Fink 2001:133). It was widely believed that the former dictator, Ne Win, felt this way, and it is thought that the rulers who have replaced him in power since 1988 share that disapproval. (The rulers themselves, as military men, wear trousers as part of their uniforms all the time.)[5] So there is some element of defiance in wearing trousers. Yet to read the practice of wearing trousers only as a gesture of political resistance is to simplify matters. It is a more explicit political act to wear a longyi of the "jade" pattern, a Kachin pattern much like the Scottish Black Watch design, since that is associated in people's minds with the oppositional party, the National League for Democracy led by Daw Aung San Suu Kyi. On recent trips to Burma, I have noticed more young men wearing tight jeans and sleeveless shirts than in the late 1980s.

Nevertheless it is young men who wish to appear cool who wear these clothes. The vast majority of Burmese males in Mandalay (and elsewhere in

Burma, including Rangoon) still wear longyi, unless they are in the military. (Motorcycle riders, of which there are more and more in Mandalay, show some inclination to wear pants rather than longyi. I suspect that they wear trousers as much to draw attention to the fact that they own a motorcycle as to assure their own convenience. Middle-aged males tend still to wear longyi even when they ride motorcycles.) This means that to wear Western-style clothes in Burma is for males a statement about how one wishes to identify oneself. To wear Western clothes is to lay claim to being a member of an international community in addition to, or more than, being just a member of a local one. It means, in a word, being modern (see Figure 10.1).

The stars of a troupe often dress in the stage show, then, in what in Burma is a highly marked, even, in the eyes of some, a transgressive style. In the straight play they dress with more restraint, but invariably they still wear trousers, although just what sort of trousers depends on the nature of the role being played. A well-heeled gangster will wear a Western-style suit, whereas a middle-class father wears jeans, and a well-bred young son might wear white trousers and a flashy red shirt. In any case a star never wears a longyi. Subsidiary characters do: older brothers, servants, and other males lacking the status of the star. But stars never do. At other points in the performance, stars dress in the aristocratic style of the prince.

Overall, the clothes that the star wears can be reduced to two sorts: the various Western or international outfits based on trousers and shirts, and the various Burmese aristocratic outfits based on longyi and Burmese-style shirts. The affinities between the clothes the star wears during the stage show and the straight play that follows actually point to a deeper affinity, between the persona of the rock star and the persona of the male lead in the straight play. The rock star appears as a single, aggressive male given over to extreme emotion and on the edge of violence. Most plays revolve around a male lead who behaves in a much less implicitly violent manner yet is still in some ways a loner or an odd man out. For example, he is a disinherited son who becomes a gangster in order to support his siblings. Or he is a young man who falls in love with a servant and suffers the wrath of his status-climbing mother as a result. Or, as in Ko Naw We's performance, he is a man abandoned by his wife who ultimately takes the law into his own hands. In each case the star becomes an agent who must act on his own, against the wishes of others.

This feature of the male lead's role will seem familiar from a great many expressive traditions, including Hollywood. Unlike in Western popular culture, however, the hero's actions are usually justified by his loyalties to family rather more than by any love interest or crusade against evil. Paradoxically, the hero must act on his own, outside the bounds of convention, that is, auton-

Figure 10.1. Ko Naw Weh poster showing traditional and modern versions of Burmese masculinity

omously, because he upholds the importance of loyalty to his kin. But the image of the autonomous male that the stage show exaggerates so extravagantly still informs the star's role in the straight play, even if the caricature of radical autonomy impersonated in the stage show is tempered in the more "realistic" genre of the play. In both cases the star is set apart as a man who is worldly, active, an independent agent—and modern. So of course he has to wear pants.

I may appear to belabor the matter of costume in these performances. But costumes clearly matter—to Burmese performers and their audiences—not just to me. A star spends an extraordinary amount of time changing clothes in the course of a performance. Each princely outfit consists of many layers of cloth, as well as jewelry and elaborate headgear, and the star of the troupe appears in several such outfits in the course of a performance. Often when the star appears on stage in yet another elaborate and colorful princely costume he is greeted by applause. But the stage show draws attention to clothes just as much or even more than the scenes in which the star appears as a prince. For each song, a star wears a different outfit. Sometimes this means changing only a shirt. More often it means changing trousers, shirt, hat, sunglasses, and shoes. Often, the star changes shirts for each *verse* of a song.

Many other members of a troupe must stand in the wings with these clothes at the ready, particularly since once the star takes the stage he rarely gives it up again. The pattern varies among troupes, but singers don't usually take turns performing. Instead, each singer comes out and sings a certain number of songs and then yields to another singer. Even if some singers do alternate on stage (facilitating their costume changes between songs), the star takes the last turn in the stage show and sings the greatest number of songs. The more clothes he has to change between numbers, the longer an introduction to the next song the electric keyboard and other instruments must play.

Alternative Masculinities

An all-night performance puts a number of male actors on the stage, and their varying roles suggest alternative possibilities of how one can "act like a man" in contemporary Burma.[6] The masculine roles taken by comics and what are called "older princes" (*min-tha-gyi*) present a clear contrast to the star's roles. These other male performers represent familiar, equally stereotyped, but not idealized versions of Burmese masculinity.

Comics participate in the opera, straight play, and duet as secondary characters, usually low-status ones, such as servants and retainers. When troupe members appear as comics, they wear archaic masculine clothes including longyi that are made out of many more yards of fabric than is standard today.

They engage in a great deal of physical comedy, ribald routines, and other standard comic ploys, and they speak in a much more familiar style than the star. They contrast with the star most strikingly in the degree to which they operate as a team. They rarely appear on stage except as a group, playing off one another, teasing, deceiving, and playfully attacking one another in conventional slapstick routines. They are unaffected, in contrast to the star's various highly stylized personae, familiar and silly in contrast to his high-status seriousness, and dependent on their superiors and each other in contrast to his individual importance and agency.

The servants actually relate to the audience very directly at points in the performance, such as when they inform the spectators of what has occasioned the performance or they make other announcements. In one performance it fell to them to promote the fabric store that the star of the troupe had recently opened in Mandalay's largest market. In the course of another, young men in the audience became so rowdy that the performers of the straight play refused to continue. Afterwards, when the play had resumed and then concluded, it was the men playing servants that gave moralizing lectures to the crowd about how to behave themselves. In doing so, they stepped somewhat out of character. But the point is that it was conceivable for them to do so—the conceptual distance between them, as low-status comic characters, and their audience was not great—whereas it would not have been appropriate for the star to do so.

"Older princes" almost always exhibit evil traits: they are ruthless, venal, or status-mongering. Or they are simply doddering old fools. Yesterday's stars must resign themselves to taking on roles as "older princes" at younger and younger ages. Whereas in the past audiences were happy to watch men perform as stars well into their forties or even beyond, the consensus today is that no male much beyond thirty can expect to hold the attention of an audience.

Unlike the comics' and older princes' renderings of mundane masculine roles, the star's appearance in the stage show, in the straight play, and as a prince, can be understood as differing versions of an *idealized* masculinity. But even these idealized roles contrast dramatically in many respects, especially the two extremes of rock star and prince. The stage show star mimes ferocity; the prince smiles seductively, or coyly, or dreamily. The stage show star moves in sudden, jerky movements, as though out of control and enraged; the prince executes difficult dance steps with apparent ease, displaying elegance and grace. Yet remarkably, these figures are played by the same person.

It would be tempting to infer that the coexistence of the various modes in which the theatrical star takes to the stage implies a range of possibilities in Burmese renderings of idealized masculinity, a range of stylistically contrasting but equally valid versions of what it means to be a man. But this puts the case rather too optimistically. The way time is allotted to different parts of a performance, and the modifications in those sections of the performance in which the star is featured, suggest otherwise.

The star of a troupe generally appears at the beginning of a performance in princely attire, usually wearing the same or similar clothes during the opera, since this relates some old tale, or at least a tale that takes place in an older time and place. But the opera is over by about 11:00 or midnight, and for the next several hours the star becomes first the rock singer and rapper in the stage show, and then the hero in the straight play. During the duet, he reverts to the princely role. But here he shares the stage with two or three other princes. His status as star is preserved inasmuch as he still comes on stage only after all the others have already appeared and taken one or more turns singing and doing some dance steps. In this portion of the performance, he remains the main attraction. But his appearance tends to be brief. Ko Naw We performed for only about twenty minutes out of the last hour and a half of his troupe's performance. In the past, the star would continue to take the princely role in the "final section" *(nauk-paing)* of the performance, which would follow the duet. This final section related some historical drama, or a Buddhist morality play, or some other traditional story with a moralizing point. But this portion of a performance is rarely presented now. So instead one may see, as I could toward the end of Ko Naw We's troupe's performance, the star's extravagant princely costume hanging over the divider of his dressing cubicle while the other princes continued to perform for the vestiges of an audience.

The diminishing time a star puts into the princely role suggests a diminishing identification of the star with this aristocratic ideal. And the aristocratic ideal itself, while evident in the stylization of the prince's costume and in the dance steps he executes, that is, in the refinement of gesture and appearance that Burmese like many others think of as somehow intrinsic to aristocratic identity,[7] that ideal, too, loses much of its primacy as the prince dances less and sings more. Alternating between holding the microphone to sing and putting it down so that he can dance, the star actually moves between two rather different modes. As a dancer, he reiterates as best he is able a long tradition of Burmese dance, one that people think of as originating in the royal palaces of precolonial Burma. But as a singer, he no longer sings any of the classical songs that share that presumed origin, nor is he even likely to sing songs of the twentieth century linked to the famous stars of the past. Instead, he sings pop songs, in the crooning style of a latter-day Sinatra, and the time he spends singing greatly exceeds the time he spends dancing. Like Sinatra and many internationally famous male singers since his time, a star in this portion of a performance affects the mode of a seductive, sensitive male. He can do this because the microphone permits him to sing in an intimate manner to thousands of people.

Older artists in Mandalay often remark to me that in the old days singers sang *loud*. Indeed, young people who wanted to become performers were told they had to be able to "yell" if they were going to become stars. Now young singers are unable to project their voices at all. Their elders blame this on microphones, suggesting that young people, knowing that they can rely on microphones to make their voices audible, are simply too lazy to develop the lung power their predecessors took such pride in. But this strikes me as somewhat off the mark. "Yelling" might be appropriate to singing classical songs. It would be out of place singing the pop ballads that make up the repertoire of the contemporary prince. Microphones not only make it possible for weak voices to carry a long way, they also make it possible to create an impression of physical and emotional proximity even in a large crowd. Singers exploit this opportunity all the more fully by holding the microphone very close to their mouths, giving the sound the feel of a very confidential communication.

The whole tenor of the relationship between the audience and the performance has shifted, in the contemporary version of the duet, because the prince no longer sings to and about a princess. This part of a performance is called a "duet" because in the past it consisted of a prince and princess dancing, individually and as a pair, and singing of their feelings, such as their love for each other, sorrow at their plight, and a yearning for their home. In a puppet performance, this would still be the organizing conceit of the duet. But over time in zat-pwe the so-called "duet" has ceased to feature a pair of performers. Instead, each prince performs a solo while a semicircle of women, the "princesses," sit or stand behind him. These women may sing a chorus to his singing, or one of them may take the microphone and sing when he puts it down to dance a few steps. The princesses as a group often clap in time to the music as well, and if they are standing, they may dance simple movements. But they are a backdrop to the prince, rather than the other half of a duet. They have taken up a position midway between performer and audience, part backup singer and part spectator, cheering the prince on. They have been demoted from costars to the status of extras, a group of modestly dressed chorus girls (see Figure 10.2).

As long as a prince and princess performed a duet together, they were ostensibly attending upon each other, and we, the audience, were onlookers. Now that the prince dances very little and pays even less attention to the princesses, what comes into focus is his relationship with the spectators. This relationship, as I have suggested above, is characterized by a seductive familiarity, in which the crooning star sings directly to "us," his audience, and does so as "himself," the star.

This impression of intimacy and interchange is made all the more vivid by the common practice in which audience members approach the stage in order to put garlands of flowers over the star's head, or to hand him bouquets of flowers, or to pin money to his clothes. Spectators engage in this tipping behavior earlier in the performance as well, during the pop music section that takes place shortly after the performance starts, and sometimes during the stage show, and they do so for other performers as well as the star. (The tempo and frenzy of the stage show generally discourage audience members from tipping in this way. If they go ahead with it, though, the effect sometimes seems incongruous: here the star is enacting stylized rage yet must bend down and bow his head while someone puts a garland of jasmine blossoms around his neck.) But most tips are usually presented during the duet, and the star usually receives the lion's share of them. Some performers make a point of acknowledging these gifts graciously; others appear only to tolerate them. The overall effect is to personalize the proceedings, rather the way that a nightclub performer in the West often inflects the nature of performances, pulling them away from the model of staged representations and toward an anonymous, but in principle "real" intimacy.

The Classical Style

The move from the older, classical style of Burmese performances to the contemporary ones I have described consists primarily in this shift from an

Figure 10.2. Ko Naw Weh and the Princesses in the opening scene of a zat-pwe (Source: Ward Keeler)

aristocratic tradition, formulated in the courts, to a "modern" one formulated largely in the mass media.[8] The contrast is stunning. Three performances I saw in 2002 provide some inkling of what the classical tradition looks, or looked, like. The Ministry of Culture's Department of Fine Arts has a troupe of performers available for hire, and one night I saw them perform next to the Mahamuni pagoda in Mandalay. Not surprisingly, they avoided what Burmese call "heavy" rock songs. (People distinguish "heavy" songs that feature electric guitars and a very rapid beat, from pop songs, played with a mix of electric and Burmese instruments in a less frenzied way, although there is still a very heavy bass beat.) Vocalists sang a number of modern Burmese pop songs, but at the point in the performance, after an "opera," when the stage show would normally begin, the troupe substituted a magic show. Then from two until four in the morning they performed a dance-drama relating the *Ramayana*. The troupe's members danced superbly. But to perform the entire *Ramayana* in two hours meant that everything had to happen very fast. I sensed some tension between a dance tradition in which movements were masterfully controlled, in the fluid yet rhythmically very precise classical style, on the one hand, and on the other, the imperative to get on to the next event in the plot. In Burma, as elsewhere, the shift from the deliberate pace of a classical tradition to a more recent imperative to keep things moving quickly marks a major difference between the older and modern styles.

This imperative to keep up a rapid tempo in performances does not mean that performances are any shorter. Most zat-pwe still last until dawn, so the length of the performance depends only on what time the sun rises. Performances geared toward tourists, however, are different. A puppet troupe that performs for tourists in the small theater next to the Sedona Hotel in Mandalay performed one of the Jataka tales in forty-five minutes.[9] (The time constraint was imposed on them by Japanese sponsors, who asked that they prepare such a performance to take on tour to Japan later in the year.) The tale, in which a queen insists that her husband bring her the heart of the famous preacher Widura enabled the troupe to include in the course of their performance brief examples of "weeping songs" *(ngo-gyin)*, songs in which a character speaks and sings in a manner expressing great sorrow. These weeping songs are sources of particular pride and pleasure among aficionados of Burmese classical arts. They can be very beautiful and moving. No one under forty seems to have any interest in learning to sing them.

I did have an opportunity to see two older stars of zat-pwe perform such songs. A famous star of the 1980s, Ko Tin One, no longer performs in public. He is in his mid-forties, and as mentioned above, it is received opinion today that audiences have no interest in seeing anyone much over the age of thirty perform. Ko Tin One therefore devotes his energies to training his nephew, Ko

Yè Màn, who now heads a troupe. But Ko Tin One was gracious enough to offer to perform a "final section" on my behalf if I came to see his nephew's troupe perform in Sagaing. It was well past four in the morning before the final section started. But Ko Tin One and his costar, Má Mùn Mùn, were dazzling in their roles as a married couple who are deceived by the gods into having children despite their own decision to live as brother and sister. Their performances differed from all other performances I saw, apart from the puppet performances, because they were so highly stylized in speech, gesture, and sentiment. These were not the conventional gestures of movies or for that matter of the straight play performed earlier that night—gestures that are also highly stylized but thought of as "realistic." They were rather a thoroughly elaborated, "old-fashioned" style, performed by people with complete confidence in the validity of the tradition they had mastered through long study and performance. It is this style, one shared in many respects by the marionette tradition, that appears to have lost its currency in Burma.

The fact that the star of most troupes, even in his princely mode, performs more as a pop singer than as a classically trained singer or dancer, as well as the fact that he performs in the princely mode a relatively short time, suggests that the allure that used to attach to the aristocratic male has largely disappeared. It has been replaced by the romantic, lovelorn crooner, who is as close as one comes in Burma to the West's "sensitive New Age male." The affinities with the older convention are real: refinement of feeling and gesture grounded the princely demeanor, just as they do the crooner's. The difference lies in the fact that the crooning pop star provides another image of a *modern* masculinity, not a classically aristocratic one: his status stems not from his mastery of a specifically Burmese version of refinement but rather on his mastery of an internationally promoted style—smooth, ingratiating—and as seen in Hollywood movies. So the distinction between the prince and the rock star is maintained, in the contrast between refinement and aggressiveness. But both partake of a modernity that places the star apart from everything old-fashioned, everyday, and familiar—and therefore little worthy of attention.

Yet the princely style, even transformed into that of the crooner, still seems secondary to the preeminent place that the star enjoys in his rock-star role. The stage show takes up so much time, and its place in the order of events—starting at about midnight, when the crowd remains very large, much larger than it will be by the time the duet takes place at three or four in the morning—makes it so much more prominent in most spectators' experience of performances that it appears to be the essential persona of the contemporary star.

As the prince in the duet turns into a pop singer, he comes to resemble the similarly modern figures of the rock star and dramatic hero. One reason for the differential weighting of these roles, or at least one manifestation of it, lies in the concentration of the star's duties. If the role of the princess in the duet has been diminished, that of the male star has been consolidated. I am told that in the past, one man performed the role of the prince in the duet and final section, whereas a different actor played the male lead in the straight play. This meant that each star honed his skills in one genre—melodrama for one, classical music and dance for the other—and slept during the parts of the performance that didn't concern him. That distribution of responsibilities no longer obtains. The star appears in all parts of the performance and gives his name to the troupe (something also less commonly practiced in the past). Pulling roles together into the single person of the star means that whatever his strengths—and today it appears that the most successful stars are those best able to sing pop songs—determines what version of the modern male predominates. It also assures that the figure of the male is, even more than in the past, the real and almost constant focus of attention.

Stylized Aggression and Powerlessness

One member of Ko Naw We's troupe, an older brother of the star, told me that their troupe is famous for having the best stage show in Mandalay. No doubt some people would contest this, but of the four troupes I saw perform in 2002, theirs was indeed the most impressive. Many of the singers were very effective: they imitated the angry, aggressive, macho style of rappers brilliantly. Ko Naw We's performance was especially noteworthy. Letting his long, thick hair hang loose, he dipped forward and straightened up frenetically while screaming into the microphone, then strode around the stage looking fierce. His backup singers, three young guys (two of whom were comics in other parts of the performance), were expertly choreographed, and they, too, made aggressive gestures and mimed ferocious anger. All in all they mounted a very convincing rendition of a loud rock music performance.

This highly aggressive style has come to stand, in the West as in Burma, for a particular understanding of masculinity. What it means to be male in this version is to be assertive, ferocious, and strong—an absolutely autonomous agent. The persona of the rock singer that the star takes on during the stage show, in which he impersonates an angry, aggressive individual unconstrained in gesture or appearance by the dictates of everyday social life or government fiat, constitutes a version of masculinity with great appeal in contemporary Burma—as it does in much of the rest of the world. We have become so inured to this characterization that we are liable to let it go unremarked. But it would be a mistake not to consider its particular impact, or irony, in Burma.

The simple truth about most males in Burma today, especially the young men who attend theater performances in large numbers, is that they are humiliatingly powerless. The Burmese economy has experienced a certain number of encouraging phases since the military took control of the country in 1962. Most recently, in the early to mid-1990s the regime liberalized the economy sufficiently to bring about a sudden upsurge in foreign investment. But continued political stalemate, along with graft, corruption, bureaucratic ineptitude, and arbitrary and byzantine procedures, have all brought general disaffection among potential investors—and among many already committed ones who have cut their losses and left. As of this writing, in early 2003, the economy is in truly dire straits, with the Burmese currency, the kyat, at its lowest rate ever, and mounting concern that the inflation in prices for basic foodstuffs has grown so rapidly that there is a real risk of civil unrest.

Economic stagnation has meant unemployment for vast numbers of Burmese. At the same time the regime has kept universities closed for much of the past fifteen years. It has permitted some older institutions to reopen for graduate students, but for the most part it has provided more support for newer universities built far outside urban centers in order to make sure that any student unrest can be easily contained. Burmese men with university degrees and some wealth may be able to drive taxis to make a living, but the black market price of gasoline has risen precipitously, making it more difficult to earn much money in this way too. Tellingly, one area in which the economy has grown robustly since the uprising and subsequent political clampdown in 1988 is in teashops, now far more numerous than before, because the vast numbers of unemployed and underemployed men spend hours in these establishments. As one thirty-year-old friend commented to me, "Everyday's a holiday for us."[10]

The economic crisis that affects so many Burmese today arouses even more resentment because of the growing evidence of accumulating wealth among certain small segments of the population. In Rangoon and Mandalay both, one sees far more cars than ten or even five years ago. And many of these cars are not the modest used cars from China and Japan that many people drive but shiny new SUVs. They are driven either by families of the ruling military or by those people who have benefited by the selective liberalization of the economy since the mid-1990s.

Of course, the vast majority of young Burmese males entertain little hope of enjoying either the wealth that the fortunate few display so prominently or the power and freedom of action—autonomy—it implies. But they can enjoy the representation of their own desire as enacted by the rock star, whose performance expresses both their idealized image of a powerful male, and their rage at its utter remoteness from the conditions of their own lives. The rock star is in charge, in a fashion—and out of control. This must constitute a very powerful fantasy for young men confronted with their own impotence.

The idea of the modern suggests a great many different possibilities. Both

Burmans and outsiders might agree to include in a list of modernity's characteristics such diverse features as economic security (probably obtained through successful participation in a market economy), some sense of political agency, access to educational opportunities, freedom of expression, and urban residence. None of these is easily achieved in Burma today. Even long-time residents of Burma's cities may find themselves suddenly forced to move far outside the city center, while economic security and political agency are out of the question.

The one feature of modernity that is at all attainable for most people is stylistic: how one dresses, how one carries oneself, how one presents oneself in public. Many Burmese, younger ones especially, are at the very least intrigued by the representation of the modern as enacted on the stage, whether or not they have the means or the nerve to take it on themselves. Freud says that a dream is both the covert expression of a wish and the covert representation of its fulfillment, and much the same might be said of Burmese theater performances: that they are the covert expression of a fantasized modern masculinity, and a covert expression of many people's rage at its denial to them.

Disappearing Females

I have described the contrast between a classical style, now largely ignored by theater troupes, and the penchant for contemporary styles taken on by those troupes' stars. I have argued that modernity as a style preoccupies Burmese performers and audiences, at least those performers and audiences that one finds at contemporary performances.[11] It might therefore be asked whether my emphasis on gender is not misplaced, whether what is at issue in performances is not how to be a man but rather how to be modern. But a striking fact about contemporary performances, as my description should make clear, is the degree to which women have been relegated to a secondary role. If performances focus on modernity, they do so almost exclusively with reference to males, not females. If performances suggest alternative masculinities, the subject of femininities seems to elude them altogether—and modernity thereby becomes a version of masculinity alone.[12]

Women do of course appear in zat-pwe performances. They dance in the opening scenes and in the "duet" near the end of the performance. They may take fairly prominent roles in the straight play. They sing songs during the initial pop music series early in the performance, and often at least a few songs during the stage show. But certain constraints make it difficult for them to claim an audience's attention for very long. First, they cannot perform as comedians. After doing research on the performing arts traditions in Java and Bali, where women often perform hilarious routines as maidservants and other low-status characters, I was surprised to find that in Burma such practice is simply unthinkable. In the straight plays, and in the opera, women become modest paragons of virtue, or older shrews, or prostitutes. In the pop music and stage show portions of the performance, they may wear miniskirts and boots, or other outfits thought outrageously revealing of a woman's form. And at the beginning of the performance, and during the duet, they dance as a chorus. These are all standardized, conventional personae, just as all the available roles for males are. But when males appear as servants, they enjoy a measure of freedom—freedom to look familiar, if inglorious—that women do not enjoy.

Even if we simply ascribe to "tradition" the fact that women are excluded from comic roles in zat-pwe, we cannot treat the duet, in which the princess's role has been severely curtailed, so complacently. I provide two hypotheses about why this change has taken place. The first summarizes what some Burmese friends suggested by way of explanation for why the princess's role has diminished. The second is my own tentative explanation.

Burmese friends commented that the audience for zat-pwe is largely female. Since women are interested in seeing men on stage, not women, they lavish attention on the prince and give little thought to the princess. So women have moved to the background in the duet. These friends contrasted this situation with *anyeint,* another popular performing art tradition, in which women dance and sing, and men perform as comedians. This genre is said to attract a predominantly male audience, which explains why it is women alone who dance, while the men provide comic entertainment, and there is no male star.

There is much merit to analyzing zat-pwe with reference to other performance traditions, particularly anyeint. As Bourdieu (1993) points out in his analysis of literature as a "field of cultural production," no development in one genre occurs in isolation from developments in other genres, and this certainly applies to anyeint and zat-pwe too. Yet I do not accept the premise that spectators for zat-pwe are predominantly female. At the performances described above, there were hordes of young men in the crowds, even if, as per standard practice, women and children made up most of the audience, sitting closest to the stage.

I suggest instead that women have lost some of their prominence in performances because the question of how to represent a Burmese woman as both feminine and modern admits of no clear answer. If a woman takes on the demeanor and dress of foreign women, particularly as seen in the movies, few Burmese, male or female, could see her as anything but a prostitute. Yet simply to represent in a contemporary performance the refined, modest, graceful princess of the classical tradition would presumably hold no more allure than representing the prince in a purely classical mold. The solution for the prince has been to turn into a pop singer. There are many female Burmese pop singers, and women do take on this role in zat-pwe performances, although less prominently than their male colleagues. But they do not do so in the duet. Instead, they fade into the background.

Burmese women must contend daily with the question of how they will live their lives in contemporary conditions: they are no more left behind, or free from stress, than Burmese males.[13] But representing women on stage poses particular difficulties. A consistent feature of the masculine role taken by the star in both the stage show and in the straight play is, as mentioned above, that he appears as an autonomous agent, a loner, an individual somehow at odds with his surroundings. The angry rocker presents this image at its most extreme; the straight play does so in a more attenuated form. When the duet turns into a solo display for the prince, and we as spectators take the place of the princess, the star once again becomes in a sense disembedded. Tensions between individual desires (often amorous) and the ties that bind one to one's elders, families, community, and so on, provide the stuff of conflict to motivate performances the world over: the conflict between desires for autonomy and desires for connectedness is an existential one. But the romanticization of the autonomous agent is a preeminent feature of popular culture in the West, and in zat-pwe at least, it has become an essential part of the understanding of what it might mean to be modern. For males, this appears to suggest a range of options; for females, the options that come to mind are largely unacceptable and therefore little in evidence. Modernity and masculinity become coterminous. Females and modernity are accommodated with difficulty.

If Burmese representations of modernity focus to a considerable degree on clothing, how women dress implicates their participation in modernity as much as masculine attire for males does. This is hardly unique to Burma. The Ewens (1992) write of how young immigrant factory women in New York at the turn of the twentieth century would find themselves trapped in the sweatshop garment factories—but who express their aspirations for greater social standing by spending their money on new-styled clothes. And Chatterjee (1993:116–134) has written of how men in South Asia show that they participate in the modern world by adopting Western clothes, while showing that their women do not by keeping them in "traditional" attire. For women to uncover their legs, or even to bare their arms fully, remains in Burma a highly charged, and highly compromising, move. Even on stage, few women appear willing to generate the unflattering associations that displaying much of their body in public would inevitably give rise to. If performances enable Burmese males to observe and identify themselves with the modern at least in dress and demeanor, Burmese females lack even this option. As modernity comes increasingly to constitute the focus of performances, women's roles diminish.

Masculinity, Sexuality, and the Sangha

Understanding idealized masculinity as equivalent to modernity and autonomy raises two final and contrasting issues: sexuality and the *sangha* (monastic order). To conceive of modern masculinity as best instanced in the autonomous individual that zat-pwe celebrate actually implicates sex very little. The romantic love that figures so importantly in Western popular culture doesn't seem to exert quite the same fascination in zat-pwe. It may motivate some of the play's plot, but it tends not to prove the focus of many of its scenes. As for the stage show, the phallic symbolism of electric guitars is not lost on Burmese performers, who vigorously strum large imaginary instruments in front of their crotches like legions of males around the world. But in Burma, as elsewhere, to idealize masculinity as consisting above all in a radical autonomy means deemphasizing sexual connectedness. There is something of a contradiction here. Potency, after all, usually implies a man's sexual athleticism. But sex requires a partner and so implies something like interdependence.[14] The misogyny of so much rock music must stem from this contradiction: men's sexual attraction to women suggests that women hold some power over them, but that power contradicts the radical autonomy upon which masculinity, in this version at least, is based. So women, rather than being celebrated or courted, are subjected to verbal abuse, or as has happened to a considerable degree in zat-pwe, written out.

But there is, finally, another important masculine figure in Burmese society, that of the monk. Conceptually, the monk stands at a great remove from all the figures I have described above, and indeed the monk rarely appears in zat-pwe performances. Pop singer, rapper, servant clown, prince, or crooner: none of these models of masculinity appears to resemble the dignified, unworldly, asexual Buddhist ascetic. Although certain monks are said to be "modern" or "up-to-date" (those, namely, who pursue an interest in development projects), the distinction between modern or old-fashioned seems less urgent in their case than in that of other, lay members of Burmese society. The monochrome robes of the monk can stand for the apparent imperviousness of the sangha to the waves of fashion and style, not just in dress, but also in what it would mean to be a man in contemporary Burmese society. Such contrasts as aggressiveness versus refinement, high status versus low, acting alone versus conforming to the dictates of family, all these oppositions that inform the ways males take to the stage in the zat-pwe fall away when one considers monks as actors in Burmese society.

Yet ironically, the figure of the monk does exhibit certain affinities with modern masculinity as personified by the zat-pwe star, because a monk constitutes a long-standing exemplar of male autonomy. Of course the monk who pursues his own spiritual salvation by abandoning his attachments to and in the world actually represents a highly contradictory figure, completely dependent as he is on the very world he ostensibly ignores. But the power of this image, however paradoxical, is real, and it should be understood as another transformation of the fascinating, attractive male upon whom so much Burmese attention centers.

That the roles of monk and zat-pwe star have some unexpected affinities became apparent to me in conversation with the star of another zat-pwe troupe in Mandalay. This young man, in his mid-twenties, had a burgeoning career as a troupe leader and in addition had a new sideline selling cloth in Mandalay's largest market. He had taken this up, he told me, on the grounds that no star remains popular for very long in the contemporary performing arts, but he told me that were it not for how much it would distress his girlfriend, he would gladly give all of these pursuits up in favor of becoming a monk. This claim is made frequently by Burmese males and is hardly to be accepted at face value. Yet it is interesting that he felt the appeal of making the claim, and so representing himself as a devout Buddhist, and at the same time he justified his not acting on the desire on the grounds that it would cause his girlfriend too much pain. A man's desire for autonomy, however virtuous, is often compromised by women's attachments.

An all-night zat-pwe performance affords us the chance to see Burmese representing themselves in a considerable range of roles. What is startling to note is how consistently attention nevertheless falls on an idealized figure: the autonomous, powerful male—and this ironically in a society where few males can hope to attain any approximation of that ideal. It remains unclear how women might regain much prominence in contemporary popular theater. For males, though, there is at least the option of dressing up in muscle shirts and jeans.

Notes

1. I don't know any stars well enough to make pronouncements about their sexuality. But I have met several stars' girlfriends.

2. What "gay" might imply in a society with a different set of terms with which to classify sexual orientations is of course another discussion, and one I cannot enter into here. See Jackson and Cook (1999) for the Thai case.

3. Princesses do, it is true, roll over, at least in some vigorous contemporary renderings of female dance. But some older Burmese friends thought this a vulgar novelty.

4. I use the word "Burman" to refer to ethnic Burmans, rather than the citizens, Burman or non-Burman, of the nation-state of Burma.

5. On the place of trousers in Burma's past and present, see Marshall's (2002) *The Trouser People.*

6. There is a growing literature on masculinity in Southeast Asia. See, for example, Fordham (1998), Peletz (1995).

7. Bourdieu (1984:11–96) analyzes the cultural sleight-of-hand by which high status is equated with an innate refinement in France.

8. The transformation has been a long and gradual one. Many important innovations were already introduced by "the Great Po Sein" early in the twentieth century. See Sein and Withey (1965).

9. See Singer (1992) for a general description of Burmese marionettes.

10. Fink (2001) provides a vivid description of life for contemporary Burmese.

11. Some friends suggested to me that what one actually sees is not "what audiences want," but rather what young, poorly trained stars are capable of performing— not at all the same thing. I am told that a son, Chan Tha, of one of the midcentury's great stars, Shwei Man Tin Maung, performs in a much more classical style and is the most popular star of the contemporary stage, able to sell out large performance sheds whenever he performs. This suggests a larger audience for more classical performances than most people admit in conversation. But I have not had a chance to see him perform and cannot comment on him or his audiences.

12. William Peterson (2001), especially 103–128, describes how some Singaporean performers have taken up the issue of what it means for a woman to be modern in another patriarchal society in Southeast Asia.

13. Changing circumstances and conditions for women in Southeast Asia have been addressed in an important and growing literature. See such collections as Atkinson and Errington (1990), Ong and Peletz (1995), and Van Esterik (1996). I have found Mills (1997) particularly illuminating for the Thai case, and Brenner (1995) and Hatley (1990) for the Javanese one.

14. Hardy (2002) analyzes British soft-core pornography with reference to this paradox.

–11–

Who's Performing What?

State Patronage and the Transformation of Burmese Music

Gavin Douglas

S tate funding of Burmese arts has increased enormously over the past decade. Music, theater, sculpture, dance, and puppetry, are just some of the arts that are currently enjoying a rise in prominence due to increased access to scarce government resources. This rise in patronage follows immediately on the heels of a repositioning of the nation within the global socioeconomic arena. Burma's reengagement with Asia, and the international arts community more broadly, began after the resignation of Gen. Ne Win following the sup-pression of the 1988 pro-democracy uprising. Since the early 1990s the newly formed military council has struggled to rebuild Burma's ailing economy by drawing in foreign investment. At the same time there has been emphasis on redeveloping and protecting a particular canon of "Myanmar tradition" in the face of the negative and Western cultural influences thought to accompany foreign capital.

The Instruments of Tradition

By the early 1990s increased pressure from Western nations to recognize the results of the 1990 elections revealed that the moral and political legitimacy of the regime was questioned both inside the country and outside it. Badgely (1994) argues that 1993 was a watershed year for the junta, a year in which it lost its hero, Aung San, the founder of the army and the architect of Burmese independence, to the democracy movement. The legacy of Aung San was, at this time, successfully detached from the Tatmadaw (the military) and came to be more closely associated with his daughter, Aung San Suu Kyi, and the democratic and liberal ideas of the National League for Democracy.

It was in this climate, when a war of signification was being waged in the capital cities (Skidmore 2004:120–146), that the regime began its own campaign of appropriating the past through the unprecedented development, support, and reconstruction of certain aspects of traditional culture. Political speeches that formerly appealed to Aung San's strength now substituted precolonial conquering figures such as King Bayinnaung and Maha Bandoola. Projects such as the renovation of historic buildings, new museums, the resurrection of traditional festivals, accelerated archeological excavations, continual and highly visible support of the Sangha (monastic order) and Sāsana (Buddhist teachings, practice, and fruits of the teaching and practice), along with several new arts projects and institutions, all further this reconstruction of the past in line with a particular vision of the future.

Patronage of the traditional arts is one of many ways that the present dictatorship valorizes precolonial Burmese culture. A strong emphasis on traditional culture and values permeates the rhetoric of the state-controlled media, yet little or no public discussion is permitted as to what constitutes this "traditional culture." In the new cultural institutions, key elements of precolonial life are carefully selected and emphasized while others are deliberately omitted. This is a conscious attempt to redirect and redefine national identity and the historical record away from freedom fighting and anticolonial themes (that incorporate notions of independent identities) towards an identity based more closely upon submission to royalty and adherence to an unchanging tradition. Excessive funding and media attention directed to this revised view of national history, at the expense of many other local histories (ethnic, folk, popular), aim to establish a courtly legitimacy for the military government.

Within the music community, three major projects began in 1993: the creation of the University of Culture, the formation of committees for the publication of standardized notations of the orally transmitted classical canon, and the advent of an annual performing arts competition. These are all projects designed to regenerate, reculturize, and re-present the music of Burma to the Burmese public and to the world. This chapter explores these new institutional frameworks and the variety of reactions and adaptations to them by Burmese musicians. In addition, the high profile of the Hso-ka-yay-ti Performing Arts Competition provides an opportunity to examine the performance and ritualization of both state-certified ethnicity and claims to political legitimacy. Just what is being performed, and by whom, at these official state events is open to multiple readings.

The University of Culture

In the decade following the 1988 uprising, many of the country's educational institutions were shut down due to fears of student-motivated political activity (see Fink 2001, Smith 1995). The school closures created an enormous backlog of students and left many in a state of uncertainty waiting to finish their degrees or to start university. It was in the midst of these closures that the Yangon University of Culture *(yin-kyay-hmu tekkatho)* was created and began offering degrees in several Burmese traditional arts.[1]

Students who have passed the secondary school matriculation exam may enroll at this university to study music, dramatic arts (including dancing, acting, and singing), painting, and sculpture. Bachelor of Arts degrees are offered in all four disciplines and the university has a consistently full enrollment of over 600 students. Close to 200 students enter the university each year, with the music department being the largest of the four divisions.

The aim of the university, as announced on the first page of the *Curricula and Syllabus,* is to instill "union spirit" in the students (Myanmar, Ministry of Culture, Dept. of Fine Arts 1999). Nationalist rhetoric dominates the official discourse surrounding the university, while little mention is made of the contributions the university makes to the understanding and creation of art.[2] Teachers are instead admonished to "train their pupils to possess patriotism, Union Spirit, and conviction to preserve and promote national culture" (Than Shwe 1998:2). Entrance to the university is contingent upon passing the 10th standard matriculation exam,[3] unlike the state school of the arts, Pan-tara kyaung, open since 1952, that requires only 4th standard. The university has an age restriction of twenty as the oldest age that a student can enter. In addition, all students undergo a background check to ensure they have no criminal or antigovernment political affiliations and attend an interview as part of the selection process. The age restrictions allow for a window of only a few years after secondary school for students to enroll. More significantly, this rule prevents older or returning students, those whose education has been interrupted by recent political events, from entering the university.

Unlike most university music departments, students are not expected to have had any training on a musical instrument prior to enrolling. Beginning group lessons are held for first-year students on the *saung-gauk* (arched harp), *pattala* (bamboo xylophone), violin, and piano. Class requirements include courses on international (Western) music notation and history courses focusing on both the Western music tradition and the Burmese court music tradition. Fundamentals of Western music theory are required. As there is not yet a standardized theory of Burmese music, reference to Burmese theory tends to appear only in practical application classes.

The University of Culture operates a "dual-education" system. Mandatory "academic" subjects, including Burmese, English, history, integrated science, geography, and mathematics, supplement the "cultural" subjects (music, art, and theater). This dual-education system assures that students achieve a base level of proficiency in academic arts and sciences by the time of graduation. English is the approved medium of instruction for all the academic subjects, while cultural subjects are taught in both English and Burmese.

"Every Student Is Assured a Job"

Boasting over 150 (mostly music) graduates a year, the university provides quite a number of young professionals to the music community. Elementary and secondary schools rarely have budgets capable of supporting music teachers, and the few performance opportunities available to musicians are unlikely prospects after only four years of training. How then, practically speaking, does the university justify their time and expense? Despite these practical problems, the dean of the music school assured me that, indeed, "all students that graduate from this university are assured jobs" (personal communication, June 1999).

According to the dean, although some students apply for jobs as musicians (performers or educators) at the state music school, Pan-tara kyaung, and at the radio and television stations, most find work in government offices. In fact, all students of the University of Culture are guaranteed work in government ministries. Training in the basic academic subjects provides the students with sufficient skills to work as civil servants in a variety of government ministries not necessarily related to the Ministry of Culture. Moreover, while most universities throughout the country have been intermittently closed throughout the past fourteen years, there is a need for a workforce with a basic postsecondary education that can be gained through the University of Culture.

Accounts of Senior Musicians

Given the confusing status of the university as a conduit for the music tradition, it has caused a quietly expressed, but nevertheless significant controversy within the music community. Interviews with senior musicians reveal strong reactions to the university. One senior musician who regularly lectured at the university for little pay, but substantial prestige, claimed that his students

> have no future as musicians at all! They are not attending the cultural university to be musicians. Their hobby is music and they pursue their hobby at the University. But they have no future [as musicians] and the govern-

ment has no plans for it . . . When someone gets a degree, a Bachelor of
Music from the University of Culture . . . where will he go? Actually, he
knows nothing about music . . . even after four years. The current situation
is bad for musicians. Only the very famous, the most popular vocalists and
some pop artists, do well. The situation is bad.

Other professional musicians comment on the absurdity of student's
beginning their music education at the University of Culture with no prior
musical knowledge, and the low musical standards that inevitably result. U
Min Gaung[4] asserts that in the state education system

> there is primary, middle, and high school. For music education there should
> be as well. Here there is no such thing! Pan-tara kyaung [the state School of
> the Arts that opened in 1952] has it. It's a primary school. The University
> of Culture, no! There is no middle level. There is no advanced level! But
> they have a university. Why do they have a university? Only when students
> get to the university do they start the basics. Is it the same at your univer-
> sity? Only those who have gained knowledge *before* they went to university
> know a bit. Otherwise they don't know anything. And it's very rare to find
> those people who have studied on their own before going to the University
> of Culture. What we need is a *pan-tara* school, then a middle school, and
> then a university. Not two primary schools.

A third musician, U Ba Pe, who also worked for the university, admitted
that very few University of Culture graduates are able to pursue careers in
music, but he emphasized that the university did offer basic educational
opportunities that could then be used elsewhere.

> Some of the first batch of graduates became teachers at the University of
> Culture, and the rest of them were given positions in government offices,
> mostly office stuff, like bench clerks. That's the kind of positions that they're
> given. Most work in government offices and a few work in private compa-
> nies. Those that want [to] work in government offices, can.

The university appears to be granting educational opportunities for appropriately vetted students who have had trouble accessing universities throughout
the 1990s. These opportunities, as seen through the eyes of senior musicians,
make very little contribution towards the development of their art.

Students of the University of Culture are encouraged to participate in the
annual Hso-ka-yay-ti Performing Arts competition. Most enter at the student
level. Musicians who patronize these performances argue that since most of

these students have been playing for only a few years, the quality of their performance is quite low. The overall reaction of civilian patrons, musicians, and judges, is that the University of Culture students are the poorest-quality competitors. Their performances are therefore very poorly attended, and they are considered the "joke" of the Hso-ka-yay-ti competition.

Standardizing Tradition

A second project that intersects with several of the University of Culture's goals is an ambitious endeavor to standardize and notate the entire repertoire of classical and modern classical songs. In Burma today oral tradition is still the primary mode of musical transmission. The canon of court-related classical songs has been catalogued multiple times in versions collectively known as the *Maha Gita*. These "Great Songs" were first compiled during the last dynasty, and musicians and scholars still meet regularly to edit and revise different versions of the texts. The accompanying music, unlike the prose, is passed orally from teacher to student and thus there exist multiple versions of any given piece. In addition, there is a high degree of variation and improvisation in the song accompaniments, which creates substantial problems in the quest for definitive versions.[5]

Present-day discourse on "traditional music culture" includes, in addition to *thachin-gyi* court music, a colonial-era genre known today as *khit-haung thachin,* or old-style songs. Khit-haung are often referred to as "modern traditional" songs because their roots lie in the precolonial court tradition, yet their increased use of Western musical instruments (such as the piano, guitar, banjo, and violin) and their incorporation of foreign musical ideas (such as chordal harmony and strophic forms), place them outside of court music proper. In addition, the introduction of recording technology after the turn of the century and the development of local markets by Columbia Records and RCA in the 1930s and 1940s significantly changed the modes of transmission and distribution of music.

Today's standardization project includes a strong emphasis on the colonial-period khit-haung pieces. Whereas thachin-gyi classical songs were written for Burmese instruments, khit-haung songs are frequently written for piano, often with a small orchestra. One can hear in these pieces a gradual adoption of even-tempered (Western) tuning, steadier rhythm, and by the 1930s we find occasional chordal accompaniments and song structures that mimic American Tin Pan Alley forms. Of the multivolume standardizations that are planned, Volume 1, which deals exclusively with khit-haung, was published by the state printing press (Yangon) in 1999.

This project, as described to me by members of the standardization committee, appears to be motivated by two goals. First, it seeks "to preserve the tradition," which implies a descriptive transcription codifying the essential elements of the piece and the style for archiving and preservation purposes. Second, it is intended "to show foreigners how to play our music," which implies perhaps a prescriptive approach concerned with the transmission and expansion of the canon. These two responses reveal potentially divergent goals behind the project. Both agendas are present, yet neither is actualized. Both the prescriptive and descriptive uses of these notations are distant priorities behind their value as a tangible symbol of the tradition.

Few musicians in Burma have a working knowledge of Western staff notation—referred to by the committee exclusively as *international* notation—and few foreigners would be able to access the volume (written in Burmese) or any of the original recordings. Nonetheless, as the military council has increasingly emphasized tradition, and their symbolic relation to it, they desire visual and tangible manifestations of their oral tradition now embodied in these notations.

Now in print, the tradition becomes real. Through the standardization project, Burmese musical traditions are recreated as a series of tangible and controllable objects such as performing arts competitions, universities, and sheet music. This standardization serves to legitimize the tradition and facilitates the manipulation of "Myanmar tradition" as an ideological tool in the creation of a modern nation. These few symbols reify the diversity of forms, meanings, and interpretations that exist in the oral canon of Burmese music, rendering only one version of the past as having salience in the present. The fact that no one uses the notations is perhaps immaterial.

The Hso-ka-yay-ti Performing Arts Competition

The State is striving emphatically to bring out and uplift the essence of national culture with aims at ensuring everlasting brilliance of good qualities and national norms of Myanmar and its people. I would like to say that, in endeavors to bring out and uplift essence of national culture like that, the Myanma Traditional Cultural Performing Arts Competitions are one of the national movements of the highest order involving participation of the entire nation. (Lt. Gen. Khin Nyunt, 2000)

In hundreds of speeches, the ruling generals state that it is the civic duty of all Burmese people to uphold unique Burmese cultural values as the only way of maintaining a sense of "Myanmarness." The junta represses all direct political activity, while at the same time urging the citizenry to participate in the Hso-ka-yay-ti competition and in other facets of "traditional culture." It is in the defense of the nation, then, as explicitly stated by the top-ranking generals, that the Hso-ka-yay-ti competition acquires its political meaning.

Since 1993 the Hso-ka-yay-ti Performing Arts Competition has been held every October or November in Rangoon. The competition is energetically profiled in the state media and is patronized daily by several members of the ruling council. These government patrons command such a degree of attention that the political agendas behind the event are easily apparent and give rise to different possible interpretations regarding the position the competition holds in present-day Burmese society. The prominence of generals, "ethnic" minorities, political ministers, and children in the media coverage of the competition, and the comparative paucity of images of musicians themselves, reflects the degree to which the music tradition is integrated into the governing practices of the present military dictatorship.

The competition is organized in such a way that critical engagement by the public with music history and with what constitutes the country's musical traditions is highly restricted. Quality assessment and the evaluation of talent are kept under the control of a small number of officials. Concurrent with this is an aggressive media campaign, unavoidable in the urban centers, that advertises the competition to the public. The particular form of the competition and the official media coverage of the event reflect the numerous ways in which the government is employing this event to affirm and expedite its agenda of national unity, respect for authority, protection from the encroaching West, and the establishment of political legitimacy.

The competition is divided into four parts: singing *(hso)*, dancing *(ka)*, composing *(yay)*, and instrumental performance *(ti)*. These divisions are spread over the four largest concert venues in Rangoon. Before the stage, prominently and visibly situated for the audience to see, sit the judges. The first rows of the auditorium are reserved for the regular visits of various officials, generals, and government ministers. Immediately behind these VIP seats are the press seats. Behind the television crews, the audience sits on wooden benches.

The material for the instrumental performance competitions is primarily drawn from the classical repertoire of the Burmese court (thachin-gyi). Kyo, Bwe, Thachin-gan, Patpyo, Yodaya, and Mon song genres, drawn from the *Maha Gita,* dominate the instrumental categories. The post-kingdom colonial period (1885–1947) genres of *ka-la-baw* (modern traditional or "the music of our times") and khit-haung are present in the dancing, singing, and composing competitions, yet are largely absent in the instrumental competition. The instrumental competition focuses on the performance of traditional Burmese instruments, such as saung-gauk (harp), pattala (xylophone), *hne* (oboe), and *pat-waing* (drum circle), as well as foreign instruments that have been Burmanized into the classical music pantheon, specifically the piano *(sandaya)* and the violin *(tayaw)*.[6]

Two other extraordinarily popular genres of Burmese rural folk music, the *o-zi* and *do-bat* drum ensembles, are performed in the Hso-ka-yay-ti competition (see Figure 11.1). These extremely popular genres consistently fill the theater to capacity. Although they have vague ties to the royal court, their traditional contexts lie in rural settings, and they are not found in any of the institutions that teach music in the country. Of all the instrumental categories, it is the o-zi and do-bat performances that place primary emphasis on theatricality, costumes, and showmanship. They are not historically patronized by the court and therefore perform a different repertoire of material than is heard in the other competition divisions. The o-zi and do-bat ensembles have a lead singer who dances, jokes, and improvises, and historically these genres have held great potential for social commentary.

In the context of the Hso-ka-yay-ti competition, the social commentary (present in many theatrical genres) does not challenge the established power

Figure 11.1. Hso-ka-yay-ti Performing Arts Competition: the popular o-zi and do-bat drum ensembles (Source: Gavin Douglas)

holders, though in traditional (nonstaged) contexts this would often be the case. Music of the royal court is Burmese and classical (and national), while all other traditions are minority and folk. The presence of the o-zi and do-bat ensembles reveals a subtle Burmanization of this national festival, since no other "ethnic" music categories are permitted. The fact that these ensembles are non-court-related contributes significantly to their appeal for the predominantly Burman Rangoon audience who have little interest in courtly symbols represented by most of the other music at the competition.

A sign announcing the state or division being represented is prominently displayed in front of the contestants prior to each performance. The names of various predetermined pieces, organized according to different levels of difficulty, are written on pieces of paper and drawn from a silver alms bowl by one of the leading judges or a recognized expert on that instrument. Names of contestants are then drawn to determine the order of play. Solo performers are always accompanied on stage either by a melodic instrument or by *si* and *wa* (bell and clapper) rhythmic accompaniment. In the younger age categories the student's teacher often plays the accompaniment.

When the judges are ready, the lead judge strikes a gong to indicate that the performance may start. The contestant begins a two-minute improvisational *let-swan-bya* (lit. "show of the hands") before entering into the composition proper. The official gong will be struck a second time if the performer has not yet finished the improvisation within the allotted time. The let-swan-bya provides an opportunity for the exhibition of technical control and virtuosic improvisational skills. These two-minute introductions prove to be the most exciting moments of the competition, as the rules governing appropriate stylistic conformity may, within reason, be broken. Each instrumental performance then lasts from four to twenty minutes, depending on the length of the piece selected.

At each of the competition venues, there are anywhere from fifteen to thirty judges, who sit directly in front of the musicians, or in the orchestra pit. A senior judge, a recognized master of the particular instrument being judged, presides visibly over the event by drawing the order of contestants and song selections from an alms bowl. He or she is centrally positioned among the judges and announces the start of each piece. Even those judges most critical of the political uses of the competition value their positions as Hso-ka-yay-ti judges. Regardless of the politics involved, it is a prominent national and public venue where musical authority and credibility are established for professional musicians. Senior musicians appoint judges, and it is considered an honor to perform this duty, irrespective of the fact that only the senior judges are paid for their services.

Ideally, fifteen judges are chosen from Rangoon and one from each of the states and divisions in the country. This brings the total number of judges to approximately thirty. In reality, this symbolic representation causes many problems, due partially to the lack of space in some of the halls and considerable organizational confusion, but also because the uneven distribution of knowledge in the country allows for certain judges to be thoroughly unqualified in their positions. The symbolic representation of all corners of the country, through statewide participation of judges and performers, and the illusion of a democratic judgment overrides quality control while theatrically presenting a picture of an ideally integrated nation (Geertz 1980).

The competition bestows as much honor on each of the judges as it does on the winning contestants. Each judge returns home with a framed certificate (at a glance, identical to the contestant's awards) that is prominently displayed on the family-room wall. All of the musicians and judges prominently display their framed certificates, and all admit that the Hso-ka-yay-ti competition is an important venue for establishing credibility among their peers. Awards granted from elsewhere, and from an earlier time in their lives, have become of secondary importance and are rarely displayed.

"Ethnic" Minorities

Each division of the competition ideally has representatives from each of the seven states (Kachin, Chin, Karen, Shan, Mon, Kayah, Arakan) and seven divisions (Rangoon, Mandalay, Ayeyarwadi, Sagaing, Tenassarim, Pegu, Magwe) of the country. Competitions leading up to the national one are arranged throughout the country in the months beforehand, but are not widely publicized. It is rarely the case that there are representatives from all of the geographic areas. Each of the minority groups with their own state, and the many others that do not have their own state, are distinct in multiple ways (including language, customs, and religions) from the dominant Burman ethnic group. The traditional music of these groups is also distinctly different from that of the Burmans. This competition, however, offers no venue for the display of non-Burman music.

By organizing the contestants geographically, one contestant from each of the seven ethnic states could, in theory, be present in any particular category. The geographic origins of the contestants are always mentioned in their introduction and on a sign placed in front of the performer. Non-Burmans are strongly encouraged to wear their "traditional costumes." These often are formal costumes worn only on special occasions or "ethnic" holidays that announce ethnicity in formalized, state-mandated ways. The bodies of the contestants are draped in the bright red striped shirts of the Karen, the dark intricate weaving of the Chin *longyi* (traditional sarong-like garment), shiny Kachin jewelry, and Shan *baung-bi* (baggy cotton pants), as they play ethnic Burman traditional music. Most of these Burman traditions, with the notable exception of the o-zi and do-bat folk ensembles, are drawn directly from the Burmese court, evoking the dominance of the Burmese Buddhist kings of Upper Burma over their subjects (read "ethnic" populations). Such symbolism contributes to the marginalization, forced Burmanization, and Buddhification of Burma's more than 135 minority groups, especially as the majority of the Christian and Muslim populations are found among the non-Burman population.

I was initially surprised to see such a large degree of minority group participation in the Hso-ka-yay-ti Performing Arts competition. Many, if not most, of Burma's minority groups claim their own canon of traditions and have significantly different kinds of music. On closer inspection, however, I began to realize that "ethnic" participation was being exaggerated. Participants representing Shan State, for example, were not always ethnically Shan, and in some cases did not even live in Shan State. Many ethnic Burmans live in "ethnic" states and can thus participate as representatives of that state.

According to one judge, some contestants enter more than one of the various advance competitions, thus increasing their chances of success by performing in states and divisions where they are not residents. He urged me to

> look at last year, in Rangoon division. Those who didn't get selected in the Rangoon division went and participated as "residents" in other divisions. So the Rangoon division lost [the Hso-ka-yay-ti competition] but those talented people from Rangoon who participated as people from other divisions, won. My grandchild, who is also my student, participated in Rangoon division but he lost [in the advanced competition] and was not selected to perform [in the Hso-ka-yay-ti]. So he went and competed for Karen division and ultimately ended up winning the national competition.

The appearance of significant minority group participation in the competition is also exaggerated in the media. During the nightly news coverage of the competition, many minorities enjoyed a much larger percentage of time on television than they did onstage during the competition. This certainly facilitates the appearance of national unity and peaceful coexistence, regardless of the actual insurgency and unrest that exists in the outlying states. My estimate would put minority participation—that is, the number playing under that rubric whose identity, however, may still be questionable—at 10 to 15 percent of the total participants, while roughly 40 percent of the news coverage focuses on them. The irony of the media emphasis on minority participation is compounded by the lack of any indigenous minority music in the event. When I asked the judges and participants why this was so, I was consistently answered with a highbrow response: "This is classical music," or, "This is 'art' music and not folk music." As most forms of non-Burman music have not been formally institutionalized and are not perpetuated through an officially recognized training system, they remain absent from the competition. A very strict line is drawn between folk and classical music, between that worthy of national recognition and praise and that which is not. Not surprisingly, this line traces the officially constructed boundaries of ethnicity in the new Union of Myanmar.

Minority groups present in this competition do not represent their own traditions, but rather perform the role of ethnic symbols in the military model of a peacefully integrated nation. Mandated and official sanctioned differences are loudly publicized, yet diluted and politically neutralized by their peripheral placement at the boundaries of the competition. Participation as a visibly identifiable "ethnic" musician is encouraged and vigorously supported, in part through the less pejorative label of "national races." Stuart Hall has suggested that hegemony does not imply the disappearance or destruction of cultural difference, but rather it "is the construction of a collective will through difference" (1991:58). The Hso-ka-yay-ti Performing Arts Competition, like tourist shows in restaurants and formalized culture shows on state television, highlight "ethnic" differences and the simultaneous unity of all participants, who seemingly cooperate and work together towards common totalitarian goals.

The "Real" Performers

In addition to exaggerating the participation of the minority contestants, the state media pays enormous regard to the patrons of the competition. Indeed, the press is significantly more concerned with the patrons than the musicians. There are currently two television stations operating within the country, MRTV (Myanmar Radio and Television) the government channel, and Myawaddy, the military station. Both of these channels run virtually identical news and broadcast only slightly different programming. Most evenings during the competition, five- to fifteen-minute articles cover the competition events of the day. These video segments are constructed primarily to show the particular generals and ministers in attendance on that day, rather than the musicians or the competition. In the case of former Prime Minister Khin Nyunt, his daily presence at the competition was consistently the most reported event in both television and newspaper coverage during the Hso-ka-yay-ti period. He was considered *the* patron of the competition, and in addition to his many political designations, he also held the title, "Chairman of the Leading Committee for Organizing the Competition." He is not a musician, and has not been educated as one, yet he was the chairman of the committee organizing the event and has visibly patronized the competition since its creation in 1993 until his arrest in late 2004.

This competition, and the prominent role of "culture" in present-day Burmese politics, is largely credited to Khin Nyunt, as are the new University of Culture and even the standardization and notation projects. Typical newspaper coverage of the competition announced Khin Nyunt's rank and his political relationship to the event. The daily newspapers showed pictures of Khin Nyunt in three, and sometimes all four, of the competition venues on any given day.

The news coverage of the composing competition is particularly revealing, as there is no audience for this event. The official media dwells on the rows of judges seated watching contestants compose in silence, while the generals look on. Closer inspection reveals traditional costumes worn by participating minority group members. Television crews are present to document the event for the evening news, and newspaper reporters appear daily to photograph the composers. Khin Nyunt spent an enormous amount of time attending daily shows, visiting with participants (usually children), and moving between the various venues: he spent as much as eight hours a day with the competition. It appeared to me, sitting several rows behind him day after day, that I was in fact watching him govern the country and that patronizing the music competition was his top priority.

During the day the military leaders, such as former Prime Minister Khin Nyunt, would arrive in uniform and make appearances at most (if not all) of the venues, visiting with the judges, and shaking hands with the contestants. In the evening the theatrical performances of the *Ramayana* and *Yok-thay* (marionette) plays are held. Again, the generals, in semiformal (traditional) evening wear, are present. As Michael Bakan (1998:458) writes of the political uses of the Beleganjur Competition in Bali, "the purpose of the competition, politically, is to make the existing hegemonic order appear to be a natural extension of local cultural interests or, to culturalize politics." Repeated appearances of Khin Nyunt, both as ruler (in uniform) and civilian (in traditional dress), reinforce the naturalized connection between culture and politics.

Through the competition and its ties to tradition and heritage, Khin Nyunt gained legitimacy by establishing himself as the connection between tradition and modernity. His associations with selected forms of "Myanmar traditional culture" implied a connection to a precolonial past with himself in the role of king. Several musicians and informants were suspicious of such king-like posturing. Numerous rumors circulated among the Rangoon musical community about Khin Nyunt's alleged aspirations to revive the monarchy and place himself on the throne. His highly visible patronage of the arts lent support to such rumors.

Public Access

There is a significant element missing from the television coverage of the Hso-ka-yay-ti competition. Footage includes moving pictures of performers, judges, and patrons. News anchors narrate what events are being performed, what states and divisions are represented, and which dignitaries were in attendance, but no other sound is heard. Such absence of sound is standard for any field footage on Burmese television, highlighting an intense desire to control information, and the music competition is no exception. The fact that a music competition is the subject of the report brings into much stronger relief the absurdity of the coverage, furthering the hypothesis that this music competition has little to do with sound.

Viewers have no opportunity to hear the music until months after the competition, when archival footage is played during one of the many music hours on television. The television stations play excerpts of the first, and sometimes second, prizewinners of various competitions. Footage from the Hso-ka-yay-ti competition is frequently shown throughout the year on both the MRTV and Myawaddy television stations. These playbacks, along with the news media, become the primary sources of public consumption of the music competition.

Several days after the Hso-ka-yay-ti competition, an awards ceremony is held at the National Theater. Only at this time do any of the contestants discover how they have fared in the competition. First and second prizes are not announced or granted at the competition time itself, but rather at the awards ceremony, by which time up to three weeks can have passed since a given performance. The awards ceremony is not officially closed to the public, but after the hundreds of contestants, judges, and officials have taken their seats, there is literally no room left in the theater for the public. The content of this event is not televised, but the evening news will report on which generals were in attendance and the results of a select number of categories will be announced in the daily newspaper.

Between the removal in space and time of the awards ceremony from the individual competitions, and the lack of sound in any media report, the public at large is prevented from gaining any insight into who is considered the best performer and what he or she sounds like. What the public does hear and see, on the other hand, is how politically important this event is, how well represented the entire country is, how peacefully and cooperatively all races can live and work together, how the youth are being morally educated, and, ultimately, who is responsible for all of it.

Adaptive Strategies

New schools such as the University of Culture, tangible codifications of tradition such as song transcriptions, and mass public events such as the Hso-ka-yay-ti Performing Arts Competition each contribute to establishing a central point of musical and cultural authority. As the Burmese dynasty fell over a hundred years ago to the British, musicians were scattered throughout the country and the institutions of patronage and musical authority were distributed among private clubs, radio stations, traveling drama troupes, foreign record companies, and moderately funded government conservatories. The University of Culture, along with the committees for standardization and notation of the canon and the performing arts competitions, appear to be reversing this fragmentation and aim to relocate and reconsolidate a single voice of musical authority.

Khin Nyunt's speech from the sixth annual Hso-ka-yay-ti competition clearly states the nationalist and moral agenda of these projects and uses the vantage point of traditional musical heritage to attack his political opponents. He considers the introduction of foreign ideas and associations with the West as nothing short of treasonous.

> It must be underscored that national unity has to be built firmer and more steadfast to be able to crush the external subversives and destructionists [who are] driving a wedge to split Union spirit in order to dishonour national dignity. . . . [Their] persuasive acts to tarnish the culture and traditions and weaken patriotism must constantly be offset by endeavours to preserve and promote culture and traditions. That is why the State Peace and Development Council has been undertaking tasks for [the] uplift of national prestige and integrity and preservation and safeguarding of cultural heritage and national character, and today's Myanma Traditional Performing Arts Competitions plays one of the most crucial roles in these tasks. (Khin Nyunt 1998)

Traditional musicians respond to the three projects discussed above with a wide array of behaviors and rarely voiced thoughts. These opinions are necessarily somewhat different from those of nonmusicians. In general, the view of these projects from the perspective of the average citizen is somewhat more critical than that of the musicians. According to this author's observations, the average public increasingly associates classical music with the regime, while traditional musicians struggle to maintain its credibility as an autonomous art form separate from contemporary politics. Several significant benefits accrue directly to traditional musicians who participate in these projects, as there is an economic element to their deliberations as well as local prestige, self-satisfaction, and a pride in Burmese music to take into consideration when listening to them stating less than complete condemnation of the changes to Burmese traditional music as a result of this state patronage.

The Hso-ka-yay-ti competition appears to be the most successful of these projects at reviving the tradition publicly and in placing the generals in positions of "cultural" authority. While many of my informants realize the overt political posturing behind the activities of the ruling generals, the competition also highlights cultural respect for traditional musicians that results in increased social and economic prestige for many of them. The pride that performers and judges have in the competition, and their participation in it, is significant. The prominent display of awards and diplomas in the homes of performers and judges attests to a tacit approval of this politically motivated patronage. The public's strong support of certain rural folk genres (o-zi and do-bat) over other more classical courtly genres is noteworthy and potentially a threat, not only to the regime's regal posturing, but also the classical musicians who have managed to keep royal tradition in tact over the past century.

The University of Culture has won the favor and approval of fewer musicians. As an institution for training future musicians, the opinions of senior musicians are consistently critical. The university, which is completely ineffective at creating musicians, is realistically only developing the hobbies of many young students. The potential of the university to grow into a musically productive educational facility is certainly possible, yet its value appears inconclusive given its infancy.

Finally, very few musicians other than those directly involved with the project show any appreciation for definitive notations of the repertoire. No musician with whom I spoke has used, or has any intention of using, any standardized version of a piece of music that is not his or her own. There is a strong belief that these standardizations have the potential to actually destroy the tradition. In the minds of its practitioners, the standardizing of an oral tradition and the creation of definitive song versions acts to marginalize much of the essence of the tradition. Of the government patronage endeavors discussed, the standardization and notation project has the lowest regard among musicians. Though many agree that standardization is, perhaps, a good thing on paper, as something concrete to be shown to the rest of the world, no musician would ever use it.

The cultural symbols and new institutions upon which I have focused are all state-sanctioned attempts to codify, organize, and simplify the tradition. Parallels to these institutions can be found in most modern nation states; indeed, they help to create the nation-state. In precolonial Burma, however, these conduits for tradition themselves did not exist, at least not in this form. Each of these is a nontraditional medium for this new tradition. The value of this music tradition to its patrons appears to be ideological as opposed to aesthetic. While all musicians agree that nothing is changing their situation faster than this attempt to preserve traditional music, the results and criticism are mixed. The profile of their art and their personal fortunes are higher than at any time before, and the regime smiles benevolently upon their willingness to serve as the backdrop to a political performance of espoused national unity and minority submission. But at what cost still remains to be seen.

Notes

1. A second campus opened outside of Mandalay in 2000.

2. "The general aim of teaching Academic Subjects and Cultural Subjects is to fulfill the objectives of the University of Culture by providing the students to gain the knowledge of:

—Keeping dynamic patriotism
—Strengthening of national unity
—Preserving and disseminating the Myanmar Traditional Culture
—Teaching Myanmar Traditional Culture customs of indigenous national races at
    Universities, Institutes, Colleges and Schools
—Upholding the spirit of nationalism
—Upbringing the good artists with high morality and nobility of international level
—High technology to promote the creative power in artist way."
("Curricula and Syllabus" Department of Fine Arts, 1999)

3. Tenth standard is roughly equivalent to the completion of high school in the West, with graduates approximately sixteen to eighteen years of age as they prepare for university.

4. All names are pseudonyms.

5. In the late 1950s a prominent musician U Ba Than, under the sponsorship of the Ministry of Union Culture, began to notate and standardize at least some of the

canon. This project ceased after the1962 military coup. Over the following thirty years, various musicians attempted their own notation collections, but government support of the project ceased until 1993.

6. In addition to the solo competitions, there exist ensemble performances of the traditional *hsaing-waing* orchestra. Several other instruments are found in accompaniment roles in the vocal competition but do not have their own competition arena. These include the iron pattala, Burmese-style lap/slide guitar, the Burmese mandolin (a six-string, single-coursed mandolin), and the Burmese banjo (four-string).

-12-

The Future of Burma
Children Are Like Jewels

Monique Skidmore

Discard only bad baskets and punnets, not bad sons and
daughters.
——Burmese proverb

The *Lokaniti* states *"aputtakam gharam sunnam"* ("a home without children is desolate" [Pe Tin Thein 1992:2]). The home, the domain of children, is the space least invaded by the surveillance apparatus of the military
government. In the parenting of children we gain a viewpoint from which to
see the impact of militarism and modernization on the national private imagination. Such a viewpoint is fraught with conflicting tensions and representations of parents and of the kinds of adults produced during the child-rearing
process. Parents were portrayed as virtual monsters by many Western theorists
of the last century, and as hagiographical icons in uncensored contemporary
Burmese writings, and children were depicted as reincarnated wise elders in
Buddhism and Burmese folk traditions, and increasingly as pudgy little emper-
ors and empresses by transnational Asian marketing companies. These images
of the Burmese family are reconcilable within a historical framework that takes
into account British colonization, the brief moment of culture and personality theory ascendancy among Western academics, the continued suppression
of publishing of serious social concerns in Burma, the increasing recourse to
religion under authoritarianism, and the partial liberalization of the Burmese
economy in the 1990s that led to a conscious pan-Asian cosmopolitan model

for parenting (Anagnost 2002) being espoused by transnational marketing companies in Burmese urban media. In this chapter I privilege the voices of Burmese parents in order to create another depiction of Burmese children: as the embodiment both of all that is valuable on the earth, and of an alternate genetic history of Burma, where value is made manifest through generational links.

The Past

One could be forgiven for thinking that the Burmese act like monsters. The English literature regarding the results of studies of Burmese parents, children, and child socialization contains pejorative labels, Orientalist constructions of "difference," and a pathological view of Burmese child rearing that contrasts sharply with the "normalcy" of Western forms of parenting. These studies were conducted by American and British psychologists and anthropologists from the 1940s through the 1960s and, for the most part, involved survey materials and interviews conducted in English or with the aid of Burmese translators. Quite often the theorists, such as Geoffrey Gorer, had never conducted research in Burma and instead reviewed the existing English-language studies. They were informed by popular theories of the day and were not limited to Burma, but can be found in the literature on other Southeast Asian nations, especially Thailand (for example, Foster [1976]; Phillips [1965]; Piker [1975]).

This particular cluster of child-related research in Burma represents the second wave of such interest by Western scholars and medical personnel. As early as 1866 Westerners were interested in why Burma was sparsely populated in comparison with India and other South and East Asian nations (see Figure 12.1 for a visual depiction of Burmese children during colonialism). Beginning their enquiry on the western fringes of Burma, doctors, scientists, and scholars such as L. H. Lees argued that in Arakan in particular, the most likely reason was "a general want of care and management" of children and a "lack of parental solicitude." Lees's concluding recommendation was that Burma required the encouragement of immigration, presumably from societies in which parents knew how to look after children (Lees 1866).[1]

The words of Lees were hardly modified over the next century, with the same sentiments pervading the literature of the twentieth century. In 1945 L. M. Hanks, Jr. served for over five months as a civilian appointed to the Office of Strategic Services on the coast of Arakan, and he later earned a PhD in psychology. He believed that in Burma there was "a connection between the unpredictability of love for a child, the negatively phrased discipline that he later receives at home and in school, and the loose, evadable authority of adult social life" (1949:285).

Hanks perceived a lack of constant tending by the mother. He wrote that it "is strange that a six-months-old child is passed from one adult to another and is only in his mother's arms for feedings or in an emergency. . . . At any moment they may hand him over to someone and depart as if he were a doll or pet monkey" (1949:289, 290). He believed that the parenting of children by an extended family meant that for a child "there is a fragility in his relations to people" and "all these attentions are voluntary . . . but since they are given without obligation, at any moment they may end like a cataclysm. There may be warmth and affection, but it lacks continuity and dependability." Adults were labeled "fastidious" for not wanting to have infants "soil" their clothes, and he repeatedly argued that Burmese parents treated children as pets (1949:290).

The transition from a very indulgent and unstructured home life to a monastic education at puberty resulted, according to Hanks, in an understanding by adolescents of the imposition of power in society and over the person as "relentless and arbitrary" (1949:291). He argued that Burmese people are prone to corruption, deceit, and intrigue because they had to control their outward emotions; behind a calm exterior face, they would plot and scheme against their enemies and engage in corruption for personal gain. Such corrupt behavior, all stemming from the transition from lax to stern discipline

Figure 12.1. Mandalay Children in Court Dress (date and photographer unknown)

during childhood, was evident to Hanks during the period when the British reoccupied Burma having driven out the Japanese at the end of the Second World War. "In the American camp a continuous problem was keeping food and clothing stores safe from Burmese scroungers who would use any simulation to obtain cigarettes or a cotton sarong" (1949:294).

The "theme of revolution," in Burma stemmed not, according to Hanks, from a repressed population whose monarch had been deposed and were subject to British colonization, but instead from these pathological childhood development problems. "Arbitrary power" had to be used by the Burmese to accomplish their deep-seated needs for personal power and security, and if they were "hopelessly blocked in orthodox channels," they resorted to gang violence and even revolution (ibid.). Here, then, we see the growing Burmese nationalist movement under colonial rule reduced to an unwillingness of Burmese women to properly nurture infants and the subsequent shock of monastic discipline imposed upon "lax" children previously treated as "pets." [2]

At the 1959 annual meeting of the American Psychiatric Association, Hazel Hitson (*née* Weidman) read a paper entitled "Family Pattern and Paranoidal Personality Structure in Boston and Burma." Hitson's point was that Burmese people have an inborn tendency towards perceiving the world as hostile and this makes them violent and aggressive. Such violence and aggression is evident in the way that Burmese men treat women and children, and the way that adults treat children. Both Hitson and Hanks saw Burmese women as lazy and lacking in a sense of duty towards their children. Hitson and Funkenstein (1959:188) argued that in Burma

> When adults are angry among themselves, they take it out on their children. When children see through their mothers' laziness, they are beaten for their own laziness in not wanting to do what their mothers did not feel like doing. When children indicate that they are aware of a mother's deception, they are beaten for talking back and accused of being too "cheeky" or too particular.

When Hitson's work was published in refereed journals, it seldom escaped criticism from the journal's editors or discussants. Opler, for example, stated that, "Miss Hitson has made a community study, with an emphasis on family form, socialization and the channeling of aggression, in a village of lower Burma, a country with a high homicide rate, and with a record of much banditry and violence in the modern period" (1959:193). Opler goes on to point out the work of Cady, Furnivall, and Brohm as giving a series of politically and economically based reasons for the "high aggression" rate in Burma, contrasting it with Thailand's relatively intact social structure, having been spared British colonization (1959:194). He also compared Burmese women's high status and autonomy with the situation in India and found it "hard to reconcile with the Hitson-Funkenstein hypothesis" (1959:196).

Oedipal repression, latent homosexuality, and the evasion of sexual situations by thousands of Burmese men ordaining as monks each year, were the bases upon which Hagen argued that lax parenting and strict monastic discipline created Burmese adults unable to engage in normal social relationships or to have relationships with anyone in a superior social situation (Hagen 1962:169–171). Underneath all of these anxieties in interpersonal relations, lay a simmering, never truly repressed rage.

> The rage built up in the individual by frustrations of Burmese childhood is so great that is seems necessary to permit the child to vent it against anyone outside the family. This solves the immediate problem, but the sanction thereby given for aggressiveness leaves such a slender margin of self-control the Burmese man apparently continually or repeatedly feels a danger that he may lose control of himself and attack anyone around him. Burmese personality may be characterized as authoritarianism with a slight paranoiac streak. The intense Burmese fear of dysentery, not paralleled by corresponding fear of other cases of sickness and death, may arise from this dread of losing control of oneself. (1962:173)

Lucien Pye correctly noted in 1962 that at the heart of Western conceptions of Burmese character and personality has been the supposed paradox of gentleness versus violence (1962:178). Since childhood was where these paradoxes were universally believed to issue from, many theorists attributed the revolutionary and nationalist movements between 1940 and the 1960s to the deficiencies of a loving and consistent childhood. Pye succumbed to the "logic" of these theorists, arguing that if children were taught that family figures were worthy of respect and must always be obeyed, then they would have to turn their repressed rage outwards to social institutions or nonfamily members. Pye took these assumptions further, arguing that the happy, gentle, and carefree side of Burmese personality was a remembrance of the infant nursing period. Agreeing with the misogynistic statements of earlier theorists, Pye argued that after weaning, the child was betrayed by the mother "who turns out to be controlled more by her own unpredictable moods than by the wishes of her child" (1962:186).

In what is, ultimately, a sanctioning and an apology for colonialism, he writes that "the sense of optimism makes it possible for the Burmese people to go through crisis after crisis with remarkably little psychic damage" (1962: 186). Pye reviewed the work of Hitson, Hanks, Gorer, and Sein Tu. He followed the line, broadly, of Hanks, and on the subject of taunting argued that "there is considerable evidence that the Burmese tend to rely heavily upon shame and ridicule in the socialization process, with the result that the child becomes extremely sensitive to the opinions of others" (1962:183).

Shame and ridicule coalesce, in these early studies, in the teasing or taunting of children. Hitson stated that "In Burma, the first basic assumption parents make is that children are to be used. . . . Children are to be treated as a form of enjoyment for elders, and a child's sensitive areas and special fears are used to make it more effective. Teasing means getting a child to cry for the enjoyment of all present. It means frightening a child to see his response" (1959:77–78).

According to Hitson Weidman (1969:272), "teasing is very frequent in Burma. Both adults and adolescents generally direct such teasing toward young children." One such fat and cheerful infant "was constantly being fed, poked, squeezed, rolled about, and made to cry through frustrations of various sorts —all because he was so appealing and loved so much." Such attentions formed part of a "complex" of pathological parental techniques that included such unconvincing anecdotes as parents shouting out to "a child keeping an exhausted chick running about" that "the little chick will die" and a child who is playing too near a cow being "told in a rough voice" that "the cow will stamp on you" (Hitson Weidman 1969:270–271).

Using Hitson's data, and her own observation's about Burma, Hagen (1962:165–168) argued that "the parents treat temper tantrums with amusement or ridicule . . . the parents can hardly be said to train the children. Rather, they rule them, perhaps laxly, perhaps amusedly . . . [The child] is not an autonomous human being to be respected, but an automaton or toy . . . his father's attitude is little more than taking pleasure in him."

The final theorist in this review, Melford Spiro, examined the work of the previous authors, and noted inconsistencies with his ethnographic evidence. Spiro disagreed with the argument that Burmese people repressed their feelings until they become explosively violent. He argued, instead, that it was the taunting of children that led to the pathological adult Burmese personality.

> Laughter at another's discomfiture or even danger is not infrequent . . .
> teasing is much more frequent. Consider the following examples, all occur-
> ring in a group of reapers. A man asks his neighbor, forced by his wife to
> return an ox that he had bought the previous night, whether he or the
> seller had decided to wear a woman's skirt. A woman falls far behind her
> fellow reapers, and they "congratulate" her on her "agility." . . . Although
> relatively innocuous from our perspective, this teasing is quite cruel from
> the Burmese point of view. (1992:205)

Burmese male hostility was also, for Spiro, the reason why Burmese people had such rich imagery and beliefs regarding spiritism and the inhabitants of the seven Buddhist hells. He believed that there was no doubt that "ghosts and demons, witches and malevolent spirits" were projections of a Burmese man's "hostile impulses" (1992:202–203). While avowing that the Burmese are not paranoid, Spiro argued that the perceptual set, "the world is hostile," is fundamental to adult Burmese society and "is a generalization from their childhood perception of their parents. . . . [F]eeling threatened by moral anxiety, the child projects his hostility onto others" (1959:247). The following was the basis for the Burmese belief in witchcraft:

> If hostility is induced by frustration, then sheer rage, which is the emotional
> basis for malevolent and sadistic fantasies, is the frustration-induced
> response of the immature ego of a child. . . . In short, it is in childhood that
> private fantasies corresponding to witchcraft beliefs develop. . . . In a society,
> such as Burma, in which lavish nurturing is followed by abrupt rejection,
> the child's frustration—and, hence, his frustration-induced rage—is
> intense. . . . [T]heir childhood fantasies concerning their own sadistic and
> destructive powers constitute the perceptual basis for the Burmese belief in
> witches. (1959:250–253)

As in the other studies, it was childhood rage that explained why the Burmese would seek independence from the British. On the one hand, British colonization decreased opportunities for the projection and displacement of this innate hostility outwards (such as in witchcraft accusations), but on the other hand it created more opportunities in the form of "pre-independence political behavior" and "post-independence political machinations" (1959:258).

To recap my review so far: all of these critiques of the treatment of children at the hands of their parents stemmed from the belief that the Burmese people, and particularly Burmese men, were inherently hostile (see also Gorer 1943 and Sein Tu 1964) and this hostility was usually repressed except during wartime and in sport (ritualized warfare). The other way in which male hostility was channeled in Burma was through adherence to authoritarian hierarchy in which Burmese men obeyed their male superiors while forcing their wives and children to obey them, a "state of sado-masochistic symbiosis which gives him a sense of strength and a sense of identity" (Fromm 1963:104–105, quoted in Spiro 1992:216–217). The perceived laziness of Burmese women and the arbitrary nature of their affections for their children and the random and cruel teasing of children were together seen as causal in creating a psycho-cultural milieu in which a hostile attitude to the world was inculcated in the next generation. The results of such a pathological childhood ran the gamut from resistance to the British under colonization, to banditry, to the cruel taunting of children, to a belief in malevolent spirits.

Mahosadha

The kinds of psychological and motivational observations made by some of the social theorists of the last century often occurred without consulting the Burmese people they were observing about their feelings for their children and their own rationales for particular aspects of child rearing. When consulted, Burmese people frequently mention the story of Mahosadha. For example, a young Chin woman who was educated in Rangoon, told me that "as children, we loved the stories of Mahosadha. He was young like us, and he was so brave, so wise, and so clever. We read his stories over and over until we had memorized them. I particularly loved the one about the female ogress *(balu-ma)* and Mahosadha's wise judgment." And my middle-aged friend Daw Shwe Shwe also told me about Mahosadha in relation to her feelings for her son. She wanted to try and communicate to me a Burmese understanding of the value of sons: not as helpers in old age, or as people whose success enhances one's own social or karmic position, but as beings unconditionally loved. She explained her feelings through a version of the Buddhist tale of the wise judgments of King Mahosadha.[3]

> Mahosadha was born to a rich family and his wisdom was so great that the king came to hear about him. (He was working as a kind of a judge in a village at the time.) The king had four advisors, *ponnas*,[4] who were jealous of him and denigrated him. One day a problem was given to the king by a *natthami* [female Nat spirit] who said, "I will give you seven days to answer the problem, or else your kingdom will suffer." There were originally four problems and this was on one them: *A person kicks you in the face. As he kicks you, you feel more than love towards him, you feel an unexplainable pleasure. Who is this?* The king and his advisors could not answer. But Mahosadha said, "It is your child who is made out of your own flesh and blood."

Value

One worthy son, one valuable gem.
                                        —Burmese proverb

A number of metaphors and key themes run through the statements of the hundreds of people I have interviewed in the past decade about Burmese attitudes toward childhood. One is apparent in the story of Mahosadha, and that is the physical connection that exists between parents and their children and the ways in which Burmese people envisage children as extensions of their own physical selves. The mother sees her child as having been formed from the "blood of the heart," and children "are valued as blood coming out of my breast." "Breast blood" *(yin-thway)* is a common term of endearment for children. Fathers provide "life from their very bone marrow" (Pe Tin Thein 1992), and the *Mahatanha sankhaya sutta* argues that a mother's red blood is transformed into white breastmilk through the intense loving kindness that mothers send to their infants (Maung Yint Kyuu 2000:4). It is common for mothers to remark that "I have given of my blood and sweat [to my children]," and regarding their daughters, "I love and value her as much as my own heart." These replies from urban parents confirm aspects of a 1965 village study by Manning Nash who found that a child's character, disposition, and strength "are somehow transmitted through the blood or bone, [and] are deep lying and virtually inextirpable" (Manning Nash 1965:258), and many informants have told me that "my child is my strength," emphasizing the reciprocal physical bond between parents and their offspring.

Although the corporeal imagery is pre-Buddhist, the conceptualization of children as bearers of human life is a strong Buddhist theme. In Burmese history, children like Mahosadha have been prophets, judges, and visionaries, such as the twelve-year-old leaders of the Army of God cult, Jimmy and Luther Htoo (Ingram 2001). In 1925 the *Journal of the Burma Research Society* reported a child tested by the author, Tha Kin, for his "prenatal knowledge" of the *Tipitaka* and his general knowledge of Burmese and Pali. Like Mahosadha, the child had begun at the age of four and a half to tour villages, preaching and administering advice (Tha Kin 1925). The Buddhist belief in reincarnation means that children are sometimes believed to be an elder reborn, and this is one reason why children are worthy of respect in Burmese culture (Brant 1954:19).

Children are worthy of respect for a variety of additional reasons: as a vessel for a human life; because elders have a duty to place that human life upon the Eightfold Path to Enlightenment; and also because children are believed to embody innocence, power, and perfection. A fifty-year-old academic relates that "I have three children and the youngest one, a boy, I call *tha-gyit*, meaning 'beloved son.' They are not only my children, but also my friends. I compare them to *bodhisattva* [buddhas-to-be] because they are innocent and powerful people like bodhisattva."

The linking of children to key aspects of Buddhism shows not only the respect given to children in Burma, but also the potential power that children embody (Pe Tin Thein 1992:1). Buddhist sacred objects are imbued with *dago*, a force that is transferred to other objects that they become associated with

(Kumada 2002). At the pinnacle of Burmese pagodas, adorned with gold and gems, is the *hti* (tiered and ornamental finial of a pagoda). The *hti* is ringed with small bells that make a tinkling sound in a breeze. This is the sound most often associated with children, and a very common nickname for a Burmese child is *hswe-le,* "little bell."

The most common metaphor used to describe the value of children is jewels *(yadana),* and the most common description of all is *"yadana su-pon."* This phrase means the gathering up of all the forms of value in the world into one thing, a child. A young Burmese woman told me that when she was a child, she and her friends dug their hands into the soil, expecting to scoop out fistfuls of rubies. As children they took literally the military regime's claims about the richness of Burma's natural beauty and resources. This is the sense of the term, yadana su-pon, in the scooping up of all that is rich and beautiful in Burma, and transmuting it into the body of one's child.

This metaphorical alchemy is evident wherever one turns in Burma. "Welcome to the Golden Land," "Ruby Tea Shop," "Precious Optometrist," "Jade Inn," "Radiant Tours," "Golden Moon Star," "Royal Diamond," "Diamond Win Co. Pest Control," "Diamond Supermarket," "Golden Crowd," "Emerald Green Restaurant," and "Treasure Hotel" are just a sample of the typical signs lining all Burmese city streets. Names are powerful in Burma, and Burmese people frequently seek astrologers, wizards, monks, and other religious and magical authorities to find names for their children and businesses. To name something is to foreshadow the future of that thing. The Burmese alphabet has twenty-eight characters divided into seven groups, with each group corresponding to a day of the week. Children born on a particular day of the week will traditionally have a name that begins with one of the letters corresponding to that day. In one village, now part of Rangoon's suburbs, Brant noted in 1950 that "boy's names usually denote strength, success or brilliance; while grace, beauty, tenderness and various precious stones are the most common meanings of girls' names" (Brant 1954:20).

Although Burmese people believe that children's futures are largely predetermined according to their karmic status, they also believe that it certainly can't hurt to give children auspicious names, as one good-humored woman explained to me.

> The nicknames of my children are Whitey, Reddish, Reddish in another
> way, and Transparent. I gave them those names that I had pulled from my
> imagination. I was poor when I was young. I wanted so very much to own
> those kinds of jewels. My first-born child was a girl, and so as to predict and
> foreshadow her future, I named her Diamond Jewel. Then the next one,
> and in fact, all of the rest, happened to be girls, and so I named them Ruby

Jewel, Sapphire Jewel, and Pearl Jewel. Thankfully I only gave birth to girls. If I had given birth to a boy, I might have named him Poe Jade [Poe is a regular male name]. Now I have a grandchild and so I named him Golden Jewel. Some people think that I'm a lunatic but I don't care. Once, during the Kyi-mano festival,[5] someone played a joke and put a street sign, "Jewel Hill," in front of my house. And as far as I can recall, all of our business dealings have gone well since then: call me superstitious!

Foreshadowing is not just about wealth creation, but also naming children to become the kinds of adults of whom one would be proud, as U Chit Phyo explained to me. "I am seventy-nine years old, and I have only two children. I wanted to have more because I knew they were going to make me feel proud, but my wife died and so I was both a mother and a father to them. My children are named Chit Maung and Ma Ma Lay. U Chit Maung was a great novelist, and so was Ma Ma Lay. I wanted my children to be scholars and that's why I named them in that way."

Children are consistently compared to jewels because of their rareness, preciousness, and because of their need to be protected or watched over.[6] Girl children and youngest children are particularly referred to in the following ways. A forty-five-year-old grocery seller was telling me about the nicknames of her children when she came to her youngest child.

The third one happened to be a girl, and I had, a long time ago, decided that I would only have three children so I nicknamed her Nge Nge, "Youngest." Her school name is Yadana—*yadana ta-ya lin*—because she's the last and most precious one to me and since I always wanted to have a daughter. The real names of my children are Sunlight *(nay-min lin)*, Moonlight *(la-min lin)*, and Jewel Starlight (yadana ta-ya lin). My children are full of light. Like jewels they are very valuable and need to be protected. Nge Nge is a girl, and I have to be watchful and protect her; that's why I compare her to jewels, and because jewels are so rare and expensive.

For most of the adults I interviewed, however, children are simply too precious to compare to something as this-worldly or material as jewels. One sixty-year-old woman told me about her daughter Pon Pon's inestimable worth.

I was married when I was twenty years old. I had two miscarriages because of misfortune and bad luck. I only gave birth to my first child when I was thirty-eight years old, and I had to have an operation [caesarean birth]. She's a yadana to me because I got her alive. I named her Su Yadana [Su meaning something desired or wished for or a reward]. At home we called

her Su Pon Chit [Chit meaning love], but then as time went on we also
began to call her Pon Pon. I don't compare my daughter to jewels because
she's too valuable to be compared to anything at all.

This woman's sentiments of longing for children are echoed in another
typical example, furnished by Daw Than Hla, an academic in her fifties.

> I value my children enormously. Sometimes I wonder how I am going to
> survive without them. I was an only child with divorced parents. I don't
> think I was ever fully loved. I guess my parents thought that half of me
> didn't belong to them and so they couldn't love me wholly. Since my child-
> hood I have always longed for a family. I chose my husband with great care.
> I looked for a family man. I was lucky; I got what I wanted. So I gave all my
> love to my children, and of course, I value them immensely. They cannot
> be compared to anything. They are too precious, beyond compare.

When asked the question, "What are children?" Burmese people will overwhelmingly answer, "Children are the future." Children represent the strength
of the present and past generations made manifest, and they are bundles of
potentiality. In Buddhism "the child is a physical body, a personality, a potential" (Pe Tin Thein 1992:1). U Chit Phyo answered the question by stating, "I
think it's obvious. They are my heritage. They are a part of me and they are
my success. I am a happy man now. My grandchildren are wonderful as well.
I cannot ask for more."

An Alternative Theory of Child Socialization

> A real ruby cannot sink in the mud.
>   —Burmese proverb

It is not my intention to romanticize Burmese conceptualizations of children
and childhood, but rather to draw attention to the culturally specific ways that
Burmese people express universally familiar feelings of love, attachment, and
the value of children. The current literature regarding children and Burma is
overwhelmingly negative: child labor, child soldiers, and child-trafficking
dominate international aid agency and media discourse. As in every country,
children are victims of a variety of terrible acts and of mistreatment.

The teasing, or taunting of children is one point of supposed difference
around which many of the twentieth-century child studies in Burma are pred-
icated. It is certainly true that many, but by no means all, Burmese adults taunt
children until they are enraged or burst into tears. How can this behavior be

reconciled with the statements of the incomparable value of children given above? The answer is not discernible through Burmese statements about the phenomena. No one I have spoken to, no matter their age or education level, can give me a straight answer, but they give enough clues that a theory can be supported. The following interview segment represents the best example of Burmese reflecting upon the meaning of taunting. It comes from Nila (Sapphire), an intelligent and educated woman. I had mentioned the question to her earlier in the day and that evening over dinner she volunteered this explanation.

> I have been thinking about your question. Some Burmese parents mock their children in order to arouse their anger because they find it pleasurable. We teach our children to be jealous from an early age, even between brother and sister: "I will love your sister more than you." Actually they like comparing people a lot: "I won't give any favors to you . . ." Sometimes it's a joke. Sometimes they visit people's homes and they like invoking embarrassment and anger (by teasing their children). The parent may also want to show the neighbors or other guests that the child loves them (and presumably the depth of that love), by provoking a display. We try to point out weak points in a person's character, not just to children, but it is important for children to understand their weaknesses.

Nila makes a series of important points that demonstrate how the taunting of children by some adults is all about provoking a display of emotion.

In Burmese Buddhist society, until puberty, children are not "scolded" or "constrained" by their parents (Pe Tin Thein 1992; Mi Mi Khaing 1962). They are not "trained" through discipline but learn rather through the examples of others.[7] Maung Hlaing (1985a, 1985b) notes that Burmese children's stories are vehicles that convey codified moral lessons disguised as entertainment. Daw Shwe Shwe and I were having a conversation once, walking home from her local market, about U Po Sein, a famous dramatist and puppeteer. Shwe Shwe told me how her grandmother would sit her down in the evenings and tell her a story that had been dramatized by U Po Sein. As much as Shwe Shwe delighted in being told stories, she also dreaded them because the stories always told about a person's inappropriate behavior, and the consequences of such behavior. Shwe Shwe's childish misdemeanors were thus never openly commented upon, but through U Po Sein's stories, told by a respected elder,[8] Shwe Shwe learned that particular forms of behavior were inappropriate.

Grandparents and parents also tell less subtle stories of doom and damnation, involving the animist and Buddhist pantheon of demons, witches, and spirits. In these stories children are told they will be transformed, in their next life, into such an entity (Manning Nash 1965:262) or that the retribution for bad behavior such as lying or stealing will be more immediate. Mi Mi Khaing notes that as a child she was told stories about witches who ate misbehaving children and "in Thanatpin I could have pointed out the actual tree in which the old witch lived, and when it grew dark both my nurse and I would shiver in each other's arms at the thought of it" (Mi Mi Khaing 1962:61).

The stories told to children are a form of moral education and are similar to other forms of moral education evident in Burmese culture. At the nation's psychiatric hospitals, for example, patients learn through the example of the "normal" behavior of medical staff and through being ignored or separated from the group when they commit indiscretions (Skidmore 1998). As children grow up in Burmese society, they come to learn that emotion, and the facial expressions that betray emotion, are heavily circumscribed in their culture. Anger, for example, is considered a sure sign of madness, and public outbursts of rage are grounds for immediate incarceration in a psychiatric facility (ibid.). The control of emotion is a familiar theme in a great many Asian cultures, and has been well documented in the anthropological literature, including for Burma (see such examples as Appadurai 1990; Aung San Suu Kyi 1990; Daniel 1996; Desjarlais 1992; de Pina-Cabral 2002; Obeyesekere 1985; Skidmore 2003a; Tamura 1983; Wikan 1990). Burmese children are believed to have the same emotional needs, moods, and responses as adults, but in miniature form as Manning Nash (1965:259) describes.

> There is little view of the neonate as plastic; rather, the prevailing definition is that babies are helpless miniature adults, who with time and care will mature into whatever their capabilities and experiences permit. . . . The relative independence of children's fate from parents' guidance makes babyhood and early childhood a time . . . where emotional and ego needs are treated as budding versions of adult needs.

Teasing evokes emotions such as jealousy, rage, humiliation, and self-pity, and leads to tears, red faces, yelling, sulking, screaming, and other forms of behavior that would be considered shocking in adults. Taunting can thus be a form of cruelty or lack of respect, but it can also be viewed as a form of moral education, where children learn to control their emotions, or a way for Burmese adults to reinforce to themselves the "rules" or code of conduct in adult society. It should also be mentioned that the members of the family who taunt children are often unmarried or divorced sisters and fictive aunts. In Burmese, the term "sister-in-law" translates literally as one who stirs things up, and such individuals make trouble when they move in or become close to a sister's new husband and attempt "to form with them an extended conjugal family"(Manning Nash 1965:51).

In his explanation of the influential social norm *a-na-de* (a feeling of compassion for others such that a consideration of the feelings of others becomes of paramount importance in social relationships and situations), Manning Nash argues that from their earliest years, children are taught, through example and guidance "a kind of indirection in most human encounters . . . a deliberate effort to . . . believe that things are really what they seem" when involved in interpersonal relations. This form of social training usually prevents "a sharply defined emotional situation, a blazing argument, a direct confrontation, a clash of persons." Of the major personality types found in the rural area where Nash conducted fieldwork, villagers consistently recommended that the ideal personality type was *lein hmade lu,* a clever person who "avoids fights and arguments, never uses harsh words, and states things so that the hearers get the point easily" (1965:269–270). Nash mentions an admonition commonly given by parents to their children—"why make someone displeased/angry with you?"—which means that children are taught not to cause disharmony but to ignore, as much as possible, offensive or irritating behavior in family and neighbors. Social harmony and village cohesion is privileged at all times.

It is also possible that adults provoke children because a-na-de and the Burmese social code means that they themselves are unable to partake in public emotional displays. "K" has suggested that the introduction of puppetry to Burma in the mid-eighteenth century served a positive psychological function because it allowed the Burmese people to see and discuss forms of behavior (such as irreverent and sexually licentious behavior) in which they themselves could not participate (K 1981:15). Children, like madmen and puppets, are able to act in ways outside the formal boundaries of "normalcy," and they thus reinforce those boundaries.

Nila is quick to remind me that not all parents taunt their children, and another friend estimates that less than one-third of parents do so. When children reach the age of twelve, girls traditionally undergo an *ear-piercing* ceremony, and boys participate in a *shinbyu* ceremony (the initiation of a boy into the Sāsana through his initiation as a novice for a short period). These Buddhist coming-of-age rituals signify, among other things, the beginning of the imposition of discipline upon them in their new status of semiadults, or adolescents, when they are believed to be old enough to understand the moral teachings of Buddhism (Brant 1954:20). The unregulated temper tantrums of childhood give way to parents and, traditionally, monastic educators meting out discipline to children who fail to show respect or who break basic Buddhist tenets such as stealing.

The Future

In their frail hands
The future rests
Muddied, stained, smeared with dust.
—(from "Children" Myo Kyaw Myint 1988:48)

When thinking about the current woeful state of the Burmese economy—the famine, misery, and social suffering that characterizes the history of militarized Burma since 1962—the bright spot for researchers and Burmese alike is children. Children embody the future in Burma, and it is Burmese children for whom the most heroic struggles for democracy will be conducted, the most degrading acts of desperation will be committed, and the most loving acts of forgiveness of the military regime will be practiced.

Mi Mi Khaing (1962:67) has written that "Burmese children do not live in a child's world cut off from reality—there is no specially created world for them. . . . No special children's parties with cakes and games for them are provided. . . . Yet no one who sees Burmese children can doubt that delight, wonder and pure joy are present in their lives." She notes that children go wherever adults go and that childhood is undoubtedly a time of much joy (and also innocence [Nyunt Way 1989]).

Childhood is an invention of the Victorian era, and the creation of a miniature pleasure world for children is well documented in the literature (Ariès 1962; deMause 1974; Plotz 2001; Stone 1983). Western childhood writers increasingly call for the collapse of the rigid Victorian distinction between childhood and adulthood, arguing that information technology has advanced to such a level that the boundaries between postpubescent child, adolescent, and young adult exist only in a fluid youth space (Elkind 1998; Hutchby and Moran-Ellis 2001; James and Prout 1997; Prout 2002; Steinberg and Kincheloe 1998). These writings argue for the recognition of the cultural and historical variables in beliefs about childhood and about parenting. The reconfiguring of childhood and parenting in societies rich in information technology spills over, through globalization and the movement of transnational capitalism, into countries such as Burma, where a new generation of Burmese writers wax lyrically about these themes as they are one of the few approved ways in which emotion can be expressed in publication in contemporary Burma.

The highly negative portrayal of mothers and of childhood by Western and occasional Western-trained Burmese writers is exceeded only by the flowery tributes by Burmese adults to their mothers. These sentiments are echoed by Hla Myo Nwe in his translation of Burmese children's nursery rhymes, such as "Let's go a-gathering *thabya* plums." A family activity representative of the "wondrous innocence of a Myanmar childhood," is revisited by the author with an almost mystical nostalgia, where such poems "are emotionally evocative of a mother's loving embrace that makes children feel warm and secure" (Hla Myo Nwe 1998:63).

This nostalgia for childhood is not unusual in a society unable to look towards the future with hope, and there is a protectiveness of their remembrance of unfettered childhood. A great many Burmese people are angered, for example, at the suggestion that forms of apprenticeship can be considered child labor. In 1997 I visited a "show room" for a Mandalay company that is well known throughout Burma as creating the finest *longyi* designs on silk and cotton. The walls are adorned with several pictures of British royalty and other foreign dignitaries who have toured the premises and presumably bought longyi there. Young girls, aged from ten to adulthood, work the looms, six days per week, for up to ten hours per day. They are, apparently, not child laborers, but instead apprentices. Children from about the age of ten are expected to work beside their parents, and when a parent dies, the eldest same-sex child assumes the economic responsibilities of the deceased parent. This child was traditionally known as the *orāsa,* meaning "the child who comes from the breast," and the Burmese *Dhammathats* (Buddhist laws) entitle this child to 25 percent of the estate of the deceased parent (Maung Maung 1963:83).

The orāsa is still a crucial economic component of contemporary Burmese family life in all but the newest and wealthiest socioeconomic groups that Schober describes as the modern technocratic elite (this volume). Among those who are not the elite, children incur a reciprocal debt of caring and providing for their parents that is delayed until the parents require help in their old age. Children may be sent to live with family members who can better provide for them, but they are also sent to elderly relatives who require help with daily chores or who require the child to contribute to family income.[9] Male children begin to repay this debt when they reach puberty and participate in a Buddhist shinbyu ceremony. The merit they accrue is transferred to their parents.

In urban areas, among the reemerging middle class and the nouveau riche military class, the children of wealthy parents are spared apprenticeships and other forms of child labor, instead finishing school and attending university or other tertiary training in Burma or abroad. The lives of these children bear more similarities to the urban middle classes of other South and East Asian cities, such as Bangkok and Beijing, than to the desperately poor families who have been relocated to the peri-urban townships and rural villages. Within the urban centers of Rangoon and Mandalay, the new international hotels and fast-food eateries such as "Mr. J's Donuts" are the scene, on weekends, for children's birthday parties. Children are increasingly the target audience of Asian advertising, and such advertisements present small nuclear families with fat children as the preferred new cultural norm. Concerned parents hover over these caricatured children who are fed Chinese vitamin syrups, Singaporean soda drinks, and Thai powdered-milk products. A modern Burmese corporate childhood is rapidly being constructed in the amusement parks, supermarket aisles, and department store toy shops of the inner city.

More than anything else, however, children embody the future. A woman in her mid-fifties who works as a health consultant and has no children articulates this simple fact.

> I value children greatly. They are an added dimension to one's existence.
> I was unlucky. The doctor I worked for forbade me to get married, and I
> thought my life was going to be wasted. But I was wrong. My nieces and
> nephews made me realize the value of life. They were brought up very well
> and well trained. But I know it isn't us who made them what they are. They
> are what they are, and they are perfect. They are going to make our genera-
> tion keep our good name. They are our future; every child is our future
> and if we don't value them, what should we value?

"What else should we value?" was the question continually turned back against my own questions. Burmese don't like to state the obvious. Their word play and language is too rich for such pedestrian wordsmithery. Frequently you hear someone remark, "Do I have to finish the sentence for you?" The Burmese people have adopted a very common strategy of resistance to military rule; they invest energy, money, and attachment in those things worthy of their respect. The Burmese do not dare openly defy the regime, and they do not want, for the most part, to cause a confrontation or conflict with authorities. Their preferred strategy is to patronize, for example, monks, monasteries, and pagodas that are morally superior to those same institutions built or supported by the military regime (Jordt 2001; Schober 1997; Rozenberg 2002; Tosa 2002).

When Buddhist parents reach their fifth decade, they renounce personal goals of affluence and a material lifestyle and redouble their efforts to provide a good example and appropriate moral environment for their children and grandchildren. Their engagement in the material world is focused through the lens of their children and grandchildren. Their attention is increasingly drawn to mental processes, to meditation, and Buddhist pursuits and domains such as monasteries and meditation centers. Burmese people, in asking "what should

I value?" are telling us about how they are deliberately turning away from the modernization and materialism of the contemporary urban lifestyle as promulgated by the economic liberalization policies of the mid-1990s. They prefer to invest in the future—in children and in Buddhism.

We see the creation of an alternate moral environment, one in which Burmese parents nurture the future, in their parenting techniques; in their communication of Buddhist tenets and respect for teachers; in their use of material possessions for nonwordly purposes; and in the provision of their children's education. They show their children not only how to be *daga(ma)* (Buddhist donors), but how to donate to morally appropriate hsayadaws, pagodas, and Buddhist projects. Their parenting techniques inculcate in future generations the importance of respect for elders, the Buddha, the Dhamma, and teachers. In showing children what they should value, we see how much children themselves are valued as repositories of hope for the future.

Although the schools and pagodas stand dwarfed by high-rise buildings, they remain inner-city havens from the traffic snarls and the overflow of the accoutrements of modernity such as the Chinese plasticware of street vendors, everywhere available, but of little value. The rewriting of Burma's history and the salience of past events is thus softly challenged by an alternate genetic history of the body, where the past of one's lineage is made manifest in the ties that bind children to their parents and grandparents. Most of the visible structure of contemporary urban life is accorded "no value": propaganda, official media, international and tourist infrastructure, and wealthy leisure precincts. Value is instead manifest in Burmese children, who embody the gathering up of all the wealth in the world in their small bodies.

Children Are Like Jewels

My aim in this chapter has been to muddy the simple readings of the art and motivations of parenting and to present numerous reasons why Burmese people raise their children according to cultural, historical, economic, and political circumstances. The enormous value placed upon education and the role of teachers; the notion of debt incurred by children, especially the orāsa; the delayed reciprocity of caring, providing, and feeding that occurs between Burmese generations; Buddhist conceptions of children and the family; as well as the increasing desire to taste the fruits of modernity as it is being conceived and presented in Burma, are some of the reasons that motivate parents to adopt particular birth-spacing strategies and to pursue certain forms of economic activity and vocation.

Fertility regulation has occurred in Burma through a number of means including the use of emmenagogues and abortion. There is no consensus among Burmese women as to the desired number of children, but in relocated townships, war zones, and other areas where reproductive health issues are of urgent concern, women often seek sterilization and to abort fetuses, and men express a desire for the legalization of vasectomies. Oral and injectable contraceptions are increasingly used by women to regulate fertility (Skidmore 2003b). Condoms have become available in the last decade, largely through international organizations and in relation to HIV infection rates (Skidmore 1998).

In neighboring countries, theorists have postulated that abortion and other forms of menstrual regulation constitute a hidden reproductive transcript (Whittaker 2003), a quiet resistance to the nation-making occurring at the level of the state and involving the state's coercive power made manifest at the level of reproductive technologies. The Burmese people do not, however, limit the number of children they have because they wish to deny the state the bodies it needs to make into model citizens. Rather, the values and morals promulgated by the military regime are left lying, as state orphans have been described in Burma, like "blossoms in the dust." Value—moral worth—resides in children, but not necessarily in a certain number of children. That particular decision is contingent on multiple factors, many of them idiosyncratic. During periods of economic hardship, some Burmese families adopt an attitude that "one child is good enough to love" *(kalay tayauk-hte chit-saya kaung-de)*.[10] One child, apparently, is enough to orient a Burmese family's moral compass and enough to provide a vessel in which to project hope into the future.

We have now come full circle *(awaing)* to arrive again at Western musings on why the Burmese fertility rate is low, as evidenced by nineteenth-century health and sanitation committee reports by the British India government. There are, however, many women who continue to have large families and never resort to menstrual regulation. Before the birth of my own children, I interviewed many women about their reproductive health in Rangoon and Mandalay, and often wondered, with some frustration, why women condemned themselves to abject poverty by having six or more children. The genesis of this chapter lies then, in my own naiveté about parenthood, as was revealed in one conversation in 1996 with a forty-four-year-old divorced woman from Mandalay who drove a pony cart to provide for her nine children. A further four children had died shortly after birth. Why, I asked her with some exasperation slipping into my voice, did she continue to have children and not use contraception? She leaned back and with a crooked smile she raised a hand to her neck to touch an imaginary necklace and said, "Because, children are like jewels."

Notes

For Isabelle, my own *hswe-le*.

The fieldwork for this chapter was conducted in part through a grant from the University of Melbourne, and the writing of the paper was facilitated by the Rockefeller Foundation and the Joan B. Kroc Institute for International Peace Studies at the University of Notre Dame. My thanks to child workers and colleagues in Burma, especially Karl Dorning and Shauj-ke, and also to Carolyn Nordstrom and Bénédicte Brac de la Perrière for their helpful reviews of this chapter.

1. Forty-five years later, Maj. S. A. Harris of the Indian Medical Service conducted an annual sanitary report of Burma as part of a larger Indian survey, and argued that the contamination of Burmese blood by Madrassis had decreased the "vitality" of the Burmese people and this fact accounted for Burma's sizeable infant mortality rate (1911).

2. Forms of violence and cruelty in Burma were believed, according to the psychologists, psychological anthropologists, and other culture brokers, to be the result of what I can only describe as a mythical autonomy of Burmese men. Hanks wrote that "cruelty occurs, and it is doubtless no mitigation to the sufferer to know that his tormentor is not a sadist at heart. He is more like a child moved by frustration to vindictive retaliation" (1945: 300). Cruelty occurred for Hanks, when Burmese men sought to ameliorate their multiple anxieties regarding the dangers of interpersonal relations by trying to seize power, often through violence. Quoting Sein Tu, Spiro writes of the "great aggressiveness" that sons have for their fathers "so that the deference required in interaction with parents (and elders in general) serves as a defense against these aggressive impulses." Spiro further echoes this theme of male autonomy resulting from pathological child rearing and leading to violence and aggression in adult society. "For children of both sexes, then, parents (and especially same-sex parents) are frustrating figures, and the consequent hostility and rage of the Burmese child no more disappears in adulthood than those of other children anywhere else in the world" (1975:129).

3. King Mahosadha is his name in Pali. In Burmese it is Mahosot who is the hero of the "Great Tunnel Jataka . . . who proves his wisdom at the age of seven by answering nineteen problems set by King Vedeha. He becomes the great minister of the king, survives the jealous plots of the other ministers and, as a climax to his career, saves king and country by tunneling into the heart of the enemy's camp" (Huxley 1997:316).

4. Ponnas are "royal Brahman astrologers" (Mya Maung 1992:39).

5. This is most likely a reference to a once-common annual festival called "Thieves' Night," that seems to have been most prevalent in Mandalay, but was also celebrated in Lower Burma. It involved stealing items from homes and businesses and placing

them in situations so as to cause laughter or embarrassment (Brown 1914; Maung Maung Than 1915).

6. "The birth of a child to the family is like the thrust of a pot of gold out of the earth, such is the joy and sense of reward" (Pe Tin Thein 1992:4).

7. "Children who can walk and speak are left free to move around the compound; older children are free to come and go nearly as they wish within the village; and smaller children are passed from hand to hand or placed to sleep or rest in the swinging cradles every household has outside in a cleared area" (Manning Nash 1965: 254–255).

8. Rebukes from grandparents are especially effective because they are held in such high esteem and with much affection by children. As Nash notes, "not only are grandparents indulgent of their grandchildren . . . but they are often active allies with the grandchild against his parents" (Manning Nash 1965:63).

9. I am indebted to Bénédicte Brac de la Perrière for reminding me of this phenomenon, and she notes that her own fieldwork contains many such accounts during the 1980s in city suburbs (personal communication, March 2003).

10. I am indebted to Bénédicte Brac de la Perrière for this expression.

References

Allott, Anna J. 1996. Censorship and Government Propaganda in Burma. Essays presented at the Burma Studies Group Colloquium, Northern Illinois University. De Kalb, IL. October 1996.

———. 1993. *Inked Over, Ripped Out: Burmese Storytellers and the Censors.* New York: PEN.

———. 1981. Prose Writing and Publishing in Burma: Government Policy and Private Practice. In *Essays on Literature and Society in Southeast Asia,* pp. 1–35. Edited by Than Seong Chee, Singapore: Singapore University Press.

Anagnost, Ann. 2002. Discussant: Constructing the Future: Anthropology and the Global Politics of Childhood. Essay presented at 101st Annual Meeting of American Anthropological Association. New Orleans, November 20.

Anderson, Benedict. 1991. *Imagined Communities: Reflections on the Origins and Spread of Nationalism.* London: Verso.

Appadurai, Arjun. 1990. Topographies of the Self: Praise and Emotion in Hindu India. In *Language and the Politics of Emotion,* pp. 92–112. Edited by Catherine A. Lutz and Lila Abu-Lughod. Cambridge: Cambridge University Press.

Ariès, Phillipe. 1962. *Centuries of Childhood.* New York: Vintage Books.

Atkinson, Jane and Shelly Errington, Eds. 1990. *Power and Difference: Gender in Island Southeast Asia.* Stanford: Stanford University Press.

Aung San. 1971. *The speeches of Aung San (17.03.1945–19.07.1947)* (in Burmese). Rangoon: Sarpay Beikman.

Aung San Suu Kyi. 1998a. The Game Rules in Burma: There Are No Rules. *Asahi Evening News.* August 25.

———. 1998b. Heavenly Abodes and Human Development. From the 11th Pope Paul VI Memorial Lecture, Royal Institution of Great Britain, November 3, 1997. Delivered by Michael Aris. *Bangkok Post.* January 4, 1998.

———. 1997. *Letters from Burma.* Second Edition. London: Penguin.

———. 1996. Letters from Burma, Number 40: Faith Eases the Mind in Times of Political Turmoil. *Manichi Daily News.* September 9.

———. 1994. Empowerment for a Culture of Peace and Development. Address to November 1994 meeting of the World Commission on Culture and Development, presented on behalf of the author and at her request by Mrs. Corazon Aquino.

―――. 1993. Towards A True Refuge. The Joyce Pearce Memorial Lecture, University of Oxford. Delivered by Michael Aris. May 19. www.burmainfo.org/assk/DASSK _1993_TowardsATrueRefuge.html.

―――. 1991. *Freedom from Fear and Other Writings*. Edited by Michael Aris. New York: Viking.

―――. 1990. *Freedom from Fear and Other Writings*. Edited by Michael Aris. Hammondsworth: Penguin.

Aung San Suu Kyi and Michael Aris, Eds. 1995. *Freedom from Fear and Other Writings*. Second edition with additional material. New York: Penguin Books.

Aung San Suu Kyi, Alan Clements, U Kyi Maung, and U Tin U. 1997. *The Voice of Hope: Conversations with Alan Clements with Contributions by U Kyi Maung and U Tin U*. London: Penguin Books.

Aung Zaw. 1995. Suu Kyi Extends Olive Branch as Convention Delayed Once Again. *The Nation*, October 13.

Badgely, John. 1994. Myanmar in 1993: A Watershed Year. *Asian Survey* 34, 2 (Feb. 1994): 153–159.

Bakan, Michael B. 1998. Walking Warriors: Battles of Culture and Ideology in the Balinese Gamelan Beleganjur World. *Ethnomusicology* 42, 3:441–484.

Barthes, Roland. 1991. *S/Z*. New York: Noonday.

Bechert, Heinz. 1988. Neue Buddhistische Orthodoxie: Bemerkungen zur Gliederung und zur Reform des Sangha in Birma. *Numen* 35 (Jul. 1988).

―――. 1973. Sangha, State, Society, Nation: Persistence of Traditions in "Post-traditional" Buddhist Societies. *Daedalus* 102, 1:85–95.

Bekker, Sarah. 1989. Changes and Continuity in Burmese Buddhism. In *Independent Burma at Forty Years: Six Assessments*, pp. 51–61. Edited by Josef Silverstein. Ithaca, NY: Cornell Southeast Asia Program.

Bha Nyunt (U). 1981. *Mran ma mi rui: phalâ dale nat sa muin* (Enlarged Burmese edition of the work of C. Temple). Rangoon: Pinya Minzu Pitula SaOk Taik.

Bourdieu, Pierre. 1993. *The Field of Cultural Production: Essays on Art and Literature*. New York: Columbia University Press.

―――. 1984. *Distinction: A Social Critique of the Judgement of Taste*. Translated by Richard Nice. Cambridge: Harvard University Press.

Brac de la Perrière, Bénédicte. 2005. Les apparences du monde. Analyse des rituels de la royalté birmanie d'après un traité du dix-huitième siècle. In *Les Apparences du monde*. Edited by M. L. Reiniche and B. Brac de la Perrière. Paris : Ecole Française d'Estrême-orient.

―――.2003. Les rituels de consécration des statues de Bouddha et des statues de naq en Birmanie (Burma). In *Rites hindous: transferts et transformations* (Hindu rites:

Transfers and transformations). Edited by G. Colas and G. Tarabout. Paris: Centre d'études de l'Inde et de l'Asie du Sud. *Purushartha*, No. 25.

———. 2002. "Royal images" in their Palaces: The Place of the Statues in the Cult of the 37 *nats*. In *Burma Art and Archaeology*, pp. 99–105. Edited by A. Green and T. R. Blurton. London: British Museum Press.

———. 1998a. Le "roulis" de la Dame aux Flancs d'Or: Analyse d'une fête de naq atypique en Birmanie centrale (Myamnar). *L'Homme* 146:47–85.

———. 1998b. "Être épousée par un naq": Les implications du mariage avec l'esprit dans le culte de possession birman. *Anthropologie et Sociétés* 22, 2:169–182.

———. 1998c. Le cycle des fêtes de naq en Birmanie centrale. Une circumambulation de l'espace birman. In *Etudes thématiques 9*, pp. 289–331. Edited by P. Pichard and F. Robinne. Etudes birmanes en hommage à Denise Bernot, Ecole Française d'Extrême-Orient.

———. 1992. La fête de Taunbyon: le grand rituel du culte des naq de Birmanie (Myanmar). *Bulletin de l'Ecole Française d'Extrême-Orient* 79, 2: 201–231.

———. 1989. *Les rituels de possession en Birmanie: du culte d'Etat aux ceremonies privées*. Paris: Editions Recherche sur les Civilisations, ADPF.

Brant, Charles S. 1954. *Tadagale: A Burmese Village in 1950*. Ithaca, NY: Cornell University, Southeast Asia Program, No.13.

Brenner, Suzanne. 1995. Reconstructing Self and Society: Javanese Muslim Women and "the Veil." *American Ethnologist* 23:673–697.

———. 1995. Why Women Rule the Roost: Rethinking Javanese Ideologies of Gender and Self-Control. In *Bewitching Women, Pious Men*, pp. 19–50. Edited by Aihwa Ong and Michael Peletz. Berkeley: University of California Press.

Brown, R. Grant. 1916. On a Method of Manufacturing Charms in Burma. *Man* 67: 115–116.

———. 1914. Thieves' Night at Mandalay. *Journal of the Burmese Research Society* 4: 229–230.

Brunvand, Jan Harold. 1981. *The Vanishing Hitchhiker: American Urban Legends and Their Meanings*. New York: W.W. Norton.

Burma Pitika Association. 1986. *Guide to Tipitaka*. Rangoon: Burma Pitika Association.

BurmaNet News. 1997a. Independent Report: Anti-Muslim Riot. Issue #700. April 14. http://www.Burmalibrary.org/reg.burma/archives/199704/msg00387.html.

———. 1997b. Asiaweek. Letter (U Hla Shwe): Looking Behind the Mandalay Riots. Issue #700, April 14. http://www.Burmalibrary.org/reg.burma/archives/199704/msg00387.html.

Butler, Judith. 1990. Performative Acts and Gender Constitution: An Essay in Phenomenology and Feminist Theory. In *Performing Feminisms: Feminist Critical Theory and Theatre*, pp. 270–282. Edited by Sue-Ellen Case. Baltimore: Johns Hopkins University Press.

Central Intelligence Agency. 2003. Burma. *The World Factbook 2002.* www.cia.gov/cia/publications/factbook/geos.bm.html.

Chatterjee, Partha. 1993. *The Nation and Its Fragments: Colonial and Postcolonial Histories.* Princeton, NJ: Princeton University Press.

Clark, Cooper. 1932. Burmese Tatu. *Man* 82:67–84.

Cohn, Bernard S. 1996. *Colonialism and its Forms of Knowledge: the British in India.* Princeton, NJ: Princeton University Press.

Committee to Protect Journalists (CPJ) website www.cpj.org.

Condominas, Georges. 1998. *Le bouddhisme au village.* Vientiane: Editions des Cahiers de France.

Covington, Richard. 2002. Sacred and Profaned: Misguided Restorations of the Exquisite Buddhist Shrines of Pagan in Burma May Do More Harm Than Good. *Smithsonian,* December: 1–4.

Daniel, E. Valentine. 1996. *Charred Lullabies: Chapters in an Anthropography of Violence.* Princeton, NJ: Princeton University Press.

DeMause, Lloyd, Ed. 1974. *The History of Childhood.* New York: Psychohistory Press.

De Pina-Cabral, João. 2002. *Between China and Europe: Person, Culture, and Emotion in Macao.* London and New York: Continuum.

Desjarlais, Robert R. 1992. *Body and Emotion: The Aesthetics of Illness and Healing in the Nepal Himalayas.* Philadelphia: University of Philadelphia Press.

Elkind, David. 1998. *Reinventing Childhood: Raising and Educating Children in a Changing World.* Rosemont, NJ: Modern Learning Press.

Ewen, Stuart and Elizabeth Ewen. 1992. *Channels of Desire: Mass Images and the Shaping of American Consciousness.* Minneapolis: University of Minnesota Press.

Farquhar, Judith. 2001. For Your Reading Pleasure: Self-Health (Ziwo Baojian) Information in 1990s Beijing. *Positions* 9,1:105–113.

Ferguson, J. P. and E. M. Mendelson. 1981. Masters of the Buddhist Occult: The Burmese Weikzas. In *Contributions to Asian Studies,* pp. 62–81. Edited by J. P. Ferguson. Leiden: E. J. Brill.

Fink, Christina. 2001. *Living Silence: Burma Under Military Rule.* New York: Zed Books.

Fordham, Graham. 1998. Northern Thai Male Culture and HIV Risk. *Crossroads* 12, 1:77–141.

Formoso, Bernard. 2000. *Identités en regard. Destins chinois en milieu bouddhiste thaï.* Paris: CNRS Editions et Editions de la Maison des Sciences de l'Homme.

Foster, Brian L. 1976. Friendship in Rural Thailand. *Ethnology* 15, 3:251–267.

Freedom Forum. 2003. Freedom Forum Announces 2002 Al Neuharth Free Spirit of the Year. www.freedomforum.org/templates/document.asp?documentID=17537

Fromm, E. 1963. *The Dogma of Christ.* London: Routledge and Kegan Paul.

Furnivall, Julian S. 1948. *Colonial Policy and Practice.* Cambridge: Cambridge University Press.

Geertz, Clifford. 1980. *Negara: The Theatre State in Nineteenth-Century Bali.* Princeton, NJ: Princeton University Press.

Gorer, Geoffrey. 1943. Burmese Personality. Washington, DC.: Office of War Studies, mimeo.

Gravers, Mikael. 1999. *Nationalism as Political Paranoia in Burma: An Essay on the Historical Practice of Power.* Second Edition. Surrey: Curzon Press.

Guillard, Ginette. 1990. *Essai sur le dessin humoristique birman, mémoire inédit de Diplôme d'Etudes Approfondies.* Paris: Institut National des Langues et Civilisations Orientales.

Hagen, Everett E. 1962. *On the Theory of Social Change: How Economic Growth Begins.* Homewood, IL: The Dorsey Press, Inc.

Hall, Stuart. 1991. Old and New Identities, Old and New Ethnicities. In *Culture, Globalization and The World-System: Contemporary Conditions for the Representation of Identity,* pp. 41–68. Edited by Anthony D. King. Binghamton: Department of Art and Art History, State University of New York at Binghamton.

Hanks, Lucien M., Jr. 1949. The Quest for Individual Autonomy in Burmese Personality, With Particular Reference to the Arakan. *Journal for the Study of Interpersonal Processes* 12:285–300.

Hardy, Simon. 2002. *The Reader, The Author, The Woman, and Her Lover: Soft-Core Pornography and Heterosexual Men.* London: Cassell.

Harris, S. A. 1911. Annual Reports. Sanitary Report IV. Burma. *Indian Medical Gazette* 46 (September): 362–363.

Hatley, Barbara. 1990. Theatrical Imagery and Gender Ideology in Java. In *Power and Difference: Gender in Island Southeast Asia,* pp. 177–207. Edited by Jane Atkinson and Shelly Errington. Stanford: Stanford University Press.

Herbert, Patricia. M. 1982. The Hsaya San Rebellion (1930–32) Reappraised. Melbourne: Monash University Centre of Southeast Asian Studies. Working Paper No. 27.

Hitson Weidman, Hazel. 1969. Cultural Values, Concept of Self, and Projection: The Burmese Case. In *Mental Health Research in Asia and the Pacific,* pp. 259–285. Edited by William Caudill and Tsung-Yi Lin. Honolulu: East-West Center Press.

Hitson, Hazel M. 1959. Family Patterns and Paranoidal Personality Structure in Boston and Burma. PhD dissertation, Harvard University, 1959.

Hitson, Hazel M. and D. H. Funkenstein. 1959. Family Patterns and Paranoidal Personality Structure in Boston and Burma. *The International Journal of Social Psychiatry* 5, 3 (Winter): 182–190.

Hla Myo Nwe. 1998. Let's Go A-gathering "Thabye" Plums (A Children's Rhyme). *Myanmar Perspectives* (Yangon, Myanmar) 3, 2:61–64.

Houtman, Gustaaf. 1999. *Mental Culture in Burmese Crisis Politics: Aung San Suu Kyi and the National League for Democracy.* Tokyo University of Foreign Studies Monograph Series No. 33. Tokyo: Institute for the Study of Languages and Cultures of Asia and Africa.

Htin Aung (Maung). 1959. *Folk Elements in Burmese Buddhism*. Rangoon: Religious Affairs Department Press.

Htun Aung Kyaw. n.d. Introduction. Civil Society for Burma. www.csburma.org/htm/about_csb.php3.

Huizinga, Johan. 1949. *Homo Ludens: A Study of the Play-Element in Culture*. Translated from German by R. F. C. Hull. London: Routledge and Kegan Paul.

Hutchby, Ian and Jo Moran-Ellis. 2001. *Children, Technology and Culture: The Impacts of Technologies in Children's Everyday Lives*. London: Routledge Falmer.

Huxley, Andrew. 1997. The Traditions of Mahosadha: Legal Reasoning from Northern Thailand. *Bulletin of the School of Oriental and African Studies* 60, 2:315–326.

Ikeda, Oshima et al., Eds. 1996. *Hashiru Obasan, Nihon no Gendai Densetsu* (Running old woman: Japanese modern legend). Tokyo: Hakusuisya.

Ingram, Simon. 2001. God's Army Twins Captured. *BBC News*, January 17. www.news.bbc.co.uk/1/hi/world/asia-pacific/1121333.stm.

Jackson, Peter A. 1993. Re-Interpreting the Traiphuum Phra Ruang: Political Functions of Buddhist Symbolism in Contemporary Thailand. In *Buddhist Trends in Southeast Asia*, pp. 64–100. Edited by Trevor Ling. Singapore: Institute for Southeast Asian Studies.

Jackson, Peter and Nerida Cook, Eds. 1999. *Genders and Sexualities in Modern Thailand*. Chiang Mai: Silkworm Books.

James, Allison and Alan Prout, Eds. 1997. *Constructing and Reconstructing Childhood: Contemporary Issues in the Sociological Study of Childhood*. London: Routledge Falmer.

Jordt, Ingrid. 2003. The Social Organization of Intention: Sacred Giving And Its Implications for Burma's Political Economy. In *Money and the Sacred: Essays in Economic Anthropology*. Edited by Cynthia Werner and Duran Bell. Walnut Creek, CA: Alta Mira Press. 2003.

———. 2001. The Mass Lay Meditation Movement and State-Society Relations in Post-Independence Burma. PhD dissertation. Harvard University.

———. 1988. Bhikkhuni, Thilashin, Mae-Chii: Women Who Renounce the World in Thailand, Burma and the Classical Pali Texts. *Crossroads* 4,1.

K (U Khin Zaw). 1981. *Burmese Culture: General and Particular*. Rangoon: Sarpay Beikman.

Kabilsingh, Chatsumarn. 1991. *Thai Women in Buddhism*. Berkeley: Parallax Press.

Kala, U. 1956. *Maha Yazawin* (The great chronicle). 3 Volumes. Rangoon: Laydi Mandain Press.

Kapferer, Jean-Noël. 1990. *Rumeurs: Le Plus Vieux Me dia du Monde*. New Brunswick and London: Transaction Publications.

Katha Nyunt Way. 1989. Children are Playing. *Guardian* 36, 3 (March 1989): 7.

Kawanami, Hiroko. 2001. Can Women be Celibate? Sexual Abstinence in Theravada Buddhism. In *Celibacy, Culture, and Society: The Anthropology of Sexual Abstinence*, pp. 137–156. Edited by E. J. and S. Bell. Madison: University of Wisconsin Press.

———. 2000. Patterns of Renunciation: The Changing World of Burmese Nuns. In *Women's Buddhism, Buddhism's Women*, pp. 159–171. Edited by E. B. Findly. Somerville, MA: Wisdom.

Kendall, Laura, Ed. 2002. *Under Construction: The Gendering of Modernity, Class, and Consumption in the Republic of Korea*. Honolulu: University of Hawai'i Press.

Keyes, Charles. 1993. Buddhist Economics and Buddhist Fundamentalism in Burma and Thailand. In *Fundamentalisms and the State: Remaking Polities, Economies, and Militance*, pp. 367–409. Edited by Martin Marty and Scott Appleby. Chicago: University of Chicago Press.

Keyes, Charles, Laurel Kendall, and Helen Hardacre. 1994. Contested Visions of Community in East and Southeast Asia. In *Asian Visions of Authority: Religion and the Modern States of East and Southeast Asia*. Edited by Charles Keyes, Laurel Kendall, and Helen Hardacre. Honolulu: University of Hawai'i Press.

Khin Maung Than (Seit Pinya). 2001. *Yui:ya nat yom kran hmu hnan dhale thom:sam mya* (Customs and Beliefs in the Traditional Nat). Rangoon: Pinwa Yon Sabe.

Khin Nyunt. 2000. The opening ceremony of the Eighth Myanma Traditional Cultural Performing Arts Competitions (opening ceremony speech). *New Light of Myanmar*. October 27.

———. 1998. SPDC consistently undertaking tasks for preservation, safeguarding cultural heritage: National Unity being further strengthened through promotion of Union spirit, to crush subversives (opening ceremony speech). *New Light of Myanmar*. October 2.

———. 1989. Burma Communist Party's Conspiracy to Take Over State Power. Special Press Conference held on 5th August 1989. www.myanmar-information.net/bcp/power.htm.

Kramer, Tom and Pietje Vervest. 1999. Introduction. In *Strengthening Civil Society in Burma: The Possibilities and Dilemmas for International NGOs*, pp. v–ix. Edited by Burma Center Netherlands and Transnational Institute. Thailand: Silkworm Books.

Kumada, Naoko. 2002. Dagò, Cosmogony and Politics: Religion and Power in Burmese Society. Essay presented at Burma Studies Conference, Burma-Myanma(r) Research and its Future, Gothenberg, Sweden, 21–25 September.

Lees, L. H. 1866. On the Probable Causes of the Sparseness of Population in the Town of Akyab and the Arakan District Generally. *Indian Medical Gazette* 1 (June): 131–143, and (July): 173–175 July.

Lefort, Claude. 1976. Le nom d'Un. In *Le discours de la Servitude Volontaire, Etienne de La Boétie*, pp. 247–307. Paris: Editions Payot.

Liddell, Zunetta. 1999. No Room to Move: Legal Constraints on Civil Society in Burma. In *Strengthening Civil Society in Burma: Possibilities and Dilemmas for International NGOs*, pp. 54–68. Edited by Burma Center Netherlands and Transnational Institute. Thailand: Silkworm Books.

Ling, Trevor, Ed. 1993. *Buddhist Trends in Southeast Asia*. Singapore: Institute for Southeast Asian Studies.

Lintner, Bertil. 1997. Burma's Voice of Democracy. *Far Eastern Economic Review*. September 11: 52–53.

Luce, Gordon. H. and Pe Maung Tin. 1956. *The Glass Palace Chronicle of Burma* (translation). Rangoon: Burma Research Society.

Mahasi Sayadaw. 1979. *The Sattipatthana Vipassaná Meditation: A Basic Buddhist Mindfulness Exercise*. Translated by U Aye Maung. Rangoon: Department of Religious Affairs.

Marshall, Andrew. 2003 Thirteen Years of Solitude. *Time Asia*. www.time.com/time/asia/features/heroes/suukyi.html. 2003.

———. 2002. *The Trouser People: The Quest for the Victorian Footballer Who Made Burma Play the Empire's Game*. London: Penguin Books.

Mathews, Bruce. 1993. Myanmar's Agony: The Struggle for Democracy. *The Round Table: The Commonwealth Journal of International Affairs*, no. 324: 37–50.

Maung Hlaing. 1985a. Themes for Children's Literature. *Guardian* 32, 6:33–34.

———. 1985b. Story-Telling: Source of Children's Literature. *Guardian* 32, 8:15–16.

Maung Maung. 1980. *From Sangha to Laity: Nationalist Movements of Burma 1920–1940*. Columbia, MO: South Asia Books.

———. 1963. *Law and Custom in Burma and the Burmese Family*. The Hague: Martinus Nijhoff.

Maung Maung Than. 1915. A Note on the Burmese Thieves' Night. *Journal of the Burma Research Society* 5:33–34.

Maung Yint Kyuu. 2000. Mother: One of the Five Great Benefactors. Translated by Aung Thein Nyunt. http://web.ukonline.co.uk/buddhism//kkmyint1.htm.

McNamara, Jo Ann Kay. 1996. *Sisters in Arms: Catholic Nuns Through Two Millennia*. Cambridge, MA: Harvard University Press.

Mendelson, Michael E. 1975. Sangha and State in Burma. In *A Study of Monastic Sectarianism and Leadership*. Edited by J. P. Ferguson. Ithaca, NY: Cornell University Press.

———. 1963. Observations on a Tour of Mount Popa, Central Burma. France-Asie 19:780–807.

Mi Mi Khaing. 1962. *Burmese Family*. Bloomington, IN: Indiana University Press.

Mills, Mary Beth. 1997. Contesting the Margins of Modernity: Women, Migration, and Consumption in Thailand. *American Ethnologist* 24,1:37–61.

Mingun Sayadaw (U Bhaddanta Vicittasarabhivamsa). 1992. *The Great Chronicle of*

Buddhas. Translated by U Ko Lay and U Tin Lwin. Volume 1. Yangon: Ti Ni Publishing Center.

Morin E. 1980. *Orleans no Uwasa* (New Orleans rumors). Tokyo: Hosei University Press.

Mya Maung. 1992. *Totalitarianism in Burma: Prospects for Economic Development.* New York: Paragon House.

Myanmar Ministry of Culture, Department of Fine Arts. 1999. *Yangon University of Culture: Proposed Curricula and Syllabus.* Yangon: Union of Myanmar, Ministry of Culture, Department of Fine Arts.

Myo Kyaw Myint. 1988. Children. *Guardian* 35, 5 (1988): 48.

Myo Myint. 1984. The Politics of Survival in Burma: Diplomacy and Statecraft in the Reign of King Mindon, 1853–1878. PhD dissertation. University of Michigan.

Nash, June. 1966. Living with Nats: An Analysis of Animism in Burman Village Social Relations. *Anthropological Studies in Theravada Buddhism.* Cultural Report Series 13, Southeast Asia Studies, Yale University: 117–136.

Nash, Manning. 1965. *The Golden Road to Modernity: Village Life in Contemporary Burma.* Chicago: University of Chicago Press.

Nattier, Jan. 1996. Who is a Buddhist? Charting the Landscape of Buddhist America. In *Faces of Buddhism in America.* Edited by Charles Prebish and Kenneth Tanaka. Berkeley: University of California Press.

Nemoto, Kei. 1996a. Aung San Suu Kyi: Her Dream and Reality. In *Aung San Suu Kyi and Contemporary Burma,* pp. 1–16. Edited by Y. Sugita. Osaka: Kansai Institute of Asia-Pacific Studies.

———. 1996b. Aung San Suu Kyi: What Does She Aim At? *Genbunken,* no. 73: 21–32. Tokyo: Institute of Modern Culture Studies, Senshu University.

Neumann, A. Lin. 2002. Burma under Pressure: How Burmese journalism survives in one of the world's most repressive regimes. *Committee to Protect Journalists Special Report.* www.cpj.org.

New Light of Myanmar. 1994a. Secretary-1 Accepts over K12 million for General Renovation of Ngahtatgyi Pagoda. March 2.

———. 1994b. Preservation of Culture, Religion and Myanma Traditions Stressed. March 14.

———. 1994c. Buddhist Culture Course of Mahasi Sasana Yeiktha commences. April 4.

———. 1994d. Minister for Religious Affairs addresses Advanced Course on Buddhist Culture. April 25.

Ni Ni Myint. 1983. *Burma's Struggle against British Imperialism.* Rangoon: Universities Press Rangoon.

Obeyesekere, Gananath. 1985. Depression, Buddhism, and the Work of Culture in Sri Lanka. In *Culture and Depression,* pp. 134–152. Edited by Arthur Kleinman and Byron Good. Berkeley: University of California Press.

Okell, John. 1971. *A Guide to the Romanization of Burmese*. London: The Royal Asiatic Society.

Old, Grandfather. 1914. A Prediction (Tanhbaung) in Burmese. *Journal of Burma Research Society* 4,1:71–72.

Ong, Aihwa and Michael G. Peletz, Eds. 1995. *Bewitching Women, Pious Men: Gender and Body Politics in Southeast Asia*. Berkeley: University of California Press.

Opler, Morris E. 1959. Considerations in the Cross-Cultural Study of Mental Disorders. *The International Journal of Social Psychiatry* 5, 3 (Winter): 191–196.

Pe Tin Thein, U. 1992. *The Child in Buddhism*. Yangon: UNICEF.

Peletz, Michael. 1995. Neither Reasonable nor Responsible: Contrasting Representations of Masculinity in a Malay Society. In *Bewitching Women, Pious Men: Gender and Body Politics in Southeast Asia*, pp. 76–123. Edited by Aihwa Ong and Michael G. Peletz. Berkeley: University of California Press.

Peterson, William. 2001. *Theater and the Politics of Culture in Contemporary Singapore*. Middletown, CT: Wesleyan University Press.

Phillips, H. P. 1965. *Thai Peasant Personality*. Berkeley: University of California Press.

Pho Kya (U). 1973. *Sum: chay khu hnac man* (The 37 lords). Rangoon: Thila Press.

Piker, S. Ed. 1975. The Psychological Study of Theravada Societies. *Contributions to Asian Studies* 8: 126–138. Leiden: E.J. Brill.

Plotz, Judith. 2001. *Romanticism and the Vocation of Childhood*. New York: Palgrave.

Pollak, Oliver B. 1979. *Empires in Collision: Anglo-Burmese relations in the mid-nineteenth century*. Westport, CN: Greenwood.

Pranke, Patrick. 1995. On Becoming A Buddhist Wizard. In *Buddhism in Practice*. Edited by D. Lopez. Princeton, NJ: Princeton University Press.

Prout, Alan, Ed. 2002. *The Future of Childhood*. London: Routledge Falmer.

Pye, Lucien W. 1962. *Politics, Personality, and Nation Building: Burma's Search for Identity*. New Haven: Yale University Press.

Queen, Christopher and Sally King, Eds. 1996. *Engaged Buddhism*. Albany: State University of New York Press.

Reporters Without Borders. 2002. Burma Bulletins. August 26; October 30. www.rsf.fr.

Reynolds, Frank E. 1977. Civic Religion and National Community in Thailand. *Journal of Asian Studies* 36, 2:267–282.

Reynolds, Frank E. and Mani B. Reynolds. 1982. *Three Worlds According to King Ruang: A Thai Buddhist Cosmology*. Berkeley: Asian Humanities Press.

Rhys-Davids, T. W., Trans. 1991. *Sigalovada Suttanta* (Dialogues of the Buddha). Oxford: Pali Text Society.

———. 1968. *Mahaparinibbana Suttanta*. Sacred Books of the East, vol. 11. Delhi: Motilal Banarsidass.

Rodrigue, Yves. 1992. *Nat-Pwe: Burma's Supernatural Sub-Culture*. Scotland: Kiscadale.

Rozenberg, Guillaume. 2002. Reciprocity and Redistribution in the Quest for Sainthood in Burma: Thamanya Sayadaw's Birthday. Essay presented at Burma Studies Conference: Burma-Myanma(r) Research and its Future, Gothenburg, Sweden, 21–25 September.

Sahlins, Marshall. 1976. *Culture and Practical Reason.* Chicago: University of Chicago Press.

Sandima, U. 1993a. *Events in the Life of Thamanya Mountain Hsayadaw* (in Burmese). Rangoon.

———. 1993b. *Serene Pinnacle of Thamanya Mountain* (in Burmese). Rangoon.

Sarkisyanz, Emanuel. 1965. *Buddhist Backgrounds of the Burmese Revolution.* The Hague: Martinus Nijhoff.

Schober, Juliane. 2004. Mapping the Sacred in Theravada Buddhist Southeast Asia. In *Sacred Places and Modern Landscapes: Sacred Geography and Social-Religious Transformations in South and Southeast Asia.* Edited by Ronald Bull. Tempe, AZ: Program for Southeast Asian Studies Monograph Series, Arizona State University.

———. 2001. Venerating the Buddha's Remains in Burma: From Solitary Practice to the Cultural Hegemony of Communities. *Journal of Burma Studies* (Northern Illinois University) 6:111–139.

———. 1997. Buddhist Just Rule and Burmese National Culture: State Patronage of the Chinese Tooth Relic in Myanma. *History of Religions* 36, 3:220–244.

———. 1996. Religious Merit and Social Status among Burmese Lay Buddhist Organizations. In *Blessing and Merit in Mainland Southeast Asia,* pp. 197–211. Edited by Nicola Tannenbaum and Cornelia Kammerer. New Haven, CT: Yale University Southeast Asia Monograph Series.

———. 1993. The Burmese State and the Purification of Religion: Scripturalism, Socialist Ideologies, and Popular Resistance. Essay presented at Humboldt University, Berlin, International Conference on Tradition and Modernity in Burma.

———. 1988. The Path to Buddhahood: The Spiritual Mission and Social Organization of Mysticism in Contemporary Burma. *Crossroads: An Interdisciplinary Journal of Southeast Asian Studies* (Fall).

———. 1984. Religious Reform in Burma, 1980–1982: Traditional Religion and the Pragmatics of Modern Statecraft. Essay presented at the Summer Institute for Southeast Asian Studies, Ann Arbor, MI.

———. 1980. On Burmese Horoscopes. *South East Asian Review* 5:43–56.

Scott, James. 2002. Hill-Valley Relations in Mainland Southeast Asia, Especially Burma: Why Civilizations Can't Climb Hills. Keynote address. Burma Studies Conference, Burma-Myanma(r) Research and its Future, Gothenberg, Sweden, 21–25 September.

Searle H. E. 1928. *Burma Gazetteer, Mandalay District.* Rangoon: Government Printing.

Sein Hsan. 1991. *Inga Weikza, yadaya, Datyaik Dathsin, Bedin Bainggyok Kyan* [The techniques of Inga Weikza). Yangon: Shweparabaik.

Sein, Kenneth and Joseph A. Withey. 1965. *The Great Po Sein: a Chronicle of the Bur-mese Theater.* Bloomington: Indiana University Press.

Sein Tu. 1964. The Psychodynamics of Burmese Personality. *Journal of the Burma Research Society* 4:224–225.

Shorto, Harry Leonard. 1978. The Planets, the Days of the Week and the Points of the Compass: Orientation Symbolism in Burma. In *Natural Symbols in South East Asia,* pp. 152–164. Edited by G. B. Milner. London: School of Oriental and African Studies, London University.

———. 1967. The Dewatau-Sotapan: A Mon Prototype of the 37 Nats. *Bulletin of the School of Oriental and African Studies* 30, 1:127–141.

Shway Yoe (James George Scott). 1989. *The Burman: His Life and Notions.* Scotland: Kiscadale Publications.

———. 1963. The Burman. *His Life and Notions.* New York: The Norton Library.

Sīlananda, Venerable U. 1990. *The Four Foundations of Mindfulness.* Boston: Wisdom Press.

Silverstein, Josef. 1993. *The Political Legacy of Aung San.* Revised edition. Southeast Asia Program Series, No. 11. Ithaca, NY: Southeast Asia Program, Cornell University.

———. 1989. *Independent Burma at Forty Years: Six Assessments.* Ithaca, NY: Cornell Southeast Asia Program.

———. 1980. *Burmese Politics: The Dilemma of National Unity.* New Brunswick, NJ: Rutgers University Press.

Singer, Noel F. 1992. *Burmese Puppets.* Singapore: Oxford University Press.

Sivaraksa, Sulak. 1981. *A Buddhist Vision for Renewing Society.* Bangkok: Thai Watana Panchi Co.

Skidmore, Monique. 2004. *Karaoke Fascism: Burma and the Politics of Fear.* Philadelphia: University of Pennsylvania Press.

———. 2003a. Darker Than Midnight: Fear, Vulnerability and Terror-making in Urban Burma (Myanmar). *American Ethnologist* 30, 1:5–21.

———. 2003b. Behind Bamboo Fences: Forms of Violence Against Women in Myanmar. In *Violence Against Women in Asian Societies,* pp. 76–92. Edited by L. Manderson and L. Bennett. London and New York: Routledge.

———. 1998. Flying Through A Skyful of Lies: Survival Strategies and the Politics of Fear in Urban Burma (Myanmar). PhD dissertation. McGill University.

Smith, Martin. 1999. Ethnic Conflict and the Challenge of Civil Society in Burma. In *Strengthening Civil Society in Burma: Possibilities and Dilemmas for International NGOs,* pp. 15–53. Edited by Burma Center Netherlands and Transnational Institute. Thailand: Silkworm Books.

———. 1995. Burma (Myanmar). In *Academic Freedom 3: Education and Human Rights,* pp. 92–105. Geneva: Zed Books/World University Service.

———. 1991. State of Fear: Censorship in Burma (Myanmar). *Article 19* (London).

Spiro, Melford E. 1992. *Anthropological Other or Burmese Brother? Studies in Cultural Analysis*. New Brunswick, NJ: Transaction Publishers.

―――. 1977. *Kinship and Marriage in Burma*. Berkeley: University of California Press.

―――. 1975. Some Psychodynamic Determinants of Household Composition in Village Burma. In *The Psychological Study of Theravada Societies. Contributions to Asian Studies*, Volume 8, pp. 126–138. Edited by S. Piker. Leiden: E.J. Brill.

―――. 1970. *Buddhism and Society: A Great Tradition and Its Burmese Vicissitudes*. Berkeley: University of California Press.

―――. 1967. *Burmese Supernaturalism: A Study in the Explanation and Reduction of Suffering*. Englewood Cliffs, NJ: Prentice-Hall.

―――. 1959. The Psychological Function of Witchcraft Belief: The Burmese Case. In *Mental Health Research in Asia and the Pacific*, pp. 245–258. Edited by William Caudill and Tsung-Yi Lin. Honolulu: East-West Center Press.

State Peace and Development Council. 2002. *Preamble*. www.myanmar.com/Union/preamble.html.

Steinberg, David I. 2001. *Burma, The State of Myanmar*. Washington, DC: Georgetown University Press.

―――.1999. A Void in Myanmar: Civil Society in Burma. In *Strengthening Civil Society in Burma: Possibilities and Dilemmas for International NGOs*. Edited by Burma Center Netherlands and Transnational Institute. Thailand: Silkworm Books.

―――. 1991. The Role of International Aid in Myanmar's Development. *Contemporary Southeast Asia* 13, 4:415–430.

―――. 1982. *Burma: A Socialist Nation of Southeast Asia*. Boulder, CO: Westview Press.

―――. 1981. *Burma's Road Toward Development*. Boulder, CO: Westview Press.

Steinberg, Shirley R. and Joe L. Kincheloe. 1998. *Kinder-Culture: The Corporate Construction of Childhood*. Boulder, CO: Westview Press.

Stewart, Whitney. 1997. *Aung San Suu Kyi: Fearless Voice of Burma*. Minneapolis: Lerner Publications.

Stone, Lawrence. 1983. *Family, Sex and Marriage in England 1500–1800*. New York: Harper Collins.

Strong, John. 2003. *Relics of the Buddha*. Princeton, NJ: Princeton University Press.

―――. 1983. *The Legend of King Asoka: A Study and Translation of the Asokarajavadana*. Princeton, NJ: Princeton University Press.

Swearer, Donald. 1992. Fundamentalistic Movements in Theravada Buddhism. In *Fundamentalisms Observed*. Edited by M. Marty and S. Appleby. Chicago: University of Chicago Press.

―――. 1995. *The Buddhist World of Southeast Asia*. Albany: State University of New York Press.

Tambiah, Stanley J. 1985. *Culture, Thought and Social Action*. Cambridge, MA: Harvard University Press.

———. 1976. *World Conqueror and World Renouncer*. Cambridge: Cambridge University Press.

Tamura, Katsumi. 1997. Hito to Tsukiau (Social relationships in the village). In *Biruma Dokuhon* (Burma reader). Edited by K. Tamura and K. Nemoto. Tokyo: Kawade Shobo Shinsya.

———. 1983. Intimate Relationships in Burma. *East Asian Cultural Studies* 22, 1–4 (March): 11–36.

Tanabe, Shigeharu. 2002. The Person in Transformation: Body, Mind and Cultural Appropriation. In *Cultural Crisis and Social Memory: Modernity and Identity in Thailand and Laos*, pp. 43–67. Edited by S. Tanabe and C. Keyes. Honolulu: University of Hawai'i Press.

Taungdwin (Hkin Gyi Pyaw). 1988. *Inga Weikza Tikagyi* (Explanations of Inga Weikza). 3 Volumes. Yangon: Pitakatdo Pyanpwaye Ponhneiktaik.

Taylor, J. L. 1993. *Forest Monks and the Nation State: An Anthropological and Historical Study in Northeastern Thailand*. Singapore: Institute of Southeast Asian Studies.

Taylor, Robert. 1987. *The State in Burma*. Honolulu: University of Hawai'i Press.

Temple, Reginald C. 1906. *The 37 Nats, a Phase of Spirit Worship Prevailing in Burma*. London: W Criggs.

Tha Kin. 1925. A Claim of Prenatal Knowledge. *Journal of the Burma Research Society* 15: 134–136.

Than Shwe. 1998. Address to Teachers. *New Light of Myanmar*. February 22.

Than Tun. 1976. History of Buddhism in Burma (A.D. 1000–1300). *Journal of the Burma Research Society* 61, 1–2.

Thanlyet. 1996. Harm Caused by One's Own Deed, Being Caught in One's Own Trap—All Should Beware! *New Light of Myanmar*. November 25.

Thant Ein Hmu. 1998. The Byahma's Head. *New Light of Myanmar*. September 19.

Thant Myint, U. 2001. *The Making of Modern Burma*. Cambridge: Cambridge University Press.

Theikpan Sòyin. 1976. *Myanmá-yingyeìhmú Thamaìng* (The history of Burmese culture). Rangoon: Sa-be Ù sa-bei.

Tin Maung Maung Than. 1988. The Sangha and Sasana in Socialist Burma. *Sojourn* 3,1:26–61.

Tin Maung Than. 1996. Journalism in Burma. Essay presented at Carleton University, Ottawa, Canada. November.

Tosa, Keiko. 2002. Weikza: The Case of Thamanya Taung Hsayadaw. Essay presented at Burma Studies Conference: Burma-Myanma(r) Research and its Future, Gothenburg, Sweden, 21–25 September.

———. 2000. *Biruma no Weikza Shinko* (Weikza belief in Burma). Tokyo: Keiso Shobo.

————. 1996. Biruma niokeru *Weikza* Shinko no Ichikosatsu, *Gaing* nitotteno *Lawki* to *Lawkoktara* (A consideration on the Weikza belief in Burma: The meaning of *lawki* and *lawkoktara* for the *gaing*). *The Japanese Journal of Ethnology* 61, 2: 215–242.

Tweed, Thomas. 1992. *The American Encounter with Buddhism, 1844–1912: Victorian Culture and the Limits of Dissent.* Bloomington: Indiana University Press.

United Nations Children's Fund (UNICEF). 1995. *Children and Women in Myanmar: A Situational Analysis.* Yangon: UNICEF.

United Nations Development Programme (UNDP). 2003. *Human Development Report 2003. Millenium Development Goals. A compact among nations to end human poverty.* New York: UNDP.

Van Esterik, Penny. *Women of Southeast Asia.* Revised Edition. De Kalb, IL: Northern Illinois University Center for Southeast Asian Studies.

Venkatesvaran, K.S. 1996. Burma: Beyond the Law. *Article 19* (London).

Victor, Barbara. 1998. *The Lady: Aung San Suu Kyi, Nobel Laureate and Burma's Prisoner.* Boston: Faber and Faber.

Wang, Jing. 2001. Guest Editor's Introduction. *Positions* 9:1:1–37.

Whittaker, Andrea, Ed. 2003. *Women's Health in Mainland Southeast Asia.* New York: Haworth Medical Press.

Wikan, Unni. 1990. *Managing Turbulent Hearts: A Balinese Formula for Living.* Chicago: University of Chicago Press.

Zaw Zaw Aung. 1998. *Primer on Literary Theory (sa-pei thfbaw-tfyà achei-kan gyan).*

Contributors

Bénédicte Brac de la Perrière is a senior research scholar and professor of anthropology at Laboratoire Asie du Sud-Est et Monde Austronésien, Centre National de la Recherche Scientifique (LASEMA-CNRS), Paris, France. She trained in anthropology at the École des Hautes Etudes en Sciences Sociales (Paris) and in Burmese language at the Institut National des Langues et Civilizations Orientales. She has been working in Burma since 1981 when she was a student at the Association for Foreign Languages and conducted her doctoral fieldwork on urbanization in Rangoon (Une communauté urbaine de Basse Birmaine, 1984). She has continued to conduct fieldwork and publish more than forty articles on issues of urbanization and the *nat* spirit cult in Burma. She is the author of *Les rituals de possession en Birmanie: du culte d'Etat aux ceremonies privées* (1989).

Gavin Douglas is an assistant professor in the School of Music at the University of North Carolina, Greensboro. He holds a BMUS degree (performance classical guitar) and a BA degree (philosophy) from Queen's University (Canada), an MMUS (ethnomusicology) from the University of Texas at Austin, and a PhD (ethnomusicology) from the University of Washington, Seattle. He joined the School of Music in 2002 and his ongoing fieldwork in Burma focuses on state patronage of traditional music and the role it plays in the political processes of the ruling dictatorship. He has presented his findings to the Society for Ethnomusicology, the Canadian University Music Society, the Society for Popular Music, and the Burma Studies Group. He has published in the *New Grove Dictionary of Music and Musicians, World of Music,* and the *Encyclopedia of Popular Music of the World.*

Gustaaf Houtman is the editor of *Anthropology Today* and deputy director of the Royal Anthropological Institute, London. After completing his undergraduate degree in Burmese language, literature, and anthropology in 1980, he received his PhD in 1990, also from the School of Oriental and African Studies, on the anthropology of Burmese meditation practices. He was visiting professor at Tokyo University of Foreign Studies, the University of Münster and Gothenburg University. He is a Burma Studies Foundation trustee. He is the author of *Mental Culture in Burmese Crisis Politics: Aung San Suu Kyi and the National League for Democracy* (1999), as well as more than ten articles on aspects of Burmese Buddhist culture, history, religion, and politics. Houtman has several edited volumes, historical chronologies, and dictionaries of Burma in preparation.

Ingrid Jordt is an assistant professor in anthropology at the University of Wisconsin-Milwaukee. She received a PhD from Harvard University in 2001 for a thesis entitled "The Mass Lay Meditation Movement and State-Society Relations in Post-Independence Burma." She has spent many years in Burma as a Buddhist nun and has published articles and book chapters about the processes of political legitimation, lay-monastic relations, and Buddhist meditation movements. She is currently working on a book entitled "Political Legitimacy in Post-Independence Burma."

Ward Keeler is an associate professor in the Department of Anthropology at the University of Texas at Austin. Keeler received his PhD in 1982 from the University of Chicago and specializes in the anthropology, language, and expressive culture of Burma and Indonesia. He is the author of *Mahagita: Songs from Burma's Royal Courts* (2003), four books and translations regarding aspects of the Javanese language, four articles about Burmese culture, and a number of articles about Indonesia. He has been conducting research in Burma since 1987, is a Burma Studies Foundation trustee, and has received numerous fellowships, grants, and awards for his research in Burma.

Jennifer Leehey is a PhD candidate in the Department of Anthropology at the University of Washington, Seattle, and lectures in the Seattle area. She has been conducting research in Rangoon since 1994. She has published on literary censorship and cartoons and is the recipient of Ford and Open Society Institute fieldwork grants.

Guillaume Rozenberg, a member of Laboratoire Asie du Sud-Est et Monde Austronésien (Paris), has been working on Burmese Buddhism since 1997. In 2001 he defended a doctoral thesis entitled "Thamanya: Investigation on Sainthood in Contemporary Burma (1980–2000)," at École des Hautes Etudes en

Sciences Sociales (Paris). The thesis explores the biographies of some living Buddhist forest monks, their work, activities, and the ways they are worshipped. Rozenberg has published several papers, in French and English, concerning the practice of vegetarianism and the importance of religious constructions in the quest for sainthood in Theravāda Buddhism. In 2003/2004 he was a postdoctoral fellow at the Asia Research Institute, National University of Singapore.

Mandy Sadan studied modern history at Lincoln College, Oxford University, and art and archaeology at the School of Oriental and African Studies (SOAS), London University. She is currently a PhD candidate in the Department of History at SOAS and is a researcher in the Department of Languages and Cultures of South Asia. She worked for the British Council in Rangoon from 1996–1999. Her recent research on Burma is concerned with minority group issues, particularly relating to the Kachin peoples of northern Burma. She has published work relating to transition in material and ritual culture and Kachin identity formation. Sadan was previously a James Green Fellow at the James Green Centre for World Art, and her present research is funded by the Arts and Humanities Research Board, United Kingdom.

Juliane Schober joined Arizona State University in 1991 and is an associate professor in the Department of Religious Studies. She specializes in the Theravāda Buddhist traditions of Southeast Asia and conducted doctoral fieldwork in Mandalay in 1981–1982 on many aspects of Theravāda Buddhism in Upper Burma. She has published on the religion, social structure, and politics of modernity and nationalism in Southeast Asia, especially Burma, and is the editor of *Sacred Biography in the Buddhist Traditions of South and Southeast Asia* (1997).

Monique Skidmore is a research fellow at the Center for Cross-Cultural Research at the Australian National University. She is a medical anthropologist with a PhD from McGill University who has been conducting research in Burma since 1994, funded by a number of grants including Wenner-Gren, Rockefeller, and Australian Research Council grants. She was a 2002–2003 Rockefeller Visiting Fellow at the Joan B. Kroc Institute for International Peace Studies at the University of Notre Dame. She is the author of *Karaoke Fascism: Burma and the Politics of Fear* (2004) and coeditor of *Women and the Contested State: Religion, Violence and Agency in South and Southeast Asia* (forthcoming 2006). She has worked as a development and medical anthropological consultant in Burma and has published numerous articles and book chapters on violence, women's health, modernity, and psychological well-being in Burma.

Keiko Tosa is a professor in the Faculty of Foreign Studies at the Tokyo University of Foreign Studies, Japan. She received her PhD in anthropology from the National Museum of Ethnology in 1995 and is the author of *Biruma no Weikza Shinko* (A study of *weikza* belief) (2000). She has published several articles on the quest for sainthood in Rangoon and in Karen state and has conducted ethnography in Rangoon and Thamanya.

Index

Page numbers in **boldface** refer to illustrations.

Abbreviations: AFPFL—Anti-Fascist People's Freedom League; BSPP—Burma Socialist Programme Party; NLD—National League for Democracy; SLORC—State Law and Order Restoration Council; SPDC—State Peace and Development Council